FIVE-PART INVENTION:
A HISTORY OF LITERARY HISTORY IN CANADA

E.D. BLODGETT

Five-Part Invention

A History of Literary History in Canada

UNIVERSITY OF TORONTO PRESS

Toronto Buffalo London

© University of Toronto Press Incorporated 2003
Toronto Buffalo London
Printed in Canada

ISBN 0-8020-4801-3 (cloth)

∞

Printed on acid-free paper

National Library of Canada Cataloguing in Publication

Blodgett, E.D. (Edward Dickinson), 1935–
    Five-part invention : a history of literary history in Canada / E.D.
    Blodgett.

    Includes biliographical references and index.
    ISBN 0-8020-4801-3

    1. Canadian literature – History and criticism   2. Canadian
    literature – Minority authors – History and criticism.   3. Multiculturalism –
    Canada.   I. Title.

    PS8023.B56 2003   C810.9'8   C2002-902597-4
    PR9185.2.B62 2003

University of Toronto Press acknowledges the financial assistance to its
publishing program of the Canada Council for the Arts and the Ontario Arts
Council.

This book has been published with the help of a grant from the Humanities
and Social Sciences Federation of Canada, using funds provided by the Social
Sciences and Humanities Research Council of Canada.

University of Toronto Press acknowledges the financial support for its
publishing activities of the Government of Canada through the Book
Publishing Industry Development Program (BPIDP).

Irenae
uxori et amicae

Contents

Acknowledgments

A number of debts have been incurred during the time in which this book was prepared. First I must thank the Social Sciences and Humanities Research Council for a research grant and the University of Alberta for a McCalla Professorship, both of which provided time for research and the financial resources to acquire the research assistantship of M.A. La Chapelle and Tatiana Nazarenko. I also wish to thank Chantal Savoie for her assistance with some of the Québécois aspects of the research. I enjoyed a sabbatical leave, which permitted bringing the book to completion. For awakening a somewhat recalcitrant mind to the necessary relationship of history and literature many years ago, my gratitude continues toward John McCormick and Joseph Frank. For personal and intellectual encouragement, it would be difficult to know how to thank the late Philip Stratford, Tony Purdy, D.G. Jones, Jacques Brault, Milan V. Dimić, Kathy Mezei, Russell Brown, Clément Moisan, Denis Saint-Jacques, and Linda Hutcheon, the latter two of whom provided indispensable commentary. I am also indebted for various kinds of technical help with proof-reading, computers, and special knowledge to Jars Balan, Astrid Blodgett, R.C. Carpenter, Kirsten Gill, Linda Hoad, and Rob Normey. A special word of gratitude goes to Miriam Skey, copy editor for the Press, for her acute and intelligent suggestions and to Frances Mundy, for her shrewdness and patience. Errors of any kind remain, however, my own. Finally, I would like to think Verlag Ernst Vogel for permission to make use of parts of 'Canada as an Alternative World' in *New Worlds: Discovering and Constructing the Unknown in Anglophone Literature*, ed. Martin Kuester, Gabriele Christ, Rudolf Beck (Munich, 2000) and *Spaces of Identity* 1 (2001). To know this country is not any easy task, and I count myself fortunate to know people who do. My greatest debt is, it goes without saying, to my wife for listening and commenting, and, most of all, for being.

FIVE-PART INVENTION:
A HISTORY OF LITERARY HISTORY IN CANADA

Introduction

Canada is not a real country. It is but a gift of the imagination.[1]

Literary History, Nation, Power

In Canada, at least, the study of history no longer carries the cachet it once did, especially in nineteenth-century Europe. Such texts as Francis Fukuyama's *The End of History and the Last Man* (1992) are perhaps an earnest of what we may expect.[2] Literary history is in some ways even more moribund, which does not mean that it does not continue to be written. One wonders, however, if anyone does more than consult such histories, and whether the interests of those who consult them are not better served through reference works. Why, then, a history of literary history in Canada, as this book proposes, especially when literary history is either rarely historical or concerned with literature in ways that do not always appeal to critics who seek relations with other fields, such as philosophy, sociology, and anthropology, not to speak of feminism, Marxism, psychoanalysis, post-colonialism, and postmodernity? As Hans Robert Jauß remarked in his seminal essay, 'Literaturgeschichte als Provocation der Literaturwissenschaft,' not only has this once honourable discipline fallen off in the last 150 years, but it was once the crowning achievement of philologists, that is, the patriarchs of the discipline. Given the date of the essay (1970), it was probably not likely that the word 'patriarch' was used either contemptuously or ironically.[3] Yet it is possible that the several fields that have risen to prominence in the academy since 1970 may have turned upon literary history simply because it was so easily understood as the domain of male scholars in their later years. Nevertheless, perhaps because of Jauß's seminal text, literary history now seems to be returning as an object of discussion, at least, to which such a text as Marshall Brown's *The Uses of Literary History* bears vibrant testimony. The issue is not, however, whether literary history is too moribund to matter. The issue turns, rather, on the purpose of literary history itself.

A history of literary history is another matter and requires, if not some justification, at least an explanation, for the problems it poses are of a somewhat different order than that of literary history. The main task of such a history, as I shall elaborate in the conclusion, is to argue that those truths that appear perfectly valid for histories conceived as the articulation of a specific group or even two groups with designedly shared preoccupations lose much of their validity when examined from a larger perspective. Exclusive perspectives perforce simplify matters and, indeed, always make the attitudes and ideologies of any group appear more persuasive than those of others. To say, however, that a history of literary history is larger in its perspective than any specific literary history means primarily that it possesses more than one vanishing point. As a consequence, such a history challenges cherished notions such as the meaning and ontological status of the nation upon which such enterprises rest, as Peter Uwe Hohendahl argues cogently in *Building a National Literature: The Case of Germany, 1830–1870*. For if the generic function of a national literary history is to construct the nation, a history which addresses the several histories of a particular nation very often can, in contrast, remove the burden of the nation from literature. Removing the burden does not, however, remove the nation. It endeavours, rather, to place it in a more manageable position.

Needless to say, not all literary history is explicitly organized around the nation. It may emphasize, for example, an author or group of authors, a region, or a province. Somewhere, however, the nation is present, if only implicitly, and in most instances the nation is the dominant. Histories of literature in Quebec are national in their conception, Patrick O'Flaherty's *The Rock Observed: Studies in the Literature of Newfoundland* (1989) addresses the writing of what was until 1949 an autonomous region, and Dick Harrison's *Unnamed Country: The Struggle for a Canadian Prairie Fiction* (1977) proposes a kind of counter-culture posed against a central Canadian ideology. The Canadian nation is not solely constructed in Ottawa but is capable of taking shape almost anywhere. What is necessary – and this is the nation's debt to history – is that it requires a narrative order to be initially understood as having a history.

It needs to start, and it needs to develop to a certain point. Both starting and developing, however much they may appear matters of casual importance, particularly to most literary historians of English Canada, are assertions of power. Nations take place in both geographical and geopolitical space, and they are acquired at a price. The nation, however, that literary texts are engaged in producing recognizes this fact only with rare exceptions, and thus such texts become statements that for the most part hide both their origins and foundations. The narrative of literary history, in contrast, does not simply tell a story; it is designed, no matter how obliquely, to argue a kind of supremacy.

Finding Order

Literary history, then, like all history, is an argument, and it should be said that its facts (literary texts) are more than simply data. They are, like the facts of history itself, as Friedrich Nietzsche remarked, aspects of an oracle, and what the past speaks is oracular. We endeavour to decipher it in order to read the present and build a future. Otherwise, the simplest modes of structure would not be possible, and the activities of the past would appear only as events occurring at random. Although they may well be merely random, historiography perceives them as enigmas that carry possibilities of enlightenment. Enlightenment is most noticeable in form. David Perkins has aphoristically remarked that there are three basic plots of literary history: 'rise, decline, and rise and decline.' Such a scheme, of course, is an oversimplification that implies that the matter of plot is a mere formality and explains, for example, the way in which conclusions are constructed. As he asserts, 'most literary histories close where they do for formal, narrative reasons – usually for climax.' Literary history in such a perspective is no more than a well-made play. No doubt, in many instances this is a valid idea. It is not true for nations like Canada, however, whose literary histories have a central character, namely, the nation, and whose role in the drama is either constantly threatened or still to be defined.[4]

The function of plot requires, then, that it provide meaning as well as form, but meaning varies according to the kinds of decisions the historian makes both about the data and their modes of organization. It might be argued that this is not a major issue in the literatures of Canada, given the limitations of the data, but such an argument would have to be based on a reading of those histories which generally choose to ignore popular literature for the sake of products of 'restricted production.' Inasmuch as the latter are deemed capable of producing alterations in the literary system, they are given the greater credit needed to construct a history, particularly if history is a story of difference. The ideological stance of the historian in the present, therefore, is of primary significance, and it is that stance that 'reads' the oracle of the past. The reading that is made is never simply an archival gesture; rather, as I argue, it is a discursive ordering of the data (literary texts and their contexts) that follows, consciously or not, certain rhetorical structures. In this I consider Hayden White's study of nineteenth-century historiographical practice especially useful in which the modes of Metonymy, Synecdoche, Metaphor, and Irony may be shown to be dominant in various historical styles. 'In history,' as White puts it, 'the historical field is constituted as a possible domain of analysis in a linguistic act which is tropological in nature.'[5] It may be, of course, that White's argument implies that history cannot be distinguished from its writing and therefore places disproportionate weight upon discursive practice.[6] His contention, to the contrary, is that he has 'penetrated to the metahistorical level on which proper history and speculative philosophy of history have a common origin.'[7]

The practice of literary history in Canada, while it always implies a variety of theoretical and ideological positions, rarely, except in Quebec, makes explicit what its position might be. Nevertheless, a common tendency toward Synecdoche is apparent; this mode tends toward, if you will, 'peace, order, and good government.' Its desire is to find a means of unifying what may appear to be disparate parts and to suggest that in the process of finding unity meaning will emerge. As White observes of the German historian Leopold von Ranke, 'Parts are analyzed out of wholes, and the wholes are reconstituted out of the parts in the course of the narrative actually written, so that the gradual revelation of the relationship the parts bear to the wholes is experienced as the *explanation of why things happened as they did.*' It is a mode that does not seek causes but rather displays an inherent design whose conclusion is Comic in character.[8]

The primary function of Synecdoche is that once it begins to find its way into a text the permeation of meaning turns narration into metanarrative. It is narrative that must explain, but explain in such a way as to appear in some way 'natural.' Thus it makes causality correspond to an Organicist, rather than to a Mechanistic manner. Not only will its tendency be toward an integration of the parts, but also it will 'be oriented toward the determination of the *end* or *goal* toward which all the processes found in the historical field are presumed to be tending.' The final end may be invisible, but 'certain provisional *teloi*, intermediary integrative structures such as the "folk," the "nation," or the "culture"' may be invoked, not to speak of the future status that is hoped for in such invocations. The end might not be known, but it is usually implicitly Comic, and to such ends the metanarrative character of the history is almost invariably directed.[9] Plot, then, is central to most national literary history, and, as I shall argue, is manifest in a variety of subplots that belong not only to theory but also to the design of this book itself.

Design as Difference

The movement toward a goal, however vague it may appear, implies a notion of change and raises the difficult problem of literary evolution as the distinguishing characteristic of literary history. It implies that history means evolution, which is the usual post-classical understanding of the term. As the Russian Formalists argued, change depends upon a continuous, dialectical relationship between norms and deviations in the literary series. Inasmuch, however, as the literary series does not operate in a zone of its own possession, this relationship is also intimately related to changes in the extra-literary series. As John Frow asserts in his critique of Formalism, however, 'Literary history is based neither on a purely immanent development, nor on a strict determination by other orders, but is a process of constant uneven modification of literary and extraliterary functions and vice versa.' It is easy to overlook the expression 'literary function' in Frow's statement, but only through such an understanding of 'literature' can its relation to history become apparent. Clément Moisan neatly summarizes the contemporary position as follows: 'Une histoire littéraire aurait pour tâche *de construire l'ensemble d'un phénomène littéraire donné* (systèmes) *dans son fonctionnement socio-historique.*' Literature can only enter history or be constructed as an historical event when perceived as a kind of activity. It is activity that is at once part of a market and part of several interacting discursive practices. Literature, then, is the site of inevitable competitive operations which belong to the operation of canonization, a primary sign of change in the literary field.[10]

Needless to say, the writing of literary history itself is one of the agents that plays a highly significant role in the formation of texts, and part of its metanarrative is to persuade the reader that its reasons for marking change are valid. Although it has only become commonplace for literary historians in Canada, particularly in Quebec, in recent years to be explicit about their methods and ideologies, the latter are always implicitly present. Because the zone of primary meaning is always to be found in the 'nation' or an equivalent collective, particularly one in an emerging condition, a common ideological stance is one akin to Jacques Lacan's notion of the mirror stage, which is the moment in which the child moves from the Imaginary, having dwelt intimately with the mother, to the Symbolic, in which the capability of discourse and the exercise of power is acquired from the father. Lacan's text first appeared in 1936 and was reworked often until 1951, that is, during moments of both Husserlian phenomenology and Sartrean Existentialism.[11] The usefulness Lacan's text possesses for literary history, especially for colonial countries like Canada, is evident when understood in a larger social and international sense. Much of Canada's national self-awareness has developed in a complex manner involving (at least) two mother countries. Internal perceptions of colonialization are also apparent in histories of First Nations, Inuit, Acadian, and Quebec writing, and the tendency in such historians as Samuel Baillargeon to identify growth as a function of crisis should be seen in this light as a metanarrative explanation of change.[12]

Closely allied with Lacanian perceptions of the alienated or liberated self are the arguments put forward by post-colonial historians, who treat the question of political alienation more directly. Nevertheless, it is evident both from post-colonial writing and its theory that the acquisition of an appropriate *parole*, a discourse that is not based mimetically upon that of the colonizer, is akin to Lacan's notion of the movement toward the Symbolic that the *infans*, the child incapable of speech, undergoes. Post-colonial theory, however, is in many ways more empirical and understands that such speech is not simply the language that the 'Father' has always spoken in Lacan's sense, but rather an ambiguous discourse that in many ways is neither of 'here' nor 'there.' It is a special vernacular that literary historians gradually build into their argument of change as difference. It may be seen as a leitmotif in all the more recent literary histories in Canada and marks them with a layer, at least, of post-colonial intent. Needless to say, the emphasis on vernacular difference, and in some instances linguistic hybridization, is most apparent in histories of literature that address First Nations, Inuit, and Québécois writing, but the last chapter of D.G. Jones's *Butterfly on Rock* entitled 'An Ancient Slang or a Modern' places his text in a kind of post-colonial context, and certainly in an existential and phenomenological context, given the general argument of the book, namely, the recovery of our 'authentic reality' through language.[13]

The metanarrative of literary history, then, may be said to be about both the acquisition of subjectivity and agency, which explains partly its desire to emplot in White's sense, to provide meaning, to canonize, and, inevitably, to commemorate the nation. The primary agent is, of course, the historian, who controls the process. Rarely, however, is the process constructed as one of constant competition in the manner that *La Vie littéraire au Québec*, written at the Centre de recherche en littérature québécoise at the Université Laval, indicates, relying in a particular way upon Pierre Bourdieu, who shares with both Lacan and post-colonial theory a preoccupation with agency. The acquisition of agency by the producers of culture may be said, in fact, to be the primary site of literary activity, and the role of literary history would be to adopt such a premise and to trace the phenomenon of literary evolution from such a standpoint. The goal of agency, however, is not simply the acquisition of power but the concomitant exercise of autonomy. Literary history is thus the means to guide the reader through a *crise de conscience* and into a cultural New Jerusalem. Cultural and political autonomy then become coterminous. When they do, the struggle, which Bourdieu posits as necessary for any sociological definition of literary evolution, seems to cease in the plenitude that such literary activity seems to tend toward.

How, then, should we qualify the notion of literary evolution in the literary histories of Canada? Or, more pertinently, one might ask, what is it for? The question implies that it is more of a metanarrative theme than a structural principle. Where, for example, might one expect to find a clear idea of literary evolution if not in a Marxist text, such as R.E. Rashley's *Poetry in Canada: The First Three Steps* (1958)? It is designed to shape a movement from immigrant alienation to the individual's identity with the group through love. Once the goal has been reached and positively valorized, the process becomes subservient to it. The implication is strongly made, in fact, that the possibility of the goal was present all along and the process was simply an operation of revelation practised by the historian. Process is controlled by an idea that the conclusion makes most explicit. The contradiction between process and goal is always present in the literary histories of Canada, and it may be that no literary history may escape it. Generally speaking, the contradiction is not seized upon in dialectical fashion so as to project a continuously open, modifying future. The final sentence of W.H. New's *A History of Canadian Literature* (1989) provides such a conclusion without closure when he observes that his 'entire book is a history-in-process,'[14] but such a pronouncement is exceptional. Endings, in any event, are no more artificial than beginnings, despite Perkins's comment to the contrary, but rather are expressions of deeply held ideological convictions. How are we, then, to account for the function of closure as such a significant aspect of literary history?[15]

First, it should be borne in mind that literary history, whether narrative or encyclopaedic in Perkins's sense, is governed by profound metanarrative designs. It has a didactic purpose that is aimed at constructing an idea of nation, and it does so by giving it a certain form in both time and space. It requires clarity of origin and precise delimitation.[16] As history, it constructs a past by selecting texts (canonization) and commemorating events so that the nation may be imaginatively shaped by the reader in such a way as to acquire meaning. As countless critics and historians note, Canadian culture is in some way 'distinctive.' Difference and meaning come into being through procedures of exclusion and the providing of direction. Thus the beginning signifies both by what it decides to forget and by what it decides to prefigure. It installs a certain trajectory whose function is to provide the signs of nation which coalesce into a kind of central protagonist that is born, grows, and reaches a certain maturity. Consequently, it is not difficult to infer that literary history is in fact a variant of the *Bildungsroman*, particularly in its German sense. Before elaborating upon literary history as a literary genre and its particular modes of emplotment, however, it might be useful to consider the question of design and the importance of form.

Senses of Beginning

Beginnings are perhaps the crucial issue in the literary histories produced in Canada. They assume three kinds. The first is the beginning that marks a certain location in space – beginning as a function of geography – which is generally preferred by English-Canadian historians. It plays upon the notion that Canada is primarily a discovery, and, hence, one of the strongest rhetorical means of calling this to the reader's attention is to appear to deny it, which is the method adopted in the opening sentence of Carl F. Klinck's *Literary History of Canada*: 'Canada was not discovered; it just grew.' W.J. Keith's *incipit* to his *Canadian Literature in English* is the more usual one: 'Canada. A country stretching over 3,000 miles ...'[17] Canada thus corresponds to Mackenzie King's vision as a country of too much geography and not enough history. The consequence is that for the English-Canadian mentality the nation is construed primarily as space, as the motto of the national coat-of-arms succinctly declares: *a mari usque ad mare.* This attitude is to be found everywhere from Elizabeth Waterston's use of photographs in her *Survey: A Short History of Canadian Literature* (1973) to illustrate history as scenes from nature to Tom Marshall's apodeictic comment that '[t]he obsession with space, with enclosure and openness, that persists in our poetry is surely Canadian.' Finally, Frye's famous question – 'Where is here?' – appears to be the inevitable question to be raised about anglophone writing in Canada.[18] The answer, which Frye provides as varieties of pastoral in his Conclusion to the first edition of Klinck's history, designs the nation as primarily a spatial artefact. Such a conclusion, however, can pose serious problems for literary history as history, that is, a culture evolving in time. These are problems, however, that do not for the most part exercise anglophone literary historians. Their use of periods, for example, serves as brackets more than as catalysts for further events. History for them is a mode of classification; it needs to be *placed* somewhere. It may be that such an attitude toward the nation as history prompts some foreign visitors to acquire the impression that nothing happens here, and that Canada is no more than a 'peaceable kingdom.' Perhaps this is also why historians still remind us that a false etymology of 'Canada' is *a ca nada* (here is nothing).[19]

Historians of the literature of Quebec approach the problem of beginnings primarily from a moment in time: something happened decisively that determines the future and its shape. The decisive moment was not Cartier's discovery of Hochelaga, but rather the conclusion of the Seven Years War: beginning is a moment of ending. Initially, the change in the political state of what was then called Canada was referred to as the Cession, and it was not until the rise of the Montreal school of historians in the 1940s that Cession changed to Conquête.[20] The change of language is significant, for it emphasizes the shift from diplomacy to military supremacy and marks the British presence in Canada as imperialistic. Although these historians of New France promoted the view that the colony had the characteristics of a nation, francophone literary historians have taken a more ambivalent position and argued that the writing of the colony was French and produced for a French audience. Part of this argument is based upon the fact that the printing press was not introduced into French Canada until 1764, thus encouraging for the first time the rise of newspapers and pamphlets for local consumption. The significance of the decision, however, to mark the early 1760s as a beginning, a decision which may appear somewhat exclusionary, is that, consciously or not, it relieves the emerging collective of French Canada from any charge of imperialism and encourages a post-colonial construction of its culture. Camille Roy, whose *manuels* dominated the teaching of literature until the 1940s, repeatedly argues that 1760 should be considered the beginning of French Canada, and the most recent history edited by Maurice Lemire, Denis Saint-Jacques, et al. gives the date as 1764 and refers to the period of colonization as 'heritage.'

Because such a beginning was either a change of political regime from one imperial power to another or – depending upon the point of view adopted – a radical ending, it carries an ambiguous connotation. It is often constructed as a Fortunate Fall because it became the catalyst that prompted the sense of a distinct people. Because, furthermore, the beginning was not simply an extension of the realm, as it is constructed in anglophone literary history, but rather a moment in time, one can understand the moment as that of an initiating foundation, reminding one of the Roman phrase *ab condita urbe*, the moment when an enterprise effectively enters history and becomes, at least in retrospect, a nation among other nations. The consequence is that time becomes structurally marked, and the future of the nation is less dependent upon its extension in space than upon the moments that shore up its continuity. The dates that follow, often corresponding to the various constitution Acts passed between 1763 and 1867, are fraught with significance and bear strongly upon what one might call the 'great expectations' of Quebec for which the dates are moments of national betrayal or triumph. Of special significance is the Rebellion of 1837–8, which made Louis-Joseph Papineau (1786–1871) a national hero. In contrast, his English-Canadian fellow-conspirator, William Lyon Mackenzie (1795–1861), was stigmatized in English Canada and bequeathed a lasting legacy to his offspring, who were subsequently branded as 'traitor's children.'[21] The date also carries greater significance in French Canada because of the chain of reactions that followed in the texts of Lord Durham and François-Xavier Garneau (1809–66). The anatomy of literary history in Quebec is significantly manifest in the various peripeties that come forward in time, and their purpose, to use an implicit biblical metaphor of its metanarrative, is to point out the slow progress of emancipation that moves from Egypt to Jerusalem. The English-Canadian metaphor, developed most emphatically in Frye's Conclusion to the first edition of Klinck's *Literary History of Canada* is, as I argue, the New Testament desire for final deliverance from the bondage of history itself. The recourse to 'space,' then, so evident in anglophone history, implies an antipathy to time and history, which its practice bears out.

The two charter cultures, which are often seen as composing a binary opposition, may be seen, rather, as complementary. One completes the other along two intersecting axes in the search for, and articulation of, the nation. The third kind of beginning, constructed in the histories of First Nations people, Inuit, and ethnic minority writing constitutes what may be seen as a sublation in the Hegelian sense of the two dominant histories. If anglophone history extends the kingdom in space, and if Quebec history puts part of the kingdom into history, the other histories retain in their distinct ways aspects of both. Common to all three is a centre in catastrophe, which relates them to the literary histories of French Canada. The beginning is a rupture, which both continues and interrupts. The urge to continue and to extend in some timeless manner relates them to histories of English Canada. Unquestionably, immigration from France and England was sufficient in the course of time to alter radically Aboriginal cultures. The significant alteration of these two cultures, as far as literary history is concerned, is the shift from oral to print culture. The other alteration, shared by both Native and ethnic minority cultures is the forced awareness that self-knowledge would always carry with it knowledge of the Other. Their cultures were no longer complete and sufficient in themselves but always riddled with the hybridization common to post-colonial societies. The beginning as catastrophe did not, however, encourage the sense of history as it did in Quebec. Its effect was primarily existential and formed a defining centre of consciousness that linked the old and the new in continuous interaction. The past, which formed so much of cultural difference, could not be written over, as it has been in French Canada in respect of New France, and therefore the same orientation toward a future of plenitude could not be cultivated in the same fashion. Time could not be given an unequivocal linear trajectory. Thus, post-colonial First Nations and Inuit societies may be said to have dilated around the core of catastrophe, and both the fact of dilation and the paucity of historical markers, at least in the manner that their histories have been constructed, relates them to English-Canadian attitudes toward space.

Ethnic minority literary history, moreover, bears a complementary relationship to First Nations and Inuit literary history. Although their role as immigrants and settlers puts them in the same general camp as that of the French and English of earlier centuries, they also carry with them the shadow of catastrophe. If it is true that few people emigrate unless they feel in some way compelled to do so – and the histories of Ukrainian, Hungarian, and Jewish writing support such an assertion – then they may be seen as sharing the notion of a radical beginning with First Nations people. The argument developed in respect of Ukrainian culture is that it was always, after a flourishing beginning, in a state of siege. Hungarian literature in Canada carries with it the memory of the Soviet invasion of 1956 in various degrees, and the deep shadow of the Holocaust appears everywhere in Jewish-Canadian writing. In each of these examples, the synecdoche of catastrophe permeates in such a way as to inhibit the projections of futures in the Quebec sense. It causes an extension of the kingdom of the spirit, but in a manner more profoundly disturbed than that of English-Canadian culture. To develop Joseph Pivato's metaphor of the echo as a way of introducing the problem of immigrant writing,[22] all of these cultures live in, and write from, the deep echoes of a past they carry with them without always being able to reach.

Shaping Space and Time

The role, moreover, that beginnings play in each of these kinds of histories have profound effects on stances adopted toward the material, in both the matter of canonization and the articulation of significance. The anglophone predilection for space and implicit desire to be free of history gives the impression, at least, of a certain kind of objectification of the nation and its growth. The recourse to voyageurs and explorers not only emphasizes this tendency, but also suggests that the writing of literary history has a kinship with map-making and surveying.[23] Canada becomes a kind of travelogue. Despite what appears to be objectification, one cannot escape the concomitant impression that Canada is the function of the gaze of these explorers and history is a record of possession of the land. The objectifying gaze, by privileging the subject, looks – and cuts – both ways. It both separates the gazer from the Other, whether it be nature or native peoples, and constructs the Other as either hostile or absent. We have already noted how Waterston prefers pictures that commemorate nature, rather than people, as if the subject as nature, were forever 'out there,' distanced from the observer, and, consequently, unknown. An exception to this stance may be found in Jones, whose understanding of Canadian writing is deeply concerned with the subject as the site of existential struggle. The struggle is articulated in respect of the subject's relation to the natural world, and 'to give it expression is the job of the poet, the artist, the makers of human culture.' As he goes on to say, 'cultural vision ... grows out of the rock.' It is a statement designed to overcome the implications of Frye's notion of the 'garrison mentality' in which the alienating Other is conceived as the natural world or surrounding space.[24] Space is to be either overcome or redesigned and given voice.

Although the current climate in contemporary anglophone culture would support Jones's position, it was new in its time, and it may be said to have emerged from his intimate knowledge of, and relation to, the culture of Quebec which, in its literary history constructs itself as fundamentally of the Americas. It may have a French origin and a Roman Catholic ideology inscribed in its past, but its history has been one of manifesting its intimate relation between the subject and the space that it both inhabits and constructs. Place, then, may be taken as a given, and what is of significance is the narration of its distinctive story.[25] The embarrassments of possession that surface in anglophone literary history, particularly in early references to space as a hindrance to extensions of the realm, are not apparent in Quebec's cultural self-reflection. French Canadians are where they are partly by choice and partly by necessity, but not, in any case, through any political fault on their part. This does not mean that its culture did not engage in struggles for survival. To the contrary, these struggles become the anatomy of a history that primarily engages the problem of past and future continuity. Unlike Waterston's *Survey*, the struggles are not evoked by references to nature, but with photographs of people, for the most part men, whose memory embodies signs of a heroic past that continues to endure.

One might assert, then, that English Canada is possessed by space; French Canada, by time. First Nations and Inuit cultures have simply been, in contrast, possessed by other cultures, and so their preoccupations are less with space and time as problems, but rather with their specific cultures and their continuity. Such an emphasis has entailed a growing sense that autonomous space is coterminous with autonomous culture, but the latter has been the predominant subject so long as the law operated against the acquisition of an autonomously held space. Clearly, for ethnic minority writing, culture alone is the issue, time and space being fundamentally issues of the imaginary, and Canadian time and space have hardly any other than practical significance. Marguerite Maillet's *Histoire de la littérature acadienne* (1983) provides a curious relation between all the histories in this category and those of Quebec. It emphatically affirms the rapport between the nation and the imaginary by citing a poem on the back cover, the first line of which is: 'C'est un pays imaginaire / Qu'un jour je me suis inventé.' Such is the intent of all national histories of literature, at least in their initial phases. Only the cultures of English Canada and Quebec, however, appear licensed to venture further into a discourse that would have a bearing upon land and the exercise of certain political powers, in other words, aspects of real autonomy. As Maillet's subtitle declares, her history is a movement 'de rêve en rêve,' and nothing more. In this respect, at least, her history is closest to those of ethnic minorities, but the historical articulation places her parallel to Quebec histories. Predominating everything, however, is the primary motivation of 'le grand dérangement,' which, as a motif of plot, is cast as part of a larger, biblical metaphor of exile from the Promised Land, thus prompting kinship with Jewish diasporas and Aboriginal enclosures.

It is probably surprising that histories prepared outside Canada and within the zone of French influence make little effort to discover the distinctive character of francophone writing in Canada. More attention is paid to the French aspect of French Canada, and in more than one instance efforts are made to construct the culture of Quebec as part of la Francophonie, a larger nation, if you will, of French-speaking citizens. Difference, then, tends to merge with similarity for the sake of a kind of new French imperial ideology. The idea of nation is not entirely lost; it is made, however, subservient to larger, international interests and in the process the essentialization of the national idea is emptied of significance. At stake always is the role of the nation, which holds a central place whether essentialized or not.

Becoming Nations

As part of a continuous, repeated, and varied narrative, nation holds the place, as I have already indicated, of major protagonist. Because the narrative is structured by a metanarrative of a didactic character, it is possible to see it as a variant of the *Bildungsroman,* a novel that developed in late-eighteenth-century Germany at the same time as the rise of modern literary history. English literary critics are inclined to translate the term as a novel of education and proffer such texts as Charles Dickens's *Great Expectations* as examples. *Bildung,* however, refers to more than the protagonist's education and the satisfactory acquisition of social position, marriage partner, and sufficient income. Martin Swales argues that the term refers to 'a total growth process, a diffused *Werden* or becoming, involving something more intangible than the acquirement of an infinite number of lessons.' The operative word here is '*Werden*' which in the life of the individual is his story, but the story, especially in the German tradition, has less to do with the social circumstances of the protagonist than with the development of the spirit. As Swales remarks, 'It is indeed at the intersection of story (history) and mind (idea) that the Bildungsroman will generate its characteristic import, one which evolves out of an artistically controlled, and frequently unresolved, tension.' As many readers have noted, the novel's tension turns upon the world of reality ('prose') and the inner life of the protagonist, which has the allure and imagery, at least, of poetry. Thus it may be asserted that 'the tension is that between the *Nebeneinander* (the "one-alongside-another") of possible selves within the hero and the *Nacheinander* (the "one-after-another") of linear time and practical activity, that is, between potentiality and actuality.'[26]

It would be difficult to overlook the implied analogy between Swales's definition of this type of novel and the distinction drawn by Roman Jakobson and Morris Halle between metaphor and metonymy according to which the former tends more toward the *Nebeneinander* of poetic condensation. For Bradford Mudge the same tension is to be found in the practice of literary history which makes it an oxymoron, implying a contradiction between 'ahistorical literary values and historical, political, and cultural facts.'[27] Just as the protagonist of the *Bildungsroman* conjoins somewhat uneasily two opposing worlds of experience, so the nation, as it is variously employed in literary history, becomes a conflicted site where texts which claim transhistorical status and gesture toward transcendent values are made to consort with the more immediate world they both draw upon and endeavour to construe. Furthermore, the narrative *habitus* of the generality of literary histories asks of texts that they form connections with prior texts and anticipate later ones; it constructs them in some kind of historical order. This may mean that the values the literary text appears to articulate are made subordinate to the values that the larger historical text promulgates in the name of some national or other governing idea that emerges from the notion of the collective that the historian constructs. The individuality of the literary text must therefore yield to larger dimensions and possibly conflicting values.

Contradiction may appear as the generic weakness of literary history, but what prevents it from becoming a weakness of insurmountable magnitude is the simple, redemptive fact that the protagonist as nation is not always constructed in the same fashion. True, there are tendencies in the several cultures of Canada to follow similar patterns, which their culture might be said to require, but their largest validity lies in their composite relationship. The nation is never the same. The problem lies not so much in tensions that literary history possesses and cannot satis-factorily resolve, but rather in the fact that for the most part the image of the nation is so ethnically restricted. Politically and culturally Canada endeavours to promote a kind of bilingualism and multiculturalism, but the response by most of its literary historians is to ignore such efforts for the sake of particular ethnic groups. As a consequence, both literary his-tory and the nation it serves, rather than constructs, suffer.

Plot as Metanarrative

This book, therefore, has its own metanarrative, which is to suggest that literary history in Canada, no matter how accomplished some of it has been in method and critical insight, is akin to the literary history of a federation that refuses to consider the usefulness and value of the feder-ation. To draw upon John Ralston Saul's distinction, it refuses to see the benefits of the 'minority system,' as opposed to 'a system which func-tions on highly developed levels of structure and law.' Needless to say, the nation is construed in some literary histories of Canada from posi-tions that are highly unified, but they must, as a result be exclusionary, essentialist, and reifying. It means that only some find an advantage, which is characteristic of societies with 'highly developed levels of struc-ture and law.' The problem for the literary historian in such a country as Canada is the need to bear in mind that 'since the eighteenth century Canada has functioned as a confusion of minorities major and minor.'[28] Minorities share minority status, and that status is something to be mutually owned and respected. Failing that, these literary histories taken together, with few exceptions, point to unresolved tensions that are more significant than those which they contain as a function of their genre. They point to the tendency, human or not, to construe the nation as single, as possessing culturally potential selves that are limited to single cultures, thus inhibiting the fullness of potential in a world that is nothing if not a form of multiple cultures – what is now called a post-national state. This limitation, of course, reflects upon the full possibili-ties that the genre might realize, while still suggesting that the means of surpassing the limitation are available.

Like any other literary history, this book has its own plot and constructs a particular canon. Since it begins and ends in Europe, some explanation for this decision is perhaps necessary. My choice of such a beginning is to suggest that the formation of Canada through the British North America Act occurred at a time when other nations were going through analogous moments of formation which are reflected in their literary histories. I choose, therefore, to explore this fact initially in order to indicate the similarity of models adopted by these new nations and those sketched in Canada. I end in Europe because of a decision to separate histories according to national or foreign audiences. In one sense, the actual trajectory of my history would appear to conclude with the analysis of First Nations, Inuit, and ethnic minority histories, but the point of the final three chapters taken together is to read Canada as alterity and to dismantle the essentializing tendencies of the two dominant cultural groups. Of course I do not hope to achieve full success, but I want to place the emphasis that conclusions have upon the matter of difference that these histories foreground. The frame is designed to place our thinking of Canadian culture outside the limits of all cultural exclusivity.

My choice of texts will be seen to be highly various, ranging from prefaces to anthologies and essays, to handbooks and histories proper. They have been chosen on two primary bases: their perceived influence, on the one hand, and their scope, on the other. Thus, I have not included, for example, George Melnyk's recent *The Literary History of Alberta* (1998–9) simply because of its provincial emphasis. My aim has been to address the construction of the sense of a nation, and given the large number of texts that announce such an intent either explicitly or implicitly, not all histories could be included. This is particularly true for histories of specific genres, and if no efforts were made in such texts to go beyond formal considerations, they have not been included. When I have changed chronological orders, as in the example of J.D. Logan, I have endeavoured to explain why. Finally, because my intent is to meditate upon constructions of nations, I have given this history a certain periodization whose weaknesses will probably be only too apparent. Choosing the British North America Act as a beginning is not entirely satisfactory from a Québécois perspective, but, as Edmond Lareau's history argues, it was not entirely unsatisfactory from a contemporary point of view. Chapter 2 clearly accepts a notion of nation-building from an English-Canadian perspective, but chapter 3 makes it apparent that the years following Second World War were filled with a spirit of national energy in both Quebec and anglophone Canada, and both shared a sense that an end of colonization had arrived. They differed, of course, in their definition of colonial power, but the impetus to be a post-colonial nation was everywhere apparent. The first full articulation of this impetus is apparent in the histories edited respectively by Carl F. Klinck and Pierre de Grandpré in the 1960s and, because of their primary impact on their own cultures, they have been treated in separate chapters.

Although my method tends to vary methodologically in response to individual texts, Hayden White's understanding of history as a rhetorical mode of emplotment predominates. As I have already indicated, the form generally adopted by literary historians in Canada is that of Comedy. Exceptions are noted, but the general rule is that of a history which seeks a happy ending, which may be seen to be at odds with Margaret Atwood's general construction of Canada as a fiction of victimization. Such a fiction is a not uncommon point of departure, but the desire for a release from bondage and the establishment of a 'pragmatically free society,' as Northrop Frye understands Comedy, is the desired intent. If my history were probed on this point, it should be said that its structure and intent is also comic, and to be 'pragmatically free' would mean to be free of the constraints of several, single, essentialized cultures that all at some time or another demonize each for the limitations by which they feel constrained. Thus the point of the trans-national frame that is not designed so much to internationalize Canada as to open it to its several selves.[29]

Chronological List of Literary Histories of Canada

Edward Hartley Dewart, *Selections from Canadian Poets with Occasional Critical and Biographical Notes and an Introductory Essay on Canadian Poetry* (1864)

Edmond Lareau, *Histoire de la littérature canadienne* (1874)

William Douw Lighthall, *Songs of the Great Dominion: Voices from the Forests and Waters, the Settlements and Cities of Canada* (1889)

Virgile Rossel, *Histoire de la littérature française hors de France* (1895)

Archibald MacMurchy, *Handbook of Canadian Literature (English)* (1906)

Camille Roy, *Nos Origines littéraires* (1909)

Thomas Guthrie Marquis, 'English Canadian Literature.' *Canada and Its Provinces: A History of the Canadian People and Their Institutions*, vol. 12, sec. 2 (1914)

Pelham Edgar, 'English-Canadian Literature.' *The Cambridge History of English Literature*, vol. 14, *The Nineteenth Century*, Part 3 (1916)

Ray Palmer Baker, *A History of English-Canadian Literature to the Confederation* (1920)

Camille Roy. *Manuel d'histoire de la littérature canadienne-française* (1920)

Archibald MacMechan, *Headwaters of Canadian Literature* (1924)

Lionel Stevenson, *Appraisals of Canadian Literature* (1926)

Lorne Pierce, *An Outline of Canadian Literature (French and English)* (1927)

J.D. Logan and Donald G. French, *Highways of Canadian Literature: A Synoptic Introduction to the Literary History of Canada (English) from 1760–1924* (1924)

Camille Roy, *Histoire de la littérature canadienne* (1930)

V.B. Rhodenizer, *A Handbook of Canadian Literature* (1930)

Albert Dandurand, *La Poésie canadien-français* (1933)

Albert Dandurand, *Littérature canadienne-française: la prose* (1935)

W.E. Collin, *The White Savannahs* (1936)

Albert Dandurand, *Le Roman canadien-français* (1937)

Jane M. Turnbull, *Essential Traits of French-Canadian Poetry* (1938)

Jules Léger, *Le Canada français et son expression littéraire* (1938)

Émile Chartier, *Au Canada français: La Vie de l'esprit* (1941)

A.J.M. Smith, ed., *The Book of Canadian Poetry* (1943)

E.K. Brown, *On Canadian Poetry* (1943)

Edward A. McCourt, *The Canadian West in Fiction* (1949)

Desmond Pacey, *Creative Writing in Canada: A Short History of English-Canadian Literature* (1952)

Dostaler O'Leary, *Le Roman canadien-français. Etude historique et critique* (1954)

Sœurs de Sainte-Anne, *Histoire des littératures française et canadienne* (1954)

Samuel Baillargeon, *Littérature canadienne-française* (1957)

R.E. Rashley, *Poetry in Canada: The First Three Steps* (1958)

A.J.M. Smith, ed., *The Oxford Anthology of Canadian Verse* (1960)

Gérard Tougas, *Histoire de la littérature canadienne française* (1960)

Heinz Kloss, *Ahornblätter: Deutsche Dichtung aus Kanada* (1961)

Carl F. Klinck, ed. *Literary History of Canada: Canadian Literature in English* (1965)

A.J.M. Smith, ed. *Modern Canadian Verse* (1967)

Pierre de Grandpré, ed., *Histoire de la littérature française du Québec*, 4 vols (1967–69)

M.I. Mandryka, *History of Ukrainian Literature in Canada* (1968)

Paul Gay, *Notre littérature. Guide littéraire du Canada français á l'usage des niveaux secondaire et collégial* (1969)

Elizabeth Waterston, *Survey: A Short History of Canadian Literature* (1973)

Laurent Mailhot, *La Littérature québécoise* (1974)

Auguste Viatte, *Histoire littéraire de l'Amérique française des origines à 1950* (1974)

Jeanne d'Arc Lortie, *La Poésie nationaliste au Canada français, 1606–1867* (1975)

Dick Harrison, *Unnamed Country: The Struggle for a Canadian Prairie Fiction* (1977)

Patrick O'Flaherty, *The Rock Observed: Studies in the Literature of Newfoundland* (1979)

Tom Marshall, *Harsh and Lovely Land: The Major Poets and the Making of a Canadian Tradition* (1979)

Clément Moisan, *Poésie des Frontières: Étude comparée des poésies canadienne et québécoise* (1979)

Auguste Viatte, *Histoire de la littérature canadienne-française* (1980)

Clément Moisan, *A Poetry of Frontiers: Comparative Studies in Quebec/Canadian Literature.* Trans. George Lang and Linda Weber (1983)

Marguerite Maillet, *Histoire de la littérature acadienne: De Rêve en rêve* (1983)

Françoise van Roey-Roux, *La Littérature intime du Québec* (1983)

René Dionne, ed., *Le Québécois et sa littérature* (1984)

Robin McGrath, *Canadian Inuit Literature: The Development of a Tradition* (1984)

William J. Keith, *Canadian Literature in English* (1985)

George Bisztray, *Hungarian-Canadian Literature* (1987)

Michael Greenstein, *Third Solitudes: Tradition and Discontinuity in Jewish Canadian Literature* (1989)

W.H. New, *A History of Canadian Literature* (1989)

Penny Petrone, *Native Literature in Canada: From the Oral Tradition to the Present* (1990)

Maurice Lemire et al., *La Vie littéraire au Québec*, vols. 1–2 (1991–2)

Diane Boudreau, *Histoire de la littérature amérindienne au Québec: oralité et littérature* (1993)

Maurice Lemire, Denis Saint-Jacques, et al., *La Vie littéraire au Québec*, vols. 3–4 (1996–9)

CHAPTER ONE

Writing Borders, 1874–1920

Early histories of the literatures of Canada would appear to be of interest primarily to scholars, not to speak of the idle and curious. They are read from a vantage that makes them appear limited because of the insufficiency of texts and quaint because of the character of their judgments. Like histories in general that are regional and chronologically closed, they seem to be substantively outdated, offering little more than ancillary assistance in the critical study of literature and a measure of contemporary reception. In such a context, the comment made by Charles ab der Halden, a Belgian historian of early French-Canadian writing, that 'la littérature canadienne est une littérature d'action,'[1] may appear oddly, if not precociously, hyperbolic to the uninitiated. Ordered within a certain continuum of texts, however, these early histories form the basis for discovering, among other things, the criteria of canon formation, raising the questions of difference, and making initial gestures toward the construction of ideas of a nation.

Before considering them, it might be of help to broach an issue which will return frequently in this study, namely, the kinds of assumptions that literary historians make. For behind those issues which historians of literature must face – the construction of a canon, the role of periodization, the function of narrative and plot – there is another issue of fundamental importance, which is the relation taken between the literature and the nation whose culture it participates in making. Such, at least, is the unspoken assumption prompting the rise of national literary histories, that literature in some way 'reflects' a people or nation, by being its expression, and which distinguishes that culture from others. In order to test this assumption, it would be useful to consider the literary histories of three other small countries that achieved national status through some sort of confederation before, during, and after the period of Canadian Confederation, and for this purpose I have chosen Belgium (1830), Italy (1872), and Czechoslovakia (1918). Each country poses differing situations in respect of its literary life and institutions, and these will be addressed accordingly.

A general presupposition that one might make about a national literary history – as about most literary histories – is that language is an unmediated given. Certainly when one considers histories of ancient literatures, one thinks of them as, for example, histories of texts in Greek and Latin, whatever the territorial extensions might be. Language is primary and, so to speak, *a priori*. René Wellek argues, however, that for the rise, for example, of English literary history three disciplines were initially necessary: biography, criticism, and poetics. Yet, the theories of language that emerged in the eighteenth century were considered analogous to, if not intimately a part of, the history of literature as it then developed. Not only were languages seen as subject to historical development, they were also, Wellek remarks, 'part and parcel of the human mind, of its development and growth, and thus of the evolution of humanity itself.'[2] As one speaks, and by extension, as one writes, so one is or, perhaps one should add, we are. Thus, histories of literature in various degrees are histories at once of linguistic groups and, therefore, cultures.

European Analogues

How emphatically this idea can be expressed may be seen from the introductory statements that orient *Geschiedenis der vlaamsche Letterkunde* (1910) by Theophiel Coopman and Lodewijk Scharpé. It begins immediately with two assertions: '1830!' and 'The Revolution was over.' The meaning of these two remarks is immediately explained. From 1815 to 1830 Belgium was a part of the kingdom of the Netherlands. In 1830, as a result of a number of uprisings in the southern Netherlands what is now known as Belgium was formed. The authors attribute this turn of events to a number of converging elements, namely, the apathy of the Flemish, the arrogance of the Dutch regime in not being sufficiently responsive to the Flemish situation, and the gradual undermining of the regime by the French. Despite Dutch efforts to make their southern provinces monolingually Dutch, the pedagogical foundations for such an endeavour were insufficient. From this failure the new Belgium arose in which two different races were to be conjoined into a hypothetical nation: 'If and how it would be possible for Flemings and Walloons, whose gifts and feelings were so divergent, to melt [*versmelten*] into one nationality, into one people [*volk*], only time would tell.' The reasons for this, it is argued, are that the Flemish were a people who had forgotten and disowned their heritage as a result of two hundred years of imperial domination. The fundamental loss was the diminution of Flemish culture, inasmuch it was thought that 'to be Flemish and, at the same time, to be respectable and civilized was considered impossible.' The cultural heart of the matter is perceived to be a problem of language, for the national sense of being a people [*volksbewustzijn*] and possessing a language may be construed as coterminous.[3] Thus language is shown to be the necessary element in a history of literature, and the apathy that gave rise to its deplorable state becomes the point of departure for a national history. The nation's virtual death and palpable rebirth are constructed as a heroic overcoming of ethnic despair. Thus writers are given a kind of superhuman status for cherishing their language as the highest expression of national being.

In a certain measure, Francesco De Sanctis's *Storia della letteratura italiana*, published in the 1870s just after the unification of the various Italian kingdoms, duchies, and provinces, takes a similar stance, but he begins in a much more disarming manner by explicating one of Italy's oldest literary documents, a song by the Sicilian poet Ciullo di Alcamo.[4] No date is given for the song, and although the poet is Sicilian, his dialect is not a Sicilian dialect, being 'uncertain and mixed with local elements.' Even if it were Sicilian, it would have been marked by the 'original sin' of not having yet acquired 'a match in the national life.' Thus philology is put to the task of determining the purity of a national character, and only the language as it is used by the subsequent poets of Italy will be seen to possess the life of the people. The foreign, whether Norman French or Arabic, as was commonly used in the court of Frederick II, is almost immediately stigmatized in such a way as to problematize the meaning of language. Dates are not significant because the formation of national character occurs 'obscurely,' and they are not, apparently, directly linked to political interference.[5]

Significantly, De Sanctis does not structure his history according to centuries or periods, but rather around those poets or schools of writers that represent or make manifest the unfolding of the spirit in time. History of literature is constructed as an aspect of the history of the spirit and, as such, reflects De Sanctis's debt to Hegel and, perhaps, even more so to Giambattista Vico.[6] The role of the historian, therefore, depends more upon the discovery of history's invisible imperatives than its actual occurrences, in which 'everything is transformed in constant progress, which is the spiritualization of the idea, a moral vision [*cosciènza*] always more clear about itself, a greater reality.' This is not a narrative of ascent in Perkins's sense, but potential ascent; and although its origins may be obscure, in its initial thirteenth-century flowering Italian culture was a place of learning for Europe. While Italy could look back upon moments of greatness, its current situation, because of the struggle for independence, is one of exhaustion. De Sanctis's history concludes, then, with the hope that Italy will emerge from foreign influence in its spiritual life, untrammelled by other languages, cultivate its own interior life, and recover its lost splendour.[7] The nation, as a consequence, is coincident with culture, which political institutions are barely able to protect.

Luigi Russo, one of De Sanctis's editors, has observed that this history depends upon a myth of decadence, and its dramatic grandeur 'rests in the contradiction between the splendour of Italy's genius and political decadence.'[8] The same myth appears to be present, without the same formal architectonics and drama, in the literary history of Flemish writing that we have considered. The latter, however, differs somewhat by being more self-congratulatory, inasmuch as its cultural ascent comes from greater depths and appears to have more momentum than nineteenth-century Italian literature. This may be attributed to the fact that, appearing some eighty years after the country was formed, success may have seemed inevitable as the cultural life of the new country stabilized. Racial purity, supported by linguistic purity, in both histories, however, is given a high degree of emphasis. Literary history, in these instances at least, is not simply a narrative of cultural achievement or decline. It is, rather, a discourse designed to affirm and support ethnic distinction. The moment of confederation may be taken, as it is in the Belgian example, as an obstacle that serves as a stimulus, or, as De Sanctis suggests, as a necessary aspect of national regeneration in order to lay down its proper borders.

The Czech example, Jan and Arne Novák's *Přehledné dějiny literatury české od nejstarších dob až do politického osvobození* (1922), departs in significant ways from both of these. While the old and middle periods of Czech history are treated briefly as narratives of rise and fall respectively, Arne Novák's contribution on the modern period (1780–1918) begins with a short statement that endeavours to clarify the sense of the new literature. First of all, the literature of this period constitutes a closed, organic whole. While instinctively related to the earlier period, its conscious efforts have been directed toward developing its own ideas and form. The essential difference between the modern period and the past lies in modernity's conscious purpose, namely, to foster national and linguistic unity, both of which are 'founded on racial unity.'[9] The sense of unity [*jednota*] is almost as strong as that of De Sanctis, affected only somewhat by the internal presence of Slovak, which Novák considers a mere dialect or regional sociolect [*nářečí*]. Furthermore, the increased secularization of the literary system has effectively made the national interest the central literary idea. Also, Czech literature had gradually become less the privilege of the learned class alone and spoke for the nation as a whole. Remarkably, Novák expressly includes women as part of the national movement. Finally – and this marks an equally significant difference from the other histories mentioned – the author constructs Czech culture as central to Europe geographically and linguistically, for its history places it at the crossroads of the Romance and Germanic traditions in the West and the Slavic traditions in the East, a recurrent theme in Czech cultural discourse. Thus the sense of ethnic development is of sufficient strength to perceive itself as both unified and organically whole, on the one hand, and culturally diverse, on the other.

Taken together, these three histories develop a number of common themes. First of all, race and language are mutually supportive. The function of literature is to articulate the self-awareness of the nation or collective order of the race. The history of literature, then, is a history of the formation, dissolution, and recovery of the self-awareness of the people for whom it speaks. The Other must in some way be demonized in order for national distinctiveness to be perceived, and so De Sanctis, can, for example draw upon biblical discourse to describe the miscegenation of early Sicilian poetry. For Novák, the Other is, to a certain extent, Slovak writing, as well as the writing of Europe in general, the former of which is a negligible threat, while the latter is a source of positive strength. In every case the notion of confederation is taken differently. For the Flemish historians, the year 1830 is thrust before the reader as a near catastrophe. De Sanctis, by contrast, does not mention the year of Italian unification expressly, as if the political fact were of less importance than the necessary realization of the spirit in its cultural expression. For Novák, 1918 is the terminus ad quem that simply marks the self-fulfilment of the movement of National Revival, which, it would seem, is tacitly assumed as inevitable and not requiring discussion, as in the instance of Belgium, or an issue that might obscure the central argument, as in the instance of Italy.

Among the three countries discussed, an exception emerges in Francis Nautet's *Histoire des lettres belges d'expression française* (1892–3). Unlike his Flemish fellow subjects, Nautet does not mark 1830 as a national disaster. Although this may be partly attributed to the hegemony of francophone culture in Belgium at the time, Nautet prefers to construct a racial situation that does not appear to evoke the necessity of exclusion. In fact, while not introducing a comparative history of the two national literatures, the author, nevertheless, asserts the bases of a shared culture. First of all, both the Flemish and Walloons possess a reticent character: among the Flemish, 'les mots s'étranglent dans la gorge; chez les autres, les plumes sont inactives.' Furthermore, 'mépris d'un côté, incapacité de l'autre, les deux réunis produisent on ne sait quoi de terne, de fermé.' Given these similarities, it is of no use, if one is intent upon finding a national character, to take the usual step to speak of francophone writers in Flanders or Flemish writers in Brussels. Belgian writing since 1830 is neither preponderantly Flemish nor French such that 'la preuve d'une patrie en voie de se créer par communion d'intérêt et de destinées semblables, depuis un demi-siècle, pourrait peut-être se faire par la preuve littéraire.' Thus, Belgian writers 'sont, sans s'en douter, l'expression d'une alliance sourde, intime, résultat d'un fait historique et politique et d'un fait littéraire, les deux combinés, et tous deux expliquant tout à coup l'éclosion de lettres indigènes, d'expression française; mais ni absolument flamandes ni wallonnes, – belges.' Moreover, during the first sixty years of confederation, both marriages and political and commercial exchange weakened older, ethnic differences, and the future of Belgium depended upon the success of bastardization ['une certaine bâtardise'] in which the characteristics of both Flemish and Walloons had to be given up. Only the Flemish retarded this process, not willing to consent to the fact that they 'ont accompli leur destinées historiques et artistiques.' Indeed, as Nautet argues by citing Heinrich Heine (1797–1856) on the German Romantics, the Flemish desire to recover their youthful glory has been so great that, succumbing to its spell, it made them both childish and naive. But romanticism is at once the problem and the cure of Belgium's cultural problem, and it is invoked to 'expliquer comment l'union artistique s'est faite entre nos deux races et comment cette union purent naître des lettres d'expression françaises ayant un cachet local et une saveur du terroir.'[10]

Because Nautet's argument rests on the notion that political relationships do not depend necessarily upon racial configurations, pointing to former ties between the Walloons and Germans, on the one hand, and between the Flemish and the French, on the other, the key to national union is cultural, not political: 'Par dualité ethnographique, nous nous trouvons au confluent des deux courants intellectuels; nous avons désormais une raison d'être littéraire. Nous sommes en quelque sorte l'endroit sensible de l'union; c'est chez nous que les deux liens se nouent.' Nautet's history, then, is a history of the new, whereas the others in various ways are histories of fulfilment and the restoration of the past. While not explicitly stated, it is, nevertheless, a history of exclusion or assimilation. For while the author is careful to employ the phrase 'd'expression française' (francophone) to designate his literature 'chez nous,' thus distinguishing it from French, he means that the national literature and, therefore, culture is, while called Belgian, to be francophone. This is one way of explaining that almost one third of the first volume is devoted to the foundational work of Charles De Coster, whose major work, *Ulenspiegel* 'est flamande si l'on veut, mais le héros est familier aux deux races.'[11] The expression, 'si l'on veut,' while perhaps not intended as such, condescends to Flemish culture to an unfortunate degree and betrays the compromise intended by the text.

Progressive Conservative History

Each of these histories was written during the early period of the writing of literary history in Canada and they serve as useful points of order for our discussion. I have treated Nautet as an exception because of the degree to which it constitutes an ideological departure from the others by projecting a history that looks more toward a future than toward a past. In this respect, at least, it anticipates issues in literary history in Canada, which also construct the old in respect of the new. Canadian ideologues have also strayed toward the prospect of two intertwined races that work to the advantage of anglophone culture, which is a question that will be examined in the second chapter. Earlier histories were either exclusive simply by omission or, as in the exceptional instance of Edmond Lareau's founding text, *Histoire de la littérature canadienne* (1874), inclusive with reservations.

1874 was not an auspicious year to publish Canada's first literary history. The Dominion was but seven years old, and it had already been forced to address rebellion in the Red River Colony, which was an event, brief as it was, that has come to haunt Canadian history, especially because of its enduring questions of race, language, and nation. The first prime minister, John A. Macdonald, had just lost an election, largely because of a loss of confidence over the Pacific Scandal, and the Liberal Party faced a period of depression and continued problems with the Pacific railway. The political situation did not augur well for the future of the confederation. One might also wonder what the point of dwelling upon the literary culture of some four million people might be. Moreover, the formal problems of such a history must have seemed particularly daunting because of the lack of models of organization.

If Lareau was aware of these questions, his history does not explore them in any significant manner. The distinguishing fact is the status of dominion that besides 'rendant au pays sa véritable autonomie et en le plaçant au rang des nations libres' also breaks colonial ties. The function of literature in such an historical moment is to serve as a record of the nation, for it is literature 'qui se fait le fidèle interprète des sentiments et des tendances qui animent les hommes.' Since literature possesses the highest human aspirations, it follows that 'les sociétés grandissent en rendant au beau le culte qui lui est dû, parce que la recherche de l'idéal est une indice de virginité nationale.' None of these aspirations can be fully realized by the imagination, however, without the intervention of a literary history, whose purpose is to direct its audience toward the understanding of the intimate rapport that exists between literature and nation. Thus it is not insignificant that this first period of Canada's literary history, which Lareau goes so far as to see as at the beginning of a golden age, coincides with the beginnings of Canadian independence. Literary history, then, is a complicit discourse designed to shape the nation as it shapes texts.[12]

Unlike some of his contemporaries in Europe, Lareau does not hesitate to assert that all civilization is an anthropological narrative: 'Comme toute chose créée, la littérature naît, grandît et décroît. C'est là le grande acte de tous les jours, l'histoire de tous les êtres.' Finally, while European literature in the nineteenth century shows signs of a moral decline, Canadian literature, it is implied, because it is a young literature, possesses both religious and national virtues. Finally, Lareau himself, bearing all the marks of nineteenth-century Christian, liberal, progressive thought, has few doubts that Canadian literature, because of the laws of human perfectibilty, countervailing those of natural life, will only improve in the course of time. Liberal and progressive though his ideology may be, however, Lareau's criteria of texts deserving of canonization may also be said to correspond to those of any worthy graduate of a French-Canadian collège classique. The Romans, for example, are superior to the Greeks because of their heightened sense of unity, gravity, and clarity; religion is valorized in medieval and early Renaissance poetry in Italy and Spain; the English have a certain grandeur, but they suffer from being cold and realistic, not to speak of being eccentric; and French neoclassicism may be termed 'incomparable.' As a whole, contemporary European literature 'prend des licences dans la forme et s'inspire d'idées nouvelles, étranges, trop radicales peut-être.' Lareau seeks a 'démocratie honnête, chrétienne, laborieuse, capable d'inspirer la confiance avec la stabilité' – all the virtues that inform the talent of Antoine Gérin-Lajoie (1824–82), a novelist assessed as on a par with the now neglected Napoléon Bourassa (1827–1916).[13]

It would have been difficult not to be Christian in nineteenth-century Quebec, and this provides the moral character of Lareau's aesthetic judgment. His liberalism forms the basis of the political character of his judgment, which permits the admission of certain anglophone texts and the denunciation of others. Although a member of the anticlerical Institut canadien and capable of assuming attitudes aligned with the political left,[14] as evidenced by his critique of Louis P. Turcotte's *Le Canada sous l'Union* (1871–2), his own approval of British government, while defending French rights during the crucial transition period from 1790 to 1841, reveals an effort to be a French-Canadian federalist. Moreover, he is prepared to consider the literature of the Canadas as the same literature because of Confederation, at the same time avowing that he is 'surtout attaché aux écrivains de la Province de Québec.'[15]

Although Confederation is the moment of organization for Lareau's history, Canada's moment of origination is the Cession of New France to England, the moment when the French settlers were transformed from colonizers to colonized. Thus, if Confederation is to be read as coterminous with autonomy and self-government, the guiding ideology of the history corresponds to that of colonial liberation, and Lareau's stance may be construed in a certain measure as post-colonial. Considering the predominant position that francophone literature enjoys in the history, it is evident that Lareau is constructing a largely francophone nation, the first phase of whose mission was fulfilled through the agency of British political structures, which, according to Lareau were, for the most part, republican. Although the period of French domination is not neglected, the author admits that there is little material for the literary historian to examine profitably. Lareau's interest is attracted less by exploration narratives than by the educational efforts of the Recollets and Jesuits. While he remarks upon the *Relations* of the latter and also the early histories of New France, he notes emphatically that 'la littérature proprement dite n'existait pas sous la domination française: l'imprimerie n'a été importé qu'après la Cession.'[16]

Casual as this remark may appear, it may be considered central to the construction of a nation through its literature.[17] In many respects, despite the overture to anglophone writing, Lareau is constructing the boundaries of a nation. These boundaries are both external, distinguishing French-Canadian writing from that of France, on the one hand, and internal, distinguishing French-Canadian writing from English-Canadian, on the other. Thus, Canada is to be distinguished in North America because it is comprised of two different idioms. This emphasis placed upon language was shared with other philologists since the eighteenth century and, as he remarks, 'la langue d'un peuple est bien l'institution la plus frappante qui l'éloigne et le sépare des autre peuples en lui donnant sa physionomie propre.' Language is the essential boundary.[18] It is not, moreover, a superficial difference, for its usage reflects the *Volksgeist* of a particular nation, distinguishing its character from others, since 'le génie de chaque langue s'imprime dans les productions des écrivains qui la parlent, et les institutions diffèrent entre elles comme les idiomes.'[19] This means, of course, that while French-Canadian writing can be no more than a tributary of French writing, it expresses its difference and takes an independent course by its use of local colour and by marking what is special in the social life of the new nation. Thus the historian of a nation's literature is tautologically related to the nation, and the history of a nation's literature is a history of the nation *tout court.*

Such a homological relationship may also be derived from the definition of literature itself as 'l'expression du dégré de civilisation chez une nation. Prise de ce point de vue, toute production littéraire est une marque pour juger des progrès intellectuels et du dégré d'avancement moral.'[20] Thus literature is the sign of the *Volksgeist* as it becomes *Geistesgeschichte.* As a consequence, Lareau does not hesitate to include any writing of a high cultural character in his history, which is a history of genres, ranging from poetry and history, the major genres, to fiction and scientific writing, and also including chapters on legal writing and journalism, thus indicating the institutional structures that make writing possible. Nor does he neglect at least passing reference to the institutional function of literary associations, particularly the Institut canadien, as well as competitions for poetry.

Considering the romanticism from which Lareau's history derives, the privileging of poetry and history is not surprising. Although 'la commencement des peuples anciens a commencé par la poésie,' New France, not to speak of the early years of English domination, had no one who could match Octave Crémazie (1827–79). Much of Lareau's praise for Crémazie comes from Louis-Honoré Fréchette (1839–1908) and turns upon Crémazie's enthusiasm for France during the Crimean War. The war awakened his inspiration, and he became the poet who, in Fréchette's words, 'chantait notre passé, réveillait nos glorieux souvenirs, couvrait de fleurs la tombe de nos pères dont il célébrait les immortels fait d'armes.' Patriotism is certainly one criterion for canonization; love of nature, the other. Thus Charles Sangster (1822–93), Canada's national poet according to his fellow English-Canadians, and his 'The St. Lawrence and the Saguenay' (1856) is considered 'éminemment nationale; d'abord parcequ' [sic] elle est descriptive des lieux enchanteurs de notre patrie, ensuite parcequ'on y trouve cette sève patriotique qui nourrit les meilleurs inspirations, les soutient et leur assure l'immortalité.'[21]

Foundations, then, require patriotism; and while many poets are given brief notices, the major poets are those from the generation of 1850 on, namely, Crémazie, Léon-Pamphile Le May (1837–1918), Fréchette, and Benjamin Sulte (1841–1923). The latter, who has gradually disappeared from the canon, is praised for reasons similar to those inspired by the work of Sangster: 'le sentiment qui domine dans [Les Laurentiennes] ... c'est l'amour du pays. C'est pourquoi ses poésies sont essentiellements canadiennes.' Given such a central criterion, Lareau did not choose to examine the poetry of the Maritime provinces, first because he did not leaf through any work before 1867, and nothing caught his attention afterward. His interest lay in the poets of Ontario because 'ils se font toujours l'expression du sentiment national' and because 'la nature des relations politiques qui existaient entre le Haut et le Bas-Canada avant la Confédération explique encore la présence des poètes ontariens dans ce recueil.'[22] A national literature consists of a certain feeling ('l'amour de la patrie'), which articulates the inner border, but which is capable of expression in the two national idioms that write other borders both inner and outer.

More than poetry, however, 'l'histoire a été de beaucoup le genre le plus et le mieux cultivé chez nous.' Furthermore, were it possible, Lareau would have preferred to have devoted his efforts primarily to the history of Canadian historiography, rather than the panorama of genres he feels obliged to provide. First of all, it is, as I have just noted, the premier genre in Canada. Second, history readily makes Canada known to foreigners and cultivates at home 'cette fleur divine du patriotisme, en découvrant la grandeur de notre passé et l'éclat des actions de nos pères.' Finally, 'il raconte le fait réel et juge les hommes et les choses.'[23] Such an assertion suggests that, as distinct from the artistry, passion, and variety of poetry, history seeks a realism associated, for example, with the nineteenth-century German master of realism, Leopold van Ranke.[24] Lareau's central practitioners, François-Xavier Garneau (1809–66) and Jean-Baptiste-Antoine Ferland (1805–65), however, belie this possibility. Lareau's Garneau has, indeed, an agenda, for, citing Henri-Raymond Casgrain (1831–1904), 'l'Histoire du Canada n'est pas seulement un livre, c'est une forteresse où se livre une bataille.' The ideology of its first two volumes, at least, is characteristic of French Canada in the 1840s, imbued with a spirit of liberalism, democratic thinking, and patriotism. Among his masters was the French historian of the Revolution, Jules Michelet, whose lectures Garneau had attended at the Sorbonne.[25] If the hero of Garneau's text is 'le peuple canadien pris dans son unité,' the guiding thread of Ferland's Cours d'Histoire du Canada (1861–5) is 'la mission providentielle du Canada,'[26] and in a certain sense the two histories bear a complementary relationship to each other, Garneau's stressing politics and Ferland's stressing ethics.

Garneau and Ferland are the historians against which all other historians are measured, but Garneau is chiefly praised, especially for his foundational character: his history 'éclaire tout le gros l'édifice, il ne reste plus que les compartiments séparés, les racoins éloignés, les retraites cachés.' Of the many others passed in review, Étienne-Michel Faillon (1799–1870), François-Maximilien Bibaud (1823–87), and Joseph Doutre (1825–86) belong in his principal group, and Bibaud appears to be the most significant, particularly because of the Biographie des Sigamos illustres de l'Amérique Septentrionale whose importance rests on the place it enjoys, along with some articles written against Faillon, in the debates on the fate of Aboriginal peoples that took place in the 1860s.[27] Despite Lareau's sympathy with Bidaud's effort to recover the special character of these peoples, his own view is that since they are gradually growing extinct, it is incumbent upon colonizing governments to provide them with 'un peu d'espace à côté de nous, un coin de bois et un peu d'eau pour la chasse et la pêche.'[28] Although we might wish to criticize the condescension inscribed in this observation, it should be borne in mind that Lareau's intent, at least, is to teach his reader respect for an alterity for which our generation still continues to manifest a certain ambivalence.

Lareau's own ambivalence is based upon his contemporary notion of liberalism and progress which inevitably conflicts with peoples 'jouissant d'une liberté et d'une indépendance absolues.' For the moderate French-Canadian liberal of Lareau's generation, the only solution to such an impasse was to take the position of colonization, shared by both the Quebec and Canadian governments, and to support those institutions which possess a democratic character. Thus such Loyalists as William Smith (1769–1847) and Robert Christie (1788–1856) are expressly rejected from his canon, and John McMullen (1820–1907), while nearest to Garneau among anglophone historians, suffers from two vices: 'd'abord il est avant tout haut-canadien, ensuite il est trop conservateur.'[29] The balance resides between the liberal thinking of English and French Canada to the unhappy exclusion of other races, and the belief in progress is sufficient to forecast the gradual elimination of native peoples.

For these reasons, one may infer that the novel contains less contested ground for Lareau. To simplify matters, his reading of Doutre's *Les Fiancés de 1812* (1844) makes no mention of native characters, and John Richardson's frontier novel *Wacousta* (1832), like Richardson himself, is not part of Lareau's corpus. In fact, with the exception of a few minor English-Canadian writers noted by name and title, only Rosanna Leprohon (1829–79) is discussed.[30] She not only is assured a distinguished place in 'notre littérature nationale,' but also 'ses opinions et ses jugements n'ont rien de blessant pour la nationalité canadienne française.' When, therefore, Lareau refers to '*nos* novellistes,' '*nos* romanciers,' '*nos* romans' and '*nos* légendes,' it is not hard to imagine that *his* fiction was primarily French-Canadian and, consequently, national, rather than European. To give this fiction a certain cachet, inasmuch as it might not have been received with much enthusiasm in France, he invokes the French classicist and medieval Latinist Pierre Daniel Huet's *Sur l'Origine du roman* (1670), in particular his assertion that romance has one purpose, namely, to illustrate virtue and vice. Thus, he can excuse the lack of imagination displayed by Canada's novelists in the nineteenth century. Indeed, 'nos romans, ou si on l'aime mieux nos esquisses de moeurs, portent un caractère primitif, qui les rapproche de l'histoire ou de la chronique.' Finally, the most original aspect of the novel is the use of legend, and the young writer is urged to read Garneau's *Histoire du Canada* (1845–8) where each page provides the theme of a beautiful novel.[31]

The intimacy, then, between the major genres – poetry, history, and

the novel – is clearly drawn. They must be nationalist in Lareau's romantic, liberal, and progressive sense, they must illustrate by suggestion or
make explicit those ethical values which illustrate the greatness of the
nation, especially the struggles of the past, and they should draw to their
advantage upon those stories that have gained the force of legend, by
linking a people to its origins through the power of oral transmission: 'Il
y a tout un monde légendaire et fantastique, tout un drame palpitant
d'intérêt dans le grand acte de colonialisation de l'Amérique. J'imagine
un homme de talent travaillant un tel sujet: sa plume crée ses person-
nages grands comme les héros de l'antiquité, des martyrs dignes des
premiers temps de l'Eglise, des défenseurs de nos libertés et de nos
droits nationaux.'[32] From these and other examples, it is evident that
Lareau, whether drawing upon anglophone texts or not, is constructing
a narrative for French Canada.

In order to develop his argument, Lareau does not begin with what is
sometimes taken to be French Canada's earliest novel, Philippe Aubert
de Gaspé, fils's *L'Influence d'un livre* (1837), which he later dismisses in a
few paragraphs, but rather Eugène L'Ecuyer's (1822–98) *La Fille du Brig-
and* (1844), which, while recommended for young women, safely lacks
the wit of French adventure novels. Patrice Lacombe's (1807–63) *La
Terre paternelle* (1846) 'se rapproche plus de nous' because of its representation of real life in Canada. A new era is marked with Doutre's *Les
Fiancés de 1812*; Pierre-Joseph-Olivier Chauveau's *Charles Guérin* (1846–
53) continues in the line of Lacombe, but lacks his moral wholeness;
and Georges Boucher de Boucherville's *Une de perdue, deux de trouvées*
(1863–4) stands forth as 'le meilleur ouvrage dans le genre qui ait été
écrit en Canada.' Like no other novel in Lareau's corpus, this one per-
fects the use of the legend, a narrative that is 'essentiellement canadienne; elle résume nos moeurs, les goûts, les tendances, les usages, les
défauts mêmes des premiers colons français.'[33]

Lareau's final ordering of novels does not alter Boucherville's central
position, arguing that Chauveau (1820–90), Joseph-Charles Taché
(1820–94), Gaspé, père (1786–1871), Casgrain, Bourassa, and Gérin-
Lajoie, each of whom possesses a talent sufficient for canonization, lack
one quality that Boucherville manifests and which can be summed up in
two words: 'il intéresse.' He is interesting because of his ability to con-
ceptualize his work and to develop it according to the demands of its
idea. The judgment is formal, not thematic, and therefore seems to
transcend the emphasis upon the legendary. This may be because the
novelist combines several qualities that appeal to the classicist and historian in Lareau: besides drawing upon the past, his eye for detail and

other effects of the real appears perfect, and his characters are clear, consistent, and recognizable from an ethical point of view. Thus the progressive in Lareau does not regret the gradual death of the legendary in the maturation of Canada 'parceque l'état de choses actuel nous a été fait par le progrès et pour le plus grand bonheur des habitants du pays.' It is no surprise, then, that the final words of the chapter are devoted to Taché, who 'mieux que personne ... a saisi le côté essentiellement canadien de la vie sociale en Canada.' He may lack the artistry of Boucherville (1814–94), but realism makes him the fictional counterpart of Garneau.[34]

The final chapters on science, law, and journalism are of interest only because of their use as part of the definition of 'literature' in Lareau's writing, and the chapter on journalism is useful from the perspective of the literary institution. It should be remarked that Lareau, when he speaks of literature (with the exception of lyric poetry), like many other literary historians means narrative. Theatre plays no role in his history. Moreover, the clearly classical stance that Lareau adopts should be remarked upon as the governing aesthetic position of his history. Contrary to his political philosophy, it is avowedly conservative. As he declares, 'Je n'ai point innové; au contraire, j'ai généralement suivi dans mes humbles et modestes jugements la tradition.' In fact, he is pleased to add that 'il existe entre elle et moi un accord assez parfait.'[35] As a good professor, finally, it is evident that he writes not so much for a general public or a handful of fellow scholars, but rather for his students. This not only adds to the moral tone and didactic character of the history, but also impels him toward a number of exhortations to this group of readers to carry the nation's torch, so to speak, into the future. For if the glory of the past were not cultivated by the nation's future, what would become of the nation? At the same time, his students are to understand that literature, like any other human activity, is deemed, in a manner typical of the age, capable of improvement. The literary moral of the history, then, is that the past provides the models of greatness which it is the task of youth to emulate in its effort to be Canadian, original, and lasting. Thus his progressivism combines with his conservatism in both his moral and aesthetic judgment.

History and Empire

The early history of literary studies in Canada is dominated by articles and prefaces to anthologies. The arrival of Camille Roy was so significant for the first half of the twentieth century in Quebec that one is

tempted to cite Nicolas Boileau's (1636–1711) famous line about Malherbe to read 'Enfin Camille vint.'[36] His articles and, in particular, his
manuels, as I shall argue below, formed a nation of readers through the
collèges. Preceded by Abbé Casgrain, the two may be said to share the
credit for initiating a deeply resonant discourse that constituted the
making of literary history in Quebec. English Canada in the closing
years of the nineteenth century was a scene of many voices that found
their way into such magazines as *Canadian Monthly and National Review*
(1872–8) and *The Week* (1883–96), both of which were supported by
Goldwin Smith (1823–1910), whose dismal perspectives on Canada's
future as neighbour to the United States, as proposed in the concluding
sections of *Canada and the Canadian Question* (1891), seem now to be
close to fulfilment. Of the many issues that engaged the attention of
their contributors, one is of significance for us, namely, Canada's literature in a national and international context. Although these articles do
not have the scope to engage fully the question of literary history, they
proved in some instances seminal for later, more extensive, polemical
surveys, such as that of A.J.M. Smith in *The Oxford Book of Canadian
Verse.*[37]

Among anthologists of the Confederation period, two stand out, and
one is worthy of at least brief consideration. The first, Edward Hartley
Dewart, whose Selections from Canadian Poets appeared in 1864, while
asserting that 'a national literature is an essential element in the formation of national character,' is primarily interested in arguing that 'the
Poet's work is a lofty and sacred work.'[38] This is not an unworthy theme
for a Methodist minister, and the introductory essay is designed to provide an ideological apologia for the selections, rather than a historical
context. William Douw Lighthall's *Songs of the Great Dominion* (1889),
however, is the first anthology that endeavours to explore a meaning of
'national character' and to relate it to a Canadian literature. Such an
endeavour is not only Victorian, but also evocative of Cardinal New-
man's argument that 'literature is both the agent and the expression of
the organic unity of a national culture, the synthetic power of culture in
action.'[39]

To place the literature Lighthall invokes the theme of imperialism,
inserting Canadian poetry firmly within a British sphere of influence.[40]
Canada is distinctive because of its being a part of 'the acquisitions of
British discovery and conquest,' on the one hand, and by its geographical scope, on the other. Few English-Canadian historians weary of developing the second theme, and many continued to delight in the first.

The French settlers are included as part of Canada's imperial traditions, as well as the United Empire Loyalists, who withdrew 'out of the rebel Colonies.' The tradition of exploration and conquest, along with the vigorous defence of late nineteenth-century British imperial virtues are then developed with a few dates in order to provide an outline of Canada's history from the perspective of nascent English-Canadian nationalism, announcing 'songs of the Empire, of its heroes, and its Queen.' The theme of heroism suggests a certain masculinism characteristic of the age, and the choice of the three major poets – Charles G.D. Roberts (1860–1943), Charles Sangster, and Isabella Valancy Crawford (1850–87) – might suggest an interest beyond the heroic. His choice of 'lady singers' falls, however, upon those who write with 'the power and spirit of masculinity,' rejecting the poetry of 'a graceful subjectivity which unfortunately is unfitted for quotation here.'[41]

Humorous as it may appear now, the emblem of Lighthall's definition of poetry is the canoe, chosen because it was for a time the primary means of spanning a continent, conjoining 'bright lakes and ... savage rivers ... till we come into the settlements.' Thus he can include Crawford without hesitation, as well as French-Canadian *chansons.* The canoe is also instrumental in keeping the border close to Britain and Europe through its connection to the St Lawrence. Thus it becomes the Canadian sign of empire that reaches into nature and represents various kinds of domination, and it may also explain his characterization of Roberts as a 'poet, canoeist, and Professor of Literature.'[42] The canoe, drawing the past into the future, becomes the necessary synecdoche that combines the several themes that the anthology presents.

It was not, however, until 1906 with the publication of Archibald MacMurchy's *Handbook of Canadian Literature (English)*, that any examination of the literature of English writing occurred in an extended fashion. It is not a history of literature in a strict sense, and for this reason it will not be analysed in detail. It is, rather, a reference work that requires consultation through its index. The format, however, is somewhat striking, its structure governed, for the most part, with marginal dates accompanying each entry, the earliest being that of William Smith, 1770. The entries vary in scope and content, depending upon the amount and kind of information the author is motivated to provide. Needless to say, it is assumed that the reader either has some knowledge of English-Canadian authors or would only be consulting the book for specific entries. It falls, therefore, into the category of the encyclopaedia and, as such, generally avoids value judgments[43] and has no controlling narrative. If nothing else, it is useful for indications of the profession and ideological tendencies of the authors. The genres selected are history, poetry, and the novel, and editors are also included. A very strange omission is Sara Jeannette Duncan (1861–1922), whose *The Imperialist* (1904), which was preceded by several other novels, should have attracted his attention.

Rupture as Origin

MacMurchy's contemporary, Camille Roy, whose role in the nationalization of French-Canadian literature has been profound indeed,[44] first engaged the problems of literature and history in series of essays published in the *Bulletin du parler français au Canada* from 1904 to 1908, gathered in 1909 into one volume entitled, *Nos Origines littéraires*. The book may be divided into two parts: the first, which addresses the question of origins (1760–1812) and the second, which examines individual authors in the respective periods addressed. For our purposes, the first part is the more significant, for it organizes the literature of French Canada as the history of a long polemic that argues for the autonomy of the French settlers next to their British rulers. It is a history, then, of the problem of origination as a movement in two parts. This problem or, as Roy puts it, the 'causes qui ont entravé, ralenti, quelquefois paralysé le développement des lettres canadiennes,' corresponds in many respects to the contemporary view of Flemish literature as expressed by Coopman and Scharpé. The two moments of origin are, first, the fact of the Cession of New France to England and the consequent separation from the mother country, during which time 'l'on peut vraisemblement dater le commencement de notre histoire littéraire.' Nevertheless, no significant writing appeared until the second phase, inaugurated by the War of 1812.[45]

The period from 1760 to the end of the century is organized for the most part as a study of the literary institution, that is, the effort devoted to the rebuilding and assertion of national life that led to the establishment of a number of seminaries and colleges. The lack of books, however, and the separation from France had significant consequences. Furthermore, the British occupation itself was sufficient to stifle memories of New France, and it is not surprising to read such statements as the following: 'entourés d'ennemis, de ces Anglais qui répétait à satiété, avec leur historien Smith, et avec Lord Durham, que nous ne valions rien comme peuple, qu'un passé plus que médiocre attestait la nullité des vaincus que nous étions; accoutumés à n'entendre retentir à nos oreilles que le terme méprisant de peuple battu et conquis, nous avons fini, soit ignorance, soit lassitude, par n'oser plus parler de notre histoire.'[46] A culture, it is implied, must become conscious of itself – an argument now made familiar in post-colonial studies – in order to become a culture. Thus Roy's own text is inscribed in the process as a later, distant mirror of an earlier, sometimes less conscious polemic.

The polemic did not, of course, take place in the journals of explorations or the *Relations* of the Jesuits. What was required was the death of what appeared to be a homogeneous community in which natives were relegated behind the barrier of the exotic. What was required was a rupture of the cultural order[47] for the first moments of consciousness to take place 'et nous forcer à ne plus compter plus désormais que sur nous-mêmes.' As a consequence, French Canada's literary origins are to be found in the various journals and newspapers that began to appear after 1764. Even there, however, the emergence of a national idea was not spontaneous but grew from the combined pressures of English repression and the divided loyalty of the French immigrés. The moment when these journals showed their true mettle occurred during the War of 1812. The poetry they published was patriotic in character designed primarily 'd'entretenir, d'alimenter et de renouveler sans cesse au fond des âmes et des consciences le foyer de la vie nationale.' A primary inspiration for this poetry was the surprise victory of a hugely outnumbered French-Canadian force that defeated the Americans at the Forks of the Chateauguay. As Roy argues, the military action and the poems that sprang from it were proof of the loyalty of the French Canadians to the British Crown.[48]

Although he does not elaborate upon this point and leaves it as the apogée of the second moment of origination, his decision to make poems of patriotism toward French Canada coincide with loyalty to the Crown contains a highly charged paradox. For, while praising the defenders and their poets, Roy implies that the British were unwilling to consider French Canadians as equally responsible for Canada. Thus both moments of origin are shaped to support a notion of French-Canadian autonomy. We are to understand, furthermore, that the intimacy between literature and nation makes the text a kind of epiphenomenon designed to reflect an idea of society as a subject, that, following Lacan, requires a movement from the imaginary to the symbolic in order to acquire agency. Literary history, then, is the inscription of agency that emerges from a sense of break, in this case clearly from the imaginary of the mother country. Moments of origination in literary history can be crucial, then, for they prepare the space for the social empowerment of a people.

Preserving the National

Just prior to the outbreak of the First World War, the first comprehensive effort was made to present Canadian culture to the nation in *Canada and Its Provinces*. This work, which the editors developed in twenty-three volumes, is remarkable for its effort to balance multiplicity with a sense of national unity, as implied in its general title. Camille Roy's contribution precedes his more well-known manuals. It is divided neatly into two sections: 'Literary Origins, 1760–1840' and 'Literary Development, 1840–1912.' The first rehearses his earlier argument, making French Canada's origins coincident with both the Cession and the arrival of the printing press a few years later. The three kinds of literature important for early French Canadians in their efforts 'to preserve as intact as possible their ancient institutions and the traditions of their national life' were those produced by newspapers and journals primarily, followed by popular songs and the verse of Joseph Quesnel (1749–1809) and Joseph-David Mermet (1775–1828). Within the period from 1760 to 1840 the figure who played the most central role was Étienne Parent (1802–74), the editor of *Le Canadien* from 1822 to 1825 and later, in its revived and more militant years, from 1831 to 1842. A moderate liberal of the type admired by Lareau, he is praised by Roy as 'incontestably the finest, most worthy and most expressive figure of that time.'[49] Moreover, the fact that some 30 per cent of the first section is devoted to Parent gives some notion of Roy's own ideological formation as a defender of the Roman Catholic Church, Confederation, the French language and culture, and Canada.[50] Thus Parent becomes a cardinal figure in Roy's history, both a man of his time and a prophet of the future,[51] a future which is to be understood primarily through its historians and only secondarily through poetry and fiction.

Garneau's *Histoire du Canada* inaugurates French Canada's second moment of origination. While unquestionably a founder and author of Roy's Quebec, his work is corrected by Ferland, who 'understood better than Garneau the religious nature of the historical origins of Canada.' Following these two, Abbé Casgrain's many histories of the religious aspects of Quebec's past 'helped greatly in making Canada known abroad, especially in France,' suggesting like others in this period that self-identity requires recognition of one's cultural point of departure, one of the necessary first steps in colonial self-awareness. Garneau is also explicitly credited with supplying the metanarrative for French Canada's 'poet-patriots,' primarily Crémazie, 'the father of French-Canadian poetry' and Fréchette, both of whom emulated Victor Hugo's (1802–85) romantic nationalism. In some respects, Pamphile Le May surpasses them both for being both 'the poet-patriot moved by the noblest inspirations of his race, and the Christian poet extolling that which is most dear to his faith and piety.'[52] The section on poetry concludes with notice taken of 'L'Ecole littéraire de Montréal,' represented primarily by Émile Nelligan (1879–1941) and Alfred Lozeau (1878–1924) and several others. The difference between these more contemporary poets and their forerunners is the emphasis placed upon personal feelings, rather than national themes. Although Roy has some appreciation for them, he gives them somewhat short shrift because, it would seem, of their profound disinterest in the national idea.

A brief section follows on the novel. Although a number of writers are mentioned, only Philippe-Joseph Aubert de Gaspé, père, and Gérin-Lajoie are considered at length. Early texts of the 1840s are not mentioned; Chauveau's *Charles Guérin* is simply passed over as 'a timid attempt.' Aubert de Gaspé is mentioned in the same breath as Homer's *Iliad* and the medieval French *Song of Roland*, both traditional, foundational epics, and he is praised as 'the true epic singer of a marvellous phase of [Canada's] history' for his *Les anciens Canadiens* (1863). Boucherville is displaced by Gérin-Lajoie in the canon for his *Jean Rivard* (1862–4), 'a social romance – a novel with a purpose,' and the latter is also credited with 'writing a book that was widely read, and creating a type that has remained as an example for all colonists.' Such an assertion is, of course, an exaggeration, and some credit might have been given to Lacombe's *La Terre paternelle*, the seminal and frequently ignored inauguration of the *roman du terroir*. Boucherville is indeed mentioned, but it is possible to infer that the final word of the paragraph devoted to him – 'popularity' – is at once a description and a mild rebuke. Among others noted rapidly, the brief mention given to Laure Conan (Marie-Louise-Félicité Angers [1845–1924]) is particularly revealing for not hinting at the existence of *Angéline de Montbrun* (1881–2), the one novel of hers that continues to find readers, partly, one might suppose, because of its ironic treatment of the national and the symbolic in Lacan's sense.[53]

Before a final section where those texts without generic classification are placed, Roy discusses the literature of journalism and oratory – the central writing and discourse through which French Canada is founded. In this section he resumes a theme developed in *Nos Origines littéraires*, namely, that French Canadians are of French origin, but their distinguishing trait is to be found in their relation to English-Canadians, whose government they respect with loyalty and pride, and Wilfrid Laurier, Thomas Chapais, and Henri Bourassa are successively brought forward to testify. Politically, then, the struggle for a French-Canadian culture culminates here and explains the importance given to texts that might be understood as less 'literary' than the novel. Roy's culture is Canadian, but in French and within the framework of Catholic morality.

Although during this period there were a number of articles by various authors surveying English-Canadian literature, the first sustained examination was made by the Edwardian poet, novelist, and historian, Thomas Guthrie Marquis, in the same series as Camille Roy's. Marquis's history, by contrast, lacks the clear, teleological structure of Roy's, and the only thing they have in common is the sense that the founders of the respective literatures were male. Both carry portraits at the beginning of the significant grandfather: Roy selects, needless to say, François-Xavier Garneau; Marquis, Thomas Haliburton. The latter choice, the well-known satirist and historian from Nova Scotia, is of the same generation as Garneau, but his work began to appear somewhat earlier. The true significance of the choice, however, lies in the difference in the ideology each writer represents. Garneau's thought is of the liberal, bourgeois character that represents the 1840s, which was capable of reaching an accord in the course of time with Quebec's clerical interests,[54] and his ideological perspective is closer to that of Lareau than that of Roy. Haliburton was always conservative and, in the course of time, acquired even firmer convictions in this regard.

Literature for Marquis consists of a variety of genres, including, besides fiction and poetry, history, biography, and exploration writings. The history has no other sense of historical order than what a simple chronology can provide and, consequently, has less of an overtly ideological stamp than Lighthall's. No particular emphasis is placed upon the British North America Act. The Other against which Marquis's Canada defines itself is not its French-Canadian compatriots, but rather Great Britain and the United States, and distinctions are drawn between 'birds of passage' and 'native Canadians,' that is, writers of European stock born in Canada. With the exception of the year 1880, which marks a renaissance in Canadian poetry, no other frames of order are provided, and within the various generic sections the authors are biographically presented with some remarks about their work.[55]

As one might expect, the longest sections are devoted to historiography and fiction. None of English Canada's historians before 1914 can be called great in the sense that Garneau was great, and while the work of the American historian Francis Parkman is mentioned as fundamental, he is not examined in any detail. The two pillars upon which Canadian historiography proper appears to rest are the works of William Smith and Robert Christie, both of whom are considered influential and valuable, and both of whom were, in contrast, held in contempt by Lareau. Marquis's interest in fiction is more lively, both because of the lives of novelists and because of the narratives themselves. Furthermore, while historians seem to do more than narrate chronological facts as they know them, novelists have moments in history itself, which are either provincial or international in scope.[56] This observation would appear to neglect his reading of Frances Brooke's *The History of Emily Montague* (1769) as a Canadian development of the style of the eighteenth-century English novelist Samuel Richardson.[57] This is, perhaps, because she is but a 'bird of passage' and, therefore, cannot be given full credit as an originator of Canadian fiction. Although Julia Catherine Hart (1796–1867) was indigenous, her work is dismissed as 'scarcely worthy of notice in a literary review.' While defending John Richardson (1796–1852) against the charge of being James Fenimore Cooper's epigone, Haliburton, the 'ardent imperialist' who 'was strongly opposed to responsible government,' is said to stand 'high above all other Canadian writers.'[58] His Sam Slick ranks among 'such immortals as Pickwick, Tartarin of Tarascon and Huckleberry Finn.' Finally, he was 'the first writer to use the American dialect in literature,'[59] and is judged superior to Mark Twain (Samuel Langhorne Clemens [1835–1910]) and Artemus Ward (1834–67). Superlative as this praise may be, Haliburton in Marquis's schema remains provincial like the notable contributors to *The Literary Garland* (1838–51). James De Mille (1833–80) and William Kirby (1817–1906), finally, are the last in the provincial category.

Seemingly unembarrassed by his expression 'bird of passage,' Marquis ironically selects the year 1890 as the dividing moment in Canadian fiction, the year in which the highly praised Sir Gilbert Parker (1862–1932) emigrated to England and began to write. Sara Jeannette Duncan (1861–1922) married Everard Cotes in the same year and subsequently left Canada, spending the rest of her life abroad, where her major novel, *The Imperialist*, was written. Marquis is on safer ground with Charles W.

Gordon (Ralph Connor [1860–1937]), a Presbyterian minister and 'in every way, a Canadian writer.' Assembling a number of characters from several ethnic groups, the 'international' character of his writing is perhaps best found in *The Foreigner: A Tale of Saskatchewan* (1919), written 'after the manner of Zola.' Although Sara Jeannette Duncan, who 'holds easily the first place among women writers of fiction born in the Dominion,' and a number of other women are mentioned, including Leprohon and Lucy Maud Montgomery (1874–1942), it is evident from the brevity of the space devoted to them, especially to their lives, that Marquis wants to privilege the 'vigorous Canadian boyhood and manhood' to be found in such writers as Parker, Gordon, Norman Duncan (1871–1916), Charles G.D. Roberts, and Edward William Thomson (1849–1924).[60]

Poetry, however, is 'the chief glory of Canadian literature,' despite the fact that Canada's poets have been 'for the most part inadequately equipped' for their task. Their themes correspond to those essayed by French-Canadian poets, namely, nature, struggles against it on land and sea, battles with 'Indians' and 'the fight for national existence during the Revolutionary War and the War of 1812.'[61] While derivative, Canadian poetry begins with Oliver Goldsmith (1794–1861), who developed some of these themes. English Canada's first talent, however, is Charles Sangster. Both Charles Heavysedge (1816–76) and Thomas D'Arcy McGee (1825–68) are dismissed as foreign, and Alexander McLachlan (1818–96) is mentioned only for 'those who care much for feeling and little for art.'[62] Thus, if 1880 is the year of the renaissance, one has to wonder what Canada's period of antiquity was. In any event, this was the year that saw the publication of Roberts's *Orion and Other Poems*, the first of those texts characterized as Confederation Poetry. Roberts was followed by Archibald Lampman (1861–99) and Bliss Carman (1861–1929), and all three are read within the implied colonial framework of such English Romantics as Shelley (1792–1822), Keats (1795–1821), and Tennyson (1809–92). Duncan Campbell Scott (1862–1947), whose prestige has grown in the course of time, is accorded no more than a clause.[63] Isabella Valancy Crawford is fairly well introduced, but her work is finally dismissed as 'worthy, if slight'; the Métis poet, E. Pauline Johnson (1861–1913) is considered 'unique'; and Marjorie L.C. Pickthall's work (1883–1922), described as 'subtle and delicate' fares only somewhat better.[64]

As I have already indicated, Marquis's history provides few temporal markers that would provide a structure, implying that English Canada is not to be construed as a culture taking place in time, but rather as a space to be filled, establishing a norm in English-Canadian literary-historical discourse. As a space it is to be defined within a clearly anglophone world whose boundaries are the United States and Great Britain from which it is 'invaded'[65] and to which its writers disappear and lose their Canadian qualities. As M. Brook Taylor argues in *Promoters, Patriots, and Partisans*, the intersection of British possession and American incursion is foundational in the early histories of Upper Canada, becoming a part of the struggle for reform. For Marquis, this is perceived as less of a struggle than as a 'handicapped' condition, producing a static, amorphous image of English Canada that is always in a state of gaining and losing, but not of possessing definable characteristics. Finally, in a tradition already articulated by Lighthall, the major shapers of this space are for the most part male and most of these are masculinist and therefore worthy of providing 'a vigorous national note' like that of the United States.[66]

A Country without a Past

In many ways the English Canadian as a conflicted site is a leitmotif that assumes archetypal dimensions in Canadian culture. It exercises Marquis and it exercises his contemporary Pelham Edgar,[67] whose 'English-Canadian Literature' (1916) tries valiantly to place a border on the country and, in the end, decides that a Canadian is a descendant of the United Kingdom 'with a discreet touch of the Yankee – but he is so shadowy in outline that no novelist has yet limned his features for us.'[68] The one author capable of doing so, Haliburton, chose to give 'us instead a Yankee Sam Slick' whose Yankeeness is, however, denied by 'distinguished New Englanders.' As part of Edgar's introductory remarks, the difficulties incurred by trying to define 'Canadian' should give one pause. English-Canadian culture is, on the one hand, an object of intuition and, on the other, instinct with an ambivalence that is never far from Edgar's argument. He cautiously accepts Artemus Ward's (1834–67) opinion that Haliburton invented 'the humour of the United States' and later adds that, nevertheless, he 'was tory [*sic*] in the extreme,' implying he was both fish and fowl. Lampman, 'without being distinctively Canadian ... is still our representative Canadian poet,' or, as he remarks elsewhere, anticipating a later definition of (English) Canada, Lampman 'was as Canadian as circumstances would allow.'[69] Mentioning William Henry Drummond (1854–1907), he asserts: 'It is a healthy sign that poetry should, occasionally, revert to the primitive conditions from which it originated, and assume its original public function as a binding force.' Nevertheless, an earlier reference to poetry 'as an affair of impulse, [which] can live, if not flourish, without a public' would suggest that Drummond's efforts might be in vain.[70] 'If not flourish' is, moreover, a finely ironic phrase that works upon the life of poetry both positively and negatively and that readily gives the impression of someone surveying the accomplishments of a literature that are, rather, *nearly* accomplishments of a country that is *nearly* a culture. So '[a] very enjoyable part of Canadian literature connects itself with accounts of expeditions into distant regions of an unexplored continent,' and, after whetting the reader's appetite for these texts, Edgar moves easily through them in a paragraph. History is Canada's most 'successfully organized' genre to which he devotes a page. Fiction is given the most striking and revealing characterization: 'There are some novels that have honestly died, and some that have never lived. Canada's fiction may, with few exceptions, may be classed in one or other of these categories.'[71] The few exceptions are, for the most part, treated either diffidently or ironically.

Acerbic in many ways as Edgar's article is, its value lies in neither his canon nor the judgments laid upon them, but rather in the elegance which masks the uncertainty with which the matter is taken up. As for Marquis, history in English Canada does not appear to have a chronological structure: its beginnings cannot be placed with any sureness, inasmuch as Canadian culture is difficult to construct distinctly separate from the United States and Great Britain. To whose history, one might ask, does that of English Canada belong? It is a complicit culture with amorphous borders. This is, at least, the manner in which Edgar chooses to construe it. As a consequence, his discursive manner more than anything else originates a Canada in such a way as to empty it of both origination and originality. The absence of telos in English Canada, so marked as compared to French Canada, inscribes a culture in which few dates and no events are significant. Paradoxically, Edgar's Canada is like Lord Durham's French Canada, 'a people with no history, and no literature.'[72] Nor does he feel constrained to invent one. Rather, his history appears to empty history of history, like Marquis's, and then to place it where its outlines cannot be grasped.

Canadian Literature as American

Ray Palmer Baker's *A History of English-Canadian Literature to the Confederation* (1920)[73] was ripe with reply. For him Canada's English culture, at least until 1867, is the culture of the United States, at least until the Revolution. In Baker's own words, 'the literature of Canada until the Confederation was that of the United States.' His thesis is based on a number of assumptions. The first is that United Empire Loyalists bear a weight greater than any influence from Great Britain. Massachusetts was the source of most of Nova Scotia's significant writing and political oratory, and Harvard was the Alma Mater of most of Canada's pre-Confederation scientists.[74] The argument is developed by devoting over half the book to the literature of Nova Scotia, in particular to Joseph Howe (1804–73) and Thomas Haliburton. By selecting them as founders of 'Canadian' metadiscourse, Baker neatly unifies and resolves a problem of Canadian culture that overstrains his argument.

Howe is exemplary because he is the son of a Bostonian, because he favoured 'responsible government,' and because he championed the cause of democracy, all of which appear to be republican (read: American) causes. Nevertheless, we are to understand that it was not, in the main, Whigs who migrated to Nova Scotia, but rather Tories from the upper classes of pre-Revolutionary America.[75] The argument implies, however, that anyone who favoured responsible government was ideologically American. Furthermore, homesick Tory exiles were also ideologically American. Needless to say, it would be difficult to define an English Canadian in the closing years of the eighteenth century, not least because of the colonial character of the country, but to define by overemphasizing oppositions seriously weakens one's thesis. In fact, what Baker cannot countenance is the hybrid complexity of Canadians, a fact that is true of most people anywhere, and not finding difference he can only construct similarity: United Empire Loyalists continued an American political ideology.

The difficulties of maintaining a position that is embarrassed by ambiguity become clear in the analysis of Haliburton, who, he concedes, may be read as either American or English.[76] Unlike Howe, with whom he shared a defining vision of the British Empire, Haliburton was notably opposed to responsible government and clearly Tory. Because he is widely hailed as the father of American humour in a particular way, the inference is that he is more American than English, for 'Slick, interrupting the tradition of subservience, is the first sign of a new civilization.' While interruption, as we have already noted in our discussion of Camille Roy, is a sign of a new orientation and a vehicle of origination, everything depends upon how rupture is structured. The rhetoric of revolution motivates this description of Slick's function as American humour and yet, as Baker and others have noted, Haliburton's intent was 'to arouse his countrymen to an appreciation of its possibilities.' Memorable as he was, Slick is a 'Yankee pedlar, the despised of despised.' The interruption, then, does not address attitudes between North America and England, but rather those that obtained between two North American countries in their infancy. Baker's Haliburton can only be English and Loyalist, the latter being 'a direct heritage of the Revolution.' Taken together, neither constitute a Canadian character.[77]

Canada's founding novelist is John Richardson. Frances Brooke's novels 'disappeared without leaving any trace on the life of the province where they were written,' and Julia Catherine Hart is mentioned only through a casual noting of her novels. While Richardson has every chance of being Canadian, because as he descends from 'the Scotch, French, and Loyalist elements of Canadian society,' Baker's discussion shapes him as American. First, Cooper (1789–1851) is recognized by Richardson as an influence, which prompts Baker to observe: 'That Cooper, who had the bitter, verbal conflict which reverberated back and forth across the Border after the publication of the *Inquiry*, appears as the godfather of Canadian fiction is a happy instance of the power of art to transcend the barriers of national prejudice.' Once the border is transcended, Baker can later remark that 'Richardson ... found his pattern in America.' Finally, 'coming from a family accustomed for generations to the perils of the Frontier, and familiar from boyhood with the most stirring incidents of Canadian history, he is fully as American as Cooper.'[78]

Bearing in mind that 'the Loyalists ... were still imitators,' which is not apparent in Haliburton's case, at least, a number of 'schools,' such as those of the English poets, Goldsmith (?1730–74), Byron (1785–1824), and Burns (1759–96), can be easily put aside, if for no other reason than that they originate in Great Britain. It might have been more judicious to speak of a 'School of Cooper,' but judiciousness is precisely what Baker's thesis lacks. Only those writers clearly indebted to the Old Colonies are valorized. Because, one infers, William Kirby (1817–1906) was born in England, he is not examined closely. In fact, *The Golden Dog* (1877) is referred to by its translated title, and although mentioning that his reputation rests on this novel, Baker discusses instead the epic poem, *U.E.: A Tale of Upper Canada* (1859). Because Kirby's sympathies toward the Rebellion of 1837–8 are with the British, Baker disapproves of the poem's ideology. The treatment of Leprohon is equally questionable, for as representative of the nationalist movement, 'she has a right to contest Richardson's primacy as the first Canadian novelist.'[79] Nevertheless, she is given one paragraph in order to present her challenge at the end of the chapter on Richardson. Unlike him, being of Irish descent, born in Montreal and married to a French-Canadian doctor,[80] her background and connections are perhaps too diverse to serve Baker's thesis. Although Baker devotes a chapter to memoirs, in which Susanna Moodie (1803–85) figures predominantly, Moodie's works that 'show the growing sense of national unity' are, nevertheless, finally shelved for being 'essentially reminiscent in mood.'[81]

With the exception of Lareau and Roy, Baker is the only historian who constructs Confederation as significant. It 'is a symbol of national coalescence' and, as such, allows him to perceive a possible difference between Canadian and American literature. There is, then, a before and after in Canadian literature, analogous to his notion of the Age of Reminiscence and the Age of Curiosity. We have seen how Moodie belongs to the former and is also a nationalist. The primary fault with reminiscence is that 'loyalty to the imperial ideal ... has narrowed the outlook of the Canadian people and retarded their spiritual development.' Implied is the notion that nationalism in Canada is an undesirable element. Whether the emphasis placed upon Confederation is a recognition of Canada's American character in a post-revolutionary manner is not clear. Once Confederation occurs, however, Baker uses the term 'American' to mean belonging to the United States: 'Though [the Dominion] is thus essentially American, it differs in mood from the work of men born and educated in the South.' 'Mood' does not, however, imply a difference in kind, but rather in attitude and perspective. Baker's argument is, therefore, continentalist in the sense that he deliberately effaces differences between the writing of Canada and the United States by blurring ideological borders. It argues against difference with the same intellectual laxity as the Monroe Doctrine. The interplay, however, between the two literatures during the First World War when Baker's book was written, had yet to be resolved: 'Even now there are signs of a literary revival on the prairies. Whether it will deepen the nationalistic groove which I have been following, or whether it will assume the characteristics of a Continental or a world literature in English' is uncertain.[82] Thus the literature of English Canada, constructed as nationalistic insofar as it is loyal to the imperial ideal appears provincial and regional. Certainly in respect of the desire in the United States not to remain 'hampered' by its own moment of origination, nationalism in Canada is something for Baker that should be transcended, like borders.

In a paradoxical way, Baker may be associated with Marquis and Edgar, despite his reservations toward their work.[83] Like them, he seems embarrassed by history. He would abandon it is an ideological inhibition; they would prefer to construct it as a kind of cultural space without intimate rapport with the events that make a nation. But where Marquis and Edgar fail to find a nation and are motivated to put up a border as a means of asserting difference, Baker sees the nation only in Confederation and implies that the cultivation of nation, in any event, is a retrograde activity. The nation includes nothing that cannot be found south of the border. Under these circumstances, is it possible to speak substantively of an English-Canadian literature? This question and the issues it implies provide the threshold and direction for the course of literature history in Canada.

The metaphor of the threshold is not only useful for this moment in the literary history of Canada, but also for the sense of Canada that urges itself upon the reader of the texts of this period. Constructing borders as a necessary first step in defining positions in Canada appears as the first order of business. The border is at once a site of geographical and geopolitical significance. It is an outer as well as an inner border that is designed to respond to the questions, where is Canada and what is a Canadian? The response from Quebec is predictable: language forms a boundary that permits another culture to develop beside a culture dominated by those of British and United Empire descent. Language becomes the basis of a nation, and the protagonists who struggled for such a nation assume major roles in its history. Another border is erected through the ordering of historical events by which a people is empowered, and Roy set a permanent example for subsequent historians of French Canada, tempered by the role of language and the Roman Catholic religion. Both Lareau and Roy, then, construct a Canada of greater clarity than what English-Canadian literary historians marked by a firm distinction between anglophones and francophones. A further border is carefully erected between Quebec and France that both separates and joins. Literary history in French Canada from its earliest texts understands its function as a discourse shaped to make a nation.

The making of a nation is often in its beginnings an assertion of one ideology against another, a declaration of independence, if you will. A well-defined sense of unity that shares a common sense of the past is important for the success of such an assertion, and French Canada has always known how to use its past for such an effect. English Canada, by contrast, often appears baffled by such an enterprise, and it may be that the very notion of a declaration of independence, so fiercely asserted by its anglophone neighbour, is one of the major reasons for its bafflement. The inner border, as a result, is often contested, and the notion of 'Canadian' is often lost in the polarities of British and American. Lighthall at the height of the Victorian Period has no difficulty in locating Canada in the Empire, but Marquis and Edgar, part of the generation of the First World War as a border, are not so certain. Marquis sees a Canada constantly invaded and drained by the seductions of larger anglophone powers and constructs a Canadian who is of native stock, preferably of British descent, and who takes a vigorous, masculinist view of the world. The border is drawn against the United States and with Great Britain. Since French Canada does not pose a threat that equals that of Anglo-Saxon expansionism, no particular border is staked out. Edgar's Canadian is both American and British, and by nature ambiguous. Borders barely separate the various cultures English Canada relates to. For Baker, ambiguity is dismissed in favour of a continentalist construction of Canada, profoundly imbued with the American aspect of the United Empire Loyalist, and so long as English Canada remained faithful to the imperial idea as the basis of nationalism the ideals of progress would never be realized. Baker's border, the liberal border, is hardly a border, and it solves the problem of Canadian difference by dissolving it. In any event, English Canada is a certain kind of geography placed geopolitically between Great Britain and the United States, and whatever meaning it possesses derives from such a placement. Events occur in that space, and its history in time appears passively acquired from what happens in the countries from which the majority of its initial settlers come. Most subsequent English-Canadian literary historians followed this understanding of history as a spatial phenomenon, finding scant empowerment in chronological order.

The border, then, is a common preoccupation for all these historians, and it is the sign of what gives their histories the kinds of coherence they have. Thus, it may be considered a synecdoche in which the sense of a border governs the sense of the whole. Such an understanding of this trope, however, should not blind one to the fact that it is fraught with ideological difference. There are many borders and they are drawn with competing claims in mind. The formal, rhetorical value of the trope, as I shall argue, is deeply inscribed by the senses of nation that it is designed to hold together.

CHAPTER TWO

The Nation as Discourse, 1924–1946

... on pose la question au niveau du discours lui-même qui n'est plus traduction extérieure mais lieu d'émergence des concepts ...[1]

The two decades that we are about to consider, which embrace the period from the end of one world war to the other, constitute a period in which a sense of national consciousness was given new energy in English Canada while in Quebec, the traditional values that Camille Roy had been supporting since the turn of the century were more firmly reinforced. Needless to say, French Canada did not feel itself particularly called upon to support what it construed as British imperialism during the First World War, preferring to hold fast to regional concerns. It did not, therefore, participate in the English-Canadian sense of maturity that the latter felt that it had acquired in the trenches of France that subsequently began to manifest itself particularly in J.D. Logan's *Highways of Canadian Literature* (1924). Furthermore, both cultures, with rare exceptions, seemed uncertain how to respond creatively to the social issues raised by the Great Depression. Indeed, all the histories that arose during the 1930s preferred positions of a generally conservative kind, despite statements to the contrary, and these positions remained the norm in the following decade.

As I have remarked, one name, that of Mgr Camille Roy, who invariably identified himself as *ptre* (prêtre), alone and unassailably dominates the writing of histories of literature in French Canada during the first half of this century. Although the revisions to his *manuels* accommodated new material, the intent to determine the sense and direction of French Canada's history was always present. This contrasts sharply, however, with the number and variety of efforts to construct histories of

English Canada's literature. It suggests that literary history, as a particular mode of semantic constructions of history, was more stable during this period in Quebec, for, despite the regular revisions to which Roy's handbooks were subject, these revisions were always within Roy's control.[2] Nevertheless, despite the number of histories published by English-Canadian literary historians during this period, the problem with history remained similar to what we have already seen. If they were more reluctant than such historians as Roy to construct a history that would argue difference, they were intent, at least for a period following the First World War, to construct a sense of 'national consciousness.'

Making a Nation

The efforts to produce a literary history for English Canada following the First World War were initially rather desultory and then suddenly fraught with academic machinations. Although Archibald MacMechan's *Headwaters of Canadian Literature* (1924) sat untouched for a few years with Glasgow Brook, after which it eventually reached McClelland and Stewart, it had to put up with the stipulation of J.D. Logan that Mac-Mechan's book be stopped from publication for six months after Logan's. Thus the first ambitious attempts *hors Québec* to provide the literature of Canada with a significant structure were marked with what appeared to be serious differences of intent and design. Although Logan's text appeared also in 1924, but before MacMechan's, I have chosen to discuss the fuller second edition (1928), written in collaboration with Donald G. French. Beginning with MacMechan permits a beginning with what E.K. Brown was later to refer to as 'the most distinguished and sensible book about the national literature yet written by an English-speaking Canadian,' a remark finely tempered by Brown's adding that his copy was dedicated to him in an 'elegant, Victorian hand.'[3] Brown had no doubt about MacMechan's ideological allegiances, and his comment firmly places MacMechan as a link to the past rather than as a sign of the future.[4] It is a summary of earlier tendencies, but as a summary it is also an occasion to confront the problem of the embarrassment of history.

Two issues, which we have already encountered, govern the structuring of MacMechan's history, namely, what is Canadian and how does the Canadian enter history? To answer the first question he draws without acknowledgment upon Marquis's distinction between 'birds of passage' and 'native Canadians.' Thus, Frances Brooke (1724–89) is not mentioned, and such writers as Susanna Moodie and Charles Heavysedge are 'denizens [who] cannot be classified as Canadian writers.' William Kirby is also given short shrift. Expatriates pose another problem. Although Arthur Stringer (1874–1950) wrote a trilogy set in the Canadian West, this is not mentioned. By contrast, however, Sara Jeannette Duncan wrote *The Imperialist* over a decade after leaving Canada, and she is still considered Canadian, along with Paul Morin (1889–1963) and Marjory Pickthall, despite their lack of a 'Canadian' consciousness.[5] John Richardson, finally, seems to arrive too soon to be noticed. Nevertheless, a notion of 'Canadian' is important insofar as without it the central notion of the argument – 'the national impulse' – would be without meaning.

The Canadian 'national impulse' is understood historically as a consequence of the British North America Act, and the structure of MacMechan's argument depends implicitly upon this fact. Confederation invests geography with a meaning it could not otherwise possess and prevents MacMechan's history itself from being the merest description of some literary events in various regions in North America. In this respect, it is the first clear continuation of Baker's history of pre-Revolutionary America in Canada until 1867. Although history in Canada for MacMechan begins in Nova Scotia, this is but 'the accident of early settlement,' nor was Halifax a city that arose either naturally or by necessity. It was, rather, 'a fiat city.' Such an origin, however, enjoins the reader to read Canada as primarily a movement from East to West, which, while generally valid from the perspectiveof settlement, is wrong, as it turns out, both culturally and politically. To obscure the truth of history, however, MacMechan credits Quebec with nothing of native significance before the year 1860, with the curious exception of Michel Bibaud (1782–1857), who is not given frequent mention in the literary histories of his native province. François-Xavier Garneau is mentioned, but almost as an afterthought.[6]

If history can be played with so as to give the impression that the period from the sixteenth to the late eighteenth century was of negligible importance, thus suggesting that the question of origin is of minimal significance, how does MacMechan choose to invest his history with *historical* significance? His answer lies in what he calls 'the literature of power,' an expression borrowed from Thomas De Quincey's 'Theory of Literature.'[7] Such a literature, as distinguished from 'the literature of knowledge' is what permits one to speak of 'the voice of the people.' The literature of power enables literature and nation to become coterminous. Thus the question of origin is shifted from a moment in time ('the accident of early settlement') to a moment in the psychological life of a people, from 'chaos' and geography to something more 'imperishable.' Thus the inner logic of MacMechan's history argues against both the expectations of the reader and conventional assumptions, that is, that the frontier moves naturally from east to west. In fact, it moves nowhere with any voluntary order until the centre of Confederation is reached, an origin from which subsequent meaning emanates. As he remarks of Garneau, 'a history is a *roman à thèse*,'[8] which is precisely the kind of novel MacMechan's own history is. His justification of Garneau follows a curiously familiar, but useful trajectory that moves from 'affront' to 'rebellion' and concludes in 'national humiliation.' It is familiar because its three-fold movement is a dialectical process that MacMechan's own history projects as the Canadian 'national impulse' as acted out in the history of Ontario. Before Confederation 'there was no common country to which Crémazie and Haliburton owed allegiance except Great Britain.' Moreover, 'the fierce, political struggles, which the union was to cure, were old, unhappy, far-off things.'[9] The new province, which appears to be at once the emblem and the catalyst of the new country, and which 'knew nothing of separate provinces,' is unified by one thing – 'loyalty to a lost cause.' Imperceptibly, the new narrative lies upon the old one in palimpsest, implying that difference in race between East (read: Quebec) and West is overcome by the similarity of cultural narrative to such an extent that conflict has become sublated through a kind of pastoral, national ritual: 'In the provincial capital, one may see on the nation's birthday, a hundred thousand people wearing the green maple leaf, the national emblem, in spontaneous festival.' From this 'centre, the fertile breeding-ground of the new national sentiment' the country acquired its final form.[10] Thus the two initial panels formed by Nova Scotia and Quebec are responded to, and given coherence by, the role played by Ontario in the making of Confederation. It is an act of truly cardinal significance parallelled by the fact that it occurs in the central chapter of the book.

The return, then, to Montreal in the following chapter is not a geographical reversal. The rise of the Montreal School of poetry is constructed rather as a figurative act of 'Revolt, self-conscious and organised' against 'the old classical school of Quebec,' and it is revealing that, in respect of Émile Nelligan, 'no wreath of maple leaves entwines his page.' Indeed, the new movement poses a genuine problem for Mac-Mechan because it not only turns away from the older French-Canadian generation, but also 'is curiously remote from national and historical influence,' despite the fact that all the poets were 'of Canadian birth and training.'[11] Rather than construe Montreal's 'revolt' as possessing any dialectical force and significance, MacMechan treats it as an anomaly: the French-speaking province is a 'chasm' opening within the Dominion, implying that Canada's 'historical consciousness,' that inspired Ontario's 'national impulse,' was, after all, the realization of a spatial instinct 'felt from ocean to ocean.'[12] Thus, what appeared to be a sense of history that allowed for conflict and that understood that significance is a function of human will concludes with the assertion that unity is a totalizing idea that overcomes change and the challenges raised against the national impulse. As a result, while appearing to challenge a notion of Canada as a function of random settlement patterns, MacMechan returns to a position analogous to that of his predecessors. While the history of Canada is dominated by the desire of English Canada, at least, to confederate, the achievement of confederation marks an end to history and, unfortunately, an apocalypse with an ambiguous gap in it. It is a gap brought about by Montreal's rejection of Quebec's earlier use of the national theme that cohered with the Canadian national theme. The loss is Montreal's, for it thus lost 'touch with the creative, life-giving, native soil.'[13]

The notion of a literature of power, then, inscribes Canadian literature, both anglophone and francophone, in a Federalist design. Deviation from the design does not weaken federalism, rather it limits the future in the ideological space of Federation of those who deviate. Opposition, then, is not sublated into new significance; it is ignored. By ignoring it, cultural difference is neutralized within the idea of the Dominion by those who generate the Canadian community: 'they all have their origin in the centre, and ... they reach out east and west to the farthest bounds of the Dominion. They are all national, not provincial ...' Origin, then, is not so much a beginning in time, despite the fact that it occurred in 1867, but a beginning as an idea, and especially as an idea of integration into a whole. Thus it corresponds to Hayden White's notion of history as Synecdoche, that is, a trope that suggests 'a relationship among the elements of a totality [here understood as the nation] – it is integrative rather than reductive.' As a result, despite his admiration for, and desire to canonize, Pickthall and Morin (the latter MacMechan's favourite among the Montreal poets), they remain ambiguous for him because of the design of the whole.[14]

Darwin, God, and History

In many respects, this is the argument of Canadian distinctiveness, a perennial leitmotif in English-Canadian metacritical discourse, and it continues in another manner in Lionel Stevenson's *Appraisals of Canadian Literature*, which appeared two years later than MacMechan's *Headwaters*. 'Concerned only with literature that is inherently of some distinctive Canadian quality,' Stevenson construes literature as a profoundly intimate sign of the writer's relationship with the nation. Unlike patriotic poetry, 'the spirit moves freely among the supreme mind of all nations.' In a claim that seems to have fallen upon deaf ears, Stevenson claims that this movement occurs 'only when the poet's country has become for him a living being, endowed with a soul, and not an abstraction of economists.' Then 'his love for her can raise his work to that lofty region.' The poet, then, by implication writes the nation, and does so by means of an organic intimacy with it (or 'her,' as Stevenson would have it). Canadian literature does not, therefore, begin in time, in 1760, for example, or in geographical space, such as Nova Scotia. For Stevenson it begins, rather, at a certain moment in intellectual history as a response to Darwinism. It belongs, however, to the rhetorical structure of the book to delay the introduction of this moment of origin until the fifth chapter, devoting the initial chapters to 'the general problem of definition.'[15] Origin thus is privileged as a primary explanation of what is construed as a general situation.

Part of the manner in which Canadian poetry is coterminous with writing the nation, as well as illustrating a general situation, is by its rarely being revolutionary and imbued, in fact, with the pioneer spirit. These are at once political and practical qualities that may only coincide, however, with the fashioning of verse. More closely related to poetry is its tendency toward idealism and pantheism. Far from being revolutionary, it manifests a certain passivity characterized by a mystical and apocalyptic bearing, and, indeed, Carman's verse is marked by 'the ecstasy of communion.' In a word, 'in Canada the primordial forces are still dominant,' in contrast to Europe.[16] Canada, therefore, appears uniquely placed between the young civilization of the United States, as exemplified in Walt Whitman (1837–1909),[17] and the old civilization of Europe, particularly England, as exemplified in the poetry of Tennyson, Swinburne (1819–92), Kipling (1865–1936), and especially Robert Louis Stevenson (1850–94). Because Canadians appear 'to be precariously perched on a monster not yet conscious of their presence ... [their] sympathy with nature is practically an inbred trait.' Nature, then, is not merely a physical presence; forests, mountains, and rivers are all signs of 'the great spirit permeating all nature, and man's insignificance in the physical world merges into his metaphysical ecstasy of unity with the spirit.'[18]

It may appear curious that such an argument would conclude that John McCrae's (1872–1918) 'In Flanders Fields' is the quintessential Canadian poem.[19] Nevertheless, it is of greater significance that much of what Stevenson asserts is later echoed in the more influential essays of Northrop Frye, notably his 'Canada and Its Poetry,' 'Preface to an Uncollected Anthology,' and certain summary remarks in his Conclusion to the first edition of Klinck's *Literary History of Canada*. Frye is, of course, more dour than Stevenson, remarking upon his continually being impressed 'in Canadian poetry by a tone of deep terror in regard to nature ... not a terror of the dangers or discomforts or even the mysteries of nature, but a terror of the soul at something that these things manifest.'[20] Frye, however, had E.J. Pratt (1882–1964) to refer to,[21] Stevenson's argument is based upon the more romantic poets of the late nineteenth century. Nevertheless, their point of departure is the same: the poetic crisis in England and Canada in the late nineteenth century did not have its origins in politics, but rather in the challenge offered by Darwin. According to Frye, 'the sombre Tennysonian vision of nature red in tooth and claw blots out the sentimental Rousseauist fantasy of the charming solitudes.'[22]

Desmond Pacey remarked in the second edition of Klinck's *Literary History* that Stevenson was 'experiencing a revival,'[23] which may be attributable to the revival of mystical attitudes in North American culture in the 1960s, and it is an argument that continues, as I shall indicate, in Tom Marshall. Although Stevenson's penchant was Rousseauist, the differences between him and Frye are differences of emphasis.[24] Thus, the Canadian poet, when faced with the dilemma of Darwin, realizes the possibilities alluded to in Stevenson's earlier themes of mysticism, passivity, and pantheism. As he asserts, however, Darwin is at once a danger and an opportunity; and although 'the poet's sensibilities would be in serious danger of quailing in horror and withdrawing itself to less terrific themes ... the idea of evolution allowed a glimpse of unity pervading nature and control directing her mysterious ways.' Thus the shapeless monster where the Canadian is perched and the chaos it signifies are paradoxically envisioned as Providence, 'a supernal plan.' Although 'rendered insignificant alike by the magnitude of the universe and the minute perfection of the atom ... [the Canadian poet's] spiritual greatness is somehow attested by his potential identity with the universal spirit'; and that spirit, as the last word of the chapter on Darwin has it, is 'God.'[25]

If one accepts Stevenson's initial assertions regarding the spiritual and idealistic character of Canadian poetry in general – and in some way they are compelling claims – the paradoxical use of Darwin is *a fortiori* stunning in its imppact. More significantly, it raises issues about literary history that prompt attention. Despite the fact that Stevenson refers to his studies as 'appraisals,' thereby suggesting that his emphasis is more on criticism than history, he sees his book in a context that begins with Marquis. He simply denies the status of his own text as 'a *comprehensive* history of Canadian literature.'[26] It is a history, but not one in the conventional sense, that is, where traces of other kinds of history – political, economic, religious, military – are to be found in it as guides. If one overlooks the praise of McCrae, one cannot fail to admire Stevenson's peremptory silence taken toward Canada's early writers, which often appear to be embarrassments for other historians, and his refusal to find any significant rapport between great poetry and events such as Confederation. His assumption is that the poetry that matters has no precursors, thus eliminating any role Sangster might have played as English Canada's first major poet, and that in Canada it emerges from the poet's perception of place and the reception of a crucial event in intellectual history. If poetry is the product of powerful motions of the mind, heart, and soul, then its origins are best found in *their* articulations.

A serious consequence of such a decision is the effect it has on modes other than poetry which may not have the ability or the interest 'to give more adequate expression to ... the eternal.' Because 'writers of prose have almost without exception lacked the profundity to achieve this philosophical point of view, and have been content with the superficial distinctiveness which Canadian settings and events provide,' the review of writers other than poets is of a desultory character, dividing discussion of their work according to such themes as nature, the native, the habitant, and the immigrant, and then ordering it geographically. Unwittingly, then, Stevenson exposes the limits of history as Synecdoche. For, while poets may approach the vision from several quarters, the vision, the integrative whole that Synecdoche produces, is not available to writers of prose. Unable 'to show [men and women] convincingly involved in man's eternal conflict with the forces that oppose him,' the novel is deemed inadequate.[27] Stevenson's standard for the novel is that it does not assume the moral clarity of romance: it prefers 'a distinct cult of unpleasant characters and an assumption of the harshness that is loosely termed realism.' It is a cult that in the end fails because of its faithfulness to the real. A possible response to such a dilemma would be to posit a more flexible idea of order in an effort to determine what the attraction to realism was. It could be suggested that the realism that Stevenson describes with its emphasis on characters that are 'ponderously manipulated marionettes'[28] is closer to Naturalism, and therefore closer to a world of (Darwinian) determinism and the large, unavoidable forces in the physical universe that have the appearance of being the obverse of Stevenson's construction of Canadian poetry. But the risk of Synecdoche, as MacMechan also implies, is contradiction. Synecdoche prefers to repress, rather than to construct, opposition as a complementary action.

History of Literature as National Self-Knowledge

While it is true that both Lareau and MacMechan made serious efforts to include the two founding cultures in their histories, Lareau was not particularly consistent and MacMechan at once includes and excludes in his treatment of the Montreal School of poetry. Consequently, when Lorne Pierce claims in his Foreword that his '*Outline* is the first attempt at a history of our literature, placing both French and English authors side by side,' it is both a valid statement and model for subsequent efforts of the same kind. Camille Roy, the dedicatee of the book, gestured in the same direction some years later, and the renewal of comparative studies in the late 1960s chose the same model without acknowledgment, with the exception of Richard Giguère.[29] Pierce's subsequent claim that 'hereafter [French and English] must share equally in any attempt to trace the evolution of our national spirit' has not, for the most part, been considered an imperative. If his *Outline of Canadian Literature (French and English)* is to be understood as 'the standard reference book for at least a decade or so,' the extent to which it sought to articulate national self-knowledge should also be understood. As he asserts in his dedication letter to Roy, 'Il faut apprendre à se connaître.' Literature is only to be construed as a sign of the nation. To order literature historically is to write the nation as a culture that is such through the exercise of self-knowledge. So firmly is this believed that Pierce constructs origins primarily in 'the constitutional development of Canada,' implying, at least, that political arrangements signify a kind of cause of the national spirit inscribed in literary texts.[30] Thus the structure of the *Outline* corresponds to White's notion of history as Metonymy in which constitutional developments would serve as agents or causes of which literature is the effect.[31] If the controlling purpose of the book is 'to acquire a greater cohesiveness' for the nation, the structure poses unre-solvable problems because 'constitutional development' has not been the scene of 'une profonde entente cordiale,' needless to say.[32]

The problem is immediately perceptible in the honesty with which Pierce addresses the issue of periodization. Although he divides Cana-dian literary history into four periods, the dating by the two founding cultures differs significantly. He begins by firmly accepting Roy's date of 1760, the year of the Cession, as the moment of origin for French-Canadian writing. Although such a date, as well as the Peace of Paris (1763), may serve one culture, it does not seem adequate for the other, and 1776 is chosen as the more appropriate date for the beginning English-Canadian cultural history. The dates do not coincide because they represent different historical trajectories, but both represent a shared theme. They represent the origins of Canada implicitly as defeat, if not a shared defeat. Although Pierce does not draw this conclusion, it might be observed that the tragedy of Canada is that its two dominant cultures have refused to recognize this element in the other. Thus in the early years following the Cession, French Canada's history is 'marked by nostalgia'; and so it is that, as a consequence of the United States's War of Independence, early Loyalist writing, which is granted greater signifi-cance than anything before it, is 'marked by a wistful longing back to their old homes.'[33] Although one initial paragraph is devoted to Aborig-inal culture, nothing of this sort is said on its behalf.

Because constitutional history, however, is a development of British history, cultural relationships with the power it represents must differ. Not surprisingly, therefore, the first three periods of French-Canadian history are construed as efforts to overcome nostalgia by recovering the past as national self-consciousness. The second period (1831–60) is devoted to the inscription of the nation in the writing of Parent and Garneau, as well as the movement to acquire responsible government. The third period (1860–1900) is devoted to the consolidation of French-Canadian nationalism that 'fused the scattered settlements and parishes into self-consciousness and unity.' The final period is imbued with 'the rise of a strong feeling of nationalism, and the integration of the social and intellectual elements of the province.'[34]

English Canada's colonial period ends in 1840 with the Act of Union, an act that was clearly a moment of closure for French-Canadian distinc-tiveness and, therefore, not selected as a period mark for its culture. Nor is any mention made of Upper Canada's role in the Rebellion; rather the War of 1812 is privileged, along with the work of Haliburton and Richardson. The second period (1840–77) is named 'The Confederation Group,' an appellation that is parallelled by 'The Quebec School'; and significantly it is not the act of parliament that is emphasized in the word 'confederation,' but rather the sense of 'organic growth.' The year 1877 is chosen as an ending and beginning because it saw the publication of Kirby's *The Golden Dog*, a novel that 'opened up a highway from Niagara to the Citadel, from the heart of one tradition to the core of another.' The third period (1880–1900) is named 'The Canadian School,' and it 'was of the English lineage.' This means it 'included Emerson, Poe and Whitman besides, but in all and through all it was essentially Canadian.' Significantly, Poe and Whitman are never mentioned again, and even more significantly, no effort is made to indicate how the Quebec School relates to the Canadian School. The final period does not begin in 1900, which permits the subsequent dispensing of a number of minor poets who scribbled during the '*interregnum*.' The impact of the First World War and the first conscription crisis in Quebec are passed over in silence, but in English Canada it is noted that the war led to 'the growth of a robust nationalism, and an increasing cosmopolitanism.'[35]

Structurally, then, the book argues against its declared intent and demonstrates, implicitly at least, that an 'entente cordiale' between the two cultures based on constitutional history is not viable. It suggests, rather, that the two cultures inhabit different times and different histories and that any structure of parallelism is specious. Things also fall apart in practice. Treating the French-Canadian novel, for example, periodization is not only forgotten, but also the decisive origin of 1760 entirely disappears: 'Although the French occupied Canada from 1535 until 1763, it is difficult to date the beginning of French Canadian literature.' Furthermore, Louis Hémon's (1880–1913) *Maria Chapdelaine* (1914) is astonishingly placed among anglophone novels, presumably because it was translated twice into English. Addressing francophone poetry, the period '1900 and After' is changed to 'The Post-War Period' with no explanation of how the war affected literature. Indeed, its major representative, Paul Morin, appears profoundly untouched by either Quebec or the war. By contrast, English-Canadian fiction is given periods. To embellish the Colonial period, Frances Brooke, who along with Oliver Goldsmith had been dismissed in the first chapter as 'properly belong[ing] to the old land,' is later reinstated at length. Goldsmith also becomes 'the first native-born Canadian poet,' and the use of the adjective immediately prompts a footnote indicating that it means 'English-

Canadian.' Such an admission makes it difficult to understand the manner in which Pierce is addressing two literatures in the concluding chapter, 'The Genius of Canadian Literature.'[36]

Imbalances in favour of anglophone writing are evident not only in respect of the novel and its periodization but also drama. This latter may be attributed to Roy, who omits discussion of theatre entirely in his edition of the *Manuel* of 1920, upon which Pierce relies. Apparently following Pierce's example, a subsection on theatre was added to the edition of 1930. Mutual admiration, of course, went further, particularly manifest in Pierce's use of the biographical sketch as the dominant mode of presentation. Since this is largely Roy's manner, I will postpone an analysis of its function until my later treatment of Roy. Like his predecessor, Pierce concludes his history with a summarizing discussion. Although he raises the question of a 'national ideal,' it does quite carry the same connotations as 'la vie nationale' in Roy.[37] Indeed, the eleven characteristics that make Canadian literature distinctive do not appear to have much to do with Canada in particular and nothing to do with 'constitutional developments' which, by the end, are forgotten. Pierce notes sincerity ('the secret of originality'), optimism, courage, the pioneering spirit, cosmopolitanism, 'rugged dignity,' nonconformity, unconventionality, realism, mysticism, and a love of nature as traits that might befit someone on the verge of maturity, like 'a nation that ... must learn to think for itself.' Such a nation requires concomitantly writers who 'will explain us to ourselves.'[38] And so we return ineluctably to Pierce's initial theme expressed in his letter to Roy: knowledge of the nation is knowledge of literature. The model of the nation, however, is the nation as ideal youth, an image which comfortably removes Canada from the conflicts of its (constitutional) history.

Canada as Aesthetics

In some respects, much may be gleaned from knowing to whom a book is dedicated, and from the manner of the dedication. MacMechan chose Sir Andrew Macphail, who held the chair in medicine at McGill for three decades, and who wrote confidently, if not always accurately, on a wide variety of subjects. He was chosen because MacMechan wished to associate him with his patriotic epigraph, *ad majorem patriae gloriam*. We have seen the esteem in which Pierce held Roy. J.D. Logan, one assumes, chose William Ernest Thompson as dedicatee for the book written for the most part by him, with some contributions by Donald G.

French. Thompson, who died in 1924, is addressed as 'Colonel,' and hailed for his staff duties in the Maritime Command during the First World War. He was also a writer and for several years the editor of the *Youth's Companion,* and one senses in the restlessness of his life and various careers the kind of flamboyance often associated with *Highways of Canadian Literature* and its author.[39]

Logan's ambitions were decidedly large. Not content with history as chronicle, his intent is to write a 'Synoptic or Philosophical' history. While the conventional understanding of synopsis is a general view or plot summary, Logan means something more structured which 'would treat Canadian Literature as a Whole in respect to its genetic bases and relations.' Furthermore,

> the synoptic method assists the imagination to view Canadian authors and their literature in an inclusive historical perspective, and thus to discover in Canadian literature the evolution of a people's social and spiritual ideals, their national and world conceptions, and how and what each individual poet or prose writer, or each group or school of poets and prose writers, has contributed to the vision of the people's social and spiritual ideals and to the evolution of these ideals in the people's social conscience.[40]

Because this declaration was initially made in 1924 when only Marquis and Baker were his predecessors, it carries a certain originality; certainly his initial chapters remain more attentive to English-Canadian history than either MacMechan or Pierce. In a general way, he always appears to accept Baker's general division: Canada begins in 1760 and, viewed as a whole, its history may be understood as before and after Confederation. In practice, however, the operative dates for the first period are 1760 to 1887, the latter date chosen because it marks, with the publication of Charles G.D. Roberts's *In Divers Tones,* 'the first "Voice" of the spirit of Canada.'[41] The second period is tripartite, consisting of a First Renaissance (1887–1907), a Decadent interim (1907–13), exemplified by Robert Service (1874–1958) and Robert J.C. Stead (1880–1959),[42] and a Second Renaissance (or Restoration) Period (1913–24). Although these terms may seem somewhat presumptuous, they constitute a method of emplotment not often used. Perkins simplified all the plots of narrative literature history into three kinds, namely, 'rise, decline, and rise and decline.' Logan is proposing a plot of rise, decline, and rise. The initial rise is expressly related to a change in the political understanding of Canada prior to Confederation during which 'the people in the British

North American Provinces were gradually coming to see themselves, their country, their civilization, and institutions from *the Canadian point of view*, and were gradually expressing, with more and more of conscious fervour and power, in prose and poetry, their growing interest in and love of Canada and the Canadian point of view.'[43]

While some may wonder how Pickthall, Robert Norwood (1874–1932), Katherine Hale (Amelia Beers Garvin [1878–1956]), and others are sufficient to be a part of a second rebirth after Roberts and the other Confederation poets, this is not as significant as the rage for order that such a structure bears witness to. The plot is a critical judgment to the extent that it determines value, as do all the other categories Logan considers necessary, such as '"Incidental" Literature' (work by temporary residents), '"Nativistic" Literature' (work by either permanent immigrants or writers before Confederation), and '"Native and National"' Literature (work by native-born Canadians).[44] Cumbersome as these categories may appear, they respond to an issue raised by Marquis, and they continue to address at least adequately the problem of such later writers as Brian Moore (1921–99) and Malcolm Lowry (1909–57). Categories, however, like plots have consequences. Frances Brooke, Susanna Moodie, and Charles Heavysedge are quickly disposed of because of the derived character of their writing. Although Oliver Goldsmith is Nativistic, he is passed over rapidly, and Catherine Beckwith Hart is ignored, as she often is. Richardson is Canada's first novelist. Nevertheless, the true founders, by general agreement, are Howe and Haliburton, mainly because of their national and international recognition.

Canada's true beginnings, however, are to be found among the post-Confederation writers, and primarily the poets. They are considered 'systematic,' that is: 'the first Canadians consciously to undertake a literary career which should be, in its way and degree, commensurate with the growing spiritual, social, political, and commercial life of the Great Dominion, and to find their inspiration chiefly, if not wholly, in the natural beauty and sublimity of their homeland, and in the spiritual import of their country and of the lives of their compatriots.' Without these writers, Canada would not be known as a national project; without being thus placed in history, Canada as a nation would have no meaning. Thus literary history and the nation, if not coterminous as imagined constructs, bear a dialectical relationship toward each other. Inclusion (canonization) and the estimation of relative worth is not a matter of 'literaturnost,' but rather the manner in which 'the slowly emerging consciousness of a national spirit and a national destiny in the Dominion' is inscribed in their work and then ordered into the larger framework of a history.[45]

As I have suggested, categories are in many respects value judgments. Thus Frederick Phillip Grove (1879–1948) is unknown to Logan,[46] and Sara Jeannette Duncan is implicitly taken to task for emigrating. The significant category, then, that in some shadowy manner governs both the plot structure and accidents of birth is the term 'Canadian.' First of all, it should be understood that the word refers exclusively to English-Canadian culture. The occasional reference to Canada's other founding culture, even if one overlooks Drummond's *habitant* poems, is tarnished by the ability to misappropriate. Thus, Louis Hémon's *Maria Chapdelaine* is included, its publication date given as 1922 (the English translations appeared in 1921), indicating its value only to the anglophone literary system. Logan's frequent use of the adjective 'Canadian,' however, is problematical as it becomes tautologically involved between a certain kind of imagery and 'the national spirit.' As we have seen, texts are chosen as Canadian because their authors fit categories of eligibility, and they fit those categories by being born after 1867 in Canada and manifesting the national spirit. The spirit does not manifest itself until at least a decade after Confederation at which time writers became 'indigenous and originally Canadian.' These are primarily poets from Roberts on, all of whom, unlike prose writers, merit a chapter each, and the greatest among them is Lampman. Lampman's poetry is praised because, unlike the Greek and English poetry, it does not '"[deck] out" Nature solely for the sensuous enjoyment of a world made lovely to look upon,' nor is it Celtic 'because the interior revealment expresses a special view of Nature and a special mode of intimate communion between the Canadian heart and the spirit of Nature.'[47] Consequently, 'Lampman "humanizes" Nature in a peculiar way, namely, by reciprocal sympathy.' Such a 'psychological phenomenon' is the significant element of 'the Canadian genius.' Carman goes further by identifying himself with Nature, and this is deemed both 'Canadian and unique.'[48]

Although I have qualified Logan's use of 'Canadian' as English, this is true only within a general tradition, for Canada's roots are defined more particularly as Scots and also Loyalist, that is, of New England descent. From these two sources the 'otherworldliness' of Canadian thought is said to derive. This cast of mind becomes Canadian from its bearing upon 'nature in Canada, [which] recalled Canadian poets from exclusive preoccupation with spiritual prosperities and great departures to thoughts of "the soul's inherent high magnificence" in daily mundane life and to the joys, consolations, spiritual transports, and peace which Nature affords the distracted human spirit.' Thus, the representatives of The Decadent Interim are rejected for their failure to conjoin, one might say, their real to Logan's ideal. Failing to do so, they 'refuse to promote the Godlike in the hearts of mankind.' While it is doubtful that this idealism has as much to do with responsible government as Logan's argument suggests, it possesses, nevertheless, remarkable convergences with Stevenson's desire to construct Canadian poetry as a dialectical response to Darwin's denial of biblical master-narrative. Their negation of negation, which Stevenson rightly does not force into a political framework, is not, however, recognized in Logan's text, possibly because it could have damaged his structure of the national as an historical code. But Logan's casual dismissal of Canadian historiography, which appears to rely on Marquis's comment that quantity is no substitute for quality,[49] tends to undermine his own efforts to historicize.[50] The problem with historiography is that 'men with the historic imagination do not exist in Canada.'[51] We have observed such a lack before, at least in English Canada, and it is evident that Logan himself construes history as a history of the spirit which allows him, beneath the appearance of historical structure, to use history as a justification for aesthetic judgment. It also prompts a question raised before, namely: Does English Canada exist in time?

Conserving the Roman Catholic Ethos

Clearly, by the end of the second decade of the twentieth century, Canadian literary historians *hors Québec* were not ready to address such a question. As we have seen, Roy is more at home with the question of history, and this may attributed to the French-Canadian ability to define itself, not in respect of cultures that use the same language and draw their tradition from Great Britain, but rather in respect of cultures that are constructed as different and not always capable of an 'entente cordiale.' The history of French Canada can thus be constructed as a dramatic act of salvation. Not only are the ideals of Roman Catholicism preserved among francophones after the Revolution, but also a French (American) way of life is continuously restored and protected. In such a history the Conquest as Fall can readily accommodate the code of theology and cultivate with it greater durability than the tradition of exile among Loyalists and Scots. After all, the latter had access to power and the discourse that sustains such power, while the French, as Roy is never

tired of repeating in edition after edition of his *manuels*, suffered profoundly from being severed from France.[52] Emplotment for Roy, then, is
entirely a story of rising, and at no point does this become so clear as in
his *Histoire de la littérature canadienne* (1930), which is marked by his
attempt to return Pierce's homage by including a section on English-
Canadian literature.

The fundamental difference between the two cultures is that, while
French Canada's history is marked by dates representing significant
étapes in the development of a national idea, English Canada has dates
that correspond to Pierce's, but they are easily forgotten, and structure
in English-Canadian literary history is frequently determined by genre.
In the absence of any explanation, one might infer, since Pierce's book
was beside him as a model, that the dates have no significance within a
French-Canadian perspective (indeed they do not), and so for Roy
nation can only be understood in a French sense and in a French-Canadian history. The absence of any concluding chapter that would either
combine the two literatures into one statement of significance or at least
summarize the sense of English-Canadian history would seem to reinforce this view. Indeed, the repetition of the concluding paragraphs
from the *Manuel* published in 1920 and the end of the French-Canadian
section in his later *Histoire* stands in sharp contrast to the absence of a
corresponding statement at the end of the book. Roy's reader was primarily a student of the collège classique, and the function of the *manuel*
was to 'nationaliser, dans la mesure où cela se peut faire sans nuire à la
formation générale de l'esprit, notre enseignement.' The insinuation of
the handbook into the process of construction of the nation is also
neatly expressed, and the self-realization of the nation is profoundly
assisted by such texts.[53]

Since Roy's *manuel* of 1920, the structure was changed in order to
accommodate the additional decade and a half of literary development.
Now there are three major periods, the first from 1760 to 1860, the second from 1860 to 1900, and the third from 1900 to the present. The
major difference, in conformity with the other *manuels*, is the use of biographical sketches and photographs of major authors in order to locate
literature within the history of lives that are illustrative in the fullest
sense, so that the writer not only represents a style of writing but also a
certain style of life.[54] As Robert demonstrates, Roy's texts are not simply
a reference; they are, rather, a grammar that the student learns to conju-
gate and, by extension, the same is true of Pierce. The student learns
that 'la littérature n'a donc pas ici une vie autonome. Elle a un rôle de

propagandiste de la nation et des valeurs nationales.' The macrogrammar of each biography is designed to indicate that 'l'œuvre est le reflet de la nation, par la médiation de l'écrivain et par le pivot de la biographie.' Thus it is possible, as Robert continues, that literature serves 'comme le reflet de la nation dans un rapport qui s'effectue par le passage du discours historique au discours critique,' a technique which is at work in any history whether biography is used or not.[55]

Each text in such histories as Roy's and Pierce's follows a pattern which, for the most part, seizes an event in the past in respect of the work and then shifts to the present in order to make a judgment. The rupture of the time-sequence in Roy is often marked by the conjunction 'mais,' which both distinguishes and conjoins the two levels of discourse. It should be noted that Pierce makes use of the same technique; unlike Roy, however, sequences of time are not so strictly observed and, as a result, the two levels of discourse are less easy to distinguish in a casual reading. Writing about Lampman, for example, he asserts that 'his poetry had deeper sources of inspiration than external stimuli.' This is a judgment, but it is given as a fact of history. Pierce continues: 'He *was* also a master of colour and contour, in a manner reminiscent of Keats, but lacking the sensuousness of Keats. Lampman's classical training *can* be seen in every page of his work ... While at one time social and political ideas of a somewhat unorthodox nature *perturbed* him, only an echo of this *escapes* into his work.'[56] Had he wished, Pierce might have used *is* for *was*, and *perturbed* might also have been in the present tense. His ambiguous ease with tense allows, to a degree greater than in Roy, for critical discourse to be inscribed into historical discourse, the significance of the discourses thus relating to each other as in a palimpsest but reversing their positions. Like Roy, however, Pierce privileges a certain style of life – the classical education, the repression of the unorthodox. Had Pierce known of it, he would have very possibly glossed over Lampman's unhappy extramarital relationship with Katherine Waddell. Writers are models, and as such they model an ideal history of the nation.

The function of Pierce's text is to serve as a teaching guide 'in the schools and colleges,' and Roy's text is similar in that it promulgates certain values, albeit Roy's are agrarian, Roman Catholic, and French. Such is the substance of Roy's *nation*, clear in every judgment. Like Stevenson, Pierce would probably agree that Canadians are not revolutionaries, and the same is true for Roy, whose petit-bourgeois audience is enjoined, as Robert argues, to accept a social order of the kind that was shaped by the Duplessis government.[57] Pierce, whose influence lasted until the Second World War, might be said, even in his shifting use of time in his style, to exemplify the constant adjustments of the Mackenzie King government's legendary efforts to muddle through.

The Handbook as Metonymy

The rather intense activity that the twenties in Canada witnessed in respect of anglophone literature was brought to an apparently unassuming close in V.B. Rhodenizer's *A Handbook of Canadian Literature* (1930). Like many of his predecessors, he is at least briefly exercised by 'Canadian' as a sign of eligibility.[58] His definition is twofold. Length of residence, 'regardless of how incidental' it may have been, is of no importance if the work 'vitally touches the Canadian scene or the Canadian people' and all 'authors born and bred in Canada,' no matter where they eventually reside, are Canadian.[59] Like MacMechan and without acknowledgment, he makes use of De Quincey's distinction between literature of knowledge and power and thus avoids some of the monotony that belongs to handbooks. The distinction is also more functional than in MacMechan, for it provides a structure: Canadian literature in English is structured chronologically as a movement from knowledge (to inform and persuade) to empowerment (to bring science and philosophy to life).

All of Rhodenizer's preliminary comments are couched beneath the phrase 'in this course,' and his text is more explicitly didactic than those preceding him. It is a function of the structure, and it is employed to guide the reader through from aspects of knowledge to aspects of power. Although indications of the didactic are everywhere, they are particularly noticeable in such chapters as 'The Short Story,' whose intent is announced with the following sentence: 'Not every story that is short is a short story in the technical sense.' Then three pages are devoted to general analysis. While such information is specifically necessary to chapter 18, it is clear that a knowledge of poetry, raised in chapter 20, requires a review of chapter 15. Because of the self-reflexive manner in which knowledge is constructed, (literary) history is also to be understood as self-reflexive. The knowledge it imparts is at once linear and recursive. A knowledge of Loyalism is necessarily raised in chapter 3, for example, in order to situate Kirby historically (chapter 10). Furthermore, understood properly, history, while part of the literature of knowledge, leads insidiously to a literature of power as it moves canonically higher from Howe's eloquence to D.C. Scott's poetry, whose work 'calls for a more cultivated and refined taste than that of any other Canadian poetry.'[60]

Such a form, of course, overlooks normal chronologies for the sake of an inner history of refinement, which is the aim of the literature of power. English-Canadian literary history has a beginning in the Maritimes in the late eighteenth century, and its more forceful directions derive from Howe and Haliburton, after which it is constructed generically, moving from knowledge (travel, history, biography) to a transition in the historical novel, animal stories, the familiar essay, and humour.[61] The literature of power begins in earnest with the short story, continues through a brief chapter on drama, and reaches its climax in the chapters devoted to individual poets. It is hard not to see a falling away of intensity in the concluding chapters devoted to Service and other contemporary poets,[62] Drummond, and French-Canadian literature.

The concluding chapter embroiders on the theme of 'national consciousness,' and it is precisely here that the double structure of literature as knowledge and power conjoins with the idea of the nation. They bear upon it mutually and perhaps self-reflexively: 'Literature that is the product of national consciousness stimulates in turn that which produced it, and so the good results of national consciousness are cumulative.'[63] The form and didactic intent of the book, then, are homologous with its desired effect. Just as Rhodenizer's book is a product of national consciousness, so he hopes national consciousness will continue to build upon itself, particularly in the matter of national unity. His history may be seen as a kind of metonymical gesture in which the text, the handbook itself, is a cause of which the effect is the sentiment of national consciousness. Both cause and effect, finally, have a dialectical bearing upon the ineluctable referent of the book, the Canadian nation, which resides somewhere within the whole metonymical process.

History as Palimpsest

In 1933 Father Albert Dandurand published the first of three texts which, had they been integrated, would have constituted a literary history of prose and poetry in Quebec. He preferred, however, to treat francophone writing in Canada according to genre. Nevertheless, his general argument remains the same, namely, that this is a literature grafted upon that of France, summed up in the triumphantly shaped exclamation, 'L'on emprunte donc à la France!'[64] A notion of his reception by the literary institution of the 1960s, a sign, perhaps, of Dandurand's sense of dependency, may be gleaned from the fact that he is not mentioned in Pierre de Grandpré's history. His intended audience, however, was the secondary school teacher, and, therefore, his texts formed part of the clerical school system. For a later literature that was addressing the issues of both autonomy and independence, Dandurand's thesis would have limited *retentissement,* which does not, of course, limit its value as a faithful witness of the 1930s.

The question of origins is broached with the same caution as his extortation to borrow from French literature, and a series of dates is proposed beginning with 1728. While precise dating is impossible, especially if one rejects Cartier, the significance of the date chosen lies in the fact the poem chosen is a pastiche of Boileau's *Lutrin* (1674). After the Conquest, the history of poetry in Quebec is ordered into three periods: 1800–60 ('période classique'), 1860–1900 ('période romantique'), and 1900 to the present ('période contemporain'). The method is to present illustrative examples with a stylistic reading that is imbricated with recurrent themes. More significant than the themes, however, is the French coloration. So Nelligan's style is shown in its diversity to include traits of Pierre de Ronsard (1524–85), Hugo, Edmond Rostand (1869–1918), the Parnassians, and François Coppée (1842–1900). The richness of intertextuality evident in Nelligan is found in varying degrees everywhere and at all times. Thus, in each of the summaries following the three periods the sense of a French shaping presence is always at hand. As a result, historical dates become charged with different, sometimes conflicting significance. The date 1860 may be taken as a kind of watershed, in which some poets, including Crémazie, are still within the stylistic zone of French classicism, while many of their contemporaries are already taken up by romanticism and share predilections for Alphonse de Lamartine (1790–1869) and Hugo. This ambiguity suggests that for Dandurand, the time of literary history is not necessarily linear; it is, in fact, recursive and double, partly that of Quebec and partly that of France. While he protests that one cannot state that this poetry is 'un pastiche français,' his brief historical statement at the end certainly confirms an increasing French presence: 'La vie politique et sociale de notre peuple a influé sur notre poésie; les luttes parlementaires ont nourri la verve des poètes de 1800, les victoires politiques, en excitant la fierté nationale, ont provoqué, pour une part, l'essor de 1860, comme le progrès du pays a favorisé l'abondante floraison de 1900. Mais l'influence de l'art français a été plus grande.' This is a construction of history as palimpsest, and from 1860 onward it is a palimpsest on many levels, projecting a literature, which, while seeking 'son génie propre,' is profoundly marked by plurality and alterity.[65]

Marxism and Rebirth

If this were a history of reception of literary histories in Canada, neither Dandurand's nor Rhodenizer's text would have been given much notice here. The same holds for W.E. Collin's *The White Savannahs* (1936), despite Pacey's accolade that it was 'the best sustained piece of Canadian literary criticism to appear up to its time.'[66] What is of significance in Collin is not the odd choice of Marie Le Franc (1879–1964) or some of the judgments that would raise Leo Kennedy (1907–2000), for example, to a level of recognition some might consider higher than he may deserve; and despite what seems to be a series of essays designed to promote the modernism of the McGill Group, ideas of history are implied which deserve to be explored. He is, if nothing else, the first literary historian of the 1930s who endeavoured to address the issue of modernity and to distinguish it from a more traditional poetry.

The White Savannahs is divided into two parts representing the past (Lampman, Pickthall, and Le Franc) and the modern (Dorothy Livesay [1909–96], F.R. Scott [1899–1985], A.M. Klein [1909–72], A.J.M. Smith [1902–80], and Leo Kennedy). They are separated by the Janus-faced Pratt, who, as it is often noted, 'occupies an intermediate position.' The distinction between the old and the modern, which allows them to bear more than formal difference and become history, is constructed from the use Collin makes of the codes inscribed in the two modes of writing. Drawing upon an opposition favoured by German romanticism, possibly drawn from Mme de Staël (1766–1817), we are to understand very early in the book that 'Lampman's sensibility was "Nordic,"' a word which, in the discourse of romanticism, means romantic as opposed to classic, subjective rather than objective, soft rather than hard. In a word, Nordic is everything to which one of Collin's most admired critics, T.E. Hulme (1883–1917), was adverse. His Nordic tendencies are related to the Celtic as it is filtred through William Morris (1834–96) and the English Pre-Raphaelites. The Celtic and the Nordic are what relate Lampman to Pickthall and Le Franc. The Celtic is particularly present in Pickthall and all those who 'are hyperromantic [and] dissociate attributes and qualities from the objects to which they belong and look upon them as persons – in order to create mystery.' It is enough that Le Franc is a Breton and associated with the thought of Yeats (1865–1939) to declare her Celtic affinities. What all three share is a tendency toward Rousseauism, referring to the dreamer *par excellence*.[67]

That Jean-Jacques Rousseau (1712–78) is seized upon as the problem should not be surprising given the importance of Hulme in Collin's thought and the general influence in North America, at least, of Irving Babbit's *Rousseau and Rousseauism* (1919). But Rousseau, Celtic, and Romantic are all components of the code that constitutes the past in Collin's narrative, as opposed to his more positive use in Stevenson. Glimmers of the new code are announced in Pratt. If the Nordic explains Lampman, Pratt 'is illumined with the heroic.' While there are Romantic heroes, Goethe's Faust being one and Byron's Manfred being another, they are not mentioned. The neo-romantic hero, who belongs to the romanticism Collin describes, is the Axel of Villiers de l'Isle Adam (1838–89), a figure whose notion of 'practical, everyday life he would ... gladly leave to his servants.'[68] Pratt's art is everything that Axel is not, and primarily it is 'young,' not epigonal, and 'muscular,' not effcte.[69] Unlike Lampman and Pickthall, he does not manifest 'soft femininity,' romantic qualities that Hulme eschewed, and which are found in qualities such as those characterizing Smith's poetry, namely, 'precision, hardness, clarity.'[70]

With an ability that now appears somewhat specious, Collin was able, at various moments, to combine Hulme's classicism with T.S. Eliot's use of James Frazer's vegetation myths with his own penchant for Marxism. Heterogeneous, however, as each of these ideologies may seem, each meets the other as a mode of empowerment, suggesting De Quincey's literature of power. As for Hulme, his 'analogies all have a constant purpose: to produce surprise, to create power.' Vegetation stories are myths of rebirth, and as a result of Marxist thought, the modern writer turns to communism, strange as it may seem, 'to quicken his creative powers and restore his fertility.'[71] For, 'in bourgeois society [the same writer] feels estranged, severed from his ethical roots.' The same organic imagery is applied to Lampman who 'like a solitary and exotic plant which finds itself removed from all its kind ... pined for literary copulation.' The code of the new, then, is rebirth, which is clearly prefigured in the masculinist discourse used to describe Pratt's verse, as well as Kennedy's where 'the very rhymes cry out with the vitality of young rams.' Masculinism, however, is not simply muscle and vitality. It belongs to a more deeply embedded code and one that is older than the contemporary fascination with the physical, but rather 'an athleticism, a *training*, of the soul,' which distinguishes it from the more physical masculinism of Marquis.[72] What Collin is at pains to celebrate are oblations to the 'rational god,' who is not Apollo, as one might have thought for anyone who may have seen traces of Nietzsche in Collin, but Adonis, the avatar of Christ, the young man who at the peak of his powers must forever sacrifice himself to be reborn. In doing so, he is the very sign of life. Thus he is the vitalistic sign of a myth that the past of Collin's corpus does not possess. Even Klein's poetry participates in this motif, whose 'soul ... is an ardent symbol of the spiritual rebirth of the Jewish people.'[73] The myth of rebirth, then, governs the modern in contrast to the past, which is constrained by the determinism of race, signified by its Celtic revery.

The new, then, in Collin is not primarily his masculinism but its role as a guide leading him to an understanding of history as the occasion of continual rebirth. In this sense, it corresponds to White's notion of history as Metaphor. The modality of Metaphor is identity, that is, the story of a return to primacy, a Palestine of the spirit, Smith's 'timeless Bethlehem.' Because the plot seeks its beginnings in a transcendence of the ephemeral and the mortal, its meaning derives from Being as the place of the absolute.[74] The absolute in Collin, however, is not Platonically generous; it is a function of his masculinism, alone capable of 'precision, hardness, clarity.' As a result, the feminine is an ambiguous sign, on the one hand, of the absolute's enemy, a sign of 'impressionism, sentiment' and the 'ephemeral,' and, on the other hand, of something eternal – 'love in all the wonder and mystery of a living principle.' It is otiose to point out how much this dichotomy owes to a division of woman as Eve and Mary in which the latter's function is to support the male myth of reproduction. Women are no more or less mortal than men, but their positive significance, as it is for men in a masculinist order of the cosmos, lies in their participation in the process of rebirth, which, for Collin, is not a function of the body but of the spirit, 'a vision of the living principle.' The displacement of the body is followed by the overcoming of time: 'Time's sovereignty is broken when Christ's body is pierced.'[75]

The crucial moment in the history of the spirit for Collin is always the death and rebirth of the god. Paradoxically, by abolishing time, he empties history of historical process. As White argues, this is the solution of Metaphor. Since 'historical thought in the modes of Metonymy, Synecdoche, and Irony ... not only is a symptom of the malady of the modern man, but also is a sustaining cause of that malady ... The immediate problem ... is to dissolve the authority of the inherited ways of conceiving history, to return historical thinking to a poetic, and specifically Metaphorical, mode of comprehending the world.' Malady is precisely what Collin's moderns address, and his choice of Pratt's lonely heroism over Lampman's passivity has other strong echoes of Nietzsche's will to power that makes the gestures toward a Marxist community appear, perhaps, contradictory. Malady functions, however, in two ways: it reinforces the theme of fertility and rebirth and places the theme in a context of struggle and conflict, in which the anxiety of influence is always evident. In that way it also plays a role in Collin's use of intertextuality which differs from his predecessors who use it as a context of definition, such as Pierce's use of Keats with Lampman, for example, who 'was ... a master of colour and contour, in a manner reminiscent of Keats, but lacking the sensuousness of Keats.'[76] For Collin, intertexts mark not only a style but also an ideology. Lampman's being Nordic prompted him to read William Morris. Such a statement marks Morris's writing as ideological. Collin's discussion of Scott is powerfully layered with references to the French decadents as well as Eliot, Edith Sitwell, and the British moderns, designed both to provide the formal context of F.R. Scott's poetry and to demonstrate difference and moral development. Inasmuch as the direction of Collin's argument is always toward the latter, that is, toward rebirth as spiritual empowerment, intertextual reference signals primarily the text as ideology. The consequence is that Collin is unable to envision any other communal goal than for art to find 'its roots ... among the deep, eternal questionings, joys, conflicts, yearnings in the soul of man.'[77] History, then, is not progress, but process, the effort to be reborn, understood as a continual conflict of discursive codes. The identity of Metaphor is its desired end, manifest in that struggle of which intertextuality is the sign.

History as Essential Unity

It is often the fate of texts written about a culture in a language other than one's own that they are known only from bibliographies. These are texts that take on a mediating role and, like many translations, are lost in their own apparent transparency. Such has been the fate of Jane Turnbull's *Essential Traits of French Poetry* (1938), despite her own recognition of her predecessors. Nevertheless, Turnbull argues that her text may be differentiated from Dandurand's and those of others because of its reification of '*l'âme canadienne*,' which she derives from Roy,[78] and her desire to construct 'the French-Canadian situation and character as productive of essential traits common to the body of this poetry.' The second chapter quickly outlines the substance of this situation and character: the three 'material factors of race, environment and occupation' constitute the basis of French-Canadian 'civilisation represented by their government, religion, and education.' How much Turnbull's argument owes to Hippolyte Taine's notion of '*la race, le milieu* et *le moment*' is not made clear. What these notions share, however, is a reliance upon a kind of determinism that is not only 'productive,' but also whose product is something 'essential.' They also share the idea that a literary text is, as Taine remarks, 'une copie des moeurs environnantes et le signe d'un état d'esprit.'[79] Yet there is a crucial difference between the final terms that both Turnbull and Taine draw upon, between 'occupation' and '*moment.*' Taine positions texts in a temporal order; Turnbull sees them as a function of a certain economy. The economy is represented by the *habitant,* who is characterized by 'serene contentment' and 'gaiety.'[80] Bearing in mind that the mark of an agricultural economy is cyclical rhythm, Taine's notion of historical moment is, as a result, largely effaced.

Not surprisingly, Turnbull evokes Quebec's provincial motto, *Je me souviens,* as a sign of French-Canadian attachment to France and the struggle to preserve francophone culture in North America in such a way as to 'ensure [its] survival as a distinct race.' Thus, history, the bearing of the past upon the present, is constructed as an unchanging order: 'the past remains fixed ... [and] it projects itself into the present by the invisible reality which it has formed.' Taine's '*moment,*' may be interpreted as *durée,* a timeless order of the past alive in the present, structuring an unchanging imaginary. Such a sense of the past is in accord with the sense of destiny inscribed in the third voice heard by Maria Chapdelaine, a voice greater than the two preceding it and composing a kind of duet half female and half that of a priest giving a sermon. Its famous statement says: 'Au pays de Québec rien ne doit mourir et rien ne doit changer.' Despite the challenge launched against this construction of Quebec since the 1960s in most quarters, the statement was reinscribed at the beginning of Félix-Antoine Savard's *Menaud Maître-Draveur* (1937),[81] and the couple of priest-woman continues as the central structure of the final section of Gabrielle Roy's *La petite poule d'eau* (1950). For the period in which Turnbull was writing, the position was not unusual, but its implication of determinism profoundly eternalizes history.

The history of poetry in Quebec, then, is the history of a struggle that is homologously related to the social and political struggle to construct and maintain a glorious past, which is the central metanarrative of F.-X Garneau's history. Although Turnbull dates the beginnings of poetry to the year 1830 with the publication of Bibaud's first volume, the true beginning does not take place before the generation of 1860, particularly in the poems of Crémazie, in which patriotic themes are developed at length. It is a poetry of memory which at once constructs a past and bequeaths it to his followers, who continued to meditate upon the France of the *ancien régime* and privilege the notion of fidelity to Quebec, a tradition carried on in the work of Fréchette and Le May. Although both were romantic, Fréchette is clearly faulted for ideologies of revolt apparent also in such 'dissentious extremists' as Papineau and Louis Riel (1844–85),[82] and Le May is considered more Canadian 'in that resignation and Christian piety rather than Romantic revolt is the dominant reaction to adversity.'[83]

The ideological choice in favour of Le May cannot be attributed entirely, of course, to destiny. It may be seen, however, as an aspect of ecclesiastical history in French Canada, which Turnbull describes as efficacious in the matter of 'conduct control.'[84] It shares with the third voice of Maria Chapdelaine the role of sociological superego, to which Turnbull subscribes in a manner characteristic of the dominant ideology of the Duplessis era. Her chapter on 'background' is none other than a metanarrative that explains a history, but the very act of explanation becomes a verity that determines essence. The narrative is controlled by the way the effort of L'École littéraire de Montréal is introduced. It is not heralded as the sign of difference with the previous generation of Quebec poets. Rather it is introduced with Napoléon Legendre's (1841–97) warnings that the new literature of realism is 'corruption' and the poetry of the Symbolistes is 'madness.'[85] The position is taken as 'normal' for the time, as indeed it was, and so the poetry is read as an aberration, but no matter how much he was a 'pioneer,' the final assessment is that Nelligan, along with Morin, compose a minority. Whether or not their work may have been better than the patriotism it endeavoured to displace, they are put in the shade by the grand majority of poets who 'were earnestly devoted [to] the creation as well as the preservation of a national consciousness, based upon traditions established by the example of devout and courageous ancestors.'[86] It is not enough, however, that Nelligan and his confrères are marginalized. In the end it is discovered that they too, if more subtly than others, are drawn into the national sphere.

In a sense, then, Turnbull's history may be considered complicitous history insofar as it accepts a particular story of Quebec history without embarrassment and without rising to the challenge of difference. In other words, change or difference is controlled by the citation only of positions that construct one possible tradition at the expense of any other. While it was evident to Turnbull that Nelligan and Morin were writing a contrary tradition, she rewrites them so that they serve the argument of essential unity. Thus, difference is not only controlled, but also history is placed at a centre of ideological significance where it can do no more than radiate. A successful plot, then, is only permitted what is proper to itself, which is a story somewhat similar to Dandurand's, except that the latter would argue that a change in the French sensibility at least brings about changes in that of Quebec, no matter how closely its text is tied to that of the mother country.

Overcoming the Regional

Turnbull closes, for all practical purposes, a decade of social and economic disaster in Canada, but one is scarcely aware of it in her text, and the poets of French Canada appear to be in the main a contented lot, a contentment that appears to be part of the distance taken from disaster and history. Can this contentment be, rather, a function of an 'English-Canadian' sensibility? Certainly, English-Canadian literary historians for the most part appear to take some satisfaction in the national achievement of their culture in its geographically and politically settled character. The experience of the 1930s, followed by the Second World War, provided the impetus to question the sense of achievement that developed in the wake of the First World War. Thus, a further question was prompted, namely: To what extent was Canada still a colonial nation? This was a question that exercised not only English Canada's intellectuals, but also certain members of the military, and the extent to which autonomous command could be wrested from the British played a not insignificant role in the future shaping of the country.

It is in such a context that the significance of A.J.M. Smith's influential anthology, *The Book of Canadian Poetry* (1943), the same year in which he published his first collection of poetry, *News of the Phoenix and Other Poems*, should be gauged. Smith had already acquired a reputation as a founding editor of the *McGill Fortnightly Review* (1925–7) and subsequently as an active member of the Montreal Group whose most famous publication was *New Provinces: Poems of Several Authors* (1936). Smith, in other words, was among the major voices of the modernist movement in Canadian poetry, and his *Book of Canadian Poetry* gave him the platform to make the movement's views known to a general public through its Introduction, head-notes to selected poets, and briefly, but trenchantly annotated bibliography. Although it does not provide a history of Canadian poetry, it takes a firm place, at least, in the process of its canonization. Indeed, Smith firmly dissociates himself from literary history in his opening paragraphs, echoing a dominant position of the New Criticism: 'The emphasis ... is not upon literary history or social background but on the poetry itself.' Nevertheless, his 'main purpose ... is to illustrate in the light of a contemporary and cosmopolitan literary consciousness the broad development of English-Canadian poetry from its beginnings at the end of the eighteenth century to its renewal of power in the revolutionary world of today.' It is a sentence full of intimations: does 'renewal of power' suggest the beginnings in the eighteenth century were powerful because of their proximity in time to two revolutions? Not, of course, in the least, for the intent of the anthology is to demonstrate with all of Smith's evident didactic skill that beginnings are only the complementary background to what is more significant in the contemporary. Thus, while Smith employs such organicist metaphors as 'the growth of Canada's self-awareness,' the design is simpler. There are two kinds of poets, we are told, some of whom 'have concentrated on what is individual and unique in Canadian life and others upon what it has in common with life everywhere.' The former endeavour to articulate 'whatever is essentially and distinctively Canadian' and the latter has 'made a heroic effort to transcend colonialism by entering upon the universal, civilising culture of ideas.'[87]

Smith's sense of history ideally has to be construed on two different planes. The first addresses the kinds of events that occurred in Canada that somehow distinguished it from other emerging countries; the second, a struggle within a literary and cultural context that would free Canada's poetry from its attachment to the colonial in its pursuit of 'self-awareness.' As a consequence, the hymns of the Puritan Henry Alline (1748–84) are disposed of readily as both 'extra-Canadian' and lacking in all but the simplest literary conventions. Charles Sangster is praised in respect of Joseph Howe because of a literary distance that can be measured in a historical context. While Howe's work evinced 'an advance along the lines laid down by the younger Goldsmith ... no important change' could be noted. His contemporary, Sangster, evinces the newer poetry of British and American poets. Literary context is, however, not a complete context. When giving his highest accolade to Charles Heavysedge as the greatest of the pre-Confederation poets, Smith notes that his themes are not Canadian but universal and 'the richness and comprehensiveness of the intellectual and moral experience out of which [*Saul*] arose' mark it as a precursor of Smith's contemporary understanding of poetry. Heavysedge is part of the agon that would overcome the colonial. So it is that among post-Confederation poets, Crawford is praised as precursor of E.J. Pratt, and one cannot avoid inferring that George Frederick Cameron (1854–85), whose 'rare gift of taking a somewhat artificial style and infusing into it a tone that is energetic, convincing, and almost colloquial,' is Smith's own precursor. Cameron is assured a central place not only because he read classical Latin, but also because its effects were palpable in his poetry, and, furthermore, 'there is no effort in him to do justice to any aspect of national scenery.' Thus the contemporary has finally given up on the late nineteenth-century poets, even Crawford and Pratt: 'the poets of today are bringing back to Canadian verse ... an intellectualism unknown since Heavysedge and a merging of personality into a classicism of form that might find its exemplar in Cameron.'[88]

It is difficult not to sense the presence here of such an essay as T.S. Eliot's 'Tradition and the Individual Talent' (1919), and, even more so, various essays by the Russian formalists that were not, however, available in translation before the 1960s, a central idea of which is captured in Harold Bloom's notion that the history of literature, especially poetry, is an Oedipal struggle that depends upon the poet entering upon the precursor and then 'emptying the precursor of *his* divinity, while appearing to empty himself of his own.' One aspect of Smith's sense of history, then, is the proper placement of emotion, and the other is the reality of rupture, which his Introduction elegantly constructs. This allows him to distance himself from earlier historians, notably Collin, who had already promulgated Smith's contemporaries without, however, establishing a context of anticipation and achievement, and Stevenson, whose willingness to accept pantheism uncritically as the dominant in Canadian poetry is rejected as providing a discourse that is no longer viable. Relations that are made with earlier poets are made primarily on literary grounds and testify to an effort to reach a shared field of interest through somewhat different technical means. The modern turn is to be seen not so much in a certain thematics, however, but in the use of a language found in both English metaphysical and modern Anglo-American poetry, and the purpose is to make Canada what Smith calls 'cosmopolitan.'[89]

The general tenor of this argument remained unchanged in the two subsequent anthologies that Smith edited for Oxford. The only substantive difference is the addition of poetry written in French, and parallels are readily drawn to indicate, in the end, the success of the cosmopolitan at the expense of the national and local. The Canadian aspect of the cosmopolitan, he remarks in his edition of 1960, 'derives from [a] position of separateness and semi-isolation' from American, British, and French poetry. The brief Preface to the edition of 1967 concludes with the triumphal observation that nationalism has been 'transcended' and Canada's poetry 'joins Canada to the world.' The three essays taken together not only inscribe the position of Smith's version of the modern (the last one taking it for granted), but also make it clear that Canada is no longer colonial. Canada now can take its place among the nations of the world by, paradoxically, no longer possessing a sense of the national, 'no longer,' as he pointedly remarks in the first Introduction, 'in the exporting business, for maple sugar is a sickly and cloying commodity.'[90]

The distinctive, then, has nothing to with its themes, and everything to do with the struggle to acquire autonomy through the use of contemporary poetic techniques. Poetry, according to Smith, is in a continuous agon to find perfection of form and clarity of diction. Northrop Frye's enthusiastic response to Smith's first anthology, 'Canada and Its Poetry,' was a forecast of the canonical position it has since enjoyed. As one might suppose, he noted Smith's point that literature responds to literature, not nature, and remarked that 'practically all important poetry has been the fruit of endless study and reading.' It anticipates by more than a decade the argument of *Anatomy of Criticism* concerning 'literature as autonomous language.' Literature is its own country, and to perceive it as such runs the risk of losing the nation, for good or for ill, in translation. As if unconsciously aware of this, Frye discovers something in Smith's anthology which is not raised in the Introduction. 'But,' he writes, according to Mr Smith's book, 'the outstanding achievement of Canadian poetry is in the evocation of stark terror.' Such a discovery allows Frye to get away from mere nature and communion with it – after all, who would want to commune with terror? Such a remark also permits him to distance himself from the major literary historians of the previous generation, and, at the same time, provides an image of Canadian distinctiveness, which Smith's Introduction appears to call for, despite its new emphasis on 'man's own social and mental world.' For one of the problems of a theory of immanent change as a model for literary history is its emphasis on the displacement of one literary system by another.[91] Under such circumstances, the nation, which no longer exports, becomes a producer of technical experts, capable of importing the right material and using it to overcome the national and local. The primary emphasis upon formal skill is sufficient to put the distinctive into clear jeopardy. Frye's discovery seemed to compensate for such a possibility. Thus nature is allowed to return, despite Smith's efforts to dispose of it, but it is a nature which is the inversion of nature as previously perceived and so put an apparently new Canadian stamp on the poetry that had seemed to leave nature behind.

To summarize, Smith's notion of history is twofold: to invent a tradition and then to absorb the old into the new. In a somewhat self-congratulatory essay, 'Eclectic Detachment: Aspects of Identity in Canadian Poetry,' Smith admits that the distinction between native and cosmopolitan derives from Lighthall's anthology, and that the difference is one between 'technically crude' and 'impersonal and objective.' The former is, in fact, a stage that prepares for the latter. The function of the historian is to recognize *literary* accomplishment. Needless to say, as he observes in the same essay, the argument of his first anthology was well received by Northrop Frye, who shared his view that literature is a closed, self regulatory system. The second anthology also met with success and so made Smith's construction of history as canonical. Although history in its extraliterary dimension is gradually effaced, this would be normal for an understanding of poetry that asserts: 'the audience a poet writes for is *primarily* other poets.' Thus the primary function of Heavysedge and Cameron is to anticipate and be fulfilled by such poets as Smith and his contemporaries.[92]

History as Palingenesis

E.K. Brown's *On Canadian Poetry*, published in the same year as Smith's first anthology, also addressed the question of the colonial. Like Smith's, his argument emerges from the general assumptions of the New Criticism and so avoids the personal in the sense of the biographical. Despite Collin's praise for the book he, nevertheless, takes Brown precisely to task for not examining the 'genius' behind the poetry. Brown's understanding of literary history, while curiously similar to Collin's own, is not, however, the story of genius, but, rather the story of genesis, which is where his theory of the true frontier, *pace* Mandel, lies.[93]

The first paragraph of Brown's book raises the question that is his central preoccupation: How does a colonial literature become post-colonial? Explicitly, it comes into being by asserting difference. Implicitly, it comes into being by having its difference assessed or, in a word, positioned, which is the function of such studies as Brown's. As he asks himself in respect of the first chapter, 'What are the peculiar difficulties which have weighed upon the Canadian writer?' By analysing the difficulties, the historian is able to place writers in a situation of emergence or genesis, a stance now made familiar by post-colonial theory. The difficulties are several. First, there is the economic problem of larger, more competitive countries, which in the instance of Canada are the United States and Great Britain. Next, the colonial writer is beset by the psychological handicap of the lack of belief in one's ability. Furthermore, the new country is a frontier country and encourages practical skills. Confronting the environment is more necessary that living an 'aesthetic or contemplative life.' Also, in North America, at least, the inhibitions of puritanism militate against the emergence of culture. Finally, 'regionalism ... tells against the immediate growth of a national literature.' But more than anything 'a great literature is the flowering of a great society.'[94]

Despite the questionable character of Brown's summary position on greatness, it should be clear that all of these cautionary remarks, while ostensibly of a sociological order, are meant to be understood as simply prefatory. They indicate the obstacles besetting the genesis of a literature, rather than the conditions by which it is recognized. His next chapter begins with the sentence: 'Canadian literature in the English language began ...' The theme is that of origination, and, drawing upon one of his prefatory remarks, he notes that the early literature of the Maritimes, being both regional and puritanical, can claim only 'historical interest.' This raises the question: What is historical in literature? For Brown, its true history, as opposed to documentary value, lies elsewhere: 'For the first poetry of lasting value one must look farther west.' There we find beginnings in Sangster and Heavysedge, but both are deemed inadequate because of inadequacies of their respective social orders that were not equipped to provide critical readings of their work. The validity of this judgment is particularly weak in view of the fact that, as most historians agree, Heavysedge's *Saul* was most probably already written in England before he emigrated. Brown then lingers hesitantly, but certainly not as long as Smith, with George Frederick Cameron whom he abandons because of the derivative nature of his work. None of Brown's premises are invoked. Isabella Valancy Crawford is considered 'the only Canadian woman poet of real importance in the last century,' but her work is often marred 'because it is carelessly conventional.' Roberts's first collections are, however, given a significant accolade: 'with them Canadian poetry begins anew.'[95] His chief merit appears to be that he has overcome regionalism, and the sensuousness he shares with his younger contemporaries would suggest the same for puritanism. Why his poems, published in the same decade as Crawford's (the 1880s), should be considered an adequate expression of an adequate society (not to speak of just or great one) is not made clear. Nor is the vanquishing of the regional elaborated upon. The stress is on the act of beginning.

Indeed, as Brown's history continues, he seems to move away from his general considerations and become more attracted to the formal qualities of poetry. Carman is rejected because his verse is 'cloying.' The problem with Pickthall is that 'when she thought of what war was thought to preserve she symbolized what she valued by a daffodil.' As a consequence, 'it was time for a change.' Such a summary statement implies that literary history has as much, if not more, to do with imaginative failure than with societal forces. In other words, Brown, like Smith, is intuitively suggesting a theory of literary development that is similar to Turij Tynjanov's notion of systemic change in literary evolution that operates without reference to other social institutions.[96] True enough, as Brown observes, the minor poets of the early years of the twentieth century were 'swept aside after the First Great War,' preparing the way for Pratt and the McGill Movement. Nevertheless, the innovation of Klein, for example, is not attributed to the social environment of Canada following the war as much as to the fact that he had Jewish culture to draw upon. Although Smith is considered the central writer of the McGill poets, his *News of the Phoenix* is praised because of the 'perfect keeping between substance and form.' Robert Finch (1900–95), however, uses 'imagery of unusual originality,' and, furthermore, 'no Canadian poet in our time has had in greater degree the love of the word or of design as an autonomous whole.' Earle Birney's (1904–95) 'David' (1942) 'is a narrative of a kind new to our poetry.' Finally, 'in Mr. Birney's work there is authentic originality; he owes nothing at all to earlier Canadian writing and scarcely anything ... to recent verse anywhere else.'[97]

Canonization for Brown appears to be hardly dependent on the discourse of the social, but rather on questions of culture and formal achievement. The new, which signals a rupture with the past, is the central grammatical element of his history. Thus when he addresses 'the masters' of Canadian poetry, a term which clearly emphasizes formal attainment, among Confederation poets we do not read of Roberts, but of Lampman, whose frequently cited remarks on Roberts are invoked by a question, namely: 'Could a nation's poetic history begin with a more charming freshness,' and whose 'art' is praised as 'the most careful that any Canadian has ever exhibited in verse – or in prose.' Although an initial effort is made to suggest the relation between Lampman and the scarcely great society of Ottawa during the second half of the century,[98] it is evident that Brown's interest is primarily in the theme of nature, the force that drew Lampman away from society, and his 'intense concern for the word and the phrase.' If 'At the Long Sault' is Lampman's apogée of 'poetic beauty,' it is so because of its 'formal resources.'[99]

The second master is Lampman's Ottawa friend D.C. Scott, who always seems to be an afterthought among the significant poets of the late nineteenth century. Scott's fame – and this after so much fine analysis of his craftsmanship – rests upon the fact that he is 'our Canadian symbol of the fragile artist worn down by the rigours of our climate and our social and economic structure.' Brown himself, however, discounts this suggestion and argues that Roberts, Carman, and Lampman constitute a relatively homogenous group because of Roberts's influence. Scott differs from them, not because of 'the rigours of our climate and our social and economic structure,' but because of a difference in temperament, theme, and form. He is, therefore, a founder because, unlike his contemporaries, he did not 'write of Canada ... as if it were a large English county.' Brown's most revealing insight into Scott's originality occurs in his reading of 'The Height of Land.' Scott's intent is to understand 'the Being that lies within nature,' and in the course of the poem 'descends to a historical explanation.'[100] The verb may not have been chosen for its negative connotations, but in a text that has some pretension to history it is startling. History in Brown's sense, however, is not construed as a true descent, for it consists of 'visions.' It is an idealist notion of history that does not culminate in the social or economic but in the religious. History is a scene of cognition in which 'the interpretative power of man will have been extended.' The analysis of this and other poems finally concludes – remarkably, as Collin notes – in a portrait of Scott in his 'exquisite maturity.'[101] It is an image designed to illustrate dramatically, if not to explain, the mystery of change, in which aspects of a life, a poem, a history are accommodated and refashioned. Despite Brown's claim that these events are 'dialectical,' we are to infer, I think, that change is not entirely rupture, as it appears in Birney, but a method of vision and revision.

The final section on Pratt begins with the clause: 'Originality has been rare in Canadian literature.' Despite his efforts to argue that the history of literature is metonymical, that is, the verbal effect of several causes,

Brown's preoccupation with beginnings suggests that the causes, the various obstacles to greatness, are only a way of explaining failure. Greatness overcomes what appear to be causes and leads us to the edge of deeper ground. Thus his recapitulation of the history of English-Canadian poetry at the beginning of the Pratt section is a rehearsal of failure. Landscape, environment, pioneer life are not here constructed, however, as obstacles, but the grist of a weak tradition. An effort to surpass these conditions in the generation of the 1880s never got beyond the condition of music. Greatness, the moment of origin, can only be measured with conditions of ambiguity that do not, however, spring from the discourse of the social, but from an ineluctable encounter between the discourses of one writer and another, on the one hand, and between the discourses of the same writer, as in the instance of Scott, on the other. So Pratt's originality resides, as it does for Collin, in his being 'our only valid link between the elder and the younger poets.'[102] Access to the origin, however, belongs to the literary historian, who provides the order and the criteria. In selecting originality, positioning a writer in a certain way in a discursive context, Brown is less metonymical than he suggests. He is, in fact, a metaphorical historian like Collin, and he constructs the history of English-Canadian literature as a series of renewals and repositionings in which the ability to renew becomes the identifying and unifying characteristic of master poets.

Socio-economic determinants, not to speak of colonial timidity, the demands of frontier life, puritanism, and the centrifugal tug of regionalism constitute the surface plot only of Brown's essay. The true plot is the continuous arising of the moment of origination. History is a cycle of renewals. Such is the significance of what might appear the somewhat redundant assertion that 'to the earlier Canadian poetry [the] first collections of Roberts' owe nothing at all: with them Canadian poetry begins anew,' an assertion that is echoed, for example, in the comment on Birney (1904–95) that 'he owes nothing at all to earlier Canadian writing.'[103] Canadian poetry, to modify a title of A.J.M. Smith, is always news from the (self-renewing) phoenix. Whether it is without debts to the past or more Janus-faced, as in the instance of both Lampman and Pratt, Brown's construction of the rise and order of history does not easily fit with Perkins's scheme of 'rise, decline, and rise and decline.' Canadian poetry is either mediocre, because it is bound by the trammels of various constraints, or it is randomly born anew. Greatness, the life of poetry, is recognizable by its ability to transcend from, rather than descend into, history or, in this case, the negatively Canadian. Like Col-

lin, Smith, and other English-Canadian literary historians that form his
tradition, Brown appears to prefer a cultural world without history, a
fact all the more surprising in Brown given, for example, his own brief
but intimate encounter with Canadian history as a member of Mackenzie King's wartime staff.

Defending Theocracy

The Second World War, as I have indicated, does not appear to play a
role in the formation of the histories of either Smith or Brown. Nevertheless, like Collin, they have been deeply affected by Anglo-American
modernism, and both manifest a desire to read Canada as a modern
nation with measures of autonomy. In Quebec the war was not perceived
with much enthusiasm, and one has the sense that the less progressive
aspect of the ecclesiastical wing of the province would have preferred
that things remain as they always seemed to have been, that is, rural,
patriarchal, and guided by the parish priest. So it is that Lucie Robert, at
the end of her final chapter on Roy's *manuels*, turns with an almost audi-
ble sigh of relief to a significant event that occurred at the end of the
1940s. 'Le manuel de Camille Roy,' she writes, 'échouera devant le *Refus
global* après une longue lutte, mais ce n'est que lorsque le manifeste de
Paul-Emile Borduas entera en classe que la défaite sera consummée.'[104]
In a certain respect, however, her observation may give a somewhat false
picture to the uninitiated. Although Borduas's manifesto belongs to literary history, it is not itself a literary historical text. Its significance
within the literary institution of Quebec occurred later, as Roberts confirms, and it was one of many indications of Quebec's emergence into
modernity. The immediate response to his text was to have Borduas dismissed from his teaching position at the École du Meuble in Montreal,
and he subsequently lived abroad in New York and Paris, where he died
in 1960. The world of literary history in Quebec was at the time
untouched, and an earnest of the true state of affairs is more apparent
in Berthelot Brunet's *Histoire de la littérature canadienne française*, which
appeared in 1946, two years before Borduas's text.

In his own self-portrait, Brunet had the audacity to remind the reader
that his work had been compared to that of the twentieth-century
French novelist Louis-Ferdinand Céline, thus anticipating Baillargeon's
comment that he 'fut une des figures les plus pittoresques de nos lettres'
and in whose temperament there was missing 'un élément *d'équilibre* et
de *stabilité*.'[105] Nevertheless, his history, as well as his fiction, was pub-

lished by Editions de l'Arbre, a house that could boast such venerable modern French Catholic authors as Georges Bernanos, François Mauriac, Jean Wahl, and Rissa Maritain, the wife of Jacques Maritain, who could not have been farther ideologically from Céline. It is a history, then, that received, at least, an unofficial imprimatur and may, therefore, be read within the tradition that Camille Roy fostered. Thus, with the exception of his particular engagement with the contemporary, his understanding of the canon differs little from that of his predecessor.

The central difference between Brunet and Roy is in the construction of the plot. Roy employs a clear historical structure which leads the nation toward self-awareness through the interaction of life and literature in the service of the nation. Brunet's general emphasis is on genre, and his plot structure is one that starts at a high level of achievement, then declines, and finally rises again. As he notes in his initial sentence, French-Canadian literary history is a story in which 'le prologue et l'epilogue ont plus d'importance que le corps d'ouvrage.'[106] Unlike Roy, Brunet is not particularly clear about beginnings, and therefore one cannot be certain about the meaning of the prologue. Jacques Cartier, Marc Lescarbot (?1570–1642), and Samuel de Champlain are precursors; the *Relations* of the Jesuits are assuredly a part Canadian literature; Marie de l'Incarnation (1599–1672) is given the same stature as Saint Theresa of Avila. While they are all French, they belong to the childhood of Canadian literature. Garneau assumes at least the place he holds in previous histories. Indeed, were all other French-Canadian texts destroyed, his would have to be preserved, for it serves as the *Chanson de Roland* of that culture. The distance in time between Garneau and French Canada's infancy is considerable, but Brunet makes no effort to indicate where the prologue begins. Perhaps we are to understand that, since 'le Canada français est un pays unique, terre de martyrs et d'une chaude et naturelle ferveur,' by articulating that passion and creating 'une conscience nationale chez un peuple assiégé en somme de toute part,' everything will naturally belong to the same prologue as it assumes historiographic consciousness. This seems to be implied by the reference to Aubert de Gaspé's *Les anciens Canadiens* (1863) as belonging to 'cette aube de notre littérature.' The chapter on poetry before the last decade of the nineteenth century is entitled 'La Poésie avant les vrais poètes,' and thus one surmises that the period from the Conquest until the rise of modernity is all part of the honourable mediocrity, as Brunet observes, of the middle period. Not until we reach the 1890s do we notice a reason why this is a significant moment: it marked the beginning of the emancipation from France, which gives substance to the phrase 'une conscience nationale.'[107]

Thus the relation of prologue and epilogue bears a certain symmetry and means, respectively, France and French Canada. Significance is accorded the manner in which writers conform to such a national structure. Garneau's role, in such a plot, is cardinal, for it writes the prologue and announces the epilogue. It also explains the ambiguous complementarity of the religious and the secular in French-Canadian culture. For while the precursors – decidedly representative of the *ancien régime* – are French, their exemplary figures are the Jesuits and Marie de l'Incarnation, modernity is moving toward the secular. Brunet's problem is that he sees the modern as an emancipation from France. Therefore, he must invent an appropriate past that will not contradict the aspirations of his present. He does so by making use of two ideas of France, that of the religious *ancien régime* and that of the secular post-revolutionary France. His French-Canadian moderns free themselves from the latter and transmute the former into legend (e.g., *The Song of Roland*). Thus, inasmuch as French Canada for a long time possessed something 'théocratique même dans sa littérature,' even its anticlercalism is prepared to admit that 'nous devons au clergé pour une bonne part ce que nous avons de meilleur.' As a result, two writers become the emblems of the prologue and epilogue, respectively, Marie de L'Incarnation, 'notre plus grand écrivain' and Gabrielle Roy, whose *Bonheur d'occasion* (1945) is adjudged unparalleled.[108]

Robert observes that Roy's last *manuel* before his death, which appeared in 1939, is a compromise between classical rhetoric and literary history and thus, she implies, articulates homologously a conflict between a middle class seeking autonomy and a reactionary movement endeavouring to maintain its power. Roy's compromise is justly termed a 'fragile équilibre' and it should be evident that Brunet's balance is equally fragile. Both texts construe French-Canadian history in such a way as to preserve theocracy, but Brunet's efforts may not be entirely a function of his lack of stability. I would argue that it is an indication of the deeper rifts in French-Canadian culture of the 1940s, a culture fraught with contradictions of which Borduas's text shows only one side. History, then, the site of the carefully constructed nation in Roy and Brunet, manifests itself as at once a necessity and a problem of which Garneau is the icon. If French Canada must have a history, what is it to be? Brunet recounts the legendary anecdote of the English-Canadian clerk who taunted Garneau with the fact that French Canadians were a people without a history (or story) to which the latter replied, 'Je la ferai, cette histoire.'[109] This is tantamount to saying that he would invent a tradition for his fellow citizens. The unwavering stature that Garneau attains in all histories of French-Canadian literature indicates that its literature is always constructed as a national-historical phenomenon. Because the latter is correspondingly construed in its relation to literature as a frequently contradictory system of ideas, the literature itself must bear the same fate as it acquires historical shape.

English-Canadian literary history, by contrast, tried to overcome its national propensity for fragile balances, by either occulting contradiction (MacMechan and Pierce), or judging its possibilities as unworthy of consideration (Logan and Stevenson), or abandoning history for the heroic (Collin and Brown). While MacMechan chose as an epigraph for his book the expression '*ad majoram gloriam patriae*,' it is evident that, as the period between the two wars wore on, the *patria* was gradually lost sight of by its literary historians. Literature and history began to operate on two different ontological planes, suggesting that Canada's literature was only Canadian by accident or invention. If French Canada seemed impelled to understand its literature by understanding its history first (after all, it came from Garneau), English Canada wanted to understand its literature as a function of genius untrammelled by the constraints of social, economic, and imperial orders. Great literature came either from nowhere or from other literature *tout court* (Smith). On the threshold of modernity, history for French Canada appeared to be an embarrassment that required a solution; for English Canada it was an embarrassment that appeared to have no solution and, therefore, could be left behind.

CHAPTER THREE

The Search for Agency, 1948–1965

Canada is a perpetual crisis.[1]

The final years of the 1940s were marked by a series of events whose bearing upon the francophone and anglophone literatures were direct and irrevocable. The most decisive were, first, as we have already seen, the publication of Paul-Émile Borduas's *Refus global* in 1948. It proclaimed the birth of new era of total freedom, attacking both the forces of capitalism and the repressive character of contemporary Quebec society. It was immediately met with denunciation. In the following year, the Johns Manville plant was shut down by a strike at Asbestos. It was a strike of such symbolic magnitude that it not only radically changed the workers' movement in the province but also divided the province ideologically. Both of these events in complementary fashion foreshadowed the Révolution Tranquille. As Marcel Rioux argues, they marked the end of 'the ideology of self-preservation,'[2] and the tone and rhetoric of Borduas's manifesto may be seen subsequently as inaugurating the sense of urgency that informs much of contemporary Quebec culture,[3] despite the fact that his antipathy to nationalism has been publicly stated.[4]

In the same year the Royal Commission on National Development in the Arts, Letters and Sciences was established. This led to the formation of such institutions as the National Library and the Canada Council, as a consequence of adopting the recommendations of the Massey Report in 1951. Indeed, without its subsequent implementation such histories as Carl F. Klinck's, not to metion countless other texts, would very probably never have appeared.[5] That such a report could be perceived as an irritant to certain elements of Quebec's intellectual elite may not be immediately apparent to anglophone Canadians, but its emphasis upon national unity poses problems. Michel Brunet argued at the time of its publication that the risk of unity carried with it the risk of assimilation. Its nationalism was, therefore, primarily favourable to English-Canadian ambition at the expense of regional aspirations toward greater autonomy. The consequence, for Brunet, would be to suffer the status of being 'une nation minoritaire,' a fate he finds ominous.[6]

Seeking a Voice

Canada's post-war, cultural awakening as a nation was inscribed, therefore, with tensions that could only aggravate the existing centralist and regionalist dialectic. It may be that the pressures of the war favoured an expanded and more powerful centre, but this locus of power inevitably prompted regional reaction. Is it unusual, then, that the first effort to articulate the regional as literature *hors Québec*, of course, should appear at this time? I refer to Edward McCourt's *The Canadian West in Fiction*, the first edition of which appeared in 1949, the same year as the Johns Mansville strike. Hence, it belongs to the growing cultural awareness of the local. In a sense, it is difficult to declare why McCourt wrote the book other than to remind his readers of the existence of the Prairies, for by his own admission the story of the region had not been adequately told in its prose fiction.[7] No writer of fiction was imaginatively prepared or socially supported to carry out the task with the exception of Sinclair Ross (1908–96) in his short stories, published during the 1930s and 1940s, and W.O. Mitchell (1914–98) in his *Who Has Seen the Wind?* (1947). Such a conclusion appears to mark McCourt's history as history of a certain kind of failure with neither rise nor fall.

The attainment of failure from a beginning of dubious achievement makes the writing of a history difficult. Moreover, that the period of time covered is at most some sixty-five years does not allow for much scope, and no serious undertaking can be perceived before Ralph Connor's personal discovery of his Presbyterian, manly West. The chapter titles would suggest, however, that migration westward was perhaps an exception, for only one, 'The Transplanted,' signals this aspect of Western writing. Yet before Nellie McClung (1873–1951) began publishing and for some decades afterward, the writers McCourt presents are immigrants. When one considers that McClung's first book was published in

1908 (*Sowing Seeds in Danny*), and that she is placed in the history after Ralph Connor, Frederick Niven (1878–1944), and Frederick Phillip Grove,[8] one wonders at McCourt's sense of chronology as a structuring principle. Structure is provided, in fact, by an organization that moves from chapters on Connor and Niven to one on Grove, which forms a kind of spiritual centre raised by the title 'Spokesman of a Race?' The answer to the question is that 'Grove is not a great novelist ... but his record of "agricultural operations and the attendant rural life thereof" is one of the most accurate in Canadian fiction.'[9] He is, at least in a certain measure, a spokesman. After Grove there are only 'others,' many of whom preceded him in time.

Chronology, then, is overlooked, and everything apparently depends upon the thesis of regionalism, which is presented in its literary guise as a preface to the chapter on Grove. Three talents, McCourt argues, are required for success in regional writing, talents possessed by the pictorial artist, the poet, and the psychologist. Together they create the landscape, the atmosphere, and the sensibility appropriate to the local. The first two combine to form a sense of environment and its effect upon character. The failure of Western prose, however, lies in its 'inability to understand people in relation to their surroundings.' Exceptions are Ross's 'The Painted Door'[10] and Mitchell's *Who Has Seen the Wind?*, neither of which are given dominant roles in the book, which suggests that the book has another function that certainly exceeds mere history, but related, nevertheless, to the question of environment.

A region, after all, is a special place, and the place is defined not only in itself but in relation to somewhere else. That somewhere in McCourt is Ontario, against which the prairie provinces are 'united in their hostility.' So place becomes an ideological centre that can construct itself, like McCourt's West, as a failure. As a result, his book becomes lament for both a nation and a region, which the concluding chapter outlines at length. Whether by conscious design or not, the final chapter is ironically entitled 'The Sum of Achievement.' The sum is, of course, a negative sum, and McCourt details a number of reasons for the difficulties of writing in the Canadian West. First is the conservatism of Canadian publishing, most of which at the time was centred in Ontario. Its conservatism is related to the need 'to create for ourselves a "culture" which shall be recognizable to all as Canadian.' As a consequence, the old colonial spirit has given way to 'a strident nationalism, which demands that the writer be aggressively Canadian,' which ironically makes the Canadian writer similar to the American. Such a situation would only be exacerbated were artists to receive government grants, a criticism and suggestion in advance of the Massey Report. Finally, he mentions the isolation of the Western writer and the lack of proximity to a society that possesses history and tradition – a point already raised by E.K. Brown – as other difficulties in the making of a regional literature in the West. These arguments do not address, however, what might otherwise be called a lack of talent, but seize, rather, upon a financial and social environment. Although 'a change is coming over the West,'[11] such a change is not evident in the book. The sentence, however, is appropriate to the rhetoric of apologia, which is what the book ends up being. Given the kind of apologia, that is, for a place that has not yet found its voice, it constitutes history as prehistory, in which the West becomes a figure in a larger, national drama that is seeking recognition of its maturity.[12]

Tory Values

The decade about to begin, while uncertain of any direction, was not particularly auspicious, at least from the perspective of English-Canadian nationalism. As if to respond to the effort of presenting that culture as 'distinctive,' Desmond Pacey, as part of his Introduction to his *Creative Writing in Canada: A Short History of English-Canadian Literature* (1952), begins by answering a charge expressed by an English critic that Canada had no indigenous culture. His aim, furthermore, was to assess, at least 'the *quality* of Canadian writing,' which is laudable insofar as, according to Pacey, the distinctiveness of Canadian literature was generally found to be a function of a unique environment. By implication, to assess quality would seem to aspire to a more universal, less regional, level of reading. Pacey, however, makes somewhat of a compromise, by which he would both analyse texts in themselves, submitting them 'to judgment by the standards applicable to all literatures,' presumably those developed by the New Critics then in vogue in North American universities, while also making allowances for 'the circumstances in which the writing was done,' a practice then considered somewhat suspect at the time. Thus environment, at least, in a broad sense is not discarded entirely, and while nothing particularly dramatic marks the story of English-Canadian history as Pacey tells it, each period that is created is introduced by references to significant social and political events. These prefatory comments, however, are not always capable of integration with the literary events of the history, which may be attributed to Pacey's expressed doubts about their integrative possibilities.[13]

Indeed, as he remarks about the Confederation Era (1867–97), 'the relations between a society and its literature are hypothetical and obscure, and no simple arrangement of cause and effect can be discerned or proved.' This is a highly revealing sentence, implying that the relations happen of themselves, and when they happen, they might be perceived as bearing a relation of cause and effect. By so glossing over his activity as a historian, namely, as the one who makes the relations, Pacey implies something we have already noted in English-Canadian literary historiography. Since what is not literature is in some respect invisible ('obscure'), it offers no possibility of hypothesis. History, of course, makes no hypotheses, and therefore Pacey does not feel summoned to make them either other than, in this instance, to suggest an analogy between a high level of 'excitement in the community, together with some powerful stimulus from outside ... [as] likely to result in the creation of a vivid and vigorous body of writing.' Because this happened in the 1820s and 1830s in Nova Scotia it could said to happen again elsewhere. The manifestation of this excitement, however, is curious. Among poets, only Charles G.D. Roberts seems moved by it, and when he did, his work was 'far from his best.' His better poetry springs from his empathy with fellow New Brunswickers, particularly in elegies drawn from rural life. It is this empathy which relates him to his cousin Bliss Carman, who 'like Roberts ... was essentially a regional poet who found in the woods and streams and tides of New Brunswick the inspiration of all his best work.'[14] Although Archibald Lampman lived in the capital of the new Dominion, his heart was clearly elsewhere, and what notice he took of Ottawa and social life was satiric.[15] No mention is made of D.C. Scott as a patriotic poet. That leaves among major novelists William Kirby, whose use of historical romance suggests a creation of the past that would shape a nation, but Kirby 'was no advocate of independence.'[16]

The first two decades of the twentieth century, which constitute the next period, are prefaced by Wilfrid Laurier's famous pronouncement that the twentieth century belonged to Canada. Nevertheless, as Pacey remarks, 'such optimism was unjustified' to a degree. Already the idea of national unity was weakened from the 1880s onward (the period of the Confederation poets), antagonism between Quebec and Canada had continually worsened since the hanging of Louis Riel, and the whole period fell into catastrophe during the First World War. Nevertheless, the regional idyll dominates in the poetry of Drummond[17] and the fiction of L.M. Montgomery and Ralph Connor. Pacey remarks of the prose: 'Instead of challenging the values of the new industrial society, these writers ignored its existence. Instead of seeking to show how the old ideals could be adapted to the needs of a new generation, they sought merely to turn the clock back.' Pride of place in both genres is finally given to Marjorie Pickthall, 'a highly derivative poet, whose work is full of echoes of the pre-Raphaelites and of the poets of the Irish Renaissance,'[18] and Stephen Leacock (1869–94), 'whose values are eighteenth century values: common sense, benevolence, moderation, good taste.' Although Pacey's admiration of Leacock as both satirist and regional idyllist is appropriately tempered – nor is there any hint of criticism for his own anachronism – it is evident his values acquire value in turn. Nor was it Leacock's fault that he was not a better writer than he was: 'The prevailing materialism was too strong even for him, for any one man, to resist.'[19]

The three decades that constitute the final period are marked in distinctive ways. The 'new nationalism' of the 1920s is perceptible in Canada's acquisition of 'status as an equal partner in the British Commonwealth of Nations.' The 1930s brought a decade of depression ended by the Second World War, which 'was, strangely enough, the signal for a sudden resurgence of Canadian literature.' No mention is made of French Canada, as if it had quietly disappeared under the weight of 'optimistic nationalism.' The two most original poets of the period were E.J. Pratt and Earle Birney.[20] Many of Pratt's poems had 'the immediate purpose of stimulating the national morale, but by the admirers of [his] best poetry it must be regretted that his energies were expanded on such occasional themes.' Nor can Pratt be located within the history English-Canadian poetry; he is without predecessors or imitators, a clear departure from earlier assessments, including Brown's. Although Birney is 'interested in the people and events of his own time,' it is not clear from Pacey's argument in what way his best poetry, such as 'David,' can be integrated with the significant events of the period as Pacey presents them.[21]

The novel does not stand high in Pacey's canonization of genres, and within subgenres of the novel – realism, the regional idyll, and the historical romance – only the former has been developed by the best novelists of the period. The regional idyll, to which I will return, mediates between the other two genres, blending both. Thus progression from romance over time seems also to carry with it a cluster of values dominant in the previous period. Although the best writing emerges from realism, the best of all finally emerges from Frederick Philip Grove. Of the others, Morley Callaghan (1903–90) suffers from 'moral flabbiness,' and Hugh MacLennan (1907–90) leans too far toward 'didacticism and self-consciousness.' Since Grove is the oldest of the three and possessing a 'reputation [that] rests firmly on his studies of pioneer life in the West,' all of which were published by 1933, it is implied that the other two do not constitute a rising plot in Pacey's history of the novel. Although the pioneer theme pertains to Canadian history, it is not presented in Pacey's introductory remarks. Indeed, what is noticed is the populist bent of regional politics in the West.[22] As for MacLennan, whose novels are more recent, a number of his novels depend upon themes that relate to twentieth-century history, notably the rise of national self- consciousness in English Canada;[23] yet none, according to Pacey, is on a par with *Each Man's Son* (1951), 'a regional study,' which, incidentally, makes it comparable to the best of Grove's work.[24]

Both novelists are at their best, then, as they border on the regional aspect of the regional idyll. The major exemplar of this subgenre is Mazo de la Roche's (1879–1961) *Jalna* (1927), a text most anglophone literary historians have either ignored or treated with some derision, notably V.B. Rhodenizer. Pacey's defence of the series is that what she does is done well. What matters is 'the degree of consistency and harmony which is maintained and the power with which the vision is projected.' The vision, indeed the moral vision, which is necessary for the novel to attain the shape of fullness, lies in its preservation of 'an ancestral British way of life against the growing pressure of American commercial democracy.' The values of the Whiteoaks cycle coincide with those of Leacock, namely, 'the traditional virtues of a landed and genteel mode of life, and against the shoddy fashions of the new commercial era.' These are values that prefigure both Leacock and de la Roche; they appear already in Haliburton, who was part of the excitement of the 1820s and 1830s in Nova Scotia and a 'Tory Imperialist' opposed to responsible government.[25]

Pacey's sympathy with such writers has interesting consequences. They show initially in his construction of the origins of a national literature in Nova Scotia. It originated in an act of colonial violence which is clearly defended:

> For a long time the English residents consisted only of a few soldiers at Annapolis Royal and a few fishermen at Canso, and the bulk of the inhabitants were French Acadians. In 1749 a slightly more positive policy of British settlement was inaugurated with the founding of Halifax and the decision to anglicize the Acadians and compel them to take the oath of

allegiance to the British Crown. When the Acadians refused to take the oath, they were expelled from the colony, 1755, and deported to other English possessions. Three years later the colony was granted a legislative assembly.[26]

In these four crisp sentences that open the second chapter British policy is affirmed, the neutrality of the Acadians is found unacceptable, and British North America's history and culture begins. If there were any native inhabitants, they are not mentioned. We have indicated how the work of a number of writers, notably Haliburton, Kirby, Leacock, and de la Roche provide an armature of conservative values in Pacey's history, and in his conclusion these values are integrated with other English middle-class values that appear to lead inevitably to a vision of national, that is, English-Canadian unity. Those writers who fit the national theme are celebrated for their attacks upon the rising commercialism of the closing decades of the nineteenth century, a commercialism usually associated with Canada's proximity to the United States. The alliance is uneasy, but where they differ, they differ in degree. Some writers look back; others look forward. To group them together as Pacey does is the gesture of a Red Tory and may have found approval in George Grant (1918–88). But social history, we find, is as nothing compared with the presence of the environment, which, unlike Frye's famous comment, does not excite terror in Pacey, but rather 'humility,' and it is this sense of awe that distinguishes Canadian from American writing, which tends to be more optimistic.[27] Here, presumably, lies the distinctive quality in Canadian writing Pacey endeavoured to find. Significantly, it transcends the events of social and other kinds of history.

And so it should, for Tory history, particularly as it looks back to the eighteenth century, is not marked by such myths as progress, but by such virtues as those found in Leacock. The challenge of history, according to Pacey, lies in the ability to prevent it from damaging virtue, which might lead, as he charges Callaghan, to 'moral flabbiness.' The function, then, of Pacey's prefatory comments for each period, is to indicate, at least implicitly, that there is a space between social events and literature and that they both exist, very possibly, in different, even occasionally, opposed ontological zones, a perspective adopted, as we have seen already, in Smith's preface to his anthology. The best writing appears to have no direct relationship with its historical moment unless it is representing moral values frequently at odds with that moment. Under these conditions, what appears in the usual sense of the term as

history in the text, such as Canada's origin in Nova Scotia, is either
accepted as 'positive' and therefore valorized as good or refused under
the guise of 'commercial fashion' and valorized as bad. True history, as
contained or produced by the 'best' writing, transcends mere events,
perhaps in moments of awe, in order to protect those virtues Pacey
admires. English Canada's history, as realized in its culture, is not history in a temporal sense. It is an ideology of moral defence.

Ecclesiastical Values

I have already referred to McCourt's text as an apologia for a region,
and a moral defence of a larger region is certainly analogous. History,
then, particularly among English-Canadian historians, is often only a
pretext. Its rhetoric is shaped to promote a structure of ethical antagonism toward the Other, whether it be Toronto or the United States,
which is the enemy of virtue, and geographical space is always transformed into centres of right and wrong. A similar argument is developed by the Sœurs de Sainte-Anne in their *Histoire des littératures française
et canadienne* (1954), which, conveniently enough, they attach to a history of French literature, implying a larger sphere of support. The
implication is never developed; France remains, however, as an impos-
ing cultural presence. It is a presence, furthermore, with a marked and
articulated past, each chapter signalling known periods, that is, the Middle Ages, the Renaissance, the Age of Louis XIV, and so forth. In apparent contrast, the literature of French Canada is structured with
organicist metaphors that imply growth and futurity. I use this term in
White's sense according to which such historiography depends upon
'the uncovering of ... *integrative* structures and processes.' Its mode of
emplotment is comic, and its ideology is conservative. As I shall argue,
these are apt descriptions of the history that the Sœurs de Sainte-Anne
produce. It proceeds from a period of fumbling about ('Essais')[28] to one
of gathering together ('*Formation*'), to Progress and, finally, Fertility.
The organic emphasis, however, is less upon growth to adulthood, a
metaphor that belongs to the same semiotic field as that of the *Bildungsroman* and favoured by Camille Roy and others, but rather upon seduction and courtship. The moment of fertility is self-engendering; hence,
the metaphor appears to depend powerfully upon the narcissistic
notion implied in the expression 'replier sur soi-même.' The movement
toward self-engendering is given point by the choice of origin as occurring at the moment of New France's being ceded to England, suggesting

that the loss of the mother country requires self-formation, which gives some point to attaching the literary histories of France and French Canada with, however, differing structures.[29]

High comedy is also didactic: its laughter is designed to correct. As narrative and plot, this history is also structured for teaching.[30] It has a bibliography and essay assignments already prepared at the end of each section, and the kinds of questions posed lend point and direction to the narrative. Thus the first question asks: 'Discuter l'opinion d'après laquelle l'histoire de la littérature canadienne-française commence avec la régime anglaise.' Elsewhere the history's religious subplot is implied:

> Mgr Cloutier a dit de Mgr Laflèche: 'Dom Benoît l'a appellé l'Athanase du Canada. Il eût été de même Ambroise si Théodose se fût devant lui, il eût été Chrysostome si Eudoxie eût étalé ses désordres au milieu de son peuple.'
> Expliquer les allusions contenues dans cette citation. Que penser de celui à qui on les applique?[31]

One wonders how many secondary students in Canada could respond intelligently now, some forty-five years later, to such a question.

The didactic level of the text is equally marked by the use of headings, often underlined, bold font, and definitions, all designed to assist the student in assimilating key concepts and words. For example under 'I. Période d'essais' we read 'Caractères généraux' and in the paragraph dedicated to describing kinds of texts we find they have a 'valeur documentaire' and that they express 'loyauté politique,' 'obéissance,' and 'fidelité intellectuelle à la France.' Elsewhere we are informed that Jean Rivard is a 'roman à thèse' and the genre provided with a definition. All of these techniques are brought to bear upon a method that provides sufficient social and political history and generic kinds (oratory, journalism, history, novel, poetry), that are in turn illustrated by various figures. The structure and method make it clear that the design is deductive, descending from the general (the period) to the particular (the writer). The final instance of the didactic is evinced in the tendency to assign grades of achievement to the writers (e.g., 'La Terre paternelle mérite ... une bonne note').[32]

The effect is to produce a discontinuous history that appears to contradict a notion of organic wholeness, but this sense of contradiction is attenuated and skilfully used to advantage by constructing a kind of imbricated metanarrative. Running along en filigrane in the text is the enormous role assigned to the making of culture in French Canada in the work and example of Étienne Parent and François-Xavier Garneau. Parent is introduced among those periodical editors who 'ont lutté, comme on le faisait au parlement, contre un pouvoir oppresseur pour conserver nos libertés les plus chères.' The same Parent provided the motto for *Le Canadien*, namely, 'Nos institutions, notre langue et nos lois,' all significant concepts in the discussion of Quebec as a distinct society. He is emphatically declared the journalist 'le plus éclairé de son époque.' Garneau, who is given considerably more space, produced a history that 'restera toujours une de nos richesses nationales,' despite reservations of an ecclesiastical character. Their presences return often in the book. Parent, for example, is an éminence grise behind the Société Saint-Jean-Baptiste, a nationalist organization that adopted his magazine's motto. Both 'Parent [and] Garneau ouvrirent les voies à un art nouveau supérieur à tout ce que les lettres canadiennes avaient produit jusque-là [1860–1900],' and without Garneau the rise of the novel would have been fundamentally different, as we have already seen. They both figure in the formation of poetic discourse from Crémazie on (1854–63), and Garneau is the point of departure for the renewal of historiography in the twentieth century.[33]

At once founders and metanarrators of French-Canadian culture, both Parent and Garneau, at least in a certain measure, overcome along with others the discontinuous form of this history. They serve as integrative elements in the narration and mark it as conservative. Their use also imparts a rhythm of what might be called precursorality, not to say prolepsis, into the text, inscribing it with a sense of inevitability. Because they were who they were then, we must be who we are now. They also encourage the sisters to give their narrative a rising plot structure: 'La littérature canadienne suit une marche ascendante,' a clause which is completed by another, namely, 'elle achemine vers l'*autonomie*.' Such an ideal corresponds to comic desire and completes the metaphor of self-engenderment. The literature of the first half of the twentieth century is characterized by its tendency toward the universal, as opposed to the regional and provincial, it is informed by a Christian spirit, and reflects the '*progrès de l'instruction* dans notre société canadienne.' The ascent, then, is progressive and didactic, despite continuous and more serious struggles between Ottawa, Quebec, and the other provinces which put at risk 'notre survivance nationale,' a theme with which the text begins and develops on frequent occasions in order to emphasize the conjoined virtues of a national culture and a Roman Catholic spirit.[34] Ideology, design, and history are thus seamlessly integrated.

An Emerging Francophonie

Everything, it might be said, about the production and preservation of culture in Quebec is designed to promote remembrance.[35] The question is how it is to be remembered. The dominant process of memorialization was conducted by members of the clergy until the latter half of the 1960s with the exception of such texts as Dostaler O'Leary's *Le Roman canadien-français* (1954), which is not a history in a conventional sense; it is rather an argument that seems to converge with Frye's in its effort to recover a repressed sensibility. Therefore, the chapter entitled 'Esquisse historique' cannot be drawn upon as an orderly succession of texts and events. Although he recalls implicitly the efforts of Émile Chartier (1876–1963) and Albert Dandurand to read French-Canadian writing in its relation to that of France, O'Leary sounds a more secular note. The leitmotif of his argument is the recovery of liberty in attitude and theme in order to lift francophone writing from the provincial to the universal. Thus the Conquest, the moment of origin, is compared to the occupation of France in the Second World War,[36] and although efforts to remain in touch with the post-revolutionary regime in France were jointly repressed by the British and the Catholic clergy,[37] that did not prevent the 'passion de liberté' from developing. In a paradoxical way, the necessity for an awakened political consciousness was the impetus of both cultural survival in Quebec and its poverty, especially from 1880 to 1930. It was necessary as a defence against 'la guerre d'extermination légale' waged against the citizens of the province, and, as a consequence, the best prose writers were attracted to journalism, rather than the novel.[38]

Such a construction of the French-Canadian past as sanction against extermination has other consequences as well, especially in respect of canonization. O'Leary prefers the early nineteenth-century novel of adventure, rather than novels that were 'pieusards et faussement patriotiques.' Preferred are novels 'des récits pleins d'imprévu, le développement pittoresque de légendes, de relations historiques mêlées d'études sur les moeurs indiennes.' In his effort to privilege a conservative ideology, Lareau is taken to task for undervaluing novels like L'Ecuyer's *La Fille du brigand* because of its penchant for adventure and fantasy. He therefore reserves most of his invective for Aubert de Gaspé's *Les Anciens Canadiens* and its reception in official francophone literary history. Noting that it has been raised far beyond its literary merit because of a pompous style that hides behind 'un aspect de bonhomie qui se voudrait naturelle,' O'Leary argues that its position in the canon sets a standard of limited ambition by emulating Eugène Sue (1804–57) and Alexandre Dumas (1802–70) at the expense of Balzac (1799–1850), Stendhal (1783–1842), and Flaubert (1821–80), all of whom, he implies, were accessible around the middle of the century.[39] Although the social novel, exemplified by Chauveau's *Charles Guérin*, hardly compares with that of France or of the United States, it is redeemed by the fact that 'Chauveau nous fait assister à l'ébranlement du régime seigneurial.'[40]

The weakness of the French-Canadian novel may be attributed, then, to a social and political situation, which prevented it from aspiring to a level of universality, represented primarily by the literature of France, and thus acquiring the freedom that would give it an international profile. Canonization could only occur 'si on acharnait à retourner le seul, l'unique thème de l'attachement à la terre, le seul qui trouvât grâce devant les professeurs et les clercs.' As O'Leary goes on to argue, that was 'l'aspect dramatique de notre littérature, et peut-être aussi de notre Histoire tout entière, au XIXe siècle.' The international success of Hémon's *Maria Chapdelaine*, inscribed with the view that Quebec was incapable of change, only confirmed and prolonged this situation.[41] Thus, while the history of the novel has its roots in the struggle for liberty of post-Conquest Quebec, its true history does not begin until it consciously asserts its autonomy in the work of Ringuet (Philippe Panneton [1895–1960]), Germaine Guèvremont (1893–1968), Gabrielle Roy (1909–83), Roger Lemelin (1919–92), and others from the 1930s and 1940s on. Its autonomy, however, is to be acquired within a history that transcends that of French Canada. Worth can only be assigned to Quebec's novelists when, along with the Belgian Maurice Maeterlinck (1862–1949) and the Swiss C.-F. Ramuz (1878–1947), 'en citant [un écrivain] canadien, les Français puissent en être aussi fiers que nous le sommes de ces noms qui illustrent le passé français.' The canon, then, is understood as a general francophone canon, and not to so understand it is to remain in an ivory tower of regionalism.[42] Although it may appear that this is an argument for a sophisticated colonialism, it would be more apt to see it, according to O'Leary, as proposing a cultural basis for what is now known as La Francophonie. It corresponds to an idea of a Commonwealth literature without, of course, the contemporary overtones of an 'empire writing back.' Nor could it, given the historically complicated relationship between Quebec and France that has prompted histories of abandonment, on the one hand, and an heroic France that supported the colonization of North America, on the other. O'Leary's France is neither of these. He hastens to valorize the story of liberty that emerges from the Revolution and a more contemporary France that suffered during the Nazi occupation. These are necessary images of France in the struggle against assimilation by the British, and an affirmation of those values that are to be seen in the long history of French culture.

The Synecdoche of Crisis

The first ambitious history of writing in French Canada, also addressed to secondary students, was Baillargeon's *Littérature canadienne-française* (1957). The title itself is revealing, for it omits any reference to history, which is clearly part of its intent to provide. Tacitly holding it in the zone of historiography, Lionel Groulx's (1878–1967) signed preface praises its historical structure. As one might guess because of its audience, its didactic character is perfectly evident, and many of the typographic effects noted in the previous history by the Sœurs de Sainte-Anne are to be found here. It differs, however, in a number of other ways, notably, its format, which follows that of the French manual (1946–53) of Pierre-Georges Castex and Paul Surer, not to mention Roy's, providing photographs; it is also, besides being replete with intertextual citations, an explicated anthology, which leads the student to specific texts and explains how they are to be read; and finally, graphics are often used, consisting of arrows that direct the student through various lives in order to represent significant moments. Like Groulx, however, I want to argue that Baillargeon's text is more interesting in respect of '*le dessin des courbes ou des époques.*'[43]

In order to answer the question whether there is a French-Canadian literature, Baillargeon proposes a bipartite response. The first is an *Étude de la formation du type canadien-français* (1600–1850) and the second is the history of its literature. The first section is further divided into the respective French and English regimes, implying that the type he is constructing is the product of a political reversal of fortune, that is, 'notre séparation brutale d'avec la mère patrie, la culture et la langue française.'[44] It also implies that the writing of these initial two subperiods is esteemed for its sociological and political character, and such an axiological position also encourages the frequently cited interventions of historians and observers of the period. The effect of the British occupation was sufficient to remove economic and political power from the *habitants*, and therefore the literature esteemed in the text's treatment of this period belongs to a literature of combat through which the colonized might recover its culture. By the middle of the nineteenth century, a distinct ethnic type emerges that differs from the French. The French-Canadian is a zealous patriot, still imbued with Catholicism, and suspicious of both the French and the English. The moment is ripe for a beginning of a distinct literature.

This is a bolder step than any taken by Baillargeon's predecessors, who usually find an origin at the moment of Conquest. It also allows Baillargeon to construct a historical rhythm of rise and fall that is frequently repeated in the text. Furthermore, French-Canadian cultural history is articulated clearly as modelled on an organicist metaphor similar to those of Roy and the Sœurs de Sainte-Anne and that operates in three phases: Birth, Maturity, and New Orientations. Its development, however, possibly affected by modern psychological theories, does not allow for continuous growth. It is marked by frequent crises, typical of a *Bildungsroman*, all of which are informed by the first crisis of Conquest. Thus the initial section on the formation of an ethnic type is itself a prototype of the historical 'curves' in the text, and even within a sub-period, such as the British regime, a rhythm of rise and fall is inscribed that runs from the first parliamentary structure of 1791, leading to several years of constitutional struggle culminating in the Rebellion of 1837–8, described as a 'crise de liberté,'[45] followed by the BNA Act, which was partially designed to preserve French-Canadian culture. Crisis appeared to be overcome.

The same crisis had other, equally well-known, effects: Garneau provided the culture that French Canada was accused of not possessing, and he is celebrated as the one who 'par l'histoire, démarre la production littéraire canadienne-française.'[46] In Quebec, at least, history, historiography, and literature are all shaped by the same forces, and it would be impossible for literary history not to feel rooted in the past and the ideologies that can be formed from it. It is a past that is always constructed so as to aim[47] toward a future perfect. To achieve such a future, since utopia is only virtual, obstacles must be surmounted, and crises overcome. Consequently, the crisis becomes the defining moment. Without it, no ideal can be reached. But since an ideal is a model and crisis can be constructed as a recurrent reality, the crisis might be called the subject of Baillargeon's argument. The crisis, furthermore, bears upon the central theme of the text: French-Canadians are a distinct ethnic type (the object of Part I), and thus their literature, as a consequence, is distinct (the object of Part II). Whatever threatens the type and its expression is deemed a crisis. In more political terms, the literature of Quebec is admired primarily because it is a cultural sign of provincial autonomy without which the French fact would not exist in North America.[48]

Crisis, however, is the principle that, in fact, animates the structural metaphor of Baillargeon's history: crisis is a moment of birth. Garneau's *prise de conscience* during the period of a united Canada gave rise to Quebec's most significant history, which in turn fathered its literature.[49] The end of the nineteenth century, according to Edmond de Nevers (1862–1906) was 'une *période nefaste*,'[50] insofar as it was the threshold of Canada's acceptance of British imperialism, and the response was an upsurge of nationalism in Quebec that intensified the production of its own culture. Crisis is therefore a growing pain, but Camille Roy rose to the occasion by providing a history of its literature '*en* pleine crise de maturation.' Sustained crisis became a norm in Quebec from 1940 on and laid the foundation for the province's contemporary orientations, and such poets as Hector de Saint-Denys Garneau (1912–43) and Anne Hébert (1916–2000) bear a homologous relationship with this crisis.[51]

Culture, then, is synonymous with crisis, and so, like Adam's Fall, the Fall of New France is constructed as a prototype of a series of fortunate falls that anticipate various kinds of redemption. Thus one might ask, as historians have often asked since Hémon posed Quebec's situation as one of immobility, whether the cycle of crisis and growth is less dynamic than it appears. Although Baillargeon is not explicit about his historical vision, his comment about historical construction is revealing: 'L'histoire est la *science des faits passés*. Comme telle, elle a besoin que son objet ait acquis une certaine *immobilité* dans le temps. Avant sa fixation dans le passé, un événement peut difficilement être l'objet d'une étude historique stricte, car l'interaction des influences humaines lui imprime des *orientations* encore imprévisibles.' As a consequence, Baillargeon cautions the reader not to expect that his judgments in turn will not be subject to the effects of time: 'C'est pourquoi l'étude littéraire de cette période [the contemporary period] ne donne que des jalons et non des traits définitifs.'[52] Thus the past is at once immobile and subject to changes of significance. Baillargeon's conservatism urges him toward the immobile which inscribes a rhythm of crisis and resolution forever into Quebec's cultural history from which there appears to be no exit. As if to reinforce the sense of immobility, writers are held in an order of static verticality in which they are named, dated, defined, given a life, a photograph, a personality, a style, a text, and an explication. Each genre is carefully placed in its appropriate literary contexts and frequently interrupted with various quotations so that even the discontinuous acquires an effect of stasis. Crisis itself is therefore implied as the norm, which redefines its role as a principle of animation and gives the impression that the plot continues only by repeating itself as if it were a romance of successive and, apparently, interminably recursive re-enactments of an originating crisis.

Nature and Marxism

As we have argued, the task of finding a persuasive historical structure for the literature of English Canada is a task of some magnitude that is not always met with conviction. The object of R.E. Rashley's *Poetry in Canada* (1958) is to find an appropriate order. That he endeavoured to do so with a certain Marxist bias near the height of the Cold War in the 1950s testifies to a degree of daring infrequently met among fellow anglophone literary historians, which may, however, be accounted for by his English upbringing. His project constructs both a rapport between history and culture (base and superstructure) and articulates them into a trifold structure that implies a certain dialectical movement. Correspondingly it has three aims, which are sociological, historical, and evaluative. The aims are, however, mutually supportive and not sequential like the three major steps that, according to Rashley, English-Canadian poetry has taken. Poets are therefore constructed as types that represent a group, and the groups in turn are defined as signal moments in Canadian history.[53] The first, divided into two phases, comprises the moments of immigration and pioneering. The second occurs when poets attempted to transform 'their physical world into the world of idea.' The third stage arises when the new group 'saw man as a social animal and occupied itself almost exclusively with the social environment.' The sequence as a whole is perceived as inevitable, and 'its origin is in the actual experience of people in Canada.'[54]

The plot, then, has at least a formal affinity with those developed in French Canada. Beginnings do not correspond, for example, with a moment of discovery, but rather a raising to consciousness of a recurrent event or situation. Each transition is described as a 'breakdown,' which constitutes a kind of crisis. That the sequence takes an inevitable shape marks it in some respects as the argument of 'vulgar' Marxism with its attendant limitations, and the weakness of the argument becomes manifest in the choice of representative poets. Assuming, for example, that Carman is such a type, it is then possible to assert:

'Carman's birth and growth in the Canada of his time require the transcendentalism which he adopted and also condition its application to life.'[55] Carman becomes tautologically useful in the argument in a way that his contemporary D.C. Scott, a more conflicted and contradictory poet in Rashley's argument, cannot. Far from demystifying the relation of culture to history, which one might expect of a sociological reading, the claim of inevitability throws all action over into the arms of destiny. The reliance on the inescapable, however, poses contradictions for Rashley which his method cannot overcome, but in its rigour tends to reinforce.

Part of the tacit adoption of the model of base and superstructure in Rashley may be seen in the relationship established between the first and second steps. The former fails because of its inability to transform the physical – the unadorned, external character of nature – into idea, nor is the group that represents it capable of anything other than achieving group consciousness. That transformation to consciousness occurred in a certain measure as Canada moved from being an aggregate of colonial regions to a confederated country. Of greater moment, however, than a changed political agreement was the reception of Darwin's theory of evolution. After evolution, what was to be done with Nature? In both instances, the change in the understanding of the base afforded a corresponding cultural transformation that encouraged the assimilation of nature by spirit, drawing both base and superstructure into a more intimate rapport. Although the initial effects were energizing and prompted a sense of Victorian moral vigour, this changed rapport positioned the subject in revery, apart from the social world, alone with the 'oversoul' where the poet is occasionally able 'to recover the secret feelings of one's own experiences with nature.' 'Nature' provided access to self-knowledge, but no more than that, and perhaps not that much. When Carman hears the wind, 'all that I had heard / Was my own heart in the sea's voice / And the wind's lonely word.'[56]

The satisfactions and moral illusions of solitude were tossed aside during the First World War and the Depression, both of which proved to be the basis of the third step, which discovered 'humanity directly seen in the light of experience and the new knowledge science had provided.' If I have followed correctly the dialectic of the movement of poetry in Rashley's argument, we are to understand that initially Nature is manifested as brute materiality for the immigrant and pioneer. Nature is raised to a second level of consciousness by the generation of the 1860s and becomes a way of defining the Spirit and providing a basis of moral order and perfectibility. In the third step, Nature is sublated as human love through which 'one loses identity or singleness to win significance through identity with man.'[57] As a result, the collective experience of the first step is recovered at a new level of consciousness, and the limitations of the second step, the hypostasis of the self, are overcome in a new synthesis; or, to simplify, one aspect of romanticism was infused with another.

As Rashley is careful to argue, such shifts in perception do not merely occur to the perceiving subject. They are rather prompted by shifts in the base, and so his argument is consistently held within a Marxist framework. As Fredric Jameson indicates, dialectical thinking is 'thought to the second power: an intensification of the normal thought processes such that a renewal of light washes over the object of their exasperation, as though in the midst of its immediate perplexities the mind had attempted, by willpower, by fiat, to lift itself mightily up by its own bootstraps.' As Jameson cannot help reminding us, however, nothing occurs at the level of the superstructure without the intervention of mind. Mind must work however, in a particular way, which returns us to Rashley's rhetoric of the imperative. The poets of the third step are esteemed because their solutions were in favour of 'humanity.' They were not stayed by the middle-class interests of middle-class individualism which has a habit of making a commodity fetish of the object and the locus of objectification itself. As Georg Lukács asserts, 'bourgeois thought ... remains enmeshed in fetishistic categories and in consequence the products of human relations become ossified, with the result that thought trails behind objective developments.'[58] So it is that Carman's failure as a poet is a function of his failure to think dialectically. Although the one 'who espouses perfection / Must follow the threefold plan / Of soul and mind and body,' these are only phases of nature. Rashley faults Carman for thinking that the three possess equal value and that they are not mutually influential, a point that Rashley infers and that Carman does not imply. If they were, and if they influenced each other properly, that is, progressively responsive to history as understood in the Marxist sense, then Carman, we are to assume, would be a better poet. We cannot, however, assume this. If we are unable to assume this, how are to assume, then, that the poets of the third step are necessarily superior because of its being possible to construe their poetry as possessed of affinities with Marxism? Rashley reveals more, however, when he asserts that as Carman becomes 'the vehicle of cosmic forces ... there is a willing suspension of intelligent control.'[59]

Does 'intelligent control' lead necessarily, however, to intelligent understanding? Poets are valorized when their thinking is in accord with the imperatives of history. As Lukács reminds us, 'intellectual genesis must be identical in principle with historical genesis.' Although there is an ontological difference between nature and history, they may be thought on the same plane. They are both capable of construction by the intellect, so that one can choose to be a vehicle[60] of either, at which point, one must assume intelligent control ceases. Thus the basis for valorizing the third group has no particular logical foundation. Perhaps this why Rashley himself reaches the surprising conclusion in the end that 'poetry outside of the marxist group makes a richer response to the world of its time.' Indeed, 'when all is said there remains "that strange precipitate" which defies reduction and destroys the accusers.' The precipitate is the humour of such poets as Pratt and Birney whose laughter dissipates the burden of necessity and inevitability. One might also remark in conclusion that during the infrequent moments when Rashley discusses Marxism explicitly, it is difficult to know what happened to the problems of economic production, constructions of class, and the issue of conflict, especially as one discovers that the 'marxist theme' possesses four concepts: 'nature as an enlargement of the richness of life, love as a symbol of humanity, racial harmony, and clarity of programme.' If this is Marxism, it is the humanitarian Marxism of liberal Canadian intellectuals of the 1930s like that of Collin, and it also calls to mind more contemporary attitudes, such as those developed by Ernst Fischer, arguing that '[a]rt as the means of man's identification with his fellow-men, nature, and the world, as his means of feeling and living together with everything that is and will be, is bound to grow as man grows in nature.'[61]

Deliverance from Literary History

During the time that Rashley was preparing his book, Carl F. Klinck was getting together the editors of, and contributors to, the first edition of *Literary History of Canada* (1965). Not surprisingly, Rashley's name was not mentioned as a possible contributor. His enthusiasm for 'clarity of programme' would not have sorted well with Klinck's approach, who 'didn't want to impose a pattern, because people would write to it, that is, write up an old concept, instead of letting the concept issue from the facts.' The same position is adumbrated in the history's Introduction: 'The divisions and periods of this history have not been arbitrarily

imposed, but have rather been discovered in the light of the evidence.'
Delicate as it may appear, the first sentence of the history proper tends
to reinforce a sense of the empirical to the point of being morally diffi-
dent: 'The New World was not discovered; it just grew.'[62] True enough,
from an indigenous perspective the New World was hardly new, but it
was new for explorers, interpreters, and settlers, and to suggest that it
merely grew is to remove onself from the responsibility of the effects
that European culture had upon that of the native inhabitants. As a consequence, by continually imbricating the imagery of the 'New World'
into the literary system of English literature, the native is constructed
merely as a literary artifact, and fortunately for English-Canadian culture, at least from the perspective of history, neither native culture nor
the exotic in what is now Canada became a part of anglophone literature before the eighteenth century. Responsibility for the negative
impact of settlement of the New World falls on Spain.[63] Needless to say,
although it would be decidedly anachronistic to expect to find the ideology of the New Literary History in a text of the mid-1960s, it nevertheless assists, at least, in positioning the history in a certain fashion.

It is tempting to refer to this history as an encyclopaedia with a narrative frame. Klinck perceives it, however, as an inventory whose project
was 'to discover what kind of "place" Canada was and is, and what has
happened here in the realm of literature and closely associated writings.' Such a statement suggests, intentionally or not, that whatever
Canadian literature is, it is a function of its location, as if Canada were a
house and its culture furniture that changed according to the season.
The historian enters and takes note, implying that the historian has little to do with the arrangement. History observes how the New World
'grew.' Despite the effort to avoid 'ready-made categories and descriptive headings hitherto solemnly accepted in Canadian literary history
[that] might prove to be part of the folklore,'[64] there is nothing remarkable about the four major divisions of the text, namely, discovery and
exploration, settlement, development, and realization of a culture. Two
points, however, arrest one's attention: on the one hand, time overlaps,
inasmuch as exploration texts are treated up to 1860 and settlement
begins much earlier, and, on the other hand, despite the profession of
pragmatism, sections II to IV are all governed by the word 'tradition.' A
determined effort is made to construct a past, which prompts the reader
to examine the kind of past that is made.

As we have suggested already, Canada's origin is presented as a random event. Not only did it, like the other Americas, just grow like Topsy,

its growth was a marginal occurrence: 'In the minds of men who saw their fondest dreams beyond the setting sun, what is now Canada was, in the sixteenth century, a mere footnote to the countries of perpetual spring farther south.' Such a statement with all its poetic allusions deliberately constructs Canada as a literary event of ironic magnitude. The first clause evokes Ulysses's brilliant parainesis in Dante's *Inferno* that urges his companions to follow him 'di retro al sol,' and the second recalls the serene beginnings of Ovid's *Metamorphoses* in which he sets forth the four great ages of which the first was characterized by 'ver ... aeternum.'[65] The first text, not widely read during the English Renaissance, condemned Ulysses and his kind; the second text, highly admired in the Renaissance, puts a favourable cachet on the temperate zones, in this instance the future United States. The irony that composes both clauses is further enhanced by the designation of Canada as 'a mere footnote.' Although Canada had begun to be construed in English literature by the beginning of the eighteenth century, it 'was merely a minor vehicle.'[66] Such a beginning denotes a plot that rises from nowhere in particular – in fact, from a margin of political and economic invasion – in anticipation of its 'realization' in the final section. Some beginnings need to be hidden, and the discourse used to do so in the opening chapter fits readily into the general fondness for organicist and, especially, spatial metaphors found in most anglophone literary history. In this instance, any moral responsibility incurred by overseas expansion is carefully obviated by holding the Spanish up as the worst example.

It is not surprising to read in the following chapter of a crucial difference between a European and a Canadian consciousness: 'European literature can be seen as a statement and a restatement of a myth within a continuous community.' In contrast, 'English-speaking Canadian consciousness faces from the start the problem of creating from direct experience, memory, and written records according to the sense of history which begins to mature within societies dominated by commodity production.'[67] The difference lies in the distinction that can be drawn between the genre of epic and the records of explorers. This is a statement of some value, because it recalls Schiller's celebrated distinction between the naive and the sentimental. Canadian literature will always be sentimental, that is, clarified by its freedom from myth and forced to develop reflexively in the world of history, a notion that Northrop Frye pursued to advantage in his concluding remarks on pastoral.[68]

While these early texts constitute our unwritten 'foundation literature,' what they founded does not begin to acquire a more literary form until the process of the 'transplanting of traditions' begins. We are advised immediately, however, not to assume that this early writing should necessarily be read as Canadian. Indeed (but here the implied difference with Rashley becomes apparent) 'twentieth-century scholars, in looking back upon the early history of Canada, may find it difficult to draw an inference of inevitability from what they see.' If there is a destiny, it was certainly not yet manifest in Canada. Such a caveat permits Alfred Bailey to pass over in silence all the writing which belongs properly to England and New England prior to 1670. The year provides a beginning because 'the peoples of English speech ... had begun the attempt to outflank the French in their pursuit of the beaver.' Origin, then, is an economic success story. One by one, obstacles like the French stronghold of Louisbourg are overcome, 'the hapless Acadians' are deported, the 'hard labour of the frontier' begins, and a 'sense of identity with Mother Country' is affirmed in the crushing of the Rebellion of 1837–8, paving the way for a period of 'national achievement from which the country has never seriously receded, and from which it has advanced to the ampler perspectives of our own day.'[69]

No one can miss the note of English-Canadian nationalism in this emplotment of fidelity to England and its rewards. The French, in a word, lose, and the indigenous people are not mentioned as a serious threat. How quickly the story of ascendence takes place is another matter. In Newfoundland everything written from 1715 to 1800 merely continues 'the literature of discovery written by Europeans about the New World,'[70] and, indeed, Frances Brooke's *The History of Emily Montague* is possibly best construed as 'description and travel literature.'[71] Thus until the end of the eighteenth century, one might well suppose that literature in English Canada was a literature of visitors who, although many stayed, preferred to describe the furniture in the rooms, to return to a metaphor already proposed. Nevertheless, whether an effort is made to situate literature in 'actual experience,' to use Rashley's expression, is uncertain. A study of Haliburton emerges in a chapter whose first sentence is as follows: 'In the two decades following 1815, the Maritime Provinces underwent a prolonged period of social and economic crisis.' Haliburton shared Thomas McCulloch's (1776–1883) view that social troubles in the colony were a consequence of recession, and they decided that the best way to reach the public seriously was to model 'their work essentially on the essay as perfected by Addison and Steele.' In their decision 'the first serious realistic Canadian prose fiction was born.'[72] Haliburton's Tory ideology was inherited, however, from his father, and inscribed in his major text, *The Clockmaker,* which appeared at the end of Nova Scotia's recession in 1835. It is described as a 'happy book,' Haliburton now being 'secure in his enjoyment of life and his faith that his gospel for Nova Scotia would ultimately prevail.' With the exception of Haliburton, however, Maritime writing from 1815 to 1880 yields more 'when considered as history and sociology than ... as literature.'[73] Because of the conditions of social and economic life in the Maritimes, typical of the frontier, literary life was limited to nostalgia and diversion.

Fred Cogswell's argument is consistent with that of making a tradition for English Canada, and it is a tradition of colonial self-awareness and dependency. The furniture that Maritime poetry – the dominant genre – saw was intertextually bound. It mirrored 'either the Victorian tradition of poetic decoration and moral edification or the Lowland Scots tradition.'[74] How much this kind of literature differs from that of the Canadas in the nineteenth century is moot. If the tradition was to be distinctive, it would have to reckon with the more powerful anglophone presences of Great Britain and the United States. The Maritimes were not particularly successful, and despite Klinck's chapters, the Canadas did not fare better. Despite the number of English immigrants, only a small minority developed 'the theme of exile or homesickness for the Old Land,' and it took some years for writers like Susanna Moodie to acquire an admiring local audience. If *The Literary Garland* is to be taken as representative of the period, its 'English and Victorian' character must be taken as 'Anglo-Bostonian.'[75] Despite an effort on the part of Leprohon and Kirby to develop the regional with the assistance of Walter Scott (1771–1832) and Alexandre Dumas, the Canadian book trade was seriously squeezed by both Great Britain and the United States from the 1840s until 1900, so that 'Canada's ablest writers, with a few notable exceptions, became expatriates and had their work published outside Canada.'[76]

More damaging, however, than the pull of English and American models and memories in the effort to make a tradition is the awareness that no matter how great 'the desire for national unity' may have been, despite the different definitions of unity held in English and French Canada, 'there is no simple correspondence between an objective record of political, social, and economic events, on the one hand, and on the other, a criticism of the arts, whose creation and appreciation are suffused with subjectivity.' Such a sentence by Roy Daniells, an editor of the volume, may appear to contradict all the efforts made to provide

Canada with a cultural tradition that takes shape within its history. The problem with politics, however, not to speak of social and economic life, is that it presents obstacles, does little to nurture cultural activity, and, by implication, places it at the mercy of the market. 'What needs to be asserted in any study of nineteenth-century Canada,' according to Daniells, 'is the primacy and autonomy of cultural tradition at that time.' In fact, Rashley's notion of 'actual experience' – a position which coincides neatly with that of Frye – prevents the student's admission 'to the centre of Canadian consciousness.' Hence, the weakness of Lighthall's *Songs of the Great Dominion* is its 'sacrificing poetic quality for representative national sentiment.' In other words, Lighthall's subservience to the centre is a manifestation of high colonialism; the true tradition is local, which justifies Daniells's rejection of Toronto periodicals and the influence of Goldwin Smith. How else explain the rise of Roberts and Carman and the impact of '[George] Parkin reading Keats, Rossetti, and Swinburne to his boys,' which proved to be 'the source of our first national literary movement.'[77] The origin of literature, more than being in a place, takes place, rather in literature itself. Needless to say, such a construction of literature continues the perspective of the New Criticism, but it may also have a lot to do with Daniells's spending most of his life in British Columbia, far from central Canadian ideologies. Pardoxically, it anticipates the later privileging of the local in such literary historians as Dick Harrison, the title of whose *Unnamed Country: The Struggle for a Canadian Prairie Fiction* (1977) marks a distinctive shift in attitude toward the local.

In the new fiction from 1880 to 1920, the local is preferred to the national, and despite Sir Wilfrid Laurier's announcement that the twentieth century would be Canada's, only 'a few Canadian fiction writers'[78] showed any interest. Rare indeed is the writer of fiction who saw beyond the moral being of the characters depicted, and 'social forces' were neglected. What was desired in the fiction of the time was ' "story," and "story" told within a framework of unexamined, idealistic values.'[79] Not surprisingly, since the treatment of poetry in this period was provided by Daniells, all the Confederation poets are positioned within either English or American poetic modes and ideas, and the minor poets that conclude the period are not weaker because of their concessions to a crasser public taste except insofar as they are 'induced by the taste of the generation to follow masters and models too far removed from the primal source of Romanticism.'[80]

A chapter on 'The Literature of Protest' would suggest closer rapport between literature and historical events, but 'the leftward swing of the 1930s produced no more permanently valuable poetry than prose.'[81] The difficulty of developing a literature of protest, it is argued, may be attributed to the conservative character of Confederation, 'conservative in the sense of attempting to preserve in the new political entity the character, traditions and advantages of its colonial components, and to avoid a revolutionary rupture with the circumstances of the past.'[82] Such a conservatism, however, is precisely the conservatism of Klinck's history, and one need only change the verb 'to preserve' to 'to construct' to take the sentence as definitive of the enterprise as a whole. Revolutionary rupture is avoided by making the history of literature autonomous, thereby transcending the oppositions of the native and the cosmopolitan, not to speak of confrontations between the regions and the centre, to such a degree that it is possible 'merely and calmly to record and appraise,' a phrase used to open the final section. Nothing could more succinctly express the notion of literary history as a controlling gaze.[83]

It may be that the distinguishing mark of English Canada, as Millar MacLure remarks, is that it is 'unhappily not an organism, but an agglomeration.' Its coherence is random, and sensitivity to this condition prevents the imposition of a guiding unifying thread other than one that stands apart from the historical. MacLure signals the apocalyptic, a theme running from Stevenson to Frye, supported by such critics as Eli Mandel and James Reaney, 'which is a-historical, and invites us to take our ancestors on our own terms.' Such an understanding of literature clearly permits the placing of poetry, at least, outside the intervention of historical event and providing it with the autonomy that Daniells refers to. Above all, however, scholarship in English Canada adheres 'to the disinterested use of words; this is the dominant element in an otherwise complex tradition.' Culture, then, is given the status of object, a conclusion MacLure draws simply because, one supposes, the history of English Canada, as he asserts in his prefatory remarks, is so diverse and so resistant to linear analysis. Perhaps its human emblem would be the 'synthetic man,' who cannot be comprehended by either horizontal or vertical order.[84] So it is that correspondences between fiction and lived experience are difficult to find. Although, finally, poetry achieved another 'renaissance' in the forties, 'the Second World War made few appearances in it.'[85]

The only person in Canada at the time qualified to find an order in Klinck's history was Northrop Frye, and he made one that was appropriate and perfectly in accord with its general tenor. In his usual dour, ironic fashion, Frye plunges in, confirmed 'in most of [his] intuitions on the subject.' He begins by agreeing with the emphases of the editors that Canadian literary culture 'is more significantly studied as a part of Canadian life than as a part of an autonomous body of literature.' A context for this remark is found in his *Anatomy of Criticism* (1957), published at the time that Klinck was assembling his team of editors. There Frye remarks programmaticly that literature must be understood as an 'autonomous language.' Thus English-Canadian literature is stripped of literary status to become, apparently, mere documentation but, as I shall argue, literature is in the process of being stripped in order to be placed into a more primal state. Its sociological function is further enhanced by permitting 'the Canadian cultural public to identify itself through its literature.' Frye is thus led to discuss those national institutions that support the process of identity, which, by extension, are available to both francophone and anglophone culture, which suggests both advantages and difficulties for Canada as whole. And so he is brought to the first large theme of his essay, Canada's beginnings 'as an obstacle.' Here he supports a number of contributors to the volume in producing a structure, in fact a binary opposition, of some magnitude, that may be constructed as resistance and compromise, conflict and preservation. The environment is perceived as object, the menace to the subject, which in turn allows for a significant excursus on the role of the gaze in Canadian culture. The gaze is rapidly transformed into a desire to control, which in turn lends itself to the perception that Canada is a Hebraic country. Among the examples given are 'its conquest of a promised land, its Maccabean victories of 1812, its struggle for the central fortress on the hill at Quebec.'[86]

If Canada is, as Douglas LePan (1914–98) declares in the title of a 1948 poem, 'A Country Without a Mythology,' a mythology must be found, and Frye finds it in his image of the 'garrison mentality,' the sign of a society that poses itself over and against the Other, whether it be the environment or something more ideological. Conviction, he argues, particularly the conviction of religion, 'has been a major – perhaps the major – cultural force in Canada.' But conviction in general, according to Frye, is also deeply inscribed in English-Canadian literature, and 'the literature it produces, at every stage, tends to be rhetorical, an illustration or allegory of social attitudes.' So he concludes the second part of his essay, and it confirms his initial thinking about the sociological usefulness of Canadian literature with which he begins. In the next section he locates this description of Canadian culture in the wider context of Western history, finding nothing in this that is particularly distinctive about Canadian literature. As a result no matter how Canadian the theme, its literature does not for this reason become Canadian. This is because 'the forms of literature are autonomous.' Thus Canadian literature finds itself in a double bind: there is no Canadian literature because its writing possesses primarily a sociological value and because its literature has no national specificity. With sovereign ease Frye then makes the observation about history that we have already indicated, namely, that Canada's cultural origins are historical, not mythical, and then remarks that 'literature is conscious mythology.' How does such mythology come into being? In two movements beginning with the separation of subject and object, a separation already grounded in the separation of subject from the threat of the surrounding environment, and a second phase that enters mythological consciousness. The separation is captured in the image of 'obstacle' as the origin of Canada. The first movement issues in reportage, a type of narrative that ranges from the reports of explorers to prose fiction and poetry. Since, however, the separation of subject and object is not truly grounded in nature or even social history but, rather, 'the primary fact of consciousness,'[87] it is only on that level that the separation and the obstacles can be overcome. On that level literature becomes mythology made conscious; it is not, to use Schiller's terms again, simply a naive expression, but reflexive and meditative, which Schiller calls the sentimental. So Frye remains within the contemporary and the historical, but he construes it romantically as another and higher level of mythological process. Despite the fact that there may be two kinds of literary mythology, one evinced in romance and the other in realism, this distinction is held by 'our own revolutionary age,' and the garrison mentality is held responsible for the proliferation of romance, melodrama, and other forms of popular literature. Thus popular literature, which is deeply inscribed with social values, puts our understanding of the sociological value of literature on a plane coterminous with literature as an autonomous language. As a result, while the public may find its identity in literature, a remark that in its initial context appears benignly sociological, Frye anticipates his programmatic observation that 'the imaginative writer is finding his identity within the world of literature itself.' Writer and public meet in literature, a conscious mythology.[88]

Without going so far as to argue that the pastoral myth is characteristic of Canada, Frye chooses appropriately to speak of 'Canada' as a con-

cept which 'can also become a pastoral myth in certain circumstances.'
Consistent with his earlier argument, the myth has two phases, namely,
one of separation ('sentimental or nostalgic pastoral myth') and the
'genuine myth [which] would result from reversing this process.' History of literature would mean, then, history of mythopoeisis or a history
of how Canadian writers have chosen at various times to articulate the
two phases of pastoral. Grounded as it is in a mentality that is characterized by its conservatism, Canadian culture, as Frye observes in his
conclusion, turns away from the revolutionary and the excesses of technology in its preference for law and history and seeks reconciliation
rather than conflict. History is a continuum, rather than an order of discontinuity as described, for example, by Michel Foucault and Frow; history as literature may be perceived 'not only as complicating itself in
time, but as spread out in conceptual space from some kind of centre.'[89]
The emphasis in the concluding essay hovers over time, but proceeds
relentlessly toward the centre, the organization of literature as 'consciously spatial,'[90] toward a 'profoundly disturbed'[91] sensibility whose
identity depends not so much upon existential self-identity, but the
identity of the subject in a certain space, which prompts the celebrated
question, 'Where is here?'[92]

I have dwelt upon Frye's modestly entitled 'Conclusion' at some
length because it is a brilliant summa of the English-Canadian understanding of the relation of literature to history. Although it may appear
too much like his own theory as expressed primarily in *Anatomy of Criticism* to be seamlessly applicable to a history prepared by many hands and
too much rooted in the modernism of the 1950s and the early 1960s to
have contemporary significance, it, nevertheless, effortlessly resolves
many of the paradoxes and contradictions met by those literary historians who preceded him. Whether one accepts the centrality of the pastoral myth or not, it is difficult not to admire the manner in which he raises
the problem of literature as merely sociological artifact into the zone of
consciousness, which has its own sociology. Nor is it sufficient to charge
Frye with the limitations of formalism as it was understood by Anglo-
American critics in the decades following the war, according to which he
evades 'the whole problem of temporality.'[93] Rather the 'Conclusion'
intimates a search for a different kind of temporality, that would find literature in cyclical revelations of the archetype, as opposed to a liberal,
progressive movement of history in sense that George Grant excoriates.
It almost suggests a fear of history in the modern sense on the part of the
conservative elites of Canadian culture, that is, those who have domi-

nated the production of its cultural understanding. In that sense, one may take Frye's essay as a central English-Canadian metanarrative of literary production. Canada 'just grew,' and the random character of that growth can be construed as a scandal to the mythologically informed imagination. So, for example, in this telling the West was not settled at random, but first brought under control by the North-West Mounted Police. Myth at its highest level is an affair of consciousness. On such a level, accidents, random surprises, can be accommodated and turned to art. History is not overcome, nor is it the sole referentiality, but it is drawn, rather, into the process of accommodation.[94]

It could also be argued that Frye's recasting of English-Canadian literature into mythopoeisis shrewdly allows him to use its literature for his own purposes. But his purposes, as I have suggested, are in many respects anticipated implicitly by other literary historians in English Canada. By arguing that literature as myth has a history apart from social, political, and economic history, Frye returns to an issue raised at the beginning of the book, and raised often in other discussions of literature in this country. It began as a culture on the margin. Does it overcome such a position simply by being made available to the kind of theoretical exposition Frye adumbrates? Is it any less marginalized in the sphere of the mythopoetic than it was in history? In a subsequent book, *The Secular Scripture: A Study of the Structure of Romance*, Frye dwells upon the mode for which he has the most affection and which claims the largest illustrative share of the Conclusion in which it articulates a 'social mythology.' The same definition may be found in *The Secular Scripture*,[95] and the coincidence should not be surprising. One might ask whether any Canadian writers are found in the new context. Only one is found, the Scottish writer R.M. Ballantyne (1825–94), whose impact on Canadian literature depends on half a dozen years spent working in the Northwest in the 1840s.[96] In the canon of romance and popular literature English-Canadian literature is not to be found, and the omission clearly adumbrates what is at stake in the removal of literature from the usual understanding of history. Worse than being marginalized, where some bearing upon the metropolis can be constructed, it can simply be forgotten.

Early in his Conclusion Frye calls attention to the relation between the two dominant cultures of Canada, remarking that to make statements about 'Canadian literature' is implicitly to make use of synecdoche, for 'every such statement implies a parallel or contrasting statement about French-Canadian literature.'[97] The two cultures either are similar or compose a binary opposition. As we have seen, however, they do not lend themselves easily to either possibility. If Canada for Frye poses itself as a geographical conundrum, an obstacle in space, the narrative of nation for Baillargeon, for example, originates in a *prise de conscience.* His is a history of alterity that, rather than just growing in some unpredictable, yet organic fashion, is founded upon the shock of loss. Thus he employs the colonial period as an opportunity to construct the development of a new ethnic type, the French-Canadian, who retains something that is French but in a changed and changing histori-cal context. The great loss of 1760 constitutes a beginning as a Fall, no matter how unmerited, which makes of alterity more than a fact: it is a definition, a motivation, and the seminal moment of an ideology. Such a construction of origin does not bear a merely oppositional relationship to the English-Canadian more casual reorientation in space. While it is true that Frye puts a Hebraic cast upon the construction of English-Canadian history, his predilection is for the apocalyptic, and his reading of it is through the New Testament as fulfilment, revelation, and, finally, deliverance from temporality and literary history.[98] Despite the Ultra-montanism that colours so profoundly much of the religious history of Quebec, it is difficult not to escape the sense that the deep structure, so to speak, of its ideological history comes closer to the period of Egyp-tian bondage, of which the most powerful motivation, since Eden is not recoverable, is the return to the promised land. The return is in history.

Whether Quebec's return is in history or English Canada is, for the most part, seeking deliverance from history in the construction of the respective literatures, they are, nevertheless, curiously related in the rhe-torical modes by which they produce order. In rhetorical terms, each of the histories examined in this chapter is fundamentally marked by its adherence to Synecdoche, that is, by the effort to find a core of motifs that operate together to form a plot. With the exception of McCourt, the plot is comic, aiming toward a positive solution to the dilemmas that the respective literatures face. Although McCourt relies upon a core of motifs, namely, landscape, atmosphere, and character, to give an account of a regional literature, his general view is not marked by a sense of upward *élan.*[99] He shares, of course, the theme of place as the domi-nant with other anglophone literary historians, but place does not reach the level of 'awe,' as it does in Pacey or take on apocalyptic significance as it does in Frye. The Sœurs de Sainte-Anne come perhaps nearest to demonstrating that the full deployment of Synecdoche is both comic and organicist. As we noted, the metaphor of growth is clearly implied in the birth and maturity of literature, and its maturity is characterized by a sense of autonomy, aspirations toward a universal ideal, the cultivation of the Christian spirit, and progress in education.[100] Although Baillargeon shares the metaphor, the central, explaining core of crisis poses certain problems. Crisis is initiated during the formation of the French-Canadian 'type' in its confrontation with the British regime. The French Canadian, as he argues, suffers from arrested development and, as a consequence, French-Canadian society and its literature is motivated by a continuous sense of crisis. Evidently, such an argument would appear to rely more upon the trope of Metonymy than that of Synecdoche. According to White, Metonomy harbours a mechanistic understanding of process: it depends upon cause and agency, and, by implication, the loss of agency.[101] The loss is raised in his discussion of Karl Marx, who constructed historical process as one of 'schism, division, alienation,' and his hope was 'the ultimate integration of the forces and objects that occupy the historical field.' Baillargeon's theme of crisis clearly corresponds to a notion of division and the desire for integration, and the sense of division is given real political and economic bases. Nevertheless, this use of Metonymy is driven by the larger ordering principle of Synecdoche. The crisis always appears as a 'window of opportunity' that lifts literature to new and higher levels of insight, edging ever nearer toward an integration of forces. The process that Baillargeon constructs is more evident in Rashley, for whom the major shifts at the material level prompt corresponding shifts on the conscious level that affects cultural production. Like Marx, as White argues, 'he conceived of the processes of the Base of society mechanistically and the processes of the Superstructure Organistically.'[102] As a consequence of the emphasis on literature in the case of both Baillargeon and Rashley, the central action of their plots remains closer to the Superstructure and, hence, Synecdoche.

The most revealing use of Synecdoche is expressed in Turnbull's reflection on history: 'The past remains fixed, as it were, by reason of the events which hallow its record [and] projects itself into the present by the invisible reality of a character which it has formed.'[103] Here is the central, radiant core treated passively by the author. The core must by necessity be a motif constructed by the historian as the indispensable mode of conjunction of past with present, making history fit the needs of the present. Rhetoric, then, is not simply formalism; it is, rather, a symptom of authorial desire and how he or she desires to articulate a signifying present. In other words, rhetoric is the sign of kinds of agency. What is striking is the fact that, on the one hand, Synecdoche lends itself to any ideology, whether Protestant, Catholic, or Marxist, and on the other hand, confirms the two dominant groups of literary historians in the tendencies that dominate their respective societies. The anglophone attachment to place appears driven, paradoxically, to overcome place in its quest for a New Jerusalem; and the francophone 'discovery' of the lack of fulfilment has its roots in history, and only history will show the way to integration. Rashley may appear an exception to this distinction because of his efforts to accommodate the extra-literary series, but his emphasis on the enlargement of the spirit through love calls to mind not only earlier historians such as Stevenson, whose emphasis is also upon the spirit, but also later historians such as Frye, who hover eagerly around moments of apocalypse. Rhetorical strategies are always at the service of what the historian wants to bring forth, and in each case the argument is repeated with culturally specific differences, and what is desired, finally, is agency, whether in respect of nature (place, environment) or history.

CHAPTER FOUR

Notre Maître le Passé, 1967–1969

le language n'est plus un instrument, *n'est plus un moyen, il est une manifestation, une révélation de l'être intime et du lien psychique qui nous unit au monde et à nos semblables.*[1]

The changes that Quebec brought about in the 1960s are in many respects too complex to be given rapid summary here.[2] Despite the fact that it has been aptly named the Quiet Revolution, it was not an untroubled period of reform initiated by the provincial liberals. Indeed, some efforts in the latter part of the decade were made to arrest it, notably in the election of Daniel Johnson and the Union Nationale, the party of Maurice Duplessis. Quebec showed itself divided between one extreme represented by Johnson's party and the other of the Rassemblement pour l'indépendance nationale. The province had reached a watershed, and its vision was divided between a past which may be plainly seen in the ideology of such figures as Camille Roy and those who desired another future, such as Paul-Émile Borduas. The two histories considered in this chapter represent the political moment perfectly, the slim volume of Father Paul Gay striving to preserve a moribund tradition, and the massive volumes directed by Pierre de Grandpré announcing the future.

The End of the Collège Classique

As I suggested in the previous chapter, arguments like O'Leary's are exceptions, and they are rarely referred to. The professors and clerics, who were the same in francophone literary history until nearly the end of the 1960s, controlled the meaning of literary culture in Quebec. The last of these was Father Paul Gay, who provided a modest *Survol de la littérature canadienne-français* in 1967.[3] Like many other histories of this kind, its audience was the collège classique, a milieu that Gay knew well as a teacher, among other disciplines, of Latin grammar. Its scope, therefore, is intentionally limited to those texts considered exemplary models in an ideological sense. In Gay's hands, literature is constructed as a series of monuments designed to awaken the student's interest and especially a sense of pride in Quebec's past. Thus its literary history from 1760 to 1850 is rapidly summarized in an Introduction by the literary sociologist Jean-Charles Falardeau as a series of constitutional arrangements, interrupted by civil war and the Durham Report, and concluding not in an approach to Confederation but the Act of Union (1840). This information is followed by a series of conclusions structured by a poignant use of anaphora: 'Les Canadiens-français *luttent* pour garder leurs droits et leur dignité ... Ils luttent par les journaux ... Ils luttent par les discours politiques ... Hélas! ...' The climax sets the stage for a plot that seems to be characterized by fall (conquest), rise (the struggle for preservation), and fall (continued illiteracy), and so reinterprets the same events as three generations in which the first suffers from ignorance, the second is resigned to it, and the third accommodates itself to it. Hence, literature is not a certain order of the best texts in an aesthetic sense. Texts are valorized, in some ways following Baillargeon with perhaps unwitting irony, as 'une prise de conscience,'[4] and it is for this reason that Garneau's history is the necessary moment of origin. No rise is possible until that moment.

It may seem surprising in these descriptions of origination that the first climax of Gay's narrative constitutes a leap from journalism and eloquence into the weakness of the education system. Language, however, is a semantically charged term in francophone history, and it is emphatically related to a political struggle inasmuch as the exchange system of a culture depends profoundly on language. If literature articulates the soul of a people, a phrase frequently encountered in literary history, its soul might be called its language. If it is true, as Lacan argues, that the acquisition of language is coterminous with both the formation of the subject and the ability to make use of a symbolic discourse, a discourse of power, it would follow that to construct a society the same argument, no matter how much *avant la lettre*, the possession of language is of primary significance. Indeed, the acquisition of the language of the Other at the expense of the one's own language as a subject can be construed as subjective dispossession. Infiltration to the point of glossophagia,[5] by which the language of the Other is reduced to the status of a dialect and constitutes the transformation of the subject into colonial object, giving rise to the image of such people as that of children.[6] The study of literature and especially its position in a history of frustrated resistance is of the highest significance in any culture that perceives itself as oppressed. Thus the organicist metaphor of birth and maturity used by Gay, not to speak of other francophone literary historians, marks this history as political rather than simply biological, as the Sœurs de Sainte-Anne imply, in order to imply that life (bios) is to be understood in its relation to a collective (polis), thus anticipating some contemporary feminist arguments.

And so the literature of Quebec is born in Garneau, and he is presented in a series of sections that address his life, his history, his worth as a writer, and his influence. Garneau's history itself is considered dated; therefore its significance lies in its message, indeed its cause, which rejoins the sentiments of Gay's introduction, that is, 'la conservation de notre religion, de notre langue et de nos lois.'[7] Gay makes Garneau both his and our contemporary by first citing Milton's lines, 'Qu'importe la perte du champ de bataille. TOUT N'EST PAS PERDU,' noted in Garneau's travel journal of 1854. He then finds the same phrase used by 'un certain de Gaulle' after the fall of France in 1940.[8] The same analogy is drawn, as I have indicated already, by O'Leary, and it is useful for Gay because it allows him to salvage Garneau despite the latter's antipathy toward certain aspects of ecclesiastical history in Quebec. Other historians are given brief mention, but clearly Garneau is given necessary pride of place, and his text constitutes the generous source of the patriotic poetry of the second half of the nineteenth century. If the most galling comments of Durham's description of French Canada in the late 1830s were their lack of a history and a literature, Garneau provided one and the poets of Quebec City provided the other. Durham is constructed as a motivator within a highly charged political situation. History and literature at the birth of Quebec's culture can be seen, therefore, as none other than political acts. What is Crémazie's theme? 'Non la nature ni l'amour, mais l'actualité politique.' Short shrift is given to all of Fréchette's work with the exception of *La Légende du peuple* (1887) of which the central theme is liberty, and whose models are post-revolutionary France and the United States. Le May is ranked as 'le poète le plus attachant' of all these poets and praised as 'le pionnier de l'école dite du terroir,' which permits a rather lengthy discussion of

Nerée Beauchemin (1850–1931) as transition to the more personal poetry of modernity. In these two poets certain values are privileged, that of 'le petit pays de Yamachiche,' conceived 'dans l'orbe de musique et d'encens du clocher.'[9] This is the theme of ecclesiastical politics: a rural Quebec whose life is ordered liturgically.

Gay's preference for a certain minimalist restraint (another sign of the context of the collège classique) is matched by his dislike of Hugo's excessive romanticism that occurs unhappily in Fréchette and by implication in a number of historical novels of the same period.[10] What is sought is the sobriety and conservation of customs and an older way of life, such as to be found in Gérin-Lajoie's *Jean Rivard* and especially in Aubert de Gaspé's *Les Anciens Canadiens*. Surprisingly, the major novel of the nineteenth century is Conan's *Angéline de Montbrun*, praised (not surprisingly) for Angéline's piety toward her father. Despite Jean Le Moyne's argument that Angéline's attachment to her father is simply unhealthy, Gay admires her because 'elle aime sa souffrance,' which is part of her feminine character.[11] Although it would not be possible to construe Conan's novel in this reading as part of a literature of struggle, it is evident that, both by canonizing it in the way he does and by implicitly relating it to the poetry of Le May and Beauchemin, Gay is using literary history to construct a Quebec opposed to the modernity represented, for example, by writers like Le Moyne. By calling French-Canadian literature a literature of struggle, he can deflect attention from his own enterprise, which is itself part of another history of struggle, namely, that of the preservation of ecclesiastical values in a rapidly secularizing Quebec.

Thus, in the next section on Quebec's period of maturation he can make it appear part of the secular struggle, by posing such questions as: 'Qui sommes-nous? Comment le passé éclaire le présent?' His answer poses off Chapais's federalism (a narrow perspective) and Groulx's nationalism. Groulx is, furthermore, not only the more significant historian, but also one of French Canada's greatest leaders. Like Henri Bourassa he is presented as a great patriot. More to his credit, however, is the fact that he is at once a priest and an apostle[12] for whom our being is our understanding of the past. Concluding the presentation of Groulx, Gay cites Maurice Séguin on Groulx, outlining the phases of his thought. To cite Séguin is strategically of interest, for he is one of the historians who argued against the implications of an agricultural economy and its promotion by the Church and proposed the thesis that both the economy and its protective ideology prevented Quebec's economic growth and competitive power.[13] Séguin is thus not only drawn into the Church's camp, but also he is used to argue that the main outlines of the 'Quiet Revolution,' that is, the secularization and modernization of Quebec, may be attributed to Groulx's influence, at least in its ethical and semantic bearing.[14]

The dominant genre of the period is poetry, primarily that of l'École littéraire de Montréal, which was comprised of those poets whose primary influence was that of the Parnassians and Symbolists, on the one hand, and those poets more regional in character, on the other. Although the former seem, because of the kind of influence they evince, to be more international than regional, Gay gradually displaces them with Alfred Desrochers (1901–78): 'Profondément enraciné dans SA terre canadienne, Desrochers est vraiment un poète canadien, alors que tant d'autres ont je ne sais quoi de copié.' Paul Morin is brought forward as a kind of balance, and he is defended against Roy's censure of his work. To do so, Gay cites Roger Duhamel, who praises him for his use of language that recalls that of the French modernists, Paul Valéry (1871–1945), Stéphane Mallarmé (1842–98), and Henri de Régnier (1864–1936), so keeping him within the initial framework of his history.[15] He not only preserves language, he moves it to a metalinguistic plane like his masters, thus manifesting Quebec culture in its maturity.

With the exception of *Maria Chapdelaine*, the genre of the novel is hardly worth mentioning from 1900 to 1914. So that the point cannot be missed, Gay praises Hémon's novel in italics as '*un roman essentiellement régionaliste*,' '*un roman essentiellement patriotique*,' and '*un roman classique.*' The assigned readings are expressly designed to stress these points a second time, and to perceive the world through Maria's eyes, 'a femme de nature, sans complication.'[16] Thus Gay suggests that the regional, the patriotic, the well-balanced are feminine characteristics without saying that they are also motifs that fit intimately an agricultural, ecclesiastical ideology, the centre-piece of which is a woman who overcomes her desire for, and flirtation with, such excess as represented by two of her potential suitors, François Paradis and Lorenzo Surprenant.[17] And not to be overlooked is the fact that it is written in 'très bon français uni au parler canadien.' This novel, however, is no preparation for Jean-Charles Harvey's *Les Demi-civilisés* (1934), which appears resolutely turned toward the future. Not wishing to appear too reactionary, Gay sees its usefulness for his history despite its execrable style and 'allure insurrectionelle.' It marks 'une prise de conscience plus aiguë'[18] than the preceding period and is designed to serve as a threshold for the contemporary, a period which continues the struggle that shapes Gay's Quebec.

The 'prise de conscience,' again echoing Baillargeon, is at once the consequence of the sudden move into modernity effected by the industrialization of the province and the impact it had upon Quebec's cultural life. Modernity altered the narratives of both history and fiction and placed poetry in a state of almost permanent revolution. Although historiography became more 'scientific' in its method, for Gay its intent had not changed when measured against that of Garneau. The point of the past is to explain 'le présent en montrant comment il s'est fait.'[19] Thus history is always contemporary and lives for its own generation, whether in the nineteenth or twentieth century.[20] The shift from rhetoric to 'objectivity' in the writing of history, however, does not change one essential fact. Their love of truth 'ne les empêche pas de rapporter leurs conclusions et de les donner en principes de vie à la patrie tendrement aimée,' because for these historians no distinction is possible between their souls, their country, and their moment in history.[21]

Needless to say, this is true *a fortiori* for the modern poets Gay selects to present. Saint-Denys Garneau's life is deeply and intimately related to his poetry, and his sense of guilt marks it as Canadian. In many respects following the same themes as her cousin, Anne Hébert represents the effort to overcome the desolation of solitude in *Mystère de la parole* (1960). The poetry of Alain Grandbois (1900–75) like that of Garneau and Hébert not only reaches into mystery, but also into the problem of being and its realization. Rina Lasnier (1915–1997), the fourth great modernist, differs from the three above in opposing the themes of solitude and death with those of joy and love. Other poets are discussed but briefly, and it is clear for Gay that the effects of modernism are best seen in fiction. Despite Gay's efforts, it is evident that it is not possible for him to find a way of integrating what he identifies as universal themes of poetry – the nostalgia for childhood, the mystery of love, sorrow, and solitude[22] – into his construction of the modern and its relation to the nation.

The novel, according to Gay, is designed almost expressly for this purpose, and this may be because the novel is addressed to 'tout l'homme et non seulement à la part d'artiste qui gît en lui.'[23] As he goes on to explain, he seeks a moral humanism. Because of the plethora of novels in the period, he proposes a series of five generic categories as a means of classification, which are arranged according to theme: Canadian material, Canadian material in a critical perspective, varieties of love, novels with a foreign influence, and the theme of the priest.[24] If space is any indication, Gay is most at ease in the first category, and the adjectives reserved for these writers place them clearly at the upper end of his canon. These novelists are primarily Savard (1896–1982), Léo-Paul Desrosiers (1896–1967), despite reservations about the heaviness of his style, Guèvremont, Roy, and Claude Jasmin (1930–). Gay's predilections appear closest to Savard, who sings 'les magnifiques et ancestrales vertus des Canadiens';[25] Guèvremont whose novels 'décrivent des moeurs paysannes et saines,[26] dans des dialogues savoureuses'; and Roy, whose *La Petite Poule d'eau* (1950) is considered 'un chef d'oeuvre de délicatesse.' In a perhaps inadvertent anticipation of novels yet to be discussed, his larger comment on the novel is telling indeed: 'Comme Péguy, Gabrielle Roy n'a besoin du mal et du péché pour faire des choses intéressantes.'[27]

None of these novelists could be said, however, to articulate a 'prise de conscience' in the modern sense so much as supporting a preservation of values threatened by an industrializing and modernizing society. They also reinforce a certain understanding of women developed in Conan's *Angéline de Montbrun* as an aspect of the patriarchal in its most conservative form. Angéline's faithfulness to her father anticipates Luzina's *hieros gamos* with Father Joseph-Marie in the concluding section of *La Petite Poule d'eau.* Those novelists that make the effort to address Quebec's modernity, however, are not given the same care he devotes to Roy. They are also introduced in an effort to appear sympathetic by arguing that the past that these writers contest is that represented by the Church and its collusion with the provincial government in an effort to maintain a submissive, childlike society.[28] Gay is at pains to argue, however, that this is only one aspect of the past, and since the Church has had its day as a dominant force, a fair look at the situation in Quebec since 1960 would suggest that the social transformation pursued by the younger generation in effect ignores the past. This argument is somewhat embarrassing in its tenor since he already gave preference to those themes that are now under attack. Furthermore, those young people who are ignorant of the past are precisely the audience Gay's history is directed toward. If they knew the cultural past of French Canada – and knew it as Father Gay would have them know it – their love for it would prompt them to give up the transformations they have embarked upon.

So it is the French-Canadian cultural history is a 'littérature de combat,'[29] but the space of struggle is as much in its historiographical texts as in those texts which are constructed to appear as the true zone of combat. Gay is hardly capable of writing interventionist history, and the ideology that he supports, while eager to appear in sympathy with at least aspects of contemporary Quebec in order to gain adherents was, in fact, involved in a doomed, rearguard action against the modern and the secular. His fear of the modern is also a fear of a general alienation of the subject, and he cites Le Moyne, with whom he otherwise is often in disagreement as too pessimistic, in support: 'La littérature pure, abstraite de tout contexte réligieux, métaphysique, scientifique et social, n'a aucun sens.'[30] The choice of the quotation is significant, since the formalism that Gay finds everywhere in Québécois literary studies is rather rare, with the exception of *Le Roman canadien-français du XXe siècle* by Réjean Robidoux and André Renaud. Although these contexts were present in the 1960s, their semantic value and relevance varied according to one's ideological formation.

Gay's conclusion does not suggest a rising plot. His culture was not one that seemed to be winning the struggle. Poetry's search for being was marred by the loss of music, the novel was seeking refuge in poetry, and the theatre seemed to be going nowhere. In some respects everything seemed too much under foreign, notably, French influence, which early in his discussion is treated metaphorically as an invasion[31] of '*existentialisme athée*,' '*matérialisme dialectique*,' '*freudisme universel*,' and '*l'amoralisme et l'hedonisme*,' none of which are valued positively. His final sentence, then, resonates in a far from neutral fashion when he writes, speaking of French-Canadian literature as the expression 'd'un peuple qui, plus que tout autre, doit surveiller la marche de son destin.'[32] What better way to keep watch than through a *survol* such as Gay's that flies over in order to survey the territory and so assist in its control?

It may appear that the length of this discussion of Gay is unjustified by the length and quality of the text. It should be remembered, however, that it represents a tradition in French-Canadian literary history begun early in the century in the work of Camille Roy. As Jean Ménard remarks in his prefatory remarks to the first edition, it should be understood as continuing Roy's work, whose final edition had appeared in 1945 with a final reprint in 1962. The histories of both both Baillargeon and Gérard Tougas[33] are expressly rejected as incapable of serving the purposes of collège and secondary school education. The former's text is of only temporary value, and Tougas, as Ménard carefully phrases it, 'perce parfois avec difficulté la muraille de Chine de la réalité québecoise.' It should also be remembered that the collèges classiques, descendents of the original collège des Jésuites (1635–1760) were already in 1967 in the process of being replaced by the emphatically more secular and more

practical collèges d'enseignement général et professionel (CEGEP).
Gay's text may be construed, then, as one of their final cultural statements, which strives to be oriented toward a future which is envisioned
as 'quelque chose de terrible et de magnifique'[34] and, as part of its subplot, turning the reader back toward a particularly directed reading of
texts that range from Conan through Hémon to Savard, Guèvremont,
and Roy, as well as Le May and Beauchemin, that would preserve a clerical ideology as the true Quebec.

The CEGEP and Literary History

With the publication of Pierre de Grandpré's four volumes, a text to
which Pierre Nepveu refers as a 'monument indispensable à l'institution
littéraire,'[35] that way back was effectively closed. It is also a history that
represents and responds to the new reality of the CEGEP. Like the latter
it is consciously interdisciplinary and its orientation constitutes a move
away from humanistic canonization toward that of literature as a sociological discipline. Its immediate relation to Gay's text may be seen iconi-
cally in the relation of façade and interior of the Pavillon Judith-Jasmin
at the Université du Québec à Montréal, which retains the old exterior
of the parish church. The inside is in a late-modern style, emphasizing
open space and an exposition of its construction. It encourages groups
sitting in various parts of an emphatically secular space to hold intimate
and intense discussion. It constitutes a radical, if binary, opposition to
everything the exterior implies of hierarchy, linearity, and direction
toward the scene of sacrifice, which spreads a unified sense through
ecclesiastical space, as seen in the narratives of Roy and Gay. Although it
may appear ironic that the interior is buttressed by such a façade, it cannot be forgotten that that is all it is, but the façade is also a necessary
trace of the past. As one enters the University, one stands for a moment
in the complementary historical space of Quebec. Once inside, however, one enters the space of a new autonomy. In the same way, the structure of Grandpré's text is exposed, and the various perspectives that it
shapes give a corresponding impression.

Consistent with its emphasis on self-analysis and accessibility, the first
volume begins with a discussion of its method and how it was derived.
First of all, the character of Grandpré's history is expressly declared to
be autonomous. To become so, it recognizes that literary history is an
apparent paradox that can only be resolved through the mutual efforts
of humanists and social scientists.[36] It is a paradox inasmuch as litera-

ture is the product of 'l'invention créatrice et le génie qui dérangeront toujours les conclusions d'une histoire étroitement sociologique.' But if, as *la nouvelle critique* asserts, the text is not the sole possession of its author, what kind of 'sympathie re-créatrice' on the reader's part is capable of recovering its sense, particularly across the distance of history? By posing the problem in this way, Grandpré immediately situates the premises of his history in the contemporary debate regarding the reading of literature and the historical question of hermeneutics. For the *nouvelle critique*, the text does not open itself to any kind of historicist reading.[37] Rather, as Robidoux and Renaud argue, 'la découverte et la compréhension de la manière d'un romancier constitue pour le lecteur la voie directe et nécessaire pour entrer dans la signification d'une oeuvre.' Reading is 'la recherche attentive de la technique, animée par le consentement à la suivre.'[38] It is hardly surprising that in the climate that was prevalent in universities on both sides of the Atlantic in the 1960s Hans Robert Jauß was led to declare in 1967, the same year that the first volume of Grandpré's history appeared, that 'Literaturgeschichte ist in unserer Zeit mehr und mehr, aber keineswegs unverdient in Verruf gekommen.'[39] Therefore, Grandpré's enterprise may be considered a genuine *prise de conscience* in a society where historical self-construction assumed, one is tempted to say, existential proportions since the founding moment of Garneau's history. If history, and particularly cultural history, is not possible in a society for whom not only self-understanding but also self-realization depend upon the narratives of the past it constructed, in what sense could that society project for itself a future?

A future is difficult to construct from the autonomies produced by the *nouvelle critique*, and thus the demise of a cultural history had radical consequences to which Grandpré refers as 'suicidaire.' To overcome this impasse, Grandpré, whose career was significantly not confined to a university career, proposes a resituating of the function of literature in its classical, rhetorical role, that is, in its power to move a reader emotionally. Those schools of criticism that forget this in their effort achieve the most adequate reading do no more than 'amuser la galérie, pour la gloire du critique-acteur.' The cost of such autonomy is the marginalization of literature. Although Grandpré recognizes its usefulness, especially in the study of contemporary culture, the pursuit of literature in its autonomy cannot go very deeply into the majority of French-Canadian texts, notably everything written before 1930. Therefore, if that literature is to be cultivated in some fashion, other methods must be considered. Although the implication of Grandpré's assumption and hypothesis is that earlier literature is of no more than sociological interest, thus unconsciously echoing Frye, his understanding of the function of sociology is of another kind. He distinguishes, therefore, a '*sociologie de l'écrit*' from the '*sociologie de la littérature,*' arguing that the former leads to a sociology of value as opposed to the book as object of merchandise. Such a distinction would require 'une sociologie attentive et nuancée des divers publics.'[40] And so he is brought back to one of the bases of the *nouvelle critique* in phenomenology as elaborated, among others, by Henri-Irenée Marrou, who privileges it as the instrument that conjoins humanists and social scientists in the mutual project of constructing a cultural history. Just as the past is understood by an act of intuition, so literature is understood by a corresponding movement of spirit. The two movements are in fact complementary, the former characterized by a deconstructive gesture and the latter by a restructuring gesture. In doing so, literary studies overcome their marginalization, and Quebec's cultural history is repositioned in a secular, modern context and given the capability of resuming its historic function of providing a means of social self-realization as an autonomous entity.

Literary history, then, is metahistory: its inner workings, like the hot-air ducts of the Pavillon, must be visible. Hence the first two chapters following the introduction make no effort to adopt a neutral narrative voice, but rather begin by expressing a certain querulousness about the project as a whole.[41] Thus, Georges-André Vachon asks at the beginning of his chapter: 'Comment expliquer le malaise que j'éprouve devant tout ouvrage qui porte le titre d'*Histoire de la littérature canadienne-française?*'[42] In a sense this is a brilliant strategy, and it suggests that literary history does not originate in time so much as phenomenologically, in a shaping gesture of the imagination,[43] for certainly Vachon is expressing a malaise that others have felt encountering texts with titles addressing the history of any literature produced in Canada. Thus the wary reader is engaged in the problem and invited to share in the project as it unfolds, and this is particularly true for the reader for whom 'la lecture se présente comme un besoin,' whom most serious readers take themselves to be. The question reaches, then, those for whom literature is not a matter of disinterest, but a necessity. The answer is provided by examining 'tous les textes écrits, en refusant de savoir, *a priori,* s'ils ressortissent à un genre littéraire différencié ... et ... d'appliquer à ces textes, indifféremment, toutes les méthodes d'approche mises au point par les sciences d'homme.' While this approach would lead initially to a history of ideas, it would lead later 'à la description d'une idéologie globale – l'idéologie étant la fonction générale au moyen de laquelle une société contrôle et ordonne spontanément sa propre évolution.' Literature, however, does not 'reflect' an ideology; it is, rather, one of several social functions that share an ideology which 'se présente toute entière dans chacune des manifestations.' The literary function becomes historical when it lends itself to the study of its emergence. Although it is not stated at the beginning what is emerging or how, Vachon is prepared to suggest how Quebec as a culture may be distinguished from France:

> Si la fièrté nationale a besoin d'un aliment, que du moins elle aille le puiser dans la reconnaissance de ce que le peuple québécois est, et non pas dans le désir et l'affirmation stériles de ce qu'il n'est pas, ou n'a pas. En domaine français, par example, Corneille et Hugo sont aussi grands, dans leur ordre, que le furent Louis XIV et Napoléon dans l'ordre politique. Tandis que nous, à un Papineau, à un Bourassa, à un Laurier, hommes politiques d'un incontestable valeur, nous ne pouvons rien comparer, dans l'ordre littéraire. Être Québécois, c'est cela.[44]

Apart from what this says about the engendering of literature (why was, for example, Marie de l'Incarnation forgotten?), it makes it clear that literature is political utterance, and political utterance as performance is literature in Quebec. Moreover, no matter how much one might distinguish these three political figures ideologically, they are exemplars of what is called 'le peuple québécois,' as if it were a single people, animated by its own national pride that turns upon the most famous of its politicians.[45]

To reinforce the implication of Vachon's argument, the following chapter analyses the birth and development of a French-Canadian *mentalité* that would constitute a basis for 'une évolution globale.' Its birth takes place in a 'climat de ferveur religieuse extraordinaire ... qui imprégnera toute notre vie culturelle.' French Canada's development both as a French colony and as a part of a British colony did not prevent it from retaining the 'structures mentales' of the French. Moreover, 'la pensée française n'a ... jamais cessé d'être présent parmi nous.' One can only conclude that 'nous sommes les Français canadiens comme il y a des Français belges et des Français suisses.' The full sense of this conclusion is that French Canadians are culturally French but their citizenship is Canadian. Consequently, the construction of a history of francophone literature in Canada only makes sense 'comme l'expression et le témoingage de nos lents cheminements sur la route de la survivance, puis de la croissance collective.' Such a statement confirms this history as that of emergence 'à moins que la culture anglo-saxonne d'Amérique ne nous submerge,' a fear that, as we as noted in chapter 1, was raised by the Flemish literary historians Coopman and Scharpé. Culture and its memory, then, are indispensable to the survival of the community, and one does not reflect the other; rather the two mutually support each other. One emerges with the other, and in the emergence it is possible to construct a 'croissance collective.' The history of which these initial essays form a guiding paratext is, like Garneau's history, a text 'qui caractérise l'émergence de la conscience historique de notre groupe ethnique.'[46] Self-reflection is in appropriate phenomenological fashion self-construction. As a result, Grandpré's history is not only an act of national piety but also a demonstration of how the nation is made as a global entity, in such a way that no text is admitted that is not Québécois, in the sense that it is part of the construction of an emergent and continuously constituent ideology. Unlike English-Canadian culture as exemplified in Klinck, the culture of French Canada cannot be made to appear merely to grow. It must be shaped, and its shape must be made manifest.

Thus, opposite the page on which Vachon writes, 'il ne saurait être question d'envisager la littérature comme le "reflet" d'une société' appears a photograph of a section of one of Champlain's maps. The visual connection with the mother culture is made immediately, and through all the volumes illustrations, particularly portraits, abound. The text itself is prepared in a variety of fonts – a technique often employed by previous francophone literary historians – to move the reader rapidly between contemporary texts and modern readings in order to distinguish past and present, but also to conjoin them according to the organizational and visual power of the narrative. We literally glimpse the past reproduced in the frequently anthologized texts, and then we are given its significance so that we may possess more easily not *a* but *the* significance of the text. In the spirit of Grandpré's introductory chapters, efforts are made to provide analyses, no matter how brief, of style and its sense, and, among colonial texts, those of Lahontan (1666–1716) demonstrate how effectively the literary and the social can be integrated.[47]

The appearance of the shape of the plot into argument is most clearly displayed in the paratextual essays which develop the text's metahistorical story. The first significant moment occurs at the beginning of the second part of the first volume. If the metanarrative of the history is the survival of French culture, the Conquest represents its first test. While

the years 1760–1830 have no literature of value, it is of utmost significance in the formation of an ethnic group. To dramatize the full weight
of what was at risk, Marcel Rioux draws upon the French historian Henri
Marrou who sees in this moment the end of the ancien régime and 'un
nouveau départ,' ... un nouveau moyen âge.'[48] Moreover, it is hardly the
Middle Ages of the twelfth or thirteenth century that Marrou indicates;
rather he describes it as the full darkness of the earlier, Merovingian
period. Although this moment is not marked as the primal origin of
French-Canadian culture, it is a beginning at a nadir.[49] Without the
founding of a number of magazines and periodicals in this same period,
following upon a long period of an oral culture, a future might have
been difficult to predict. They were, however, 'à la source des oeuvres à
venir.' Two events were required for French-Canadian culture to find a
beginning,[50] namely, Papineau's revolt and Garneau's L'Histoire du Canada, and drawing upon Vachon's metaphor, 'la littérature émerge peu à
peu, sous le signe de romantisme.' Emergence, then, is to be construed
as a gesture of liberation within a political sphere, and it constructs a
society similar to a number of European countries in the nineteenth
century that, with the 'emergence' of a stronger middle class, either
attacked monarchical rule or strove to separate themselves from imperial rule to form autonomous ethnic nations. Thus Garneau's history is
conceived under the sign of ethnic difference as developed by the
French historian Augustin Thierry, and like him Garneau 'pratique la
théorie de l'antagonisme des races, qui fait de l'histoire un instrument
de combat et de foi nationale.'[51] Papineau is equally rooted in the people of whom he is said to have incarnated 'la volonté et le génie,' and
whose greatest moments emerge in his oratorical flourish.[52]

As we have often seen already, cultural origin in French Canada is
consciously understood as the inauguration of a certain discourse, and
for this reason oratory always holds a special place in its history. Its persuasive power in fact expands when that discourse is developed on the
metahistorical level of the text. While historians like Camille Roy are
always prepared to recognize, for example, the significance of Garneau,
they often temper their enthusiasm by referring to the 'more solid'
ecclesiastical knowledge of Ferland. In Grandpré the latter is related to
Garneau briefly in an introductory rubric on Bishop Laval, but not so
much to correct Garneau as to praise Laval. Ferland is otherwise summarily dispensed with in a paragraph. Garneau's role as father and
therefore initiator of French Canada's discourse of empowerment is
assured and implicitly underlined. The problem, however, was whether

the nineteenth century in Quebec was ready for him, that is, ready for his favourite themes of 'peuple, patrie, liberté et inquiétude,'[53] which were as much his themes as those of the 1960s in Quebec. Grandpré's history is constructed to suggest that it was not. Thus, literary texts in the period like the novel, because they evince a certain conservatism that has nothing 'd'incendiaire ni de neuf,' are rapidly dismissed; and it is revealing that their preference for 'le passé narratif et la troisième personne ... semble paralyser l'expression personnelle et de la sensibilité dans un art qui nous apparaît aujourd'hui en grande partie fondé sur le "je" ou le "moi."'[54] Poetry, especially that of Crémazie, despite its loss of interest for modern Quebec at least celebrates *la patrie* and makes occasional use of the first person. Emergence, however, depends upon a coincidence of the present in the past in a certain way, and in his *Survol* Gay cites Guy Frégault's observation that 'l'histoire est une hypothèse permettant d'expliquer les situations actuelles par celle qui les ont précédées.'[55] The metaphor of emergence depends upon a construction of what has emerged in order to construct the process of coming to light. Thus the present explains the past or, to use a more political term, it colonizes it, so to speak, thereby compelling the needs of the past to be those of the present.

The structure of Grandpré's plot, then, depends upon its orientation toward the 1960s. The Confederation Period is described under the chapter heading 'Le Repli traditionaliste,' a title which immediately marks it negatively, arguing that the Ultramontanism that provided its hegemonic discourse was attacked by liberalism because of the former's opposition to modernism. In the chapter on oratory, the figures presented are preponderantly of a liberal persuasion. If one is a liberal, to stray, like Laurier, into federalism is considered opportunism[56] and betrays a false sense of the future; if one is ultramontantist, like Bishop Laflèche, to manifest such qualities as patriotism and a love of the people puts one on a better track. All are valorized according to the way they can be oriented. In the same way, the nineteenth-century novelist has 'le regard résolument tourné vers le passé pour construire l'avenir.'[57]

As an introduction to the twentieth century, the previous history is recapitulated in the second volume as an 'exceptionelle conjonction d'obstacles.' The theme of a new Middle Ages is raised again and now extended from 1760 through the course of the nineteenth century, the only moment of light being the three decades from 1830 to 1860.[58] The significance of the Conquest is now raised more intensely than in the first volume, in which the years from 1760 to 1830 saw that French-Canadian society, 'amputée d'une partie importante de ses élites, va devenir plus homogène,' at the same time is accentuating its traditional character.[59] In the second volume, Frégault is again invoked to argue that French Canada was not simply conquered, but defeated. As a result, history did not continue; it started all over again. Unquestionably, Frégault represents a shift in French-Canadian historical thinking that came to the fore during the 1940s and 1950s, and it can certainly be seen as a shaping influence on Grandpré's history. He helps construct not only a beginning at the bottom, but also the beginning of a new ethnic group. By accepting the thesis held by Groulx and the Montreal School of historians to describe this new, if inchoate, society as 'rétrospectif, déphasé, sentimental' was implicitly to provide a measure of its success in overcoming the obstacles before it in its effort to endure 'l'apprentissage du présent et du réel qui lui avait manqué jusqu'à [the end of the nineteenth century], un art et une pensée de nouveau pleinement accordé à leur temps.' Acquiring a future means, then, to phase into contemporary history as it is in a secular, industrialized society. Such an acquisition also has implications for the recovery of a spatial dimension for a society that possesses a colonial character in which one is an exile in one's own country.[60]

The structure of the second volume is in many respects governed by Falardeau's introductions to its two major parts (1900–30 and 1930–45). The theme of obstacles is given two differing orientations, one bearing on events in Canada as a whole, and the other on the political situation in Quebec. Since the moment of Confederation, Quebec's history, it is argued, took a turn for the worse, and Falardeau rehearses the history of Riel, the support of British imperial ventures, the Manitoba schools question, the subsequent withdrawal of support for education in French in Ontario, and the Conscription Crisis of 1917. The industrialization of the province, moreover, only increased the sense of alienation among French Quebeckers, inasmuch as the direction of economic power was controlled by the anglophone minority. After celebrating Groulx as a second Garneau, Falardeau concludes that Canada 'se scinde en deux nations,' and its future is unpredictable. In his second essay, he notes the shift from Quebec's concern with its relation to the other provinces toward a greater emphasis on its own internal evolution, largely as a result of the Depression. The second introduction completes the implications of a comment made at the beginning of his first essay in which he laconically stated: 'Le Québec se résume dans deux traits antithétiques: fixité idéologique au sommet; remous économiques et sociaux à la base.' The rhetorique of Marxism cannot be missed here as one of the ways of articulating how a society can be 'déphasé.' But beneath these implications is another set of relations, namely, ideological rigidity as reflected in the collusion of the provincial government with American and English-Canadian capital. To be *maîtres chez nous* the economic and social movement that constitutes the base must take into its own hands the capital that controls it. This would be at once an act of liberation and a movement toward democracy. Groulx is once again celebrated, and in his discussion of the periodical *L'Action française*, edited by Groulx from 1921 to 1928, Falardeau's grammar implicates his own sympathies with the views expressed: 'La revue ne propose pas une rupture prochaine ni violente du pacte de la Conféderation, mais elle opte pour un État français libre. Seul un tel état réaliserait – réalisera? – la logique de notre destin, et nous devons en préparer l'existence. Il ne semble pas que le Québec doive se séparer de la Conféderation. On ne pourra cependant éviter d'envisager la séparation à plus ou moins brève échéance.'[61]

Destiny is not, as often and paradoxically happens in English Canada, constructed as random events occurring as if by chance; for Falardeau it has a logic, and the logic is inscribed in the recitation of unforgettable 'ancienne blessures.' Laid over that history is the logic of kinds of responses, one of which is the contribution that *L'Action française* made to the founding of 'le Bloc populaire, qui incarne l'opposition nationaliste québécoise aux politiques militaires du gouvernement canadien.'[62] As White argues, this is the logic of metonymy, a logic of cause and effect to both articulate and explain not only the present, but also the past and how it can be overcome in order to construct an emancipated future.[63] As Groulx remarks in one of his poems, to take possession of the past is to seize the future: 'Ils gardent l'avenir ceux qui gardent l'histoire.' The final line of the quatrain reads: 'À l'âme des vivants mêlent l'âme des morts.'[64] The image projects a utopian society in which alienation from an ideological past is overcome, suggesting, in White's sense, the unified order of Synecdoche.

History so conceived does not allow for unforeseen directions. Nelligan, who has sometimes been reproached for not being a particularly Canadian poet,[65] is now celebrated for his mythic qualities, the first French-Canadian to confront the modern world and clearly a precursor of subsequent poetry in Quebec.[66] For the first time the importance of Albert Laberge's *La Scouine* (1918) is recognized and implicated as a precursor of Ringuet's *Trente arpents* (1938).[67] The history of theatre in Quebec is given a significant beginning in Louvigny de Montigny's *Les Boules de neiges* (first produced in 1903) because it both illuminates the *mentalité* of Quebec at the turn of the century and foreshadows a contemporary debate on the use of 'canadianismes.'[68] While the value of Robert Choquette (1905–91) now appears limited to the period between the wars, and Desrochers has also disappeared into history, the poetry of Jean Narrache ([Émile Coderre] 1893–1970) is canonized because 'elle est née de la crise économique et encore aujourd'hui s'élève, non seulement contre la misère, mais contre ceux qui en profitent.'[69] He is a poet of the people, and his language is its witness. For Baillargeon François, 'Hertel n'est pas un grand poète';[70] in Grandpré's history he may not be moving, but one infers that the very fact that he gradually broke away from the 'statisme de notre réligiosité' is major compensation for his lack of talent. A number of women poets are grouped under the heading 'Le Romantisme féministe des années trentes,' bestowing a cachet that makes them a prefiguration of some twenty women novelists of the next generation who will be 'libérées d'entraves excessives.'[71] The 1930s in fiction is also construed as 'le seuil où la longue préhistoire du roman canadien-français débouche enfin sur son ère moderne.'[72]

History, then, has its absences, its tendencies, its plenitudes. The first two volumes of Grandpé place these aspects of history's movement on a diachronic plane, announcing plenitude as a proximate future. The final volumes, especially the third, place them on a synchronic plan, intimating that Quebec's true cultural history does not begin until after the Second World War in the years of the *Refus global* affair. Plenitude requires originality, and the preface to the third volume turns on the problem of Quebec's culture in its relation to that of France, not to speak of that of the United States. Francophone Canada, it is argued, failed, metaphorically, to kill its father in order to become what it is.[73] Its French heritage and participation in American culture, are precisely where its originality is to be found, and the texts analysed in the final volumes are constructed as 'annonciatrices et garanties d'un avenir plus fécond encore.' Dumont's essay, which introduces the reader to the sociological situation of the postwar era, argues that 'nous étions engagés, de gré ou de force, dans les voies nouvelles de la connaissance de soi,' a collective enterprise that equates self-knowledge with self-construction, thus implicating a society in a phenomenological project. It does so at a moment that is perceived as an ideological vacuum, that is, a moment of intellectual and even metaphysical absence, which 'confère aussi à notre littérature, depuis la guerre, son originalité.' It is a moment when one is provisorily 'liberée de ses racines' and in that moment of emptiness acquires a discourse, in a kind of Husserlian *epoché* where emptiness is entered and meaning is uncovered.[74] As Paul Ricoeur puts it, at such a moment 'everything happens as if, in order to enter the symbolic universe, the speaking subject must have at his disposal "an empty space" from which the use of signs can begin.' Origin, then, is in a discourse of self-construction and, as Dumont exemplifies it in his relation with his almost inarticulate father, the culture of Quebec begins with 'un devoir certain: celui de *dire*.'[75]

So it is that the orientation toward the future perceptible in the poetry of Grandbois and Saint-Denys Garneau coincides with the effort to reach the source of the world in both the latter's work and that of Hébert. Lasnier achieves 'la parfaite contemplation de soi dans l'acte même de créer,'[76] and all four poets are placed in a world of signification that in some way engages their struggles with language as the sign of being. It is as if two discourses were weaving around each other, one the language of poetry and the other the language of being, suggesting a homology with the text of Grandpré's history itself in which his history is in a struggle to draw the discourse of the past into alignment with the discourse of the contemporary. That struggle loses its intensity somewhat in the last two volumes as plenitude – the coincidence of the discourses of the visible and the invisible – more frequently coincides with itself. 'L'Âge de la parole' is the title that Roland Giguère (1929–) gave to one of his poems in 1957, and it served as both the title for his first collection and his collected works. The expression serves not only to declare cogently the tendency of Giguère's poetry but also to embrace the central movement of the contemporary in poetry, most of which was published by Hexagone. It suggests a search for an absolute, phenomenological origin in language, and finds its source in both Borduas and French surrealism, both discourses of romanticism and revolution.

The significance of *Refus global* in Grandpré's history is its ability to inaugurate not simply a discourse of revolution but to write a moment of reorigination by returning to the Conquest in order to destroy it as a beginning. The announcement that 'notre destin sembla durement fixé' implicitly challenges Hémon's construction of Quebec in *Maria Chapdelaine*, as well as challenging ideologies of the spirit, such as Jansenism, which have successfully created 'un petit peuple serré de près aux soutanes restées les seules dépositaires de la foi, du savoir, de la verité et de la richesse nationale.'[77] The value of the manifesto as a metanarrative gains part of its power from the fact that this is the first discussion devoted to it in histories of French-Canadian literature. Its full power, however, lies in the coincidence of its desire to replace the past by the present with a corresponding desire on the part of Grandpré and his collaborators. History for Borduas, as well as Grandpré, is a pretext for the true text announcing a future of magic, mystery, love, and other necessities. It provides the orientation that makes whatever is canonized in the past a threshold of the future, which is why the conversation that Dumont dramatizes with his inarticulate father is so emblematic of the enterprise as a whole. Without such a repressive and silenced past, the desired future would not have been so intensely envisioned, and so the past is necessary, and its prefigurations are fervently loved, but largely for the energy they provide in creating a new country *ab ovo*. Thus Borduas provides the discourse for the poets who emerged in the 1950s to found their work only 'sur l'instinct, la sensation, l'intelligence en acte, l'intuition vive élevée de bien des dégrés au-dessus de la conscience intellectuelle et de la sensibilité,' to begin, in other words, to write the body and 'faire venir le monde à soi.'[78]

The overture to Borduas and the Hexagone poets is placed virtually at the centre of the third volume, where it constitutes both a climax and displacement of everything preceding it, arguing against the influence of the Symbolistes and eclipsing the other kinds of poetry practised by their contemporaries, who, at best, can only play prefiguring roles. The first task of the Hexagone poets was to find a language that would 'rendre l'homme à lui-même, de le *déshabiller* pour lui donner l'intelligence des signes nus,' in a word, to uncover 'la parole nue,' as Gilles Hénault (1920–) put it.[79] The desire is to stand, as Giguère declares, 'accoudée à la dernière barrière de l'être,'[80] where a new cosmos has the power to rise in a *parole* liberated from an arrested past. To emerge, however, which is the object of Grandpré's history, is to find the place where 'l'homme avance dans l'espace qui lui-même est genèse.'[81] A poetry that is construed to play upon the synchronicity of absence, tendency, and plenitude has no difficulty with a moment of apocalypse (the naked word) reconfiguring itself as genesis (the space of beginning). This is the language of both surrealism and revolution that coincide in the convergence of past and present.

Place, however, is both a discourse and a project, which is to 'remodeler le monde' as the locus of an absolute poetry. Thus the second task of these writers is to write 'le pays "reinventé,"'[82] and in so doing finding a place for Jacques Brault (1933–), Gaston Miron (1928–96), and anticipating Jean-Guy Pilon (1930–), Gatien Lapointe (1931–83), and Paul Chamberland (1939–). With the announcement of this theme and reserving it for the final chapter, one trajectory in the volume becomes clear from Alain Grandbois and Saint-Denys Garneau, from their 'difficulty of being' to the recovery of being in the poetry of Gilles Vigneault (1928–).[83] To live is a two-fold task: to be in language is to be in the world. The world is construed as Quebec, but a Quebec as it is inscribed with all the discourses of the modern, where everything depends upon the fact 'ce n'est pas que rêve de pays, c'est parole à inventer.'[84] The process, the articulation of the virtual, is where Grandpré's Quebec is placed, and 'la parole essentiel, la poésie ... est agent et signe primordial d'existence spirituelle au sein d'une collectivité.'[85]

The inspiration that animates the third volume is distinctly lacking in the fourth. Although the novel is the dominant genre of the volume, the novel in turn is dominated by those subgenres that bear upon a certain social reality. Those novelists that would complement the kind of poetry that dominates the third volume are only rapidly surveyed, and no reasons are proffered for the general rise and development of the novel.[86] As a consequence, the history assumes a more encyclopedic character. The design of the third volume confirms, however, the phenomenological orientation of the other volumes. The meaning of this orientation for history is that, no matter when a set of events takes place in time, their significance lies in the order and shape bestowed upon them by the reflecting subject. Social and economic forces, as Dumont constructs them through the perceptions of his father are, as Maurice Merleau-Ponty would say, 'telles que je les porte en moi, telles que je les vis.'[87] The sense of history, then, does not begin elsewhere and in another time, but in the *kairos*[88] of the conscious subject reckoning with the world as it is taken in.

What does it mean to suggest that Grandpré's history and the kind of writing it represents possesses a phenomenological bearing? To answer that question let us consider some of the themes of phenomenology and their development in Merleau-Ponty. It might be said that the primary bearing of our consideration is the position of the subject particularly in respect of language, time, history, and being. Phenomenology begins with the question of where the subject is and answers that the subject is in the world and that it knows itself not as a given but as a process: 'la phénoménologie ... étudie l'*apparition* de l'être à la conscience, au lieu d'en supposer la possibilité donnée d'avance.' If the subject is constituted by an act of recognition, its recognition, nevertheless, comprises what constitutes it. As a consequence, with more than a glance at idealism, 'le centre de la philosophie n'est plus une subjectivité transcendentale autonome, située partout et nulle part, il se trouve dans le commencement perpétuel de la réflexion, à ce point où une vie individuelle se met à réflechir sur elle-même. La rélexion n'est vraiment réflexion que si elle ne s'emporte pas hors d'elle-même, se connaît comme réflexion-sur-un-irréflechi, et par conséquent comme un changement de structure de notre existence.'[89] The subject then, is not only in time, but also continually reshaped by it through the interaction of self and world in the process of reflection.

The bearing of the subject toward history in such circumstances becomes manifold, but for our purposes the shaping of history in the conscious mind and the corresponding shaping of the conscious subject in history are of primary importance. If 'c'est toujours le présent que nous sommes centrés,' how do the past and future 'emerge' in our consciousness so as to permit the construction of a history? It is effected precisely through the process of grasping our present: 'En assumant un présent, je ressaisis et je transforme mon passé, j'en change le sens, je m'en libère, je m'en dégage.' If such a bearing upon the present avails psychologically, it avails for our construction of history in an analogous fashion. This occurs in our awareness that our present is inextricably related to our past, no matter how subject it may be to transformation in reflection upon it. We know that our past was once a present for us, but, for an analogy to be drawn between them, 'il faut que [le présent effectif] ne se donne pas seulement comme présent, qu'il s'annonce déjà comme un passé pour bientôt, que nous sentions sur lui la pression d'un avenir qui cherche à le destituer, et qu'en un mot le cours du temps soit à titre originaire non seulement le passage du présent au passé, mais encore celui du futur au présent.' This is tantamount to saying, as Merleau-Ponty aphoristically asserts: 'Si l'on peut dire que toute prospection est une rétrospection anticipée, on peut dire aussi bien que toute rétrospection est une prospection inversée.' Thus, in sum, 'la conscience déploie ou constitue le temps.'[90]

The movement of the subject from psychological to historical time is a transpositional act in which one understands oneself as part of one of several social and economic classes, each of which has several differing trajectories and ideologies. However we valorize ourselves, it involves 'un projet implicite ou existentiel qui se confond avec notre manière de mettre en forme le monde et de coexister avec les autres.' Once implicated, however, we are more than psychological subjects, if only as a result of valorizing ourselves in our coexistence with others. It is still true that 'nous donnons son sens à l'histoire, mais non qu'elle nous le propose. La Sinn-gebung n'est pas seulement centrifuge et c'est pourquoi le sujet de l'histoire n'est pas l'individu.' One enters history through the kinds of decisions one makes about oneself, and the result is that whoever I am I become in that moment 'un champs intersubjectif, non pas en dépit de mon corps et de ma situation historique, mais au contraire en étant ce corps et cette situation et tout le reste à travers eux.'[91] The historical subject is, first of all, a subject in the present capable of constituting time into past and future within certain constraints, but these very constraints participate in the act of constitution. Significantly, the past and the projected future are never elsewhere but in us, and they take shape in a bursting forth of awareness, rather than simply being rationally conceived. Is it not possible to see here a coincidence between cultural history written, according to Vachon, as a consciously exposed study of emergence, announced in the first volume and reiterated in the last?[92] The past is not static and composed of events that have 'acquis une certaine *immobilité* dans le temps';[93] history is constituted in its 'originary shape,' as a movement that relates past, present, and future. But it is centred in the moment of its execution, and history has no sense apart from our participation in it: 'l'histoire n'a pas par elle-même de sens, elle a celui que nous lui donnons par notre volonté.'[94] Sense in Grandpré is conferred by the manner in which retrospection and prospection coincide in the present of the text through the technique of making all texts useful in a cultural order that shapes the emergence of that present, which is constructed as the threshold of a desirable future. Inclusion and exclusion, the process of canonization, is one that confers existence and non-existence and, in a word, engages the question of being. This means that it is possible, then, to describe the construction of history in Grandpré as an overarching process of rising emplotment, despite obstacles that appear to prevent the gradual prefiguration and emergence of plenitude. The desired future is envisaged as plenitude because it is then, presumably, the society forecast by Borduas and considered by Grandpré as the significant apogée of Quebec's will to overcome the difficulty of being.

History-in-process is engaged by placing all significant texts on a plane of equal semantic value. Thus, figures such as Garneau, Bourassa, Borduas, and Giguère, all of whom bear upon history in differing ways, are nevertheless all construed as synecdoches of a collective enterprise. As a result, Bourassa's nationalism can prefigure Borduas's desire to shape a particular future, as well as Giguère's engagement with being. The problem of the relation of culture to politics and social organization is resolved by their all being central protagonists in the same drama. All of them, to use Merleau-Ponty's expression, dispose of 'une parole originaire.'[95] All of them as *texte-actants*[96] express and compose a history, and so originate it. But to express is 's'assurer, par l'emploi de mots déjà usés, que l'intention neuve reprend l'heritage du passé, c'est d'un seul geste incorporer le passé au présent et souder ce présent à un avenir,'[97] an act which is imitated metahistorically in the way Grandpré's history is conceived, executed, and exposed. Its intention seizes upon what it constructs as tendencies and shapes them toward the desired future that is opened toward being, rather than the absence, alienation, exile, or non-being of the past. By ordering the present, the speaking position of the subject, as the period from 1945 (the same year, incidentallly, that Merleau-Ponty's seminal text appeared), and allowing Borduas as a *texte-actant* to provide a bearing both toward the past and future, history can be perceived to begin in that *now*, that *kairos* that permits being, the world, and time to appear significantly to the conscious mind of the historian.

The text of poetry is particularly powerful in this regard not only because it is the object of the defining volume of the series, but also because of its originating ability. It projects a desired future simply because its language, as Merleau-Ponty asserts, is not an instrument but because '*il est une manifestation, une révélation de l'être intime et du lien psychique qui nous unit au monde et à nos semblables.*' As a result, the great French-Canadian poets of the twentieth century are synecdoches of Quebec's aspiration to be. This can only occur 'now,' for 'le présent (au sens large, avec ses horizons de passé et d'avenir originaires) a ... un privilège parce qu'il est la zone où l'être et la conscience coïncident.'[98] Thus poetry in its originary relation to history overcomes the problem of beginnings and endings, as well as the silences of the past, by becoming a signifying intention that exculpates Quebec from the possible opprobrium of having been a colonizer, of having collaborated with its colonizer in turn, and with having, as a result, strayed into the non-being of an unworthy, not to say, false past and false consciousness. This is literary history as a triumphal act that, by 'assuming' the present, is capable of transforming the past so as to find a way out of it and so remove a future whose arrival seemed a kind of closure. In such a moment, culture finds its necessity as the harbinger of freedom in a new order of origination.

CHAPTER FIVE

Literary History as *Heilsgeschichte,* 1973–1983

If time has a direction, it also has a meaning for the salvation of all mankind and of each man in particular. History is *Heilsgeschichte.*[1]

The burden and meaning of freedom in Canada is, at the very least, ambiguous. Quebec's sovereignty movement desires freedom from English Canada, and it relies upon a close reading of history to demonstrate why knowledge of history is necessary for a proper understanding of its literature. English Canada, in contrast, appears, with few exceptions, bent upon freedom from history itself, which may be part, as I have argued, of its liberal, protestant heritage. Neither of these inclinations was particularly new in the early years of the 1970s, but they were sharply drawn into focus by the enforcement of the War Measures Act in 1970 and the war in Vietnam, which tended to sharpen an English-Canadian sense of difference, at least. Not surprisingly, histories of literature in English Canada did not dwell upon either of these issues to any noticeable degree. Characteristic, perhaps, of English Canada's position is the initial sentence of D.G. Jones's *Butterfly on Rock*: 'Having reached the Pacific, Canadians have begun to turn back on themselves, to create that added dimension that Teilhard de Chardin calls the *noosphere* or, to put it more simply, Canadian culture.' It is a remarkable articulation of English-Canadian thinking that can leap from space ('the Pacific') to nation ('Canadians'), and then from *noosphere* to Canadian culture. As an elaboration, Jones goes on to observe: 'more than ever before we have arrived at a point where we recognize, not only that the land is ours, but that we are the land's.' Thus, any division between nature and culture, typical of both a colonial mentality and Western civilization inhibits the plenitude of self-knowledge but also, *mirabile dictu*, a return to 'the first days of Creation,' which would provide both a discourse and 'a fundamental view of life.' At that moment we will learn 'more about that obscure landscape that is our life and the world's.'[2]

Leaving aside Jones's expressed debt to Northrop Frye, not to speak of some of the Hexagone poets whom he was later to translate,[3] a certain number of similarities shared by other English-Canadian critics[4] and literary historians should be evident. First, Canada is a function of spatial configurations; second, the emphasis is psychological and phenomenological; third, and as a consequence, Canada is an object capable of becoming the language of the subject; and finally, Canada is capable of translation into the time of myth, delivering the Canadian from the false dichotomy of subject and object. Time is the place of deliverance. In becoming so, it permits Jones to draw a contrast between Canada and the United States by remarking in the final paragraph of his book that such a possession of the Other is a sacrificial act of affirming identity and, while appearing revolutionary when compared to American attitudes, it is, in fact, 'radically conservative.'[5] Certainly George Grant would have both agreed and approved.

Surveying Canada

While Grant was not indifferent to history, he considered its contemporary, liberal aspect at best a *pis aller.*[6] Since Grant was symptomatic of much of English-Canadian thought of his time, it is hard to imagine what the function of the *history* of literature was in the anglophone literature system for those who continued to write it. Notable is the Prologue of Elizabeth Waterston's *Survey: A Short History of Canadian Literature* (1973). The word 'history' occurs twice, once when she wonders whether Canada is 'a fossilized bit of history,' and once in the phrase 'Canadian history of literature,' both of which are raised as objects to be probed. Her emphasis is on 'Canada,' 'literature,' and 'the relation between them.' Waterston states: '*Why* certain topics caught the consciousness of writers in this country at particular periods; *how* particular writers or groups of writers shaped those topics into artworks: this is our subject.' Time is quickly subordinated to the relationship between psychology and production, and in a certain respect the title of the book signifies all of this. It is not 'a survey' but simply 'survey.' Thus, as a title, this is a curious, semiotic gesture. At first reading, it strikes one as a verb in the imperative mood, rather than being a noun, and the author represents herself as somewhat embarrassed by the word when she asks: 'But can we line up creative art and "survey" it?' She evades an answer by discussing the individual freedom of the artist, but the word expressly identifies literature as object, as part of a scene that seems to require arrangement. The phrase 'line up' refers to the placing of literature in either time or space, and the whole metaphor is a geometrical one from which time is abstracted. To illustrate the full meaning of the Prologue, Waterston considers W.O. Mitchell's novel *Who Has Seen the Wind?* as a parable in which the major themes of 'process, change, and death' are held in suspension 'in his environment, and in himself.' In other words, whatever happens in time is contained by both the subject and the space in which it is extended as artist, character, reader, and 'Canadian thought and feeling.'[7]

Moreover, just as time is held in suspension, the use of photographs to introduce each chapter reinforces a sense of space in which movement is arrested. The first picture, for example, is of four children on a raft on a pond who will never reach the shore. The final picture is of a butterfly on a hand, not exactly in the image Jones uses to entitle his study, suspended from flight. The rest of the pictures either open upon the space of Canada or capture a moment in time. The only things given the appearance of movement are the dogs at play in the picture that begins chapter nine. True enough, no one has seen the wind, and with the possible exception of the photograph that opens chapter one, where the sun appears to dance on a mountain lake, no dramatic effect occurs. Space appears, then, to illustrate the point about time and history. It is also held in suspension. As a consequence, the reader gradually understands that what appears to be a linear movement in the text that is marked by dates at the beginning of each chapter, framing the book from 1600 to 1970, is also an illusion. With few exceptions, no reason is given for the choice of dates. The year 1812 is appropriate for a certain reading of 'The American Presence' (chapter 4), but it is only such at the expense of the Loyalists. Moreover, 1885 is certainly fair for the 'Interlude' in the completion of the transcontinental railway, and 1867 and 1914 are certainly inevitable. Although 1763 is chosen as the inaugural moment of French- and English-Canadian relations, marked by the Treaty of Paris, it tactfully avoids the highly changed year of 1760. It is thus implied that the creation of British North America occurred elsewhere, removing a level of responsibility. If origin is perceived as elsewhere, one can happily get on with one's business of locating art which, we discover at the beginning of the story, takes place on a double hook. The artist too is caught in the process of casting either into natural space ('landscape and society') or into psychological space.[8]

Although history happens, its occurrence is emphatically subordinate to what artists choose to do in their exercise of 'free human activity.' Thus they are excused from history: their only responsibility from the beginning is to observe. The world that is observed is, as I have suggested, not extended horizontally through time, but rather suspended vertically in a kind of space. Each chapter is given a title chosen from the title of books contemporary with the text. It is a thematic rubric which not only removes the messiness of history but also aesthetically controls it. Native people, for example, are captured forever as 'beautiful losers,' and Leonard Cohen's expression, taken from the title of his 1966 novel, becomes a lens through which they are perceived. While it appears as the controlling lens, it is, however, one of several. As the chapter proceeds, it becomes evident that the Aboriginal is simply an image whose semiotic function fluctuates continually from a sign of derision to that of 'Noble Savage' until becoming almost invisible by the end of the last century. At that point the Aboriginal is in a sense reborn in legend, a clear semiotic release from history into an *illo tempore* of poetry in which Isabella Valancy Crawford, 'the writer with the *least* personal experience of Indian ways seems to have written best and most sensitively' about them. Not surprisingly, contemporary revisions of the disappearing Aboriginal 'illustrate ... new uses,' and 'Indians have appeared strongly among our new poets and painters.'[9]

Although history is transposed into space and space into a collage of imagery, it is possible, nevertheless, to discern a plot in the narrative. It emerges from the emphasis on the artist and the work which is announced in the Prologue and developed in the Epilogue. Canada is a story that moves from the practical reports of travellers to a land of myths (chapter 10) and textuality (chapter 11). Indeed, as it approaches its conclusion, we find it circling about its beginning. If W.O. Mitchell as parable provides 'some insight into the more mysterious winds of free human creativity,' Marshall McLuhan's messages are invoked, and 'among the messages most powerful in the electronic age is a surprising insistence on mystical individual experience.' Furthermore, a 'return to nature in search of enhanced quality of life is a common theme in poems and stories.' Bearing in mind that 'the new media are extensions of man,' it is possible to infer that Canada is, and always has been, a text where subject, space, and time are interwoven, which is how nations are constructed.[10] This is the plot of heightened perception and developed technology to which history is subordinated as the place where things took place, where they are perceived and held in art. The dates serve, as a consequence, primarily as a filing system.

The Acquisition of Difference

The initial sentence of Waterston's Epilogue is a reminder that 'Canadian pioneers used to talk about "making land."' Although the expression also exists in French (*faire de la terre*) and motivated the genre of the *roman du terroir*, land in the French-Canadian mentality is at once place and time, and its making takes place with a strict and unequivocal observance of when it occurred. Thus, when Jeanne d'Arc Lortie frames the argument of *La Poésie nationaliste au Canada français* (1975), she can assert: 'Le pays de a Nouvelle-France est devenu le pays des Canadiens, et leur poésie exprime cet aspect de leur patriotisme. C'est cette nuance que nous voulons marquer par l'emploi de l'epithète "nationaliste."' Nationalism is not only defined as 'l'*unité*, la *spécifité*, le *culte de la patrie* et l'*indépendance*,' but also understood as developing over time through 'les états successifs de la conscience et de l'idée nationales.' The primary matrix for the formation of such awareness is the role played by the land itself, 'la réalité qui attache le plus fortement un peuple à sa nationalité.' The land, however, is immediately coded with a number of other elements, namely, the cult of royalty, social and economic institutions, religion and intellectual development. In short, concrete as the land was, it was also a semantic field in which a culture originated, particularly during the years between 1713 and 1744, that gave New France all the contours of a nation.[11]

The decision to find a beginning of history before the Conquest constitutes a significant shift in the construction of a historical semantics for the development of French Canada, and it testifies to the period of gestation of Lortie's text, which had its own origins in 1950 as part of a course on nineteenth-century national movements in Europe.[12] Its debt to such nationalist historians as Guy Frégault, Marcel Trudel, and Maurice Séguin, whose work began to appear toward the end of the Second World War, not to mention that of Lionel Groulx, is everywhere evident.[13] Such a thesis cushions to a certain extent the full impact of the Conquest, inasmuch as New France was given time to establish a cultural foundation. Once the relevance of France is established, the overture to national movements elsewhere in Europe gives a cachet of legitimacy to French Canada's self-awareness and historical development that is sufficient to embed its nationalism in a larger sphere. The legitimate aspirations of the province are, therefore, naturalized, since they run parallel to, and are fed by, the several revolts of 1830 and 1848. The forum for much of the developing awareness of a common aspiration was newspapers and journals, a source of both the latest news and poetry. Thus, contemporary events and poetry are intimately related in the emergence of the nation, giving poetry a pronounced historical function. Poetry is thus constructed as both history and the sign of a continuously shifting sensibility that articulates a 'conscience collective.'[14] As Lortie argues in respect of folk songs and also for the anonymous poems later published in newspapers: 'Les principaux éléments de cette conscience apparaissent ... : le sentiment d'être "Canadiens," le vouloir-vivre collectif, l'attachement au pays et à la couronne française, le besoin de liberté et la sauvegarde des droits.'[15]

The coincidence of anonymity that both folk songs and much of the poetry in newspapers shared invest them both with the character of a collective voice. Thus the decision to make such an archival study of the early poetry of French Canada makes it an historical phenomenon whose significance was hitherto overlooked. The poems are thus appropriately constructed as positions in the long, internal debates that articulate a dynamic and constantly changing condition as the various poets addressed the British regime, the American and French Revolutions, and the War of 1812. The shifts, the entries into the debate, the erosion of cherished ideals (such as the devotion to the Crown) are such that moments of origination gradually form an irrevocable order of historical significance: the first poetry composed in New France occurs in 1658, patriotism is born in 1690,[16] by 1760 the colony acquires, citing Frégault a 'personnalité distincte,' the first étrennes (broadsheets of poetry distributed on New Year's Day) appeared in 1767, in 1797 the word patrie as a signifier of Canada appeared. The most significant moment, however, is the end of the seventeenth century when 'la poésie prend en France une voie nouvelle, celle d'auxiliaire de l'histoire,' and the same was true for the colony itself.[17]

Texts, then, become actants, as I remarked in the last chapter, and even witnesses, in a story of explanation designed to articulate the originality of the nation. Acquiring such a shape involves struggle, and so the period of New France is invested with a significance often marginalized by other historians. Thus the long appearance of peace from 1713 to 1744 provided time to cultivate a 'conscience collective' as the colony dealt with the menace of indigenous inhabitants and the continued rivalry between the French and English for dominance in North America. From such an origin Lortie constructs Quebec, citing Jean Bruchési, as 'un *casus belli* permanent.'[18] Resolution of this kind of state of affairs can take a variety of forms ranging from annihilation to independence, and it is within these possibilities that the debate of French-Canadian poetry is given a certain trajectory, gradually replacing an early ambivalence with a sense of homeland. The period of consolidation is placed in the years following the restoration of the French monarchy in 1815 as French-Canadian thinking gradually gave up its allegiance to royalty, whether British or that of the ancien régime, as a consequence of its fear of union in a single polity.[19] In contrast to other narratives of French Canada's history, anxieties about union appear deeper than the trauma of the Conquest. In fact the latter is initially considered by Lionel Groulx a 'régime de collaboration.'[20] The poetry of the restoration period, however, is marked by 'un revirement complet'[21] in which an earlier anti-democratic and anti-bonapartist spirit yields to the desire for freedom.

The significance of Lortie's argument lies in the repeated assertion that Quebec is not to be seen as a province in a larger political jurisdiction, but rather a nation with clear analogies to European nations dominated by larger, imperial regimes. Thus at each stage of Quebec's growth of awareness, similarities are adduced, and her question is not entirely rhetorical when she writes of European and Lower Canadian struggles in the 1830s: 'La réssemblance évidente entre le nationalisme romantique du Bas-Canada et celui des peuples d'Europe est sans doute plus qu'un simple parallélisme. Ne pourrait-on pas croire aussi à une certaine parenté?' French Canada is represented as moving in tandem so to speak with Europe, which, by implication, marks the British regime as an imperial presence standing opposed to natural aspirations. Thus while the English-Canadian story involves steady negotiations with the Mother Country in order to acquire responsible government, dominion status, and eventual autonomy, Lortie's narrative perceives negotiation as a struggle for survival, not against a mother country, but against a colonizer that had annexed a people on the way to its own nationhood. Although the Conquest was a defeat, it was, as we have seen before, also a Fortunate Fall that prepared French Canada for eventual shifts in European history. Thus, while the second defeat of the Rebellion of 1837–8 may appear as a second Conquest, it was not so constructed by contemporaries who could take heart in the corresponding situations in Europe and elsewhere. Indeed, 'à peine l'union des Canadas est-elle réalisée en 1841 qu'un jeune Canadien invite ses contemporains à suivre l'exemple du poète écossais James MacPherson, en recueillant les contes, ballades ou complaintes, connus des voyageurs canadiens.'[22]

Despite defeats, each turn of Lortie's emplotment is one of gradual success, that is, the growing conception of a 'patrie concrète.' The collaboration of poetry and historiography in the nineteenth century, which other literary historians have recognized, is constructed as the catalyst of the nation, and 'alors qu'en France [le poète] est le guide de la société, au Canada français il est celui de la nation.'[23] Thus a history of poetry from the seventeenth century in New France until (at least) Confederation coincides intimately with a history of the nation. Thus the privilege that all literary historians bestow upon Garneau as father of French-Canadian literature is, in the light of Lortie's argument, somewhat inflated. He, along with Crémazie, are simply the climax of a long movement of the 'conscience collective.' Symbolic as the arrival of La Capricieuse in 1855 may have been, especially for Crémazie, the ship's arrival was only the sign of a struggle taking on a new and more hopeful direction.[24] If nothing else, it legitimized transatlantic connections that for almost a century could only be maintained by mail, visits, and newspapers. Having refused the temptations of annexation to the United States and developed a defence against British imperialism, Quebec was positioned in Lortie's argument to draw the upon the sustenance of solidarity with the emerging nations of Europe.

As she notes in her conclusion, the same theme returned in the 1960s as part of a persistent phenomenon.[25] One cannot help, then, reading her text within the context of the final dissolution of the British Empire. As a consequence, the intimacy between her argument and her examples is closely, if tacitly, established, lending it an increased persuasiveness, especially in the reminder that nationalism in Québécois poetry is not new.[26] Most significant, however, is locating the history of nationalism in a European context in an effort to distinguish French-Canadian nationalism from that of English Canada. To a certain extent it is also distinguished from that of the United States, a largely anglophone nation with a different cultural tradition that did not possess European models for its war with England. Such a history of literature in Quebec is a history of the acquisition of difference and nationality.

The contemporary character of Lortie's text, which is never insisted upon but certainly implied, inscribes a post-colonial trajectory in the history of Quebec. Certainly the marks of various colonial moments are present, not the least of which was the repression that followed the revolt of 1837–8, which brought French Canada close to complete assimilation.[27] The response, notably, but not exclusively, of Garneau's history, recovered the territory of culture and engendered a subject. The self-affirmation of French Canada in the nineteenth century is consistently modelled upon the emergence of ethnic distinction and national territories in Europe, notably in Poland, Hungary, and Italy. If the nation is the dominant in the poetry of the 1960s and 1970s – and there is much evidence to support such a position in the work of the Hexagone group of poets – the relation between the nationalism of the nineteenth century and movements of twentieth-century colonial liberation is not difficult to infer. Thus the struggle of self-affirmation, Lortie's central thesis, is an incontrovertible reflection of its own moment in Quebec's history.

The West as Canada

In a country, however, in which the expression 'peace, order, and good government' possesses foundational privilege, it may appear surprising that the subtitle of Dick Harrison's *Unnamed Country* (1977) is *The Struggle for a Canadian Prairie Fiction*. 'Struggle' is the central metaphor of the text, and in that respect, at least, it is similar to Lortie's argument, implying a post-colonial stance. Moreover, the use of the word 'Canadian' in the title may suggest something of an anti-American Canada, characteristic of the period, engaged in the effort of articulating its autonomy.[28] Like Quebec, the Canadian West is capable of construction as an aspect of empire, and the 'sense of being part of the imperial community provided the basic guidelines for the development of the new society in the North West.' The difference, of course, with Quebec is that, according to Doug Owram, Canadians participated 'in deciding the future of their own West.'[29] Although this remark was made at a time when revisionist history of North America was not entirely in its infancy,[30] Owram's observation leaves little room for Aboriginal and French-Canadian decisions. Thus, Harrison's consideration of the West, while it at least gestures toward an awareness of 'other traditions' (the title of chapter 6), positions its sense of the post-colonial within a monolingual context, and thus his study is part of a general, contemporary effort toward replacing the centre with the region on the margin,[31] making of the west 'a typically Canadian problem.' As I shall argue later, Harrison's desire to construct the West as typical does not contradict the possibility that this is an essentialism of a theoretical kind; nevertheless, the themes of naming, language, and place, which permit the empire to write back[32] are central to Harrison's thesis and mark it as post-colonial. In this respect it also differs from McCourt's history, which is content simply with clearing a space.

The other keyword of the title is 'unnamed.' What is the language that most accurately designates place? The struggle is to find the appropriate language, which distinguishes the initial attempts of settlers to construct a West with a cultural lexicon that does not fit. In many respects, the West, like other colonized regions in the world, has been forced to struggle against becoming the object of continuous 'image management' in order to find a way to live in it (the thesis of Owram's *Promise of Eden*), and therefore the challenge to the writer is to find the image, indeed the myth, that expresses it. 'Wilderness' and 'commodity' were the dominant possibilities of the nineteenth century, and they were replaced toward its end with the myth of the garden.[33] In the eyes of settlers these images were hardly adequate, but this imaginative inadequacy,[34] the expressed thesis of Harrison's text, is related to the equally significant notion that the history of anglophone writing in the West originates elsewhere, marking the struggle between here and there. As Harrison argues, the Canadian was not only denied 'the freshness of beginning' (as if this were possible in a historical world already proposed in Klinck), but also the patterns of perception construct a subject as exile,[35] one of being neither here nor there.

The imaginative means by which exile is addressed only exacerbates the problem, especially through the use of such modes as romance, comedy, and irony as they are drawn upon by immigrant and, later, native-born writers. Romance, which dominated the fiction of the first two decades of the twentieth century, drew heavily upon the implications of the myth of the garden, which fitted well with both imperialism and the need to find a language of place, but concluded in the discovery that it was not wholly adequate to the place. Although the tragic mode has been primarily emphasized by the literary institution since the middle years of the century, Harrison is right to argue that the central fiction that represents the West in the most perdurable fashion is that of adventure and sentimental romance, the latter elaborated on in sentimental comedy.[36] The contemporary, represented by Margaret Laurence (1926–87), Robert Kroetsch (1927–), and Rudy Wiebe (1934–), is engaged in the often ironic enterprise of unnaming and renaming the various images and myths of the West.

In their different ways, each of these writers may be considered out-side the dominant minority of western writers, especially if we make an exception for Laurence's Scottish background. Each of them is also con-cerned with either dominated minorities, such as the First Nations peo-ple, or the stereotypes of British immigrants and culture. Therefore, Harrison's conclusion is in a post-colonial vein.[37] It dwells upon the efforts of ethnic-minority immigrants both 'to re-write [prairie] history ... [and] to approach the central mystery of life that is in it.' This consti-tutes 'the first necessary step' toward overcoming cultural appropriation by finding an appropriate discourse. Nevertheless, his reliance upon modes, conjoined with a use of flat characters and archetypes in gen-eral, as a means of explicating how a reality is constructed, testifies to a tacit reliance upon Frye's *Anatomy of Criticism* and places him in marked contradiction to the post-colonial movement of Lortie. The difference is that, to use White's terms, Lortie's struggle is placed within a metonymi-cal order of cause and effect and Harrison's struggle is conceived meta-phorically. As I argue, one reason for this difference lies in the fact that history in French Canada is constructed as a succession of traumatic events, while history in English Canada, at least as constructed by liter-ary historians, is no more traumatic than geographical space and weather.

Such a generalization is often implied in Harrison, beginning with the central figure of Sir William F. Butler who, when cited, turns to the seasons and is overwhelmed by 'the silence, loneliness, and isolation.' The encounter with the Other, as recounted in Alexander Mackenzie's *Voyages*, is characterized by a desire 'to "civilize" the Indians.' Butler and Mackenzie, of course, never lost anything except when they failed to understand their environment, something Mrs Abercrombie learns at the end of W.O. Mitchell's *Who Has Seen the Wind*. As colonizers, no suf-fering on the part of the settler community is evident. If one considers the tragic novels of the prairie, we discover that much of Mrs Bentley's trauma in Sinclair Ross's *As for Me and My House* (1941) springs from the presence of 'an overwhelming environment.' I would accept, however, Harrison's argument that central to the novel is 'not so much ... the environment as ... a long cultural tradition of inadequate response to it.' Nevertheless, it is the environment which prompts the problem and the anguish. Nothing fits better with Frye's theory of modes than the pres-ence and passage and return of the seasons, which shifts critical empha-sis away from history to cycle and myth.[38]

The absence of history in the western imaginary, as well as in that of

English-Canadian literary history, is attested in Harrison's comment
that, with rare exceptions, the western novel does not take much
account of the public world.[39] Later, he observes that western people
have an 'unusual sense of time, of not existing in history, and their alter-
nately apocalyptic and millennial conception of their own position in
cosmic time is probably the most basic element in their mythic awareness of themselves.'[40] Indeed, God is an Old Testament figure, and the
prairie itself 'resembles the desert of the Old Testament.' This is a language which bears close similarity with that of Frye and certainly suggests that the writing that would issue from such a context is one that
would seek either revelation (a radical unnaming) or deliverance.
When Harrison speaks of time and of the desire of contemporary fiction writers to replace the older construction of the West as space, he
means that their desire, paradoxically, is not so much to reconstruct
time but rather to overcome it. Part of Harrison's apparent difficulty in
clarifying this point lies in his reliance first on Hazard Lepage's comment in Kroetsch's *The Studhorse Man* (1969), viz.: 'It is then *time* that I
must reconstruct, not space.' He then goes on to argue that the prairie
before the 1970s was primarily a matter of space, adducing Kroetsch
again to say: 'There's very little credence given to the notion that we
exist in history, in time.'[41] It is not clear why Hazard Lepage was initially
introduced, unless to suggest that the purport of the comment would be
developed. His comment is in fact contradicted, concluding the paragraph with a nod toward *As for Me and My House*, which takes place outside of history, and to Grove's heroes who 'are confident that they set
foot on the plains on the last day of creation, but ... gradually discover
they are taking part in the story of the Fall.' Admittedly Ross and Grove
are not of the 1970s, but there is nothing to suggest that myth yields to
history in the later writers. Rather, on the contrary, later writers seem
even more intent upon constructing their fiction along mythic lines,
especially in their intent to claim identity with a pre-colonial world, primarily in the Aboriginal 'as the one potential "ancestor" who is close to
the soil, organically and elementally connected with it, and whose culture may reveal what the land has been trying to tell us from the beginning.'[42]

'From the beginning' is the significant phrase, for it clearly emphasizes a position closer to Genesis than history. Furthermore, the desire
to claim identity with an ancestor that will overcome the stretch of time
is not only apparent in the authors cited, but also in Harrison's own
design which tellingly returns to Butler, who saw what Kroetsch saw a

century before, and Harrison marks it as a formative moment.[43] They would seem to share a vision of 'original chaos,'[44] which is part of the irony that plays through the final authors Harrison examines, and which also constitutes the end of Frye's cycle of myths. Just as Frye places irony at the end and the beginning, so Harrison's concluding authors are ironically making 'the first necessary step.'[45] Irony is a mode of thresholds; it makes identities of things in apparent opposition and so is akin to metaphor. The grand pattern emerges as an allegory of mythical beginnings and endings that are often based upon a biblical structure.

How the Bible is read, however, constitutes another difference between Harrison's mode of post-colonial history and that, for example, of Lortie. Despite the fact that it is often noted that both English and French Canada appear divided by faith, their respective adherence to Puritanism and Jansenism give them something in common.[46] Nevertheless, it is evident the Bible is a metanarrative to which both cultures refer in a different manner. As we have seen, anglophone literary historians prefer an allegorical reading that corresponds to the theological notion of *Heilsgeschichte,* to history as a story of salvation.[47] This means that such a history is a special kind of speech act that can be both, following J.L. Austin, illocutionary and perlocutionary, that is, one that implies both warning and achievement.[48] The ordering of literary texts is not primarily designed to establish a canon, but rather to draw certain consequences from the proposed canon. The consequences are of an implicitly transcendent kind, anagogically shaped, even if only metaphorically, toward apocalypse. Its roots of salvation history are, of course, Christian and certainly unthinkable without the New Testament, and its secular course may be traced as far as Marxism. It is characterized by an understanding of history as divided into its period of darkness and its period of light, in which everything is clarified in its proper order.[49] Thus, to reach the light we are summoned through the illocutionary use of discursive practices, and the assertion of that attainment is couched in a perlocutionary language. Literature in English Canada is 'ordered' toward such an end. Although francophone literary history flows from the same source, its movement, even among its ecclesiastically ordained historians, has been of a different character. It hints, and sometimes in an explicit fashion, at deliverance, but by deliverance it means political autonomy or independence in a clearly secular sense. Thus it eschews the atemporality of allegory which simply seeks 'to unhide the hidden,' to use Kroetsch's expression, based on Martin

Heidegger, for apocalypse.[50] It does so by carefully displaying what is already unhidden, by ordering events into a secular and sequential order in time, so that history becomes the place of apologia. Such French-Canadian literary history says: This happened, and it has meaning and consequence. The text bears testimony, rather than serving as palimpsest for another order of psychological, ethical, anagogical bearings.

Both canons bear witness as martyrologies: one is designed to summon the reader toward a semantics of the hidden in which the world is de-composed,[51] the other, toward a semantics of the temporal in which the world bears upon plenitude. It may be that the difference lies in the difference of self-construction. English Canada begins at a moment 'always-already' given, a fact that Harrison complains of. History, then, becomes a system of adjustments within an atemporal order, akin, one might say, to constitutional discussions in Canada. History, for French Canada, by contrast, begins, admittedly with a Fall, but the Fall is not attributed to any hamartia on the part of French Canadians. After all, the Seven Years War was lost in Europe, and the peace settlement was determined by others. This makes the Fall decidedly political. The narrative of struggle, with which francophone literary history is variously structured, testifies to a continuous situation of virtuality, of working toward the plenitude of the real in a secular world. Nothing is 'always already,' because it has yet to happen. 'A people with no history'[52] has no recourse but to invent one, for without one one's ontological status is indecisive.[53] Without a history, the abrogation of authenticity is barely possible.[54]

Comedies of Heaven and Hell

Although Harrison is writing a history of 'an indigenous prairie fiction,' he desires it to be understood, expressly agreeing with the novelist David Godfrey (1938–), that the prairie 'is the archetypal region of Canada.'[55] It is not so much significant that such a statement essentializes the margin as the centre, but rather that it becomes a sign of the nation. Statements that are valid for the prairie are true for Canada, and (English) Canada, as I have argued, becomes, as a result, an allegory, rather than a place. No such claim is made by Patrick O'Flaherty in his *The Rock Observed* (1979), a region that did not become part of Canada until 1949 and whose history was more closely related to that of Great Britain. It is, as Farley Mowat (1921–) noted, 'a race apart.'[56] The operative word in the title is 'observed,' inasmuch as it is O'Flaherty's intent 'to provide a survey of literary responses to Newfoundland and Newfoundlanders over the centuries.'[57] Literature subsumes writing by historians, travellers, missionaries, pioneers, and imaginative writers.

Such a broad view of literature would suggest that O'Flaherty's text would be mostly of use as a manual. It has, however, an argument and a design that orders all his texts into a homogeneous shape. The kinds of writing that Newfoundland has prompted fall into three categories, and they bear a kind of dialectical relationship. The first arises from the fact that Newfoundland is a harsh land with a bitter climate that has brutal effects upon the inhabitants. At the conclusion of the eighteenth century, for example, their situation is summed up by O'Flaherty, with a nod to Thomas Hardy (1840–1928), as follows: Newfoundland is settled by 'ordinary men and women crawling in labour and obscurity to their graves, caught in "the monotonous moils of strained hard-run Humanity."' Similar views are expressed in twentieth-century fiction, notably in Percy Janes's depiction of 'alienation and dismay.' These are perceptions, however, that are countered frequently by a more sentimental attitude, found in writers as disparate as E.J. Pratt and Farley Mowat. Mowat is indeed dismissed for his *A Whale for the Killing* (1972), and his intrusion in the life of an outport is turned upon as 'sentimental excess,' 'the mass publicity' that accompanied it was 'obscenity,' and his lack of knowledge of the necessities of outport life is treated as 'the luxury of sentiment.' Pratt, while approached with greater respect, is looked upon with a certain regret. Becoming the national poet 'meant throwing off parochial themes: the Canadian Pacific Railway rather than Newfoundland's narrow gauge line.'[58] Moreover, while capable of expressing the harshness of Newfoundland life, he is also capable of 'romancing and strutting.' Pratt's Newfoundland possesses the inaccuracies of something 'jettisoned, and half-remembered.' As O'Flaherty suggests, the sentimental is often another aspect the contemptuous, and writers like Harold Horwood (1923–), who had a friend in Mowat, waver ambivalently. By comparing the draft of *Tomorrow Will Be Sunday* (1966) with the published version, O'Flaherty persuasively indicates the shift from a 'sympathetic, and indeed at times poignant and beautiful' depiction of outport life to one that shows a place 'where ignorance, intolerance, and fanaticism reign supreme.'[59]

For O'Flaherty, these two positions, which are fairly constant throughout the history of the province, are limited by the extremes they evince. As he implies, they can also be prompted by views of history that are irrelevant to Newfoundland. The problem with the barbaric view is that it suggests that Newfoundlanders are not simply 'race apart,' but in some ways not part of the human race at all. The problem with the sentimental view is that it is tainted with the progressive view of history. Thus, Patrick Morris, an early nineteenth-century merchant, is represented as a victim of a 'turbulent imagination and zeal' and of a 'rhetoric [that] embroiled him in awkward paradoxes which he side-stepped only with some difficulty.' His flaw was that he was 'a progressivist, holding out to the people the prospect of triumph over imagined oppressors and repressive laws.' Edward Chappell is similarly dismissed as suffering from romanticism and snobbery and for also 'being one of the first writers to caterwaul in public over the fate of the Beothucks.' Sir Richard Bonnycastle, who served in the campaigns of 1812 and 1837, abandoned 'common sense for imperial bluster and imperial pomposity' in his report on the colony in 1842. As a result, in his 'unrelenting rhetoric, Newfoundland history was lumbered with imperial and progressivist baggage, another addition to the welter of delusions already clouding the colony's past and future.' Rhetoric and progressivist thought are equally manifest in the work of the Victorian missionary Moses Harvey. The idea of progress as a design of history is for O'Flaherty simply cant: Newfoundland history in the nineteenth century – the real history, that of the common people – seems to exhibit continuity rather than progress. Whatever took place in high-level discussions in London or St. John's, for the mass of the people the essential conditions of life remained unaltered.'[60] 'Real life' is a function of place and climate, in which reversal of fortune was more prevalent than progress.

How, then, is Newfoundland to be properly represented? Its true image is to be found in the concluding chapter of the book that records the case of the sea captain George Tuff, which is given as 'a symbolic moment' in Newfoundland literature. For whatever reasons – loyalty, fatalism, manliness – with full knowledge of the consequence, he led some seventy-seven sealers onto the ice, obeying the orders of his superior, and all of them froze to death. The story is summed up thus: 'The long history of the Newfoundland people includes more than storytelling in the twine-loft and cavorting in the landwash. It includes seventy-seven frozen bodies of the *Newfoundland's* dead sealers. And George Tuff's tears.' The moralitas of this exemplum is clear: 'To look closely at Newfoundland life as it is lived, rather than fancied, is to be struck with the force of continuity rather than change.'[61] What O'Flaherty is seeking in the anecdote is, to use a word frequently encountered in English-Canadian critical discourse, the 'distinctive' character of Newfoundland, a common thread that represents 'life as it is lived' or, as the nineteenth-century German historian Leopold von Ranke put it, 'wie es eigentlich gewesen.'[62] To infer as much places O'Flaherty, if not entirely within the mold of Ranke's positivism, at least within a certain frame of reference that marks his sense of historical order in a certain way. Continuity does not mean, of course, that nothing happens, but rather that certain values are maintained that make Newfoundlanders 'distinctive.' To seize the ordinary, rhetoric and sentimentality have no place, and the accurate observer in the early twentieth century will note that 'despite its near anarchic condition over the centuries, and despite the lack of a common historical or political struggle in the distant past which could have united the people, the colony was becoming a nation and to some extent beginning to sense that it was one.'[63] Assuming that such a gathering together is not exactly progress, it is, nevertheless, a movement of a certain kind that confers unity upon both the province and the text.

The achievement of unity is wrought by a design that is also an echo of Ranke's favourite plot structure. O'Flaherty's history is written under the sign of the comic mythos, no matter how much he might spurn notions of progress, and its intent is rational, integrative, and illuminating within the lights of the ordinary. The larger design is one that presents a world of often grim savagery that is countered by another of sentimental cant. The parable of Captain Tuff is shaped both to deflate and to sublate the extremes of both positions in the image of Tuff's frozen tears, which, perhaps not unintentionally, recalls the frozen tears at the end of Canto XXX of Dante's *Inferno*.[64] Tuff's tears are those of a hero, who, while tragically placed in Hell, is admired as sufficiently exemplary as to transfigure Hell. And Hell is where O'Flaherty's history begins, in images of cannibalism that also tacitly recall Canto XXX. Cartier is cited for having mused that Labrador was 'the land God gave to Cain,' which in the *Inferno* is the first division of the ninth circle of Hell, where betrayers of the family are placed. Posed against these early images are 'lies,' which anticipate later sentimentalizing of the colony. While the story of cannibalism may have been true, its inclusion in the general history of brutality adds to what is finally dismissed as prompted for the most part by 'superciliousness.' Sentiment is similarly marked by an inability to see soundly. What both positions lack is the clarity of true knowledge or, to use Frye's word, *gnosis*, which is knowledge based on the real as adequately and intelligently apprehended. Such knowledge in the comic plot is required to resolve false positions and to liberate the protagonists from positions of 'ritual bondage,'[65] as a result of which opinions are repeatedly expressed that deviate from the way things 'really are.' The valid position is expressed by a Synecdoche, in this instance 'the rock,' to which the protagonists are committed and which unifies the comic vision.[66] In this instance, the commitment to stoic values permits a proper and well-balanced perspective, which is the vision the narrator supports in the parable of Captain Tuff. This is the vision that reconciles the savage and the sentimental, and it is articulated in a style represented by that of George Cartwright, whose 'temper was even and sober, his eye fixed on the particular, his will dedicated to the common instincts: to endure and, if possible, succeed.'[67]

History, then, originates in ethics, and, in the play of darkness and the light that emerges in deadly serious comedy, intimates such larger comedies as those of Dante. The accumulation of trauma is not inscribed in specific moments of time, but rather in the force of those tempers that are shaped to survive a certain environment. Since the semantics of endings are already anticipated in such eighteenth-century figures as Cartwright, the protagonists are in fact avatars that diminish the necessity of finality. By the same token, moments of origin are not as significant in time as they are in human behaviour. Thus, historical beginning is attenuated as opinion: 'On 24 June 1497, John Cabot ... saw what most authorities think was the Newfoundland mainland.'[68] There is no certainty here, and the date simply serves as a catalyst. The beginnings are, first of all, discursive statements and, second, tales of horror and fantasy. The object of history is to find the truth, particularly as it bears upon human reality. But it is a truth enhanced by the strategies of fiction and amenable to transcendently signifying designs.

Continuity is a controlling idea in O'Flaherty, and we find it again in Tom Marshall's *Harsh and Lonely Land* (1979): his intent is to observe 'the development of certain Canadian and formal continuities,' since he perceives 'Canadian poetry as one evolving organism.' As White has argued, it is precisely the integrative function of Synecdoche that may be understood as organicism, and which is realized in the comic design.[69] Thus, while Marshall's text, as he says somewhat defensively, 'is not, strictly speaking, a history of Canadian poetry,' he, nevertheless, 'proceeded chronologically,' and there is a plot. It operates in four phases, beginning with those to whom he refers in the title of Part I as 'half-breeds,' who are the pioneers, and moving toward the modernists and the inheritors, concluding with poet-novelists of Part IV, who 'quest into darkness.' In a sense the order is not so much progressive as chiastic in which the pioneers form a frame with the later questers. Within the frame the second group 'rejected vociferously the lingering influence of the Confederation school,' and their work is dialectically developed 'by the inheritors and assimilators' of the third group.[70] The plot may thus be schematized: A–B:(B)–(A). It is a pattern that is at once integrative and organic. It also anticipates, as I shall argue, the order of comedy.

Not unlike other histories of English-Canadian writing, Marshall's text is quick to locate space as the dominant element, a space which is translated into a structural relationship by reading it as 'an obsession ... with enclosure and openness.' When time is raised, it is placed in the context of A.J.M. Smith's 'dictum that Canadian poets ought to pay more attention to their position in it.' As Marshall goes on to observe, however, time is to be understood here as 'the new technical directions of current British and American poetry.' But just as space is construed as a part of a binary opposition, culture is marked by a 'thoroughly Canadian double-vision.'[71] Thus a number of themes are raised within this matrix: half-breed, fact and dream, heaven and hell, native and foreign, myth and reality, Apollonian and Dionysian, combined with male and female. All of these oppositions are summed up in a metaphor we have already seen in Waterston, namely, that of Sheila Watson's (1909–98) double hook.[72] The image constitutes 'the world's ultimate mystery,' and while a preoccupation with such ambivalence is Canadian, the corresponding preoccupation is to overcome ambivalence in a *coincidentia oppositorum*. Thus, the canon is marked by texts that manifest both the play of opposition and synthetic ordering. The champion of finding coherence in ambivalence is Al Purdy (1918–2000), who 'articulates both isolation and connectedness.' Following Dennis Lee (1939–) and Robin Mathews (1931–), Marshall hails Purdy as 'the first Canadian poet to embody both Canadians' sense of themselves groping in space and their confused questing for a mode of existence different from both the European and the American *in a wholly appropriate form.*'[73]

Purdy's groping is couched in a reference to Heraclitus by which Marshall reminds us of the most famous aspect of his thought, that is, the idea of 'flux and flow' which he finds characteristic of both 'Canadian space' and the Canadian 'problem of identity,' which Purdy's poetry transcends.[74] Although Marshall does not pursue the overture to Heraclitus, it should be observed that Heraclitus believed also that the flow of things, an idea attributed to him by Plato, was in fact a war of oppo-

sites that possessed a unity in the idea of the logos occasionally represented by God.[75] Such knowledge would have served Marshall's
argument. As he himself observes, implicitly following Lionel Stevenson, the play of oppositions reflects both the reality and appearance of
things in the world which 'in Canadian poets ... [is] an essentially religious longing for unity with the world.'[76] Beneath the appearance, then,
of oppositions, a harmonious unity is inferred,[77] and in Marshall it is
posited as a 'holy, or "fabled," city.'[78] Such an image departs from Heraclitus, owing more to the notion of the heavenly Jerusalem that emerges
from the vision of the Apocalypse. Temporal or perhaps secular incoher-
ence is only the phenomenal flux that must be entered in order to reach
the place of harmony among peoples, which, needless to say, is the
achievement of the comic order.

Removing Borders

As I shall indicate later, one of the problems of literary history in
Canada is its mimetic reflex of a larger cultural problem, which is the
disinterest manifested by the dominant ethnic communities toward the
Other. They are deeply marked by closure and exclusion. As an effort to
make 'a bridge of sorts.'[79] Clément Moisan's *Poésie des frontières* (1979)
represents the first careful attempt to find a way to interrelate the francophone and anglophone poetry of twentieth-century Canada into a
coherent history, following in the path of such pioneers as Lareau, Mac-
Mechan, and Pierce. The title itself calls attention to the question of
exclusion, and in doing so touches upon a central theme of English-
Canadian writing, at least, which Marshall McLuhan summed up in the
title of an essay called 'Canada: The Borderline Case.'[80] For Moisan the
border is the sign of ambiguity, for the line of exclusion is also the place
of encountering the Other.[81] As Moisan goes on to argue, borders are
everywhere in the Canadian and Québécois sensibility, and thus it
becomes a metaphor that controls the structure of the book and the
implied sense of history that emerges from it.

The structure is a kind of Hegelian triadic formation. Poetry in Canada since the 1930s has followed a pattern that begins with gestures of
clandestiny, and then moves to a higher level of consciousness and
performance in a poetry of resistance that finally issues in liberation.
Each movement implies the overcoming of various kinds of barriers
that belong to the difficulty of being in Canada, and therefore imply
that history is where the ontological unfolds into an increasing pleni-

tude. Moisan constructs history as a series of ruptures and moments of *prise de conscience* that give it the dynamic shape it acquires. This is a sense of history he shares with Baillargeon and other francophone historians for whom historical moments are where its semantics are to be found. Everything begins, then, with a '*tournant décisif*' that occurred sometime in the 1930s, during the moment of modernity in English Canada and the period of 'les grands aînés' in Quebec. Because, as Moisan knows, Canada has at least two histories, moments of rupture only coincide accidentally; and thus, while certain decades may move in a parallel manner, as in the 1960s for example, continuous coincidence must be based upon textual analogies.[82] Consequently, the two poetries retain the ambiguous relationship that Moisan's initial sense of border asserts.

A central, shared theme is that of the garrison mentality, first raised by Frye in his Conclusion to Klinck's first edition of *Literary History of Canada*. Consistent with the ambiguity of the border, the garrison mentality is at once that of the keeper and the kept. The garrison excludes by holding those inside in a state of colonial inhibition. The two literary systems, however, worked within discourses that raise differing preoccupations. The inward turn in francophone poetry, announced in Saint-Denys Garneau, was later powerfully enhanced by the inscription of surrealism. English-Canadian modernism announced itself by the turn taken against the late-romanticism of the Victorian period. Thus, while the use of language differed, there was a similarity of effect. In the initial phase, the garrison is projected as a psychological condition that reflects a social order, and 'le lieu clos, la maison fermée, la prison, les geôles' are dominant images that guide the reader through the closure of the subject, a 'retour sur soi, mais sans promesse de départ vers le monde.' The difference between the first moment and the second lies in the fact that the latter, as exemplified by Irving Layton (1912–), 'n'est pas cachottière, ni refuge, ni abri; elle est oeuvre d'agression et d'opposition. Elle offre une résistance ... à un monde irrémédiablement voué à son propre anéantissement.' In other words, it refused to look upon the garrison as mortal protector. Although the direction set for resistance came in English Canada from the poets clustered about the *McGill Fortnightly Review* (1925–7), the decisive moment did not occur in Quebec until the appearance of Borduas's *Refus global.* For the sake of historical coherence, however, he argues that the poetry of resistance emerges in both literatures after the Second World War. The third moment of liberation, perceptible in the poetry of the 1970s, seeks the liberation of mankind 'dans son existence politique, mais aussi dans sa mentalité et sa conception de la vie. En récuperant l'essentiel de la poésie antérieur, la nouvelle lui donné une dimension plus large, embrassant l'homme entier, surtout l'homme intérieur.'[83]

Thus, Moisan's history ends in a sublation of plenitude which, in its contemporary forms, marks a 'retour à soi' in which the borders of death and solitude are opened, and one is permitted 'un retour en arrière dans le temps, à l'enfance du monde et celle du poète.' The coincidence of this view in a general way with that of Harrison and Marshall and more particularly Jones at the end of *Butterfly on Rock* is not exactly fortuitous in light of the frequent overtures made to Jones's own meditations on the garrison mentality. The two communities, according to Moisan, reach these 'first days of Creation' by differing routes: 'l'une doit sortir du songe, du monde irréel, pour rattraper la vie; l'autre doit abattre ces barrières qui séparent du réel, qu'il faut comprendre et assumer.' The former is the route of French Canada; the latter, of English Canada. Both arrive, however, at a point where they can overcome 'l'impossibilité de vivre,' the difficulty of being.[84] As Moisan emphasizes in his Conclusion, this takes place 'dans l'Histoire, avec un grand H,'[85] which carries a special explanatory force. As a result, History is constructed as the central barrier that prevents Canada and Quebec from emerging from the dead hand of the past. In order to be, History must be encountered and overcome, a gesture which corresponds to Jones's 'sacrificial view of life.'[86] To live, death (History) must be endured.

I hesitate to call this a 'renaissance' construction of history, for Moisan is arguing that Canada is simply emerging from death and non-being in the discourse of contemporary poetry. In this sense, it is a remarkably ambiguous use of history that understands it as the necessary explanation of how things are, which is a French-Canadian perception of history, and the place from which escape must eventually take place. As a number of English-Canadian histories imply, such a leap is the desired end of literature. While it is not an ending in Apocalypse, it is an ending in the promised land of the spirit, a kind of compromise between two ideologies, intimating Moses leading his people back from the History of Egypt into another, timeless world of plenitude, echoing the argument of Grandpre's history in a certain fashion. The plot follows the order of comedy and, as I have intimated, it is Hegelian in its structure. The history it subtends ends in a movement of transcendence by which it escapes from itself. As White remarks of Hegel's structure of history, '*The necessity of every civilization's ultimate destruction* by its own hand is sublimated into an apprehension of that civilization's institutions and modes of life as only means, abstract modes of organization, by which its ideal ends are realized.' The best that could happen, then, to Canada and Quebec would be to overcome their mutual origin in the dead metaphor of the garrison, where both experienced the repression of colonization in various degrees, and come to an end in Being. Origins and endings coherently and paradoxically relate. If the origin is to exist, drawing upon an expression of special power in French Canada, 'replié sur soi,' the end is a 'retour à soi' in the moment before history begins.[87]

Acadian Ironies

Origins for Marshall may be located in 'the incongruity [of] Canadian subject-matter and English Romantic-Victorian poetic idiom,' an opposition capable, nevertheless, of finding resolution in an 'American language.' As the subtitle of Marguerite Maillet's *Histoire de la littérature acadiennne* (1983) asserts, Acadia is a movement 'de rêve en rêve.' The dream of the past is brought into phase with the dream of the present by always remaining Acadian. Dream, therefore, is the controlling word that would connect 'nation' and narrative. It is hope, and it is a sign of the *pays imaginaire* (back cover) and a *pays fictif*, a country invented by fiction and faith. Earlier, I suggested that history may be likened to a speech act, and in the instance of Maillet it may be suggested that hers could be considered an illocutionary act, expressing a certain intention.[88] To move, however, from dream to dream is not to realize a dream, and thus Maillet's history does not, as Lortie's, announce 'une patrie concrète.'[89] It is a history of virtuality, and it operates in three major phases – 'du rêve à la réalité,' 'sur les chemins de l'histoire,' and 'sous le signe du souvenir' – each of which serves as a title for parts 1 to 3. This first movement is divided into two pivotal chapters, one addressing the promised land (1604–1754), and the other reflecting upon a paradise lost (1755–1866). The function of history and folklore (the second part) is to write the history of a people. All of Acadia's history reaches a kind of conclusion in 1955, two hundred years after the trauma of 'le grand dérangement' in the 'Cantate du bicentenaire de la Déportation' of Napoléon-P. Landry. After his poem, 'les auteurs acadiens, en général, vont se tourner vers des préoccupations ou plus universelles ou plus actuelles.'[90]

Because Maillet's text is a regional history, it poses some of the same problems as that of Harrison and O'Flaherty: the term 'literature' must be broad enough in its connotations to include history, folklore, oratory, the letters of missionaries, and journalism. Since the region is Acadia, it must also contend with the consequences of the deportation and slow return, which left a large gap of silence in the history. Finally, because its status as a colony was never recovered politically, the history of its culture poses questions about its difficulty of being unlike other regions and provinces. Thus, the moment of the deportation is a trauma that cannot be properly exorcised. Sovereignty is not a viable option, and the lack of provincial boundaries dissipates a sense of 'national' territory. An existence in space, so dear, for example, to anglophone cultural history, is, therefore, unclear; an existence in time appears only available, as the subtitle suggests, as dream and fiction, as an imagined country. Thus, it is appropriate that Maillet's story of origins is ambiguous. Acadia's beginning is 'un grand rêve français.' In Marc Lescarbot's *Histoire de la Nouvelle-France*, published remarkably in 1609, it is asserted that New France is a complex of myths in which Acadia, Eden, and the Promised Land are superimposed.[91] Needless to say, Lescarbot could not have known that he was unwittingly providing a metanarrative that was to be enacted a century and a half later, a story patterned on both the Fall and the period of bondage in Egypt that would return the Hebrews to the land of their dreams. The story is further complicated by the fact that Lescarbot's use of 'Eden' would have been a sign of paradise alone, just as his use of 'Promised Land' would have corresponded to the promise fulfilled. Before 1755 Acadia was Eden before the Fall and after the return. At the beginning, all hopes are already fulfilled and, as in Eden, time has not begun. Acadia's period as a colony, then, is constructed as dream, threshold, prehistory, in a word, an unrealized project. The failure of the project is partly blamed upon French ineptitude as colonial administrators, and partly on Thomas Pichon's role as a double agent in the fall of Fort Beauséjour (1755). The use, therefore, of France as a point of departure is itself ambiguous. France legitimizes the French culture of Acadia, on the one hand, and, on the other hand, is perceived as one of the reasons why, in a clever pun, 'le rêve a été crevé.' This ambiguity permits the inference that the deportation was a Fortunate Fall in which trauma and *prise de conscience* coincide. Taken together, they assist in the composition of the history's plot 'de l'enthousiasme à l'exil, à l'isolement, puis à la lutte pour la survie dans un paradis perdu, et finalement à des revendications en faveur d'une vie à part entière dans un pays à nommer.' Such a plot, like that of Quebec, contradicts Perkins's assertion that history always originates in either an ascent or a descent.[92] As I have suggested, enthusiasm is not only tempered, but also prehistory becomes a motivating instance. The descent, which appears the true beginning, is also ambiguous: it is a fall that instigates a rise in which no movement 'forward' is possible without a return to the cause.[93]

It is significant, however, that the construction of Acadia as a nation with a unified plot was not the work of its long attestation of oral literature whose principle theme was love. Only 'l'écrite veillera à ce que les Acadiens n'oublient pas les événements de 1755, et elle nourrira un mythe créé, par un étranger, autour d'une héroïne de la dispersion.' The reference is, of course, to Henry Longfellow's 'Evangeline' (1849), translated into French by Pamphile Le May (1870), the historical veracity of which has been contested. As Ernest Martin argues, it provided the 'souffle nécessaire' that brought a dying dream new life.[94] Nor was it alone, but it gives fair evidence that oral traditions may not be sufficient to lift a distinct culture to collective consciousness, and without the intervention of the literary institution cultures lose semantic weight. Thus, literary history itself is primarily engaged in both the ordering of testimonial texts and investing them with a sense that often exceeds their individual presence. It actualizes collective self-knowledge by 'showing' how self-knowledge is made.[95]

In this instance, self-knowledge, the function of successive *prises de conscience* in its awareness of the meaning of the French regime, the enactment of British imperial policy, and the construction of Acadian myths by non-Acadians, makes the *prise de conscience* itself the place of cultural contestation. To announce a movement from dream to dream is to demonstrate perfect awareness that, while Acadia is a nation yet to be named, it is still primarily an imaginative construction. The lost country and the found people coincide, as Dyane Léger remarks, in 'l'Imaginaire ... le plus pur du réel,' an assertion that concludes the final chapter. Nevertheless, the development of events in time is not neglected, and this is because of the way the notion of struggle is inscribed into the plot. It is not a struggle with the environment, the leitmotif of anglophone cultural history but, paradoxically, with a people that would sing of love. Acadia is the result of conscious, didactic gestures that would reconstitute loss, and the years 1864, 1867, and 1881 (the Confederation Period elsewhere) marked 'les débuts d'une renaissance en Acadie – premier collège, premier journal, première convention nationale.'[96] The dates signify the act of recovery and, therefore, differing from anglophone practice, do not disappear behind the construction of continuity. Self-engendering occurs metonymically, each event prompting another.

The implications of metonymy are significant for, as White argues, events do not merely happen in such a paradigm, they are, rather, caused, and frequently by agencies beyond our control.[97] Belief in such a paradigm removes from one a sense of agency and prompts a corresponding feeling of the subject as victim. At the end of Maillet's history, despite efforts of contestation in the 1960s and 1970s, Acadia still finds itself, like Quebec, bearing witness to a certain 'difficulté d'être.'[98] The dream is incapable of achieving realization. The space between the desire and the reality possesses all the characteristics of irony as a trope that White attributes to its emergence from Metonymy. It evokes Frye's phase of 'unrelieved bondage,'[99] in this instance bondage to a past that at once traumatizes and instigates self-realization, which leaves contemporary Acadians in a contradictory and colonized situation.[100] The mention of such a situation, however, only serves to confirm the manner in which the colony's beginnings are constructed between the two grand images of Promised Land and Paradise Lost, marking a kind of permanent irony informing the cultural history of Acadia, which at once constructs and confirms the irony it would overcome.

It used to be commonly accepted that the name 'Acadia' derived from the word 'Arcadia,' the name Verrazzano gave to Kitty Hawk, North Carolina, in 1524.[101] The maps that Champlain had at his disposal simply dropped the 'r' and extended its range to include Nova Scotia, New Brunswick, and part of Maine. Another explanation holds that the word may be derived from the Algonquian language.[102] Needless to say, for the sake of unity Maillet's history retains an ethnic focus: 'Acadia' is a geographical place where Acadians lived, left, and returned. If the word is indigenous, a larger irony is unwittingly inscribed into Maillet's history, for all North American colonies, whether subsequently colonized or not, were initially colonizing. Thus the concluding sentence of the book, asserting the 'Acadian' 'désir de vivre pleinement chez lui, en Acadie'[103] is, to put it mildly, embarrassing, and Maillet's silence on this point while addressing the silence of (francophone) Acadians captures the moral dilemma which lies at the heart of those Canadian cultural histories that aspire to national construction. They always speak of aspirations which, enclosed by linguistic and ethnic preoccupations, cannot be realized in isolation. For this reason, as I shall argue later, the Balkanization of culture which lies at the heart of Canadian history explains the shared 'difficulty of being' that all the ethnic communities which constitute the country suffer from.

Writing Memory

In some respects, Françoise Van Roey-Roux's *La Littérature intime du Québec* (1983) appears free of these claims. As a study of kinds of self-construction, relations toward other ethnic groups are not primarily at issue; they are, however, implied. As she notes in her Introduction, the writing of the subject relies upon the fact that 'la mémoire du groupe est le plus sûr garant de la mémoire individuelle.' Collective memory has a number of functions. It is the means by which the group coheres, especially since its earliest formation. It is also the surest obstacle to change, for change is the sign of a loss of cohesion and an act of aggression that manifests itself as progress. Consequently, 'la vie à la campagne est le rempart contre le mal.' It also constitutes protection against the menace of assimilation. Thus, this kind of literature not only constructs a subject but also traces and enshrines the life of a particular ethnic community. The subject is the sign of the collective. Although one might infer that such writing is a kind of fiction which blurs borders between fiction and non-fiction,[104] this is an issue that remains unexamined in Roey-Roux who assumes, with the troublesome exception of the memoir, that she is addressing 'un témoignage direct sur une vie.' To define the genre, then, requires certain exclusions, such as poetry, autobiographical novels, travel journals, because there must be a clear relationship between 'l'auteur réal' and 'celui dont le nom s'étale largement sur la couverture.' The genre so defined permits 'l'histoire vivante de la nation,' which accords with the general desire of those who write memoirs, which is to leave behind 'un héritage culturel.'[105]

Because of the emphasis on the private as a reflection of the public life of the community, certain questions of history, ideology, and gender arise.[106] Given the author's definitions, nothing in New France is pertinent. Because of the general agreement that Jean-Jacques Rousseau's *Confessions* (1782) represents the beginning of the vogue of intimacy,[107] the point of departure is 1760. The ideology of Jansenism played, furthermore, an inhibiting role in a society that frequently echoed Pascal's dictum that 'le moi est haïssable.' As a consequence, autobiography was not a major genre before 1960. Finally, before 1950 women rarely revealed themselves in print, and not until the 1970s were their stories told in increasing numbers.[108] One can only conclude from this that the cover illustration, showing a young woman in modest décolleté in a wicker chair reading what appears to be a letter, is semiotically designed to suggest a coherence between intimacy, women, and the erotic. Nothing could farther from the truth. The writings of men dominate the text, and the preference in private diaries and memoirs is for the public life.

Roey-Roux's general method is, for the most part, a structuralist one. 'Intimate literature' is divided into generic categories that distinguish the diary from the memoir, and autobiography from a *souvenir*. The study concludes with a chapter on letter-writing that avoids theoretical distinctions and simply provides a survey of collections. The distinctions rest upon questions of point of view, particularly how the narrator is positioned with respect to time and whether the narrator prefers the public to the private world. They are further distinguished by their themes. For example, the diary frequently turns upon war, religion, and prison experiences, whereas the memoir is characterized by its accent upon professional life, particularly that of politics. Because of the decision to theorize the problem, as well as to provide certain chronologies, her history is, in fact, several histories which constitute archaeologies of private life. The author, then, is less interested in using her text as a means of constructing a coherent life of the community, which is a shared goal of national histories, than theorizing the varieties of ways in which it can be done within a specific genre. One of the consequences of this procedure is that history does not appear so much as a linear unfolding of events than as a complex of intersecting trajectories in which periods and dates are assigned different semantic burdens according to the relation to the various types of writing examined. Thus the memoir, which thematizes the political life, is found frequently after 1791, the year in which French Canada in the British regime enjoyed its initial measure of political mobility as a result of the Constitutional Act.[109] Personal diaries, because of their interest, for example, in war, are clustered around the years of the American Revolution, the Rebellion of 1837–8, the Metis uprisings in the Northwest, and the two world wars. Autobiography, by contrast, is most common after 1960 for ideological reasons. The *souvenir*, 'le récit d'un fait isolé de la vie de l'auteur,'[110] overlaps thematically with some of the other types in its interest in the recollection of a military exploit, a professional testimony, and a reflection upon a childhood experience. It too has its preferred moments: the collective *souvenir* was popular at the turn of the century and since the 1960s has recovered its former prestige; the recollection of childhood has been in vogue since the turn of the century.[111]

Because such types as Roey-Roux examines have their own moments, and therefore correspond to the norms of generic mutability within a hierarchy,[112] history becomes plural or is structured semantically at different levels. It is also subordinated to literary kinds and appears to lose its unifying force. The function of the literary type is to give history its meaning, rather than vice versa. Thus, the emphasis particularly on a linear plot is minimalized; and although history is sequenced in each chapter, its design is constantly adjusted to meet generic requirements. Thus origin is not so much 1760 as 1782, the year of Rousseau's *Confessions*. This does not mean that gestures toward a sense of the nation are not made, as they are in the Introduction and elsewhere. For example, commenting on the rise of the *souvenir* in the 1960s after a period of dormancy, the author enquires: 'Faut-il y voir une forme de nationalisme?' But national heritage is inscribed in the genre as whole, and one is prompted to assert that such questions are subordinate to the issues the genre raises. The abrupt ending reinforces such a position. There is no concluding chapter. Rather, she ends in a question concerning the inclusions of letters at the end of an author's collected works. If the formula of such inclusion, she opines, 'offre fréquemment le mérite d'éclairer l'oeuvre, elle devient en soi une tentative de démystifier le personnage officiel, de le faire descendre de son socle. N'est-ce pas d'ailleurs le même désir, généralement inconscient, qui attire autant de lecteurs vers les autobiographies et toute autre forme de la littérature intime?'[113] Such a conclusion is based primarily upon literature as part of a communications model. It may have themes that summon the national, but these are themes that are to be understood as part of a theory. They are not rewritten into the structure of the argument. Gestures, finally, do not carry the force of organization as nationalism does in Lortie, and the impulses toward history as salvation appear at this moment to be distinctly dampened.

The other histories published in the decade from 1973 to 1983, however, share in an effort to overcome the constraints of history and articulate, for the most part, a comic vision of the future. We may attribute such emplotments to the various moments of energy arising from the preceding decade, such as the flush of federalism that hung over the centennial celebrations of 1967 and the nationalism that acquired renewed intensity in Quebec as a consequence of the War Measures

Act's being invoked in 1970. Such contexts are appropriate for both Lortie and Moisan, and both authors seek varieties of freedom from traumas of the past. The gestures are not entirely new, however, but elaborations, rather, upon themes I have already noted in earlier chapters. Quebec's autonomy is a perennial preoccupation, and efforts to draw the two charter cultures together may be remarked in as early as Lareau. Harrison's history may be related to that of McCourt, except for the fact that Harrison's does not share his sense of failure. Moreover, Harrison is quick to argue that the West may be taken as a microcosm of English Canada, thus enhancing the significance of its literature. Such a claim is validated by the fact that he shares with other anglophone literary historians a shared desire, in this instance a desire to understand the history of western Canada as a search for deliverance from history. O'Flaherty's history might also be passed over as regionalism except for its belief that Newfoundland represents an idea of the nation, and especially a nation that endures under apocalyptic conditions, marking a kinship with both Harrison's West and Marshall's Canada. Maillet's Acadia, finally, exists as a nation of the mind that derives its contemporary self-awareness from the renewal of intensity around autonomy in Quebec, for it has become increasingly evident that the Acadians have been left to fend for themselves. It is a history of national aspiration that is constructed to lead toward a salvation that is forever frustrated. What is desired, echoing Moisan somewhat, are 'the first days of Creation,' a desire that motivated the repeated 'lutte pour la survie dans un paradis perdu.'[114] With the exception of Roey-Roux, all these historians are exercised in some manner by such a struggle.

CHAPTER SIX

Autonomy, Literature, and the National, 1991–

Qui dit temps dit également identité et conscience.[1]

As we have had frequent occasion to remark, literary histories carry the mark of their period of gestation with them. The ambitious multi-volume *La Vie littéraire au Québec* (1991–), under the general editorship of Maurice Lemire, and since Volume 3 co-edited with Denis Saint-Jacques, not only represents fully the developments in literary theory that took place in the 1980s in North America, Europe, and Israel, but also in many respects it may be considered a summa of the tendencies of most literary histories of Quebec. Because the first volume appeared some four years after the defeat of the Meech Lake Accord, one might surmise that the debates held around it may have furnished part of its historical context.[2] Given, however, the limitations of the Accord, its appeal to those who sought a genuine autonomy for Quebec was minimal.[3] A more accurate context for this history would be the developments in literary theory that form its operative assumptions. In that respect it constitutes the most significant contribution to the study of literary history yet attained in this country and, in doing so, responds to many of the issues left unfinished, particularly those raised by Grandpré's history.

The guiding approach taken to literature in Grandpré's history was designed both to foreground the reader and to embed the question of reception into the assumptions of phenomenology. As Peter Uwe Hohendahl has persuasively argued, the various reader-response theories, including those of Wolfgang Iser that are clearly grounded in phenomenolgy, cannot, finally, 'mediate between the linguistic-literary and the social realms.'[4] For Hohendahl the significant solution to the aporias of reception theory are provided by the theory of the literary institution, which draws both production and reception into a larger whole. It would address the conditions of reading and writing, examine the conditions systematically, clarify the relation of the literary institution to other kinds of institutional activity, and finally 'historical specificity [would] be taken into consideration.'[5] Lemire's history is the fullest answer to the problems raised by previous francophone histories, and it readily satisfies the conditions that Hohendahl outlines.[6] Expressed as simply as this, however, it is difficult to acquire an understanding of the complexity of the task, but we are fortunate in the case of this history to have records of the discussions that it prompted.

The title, '*La Vie littéraire*,' states immediately and precisely the theoretical distance this history has taken in respect of other literary histories produced in Canada. It signifies the position of the Centre de recherche en littérature québécoise (hereafter CRELIQ) as a research team, and what is striking is the manner in which the guiding methodologies are drawn into the history and the questions they raise. The main approach was developed through a careful study of the several lines of thought that converge in what Itamar Even-Zohar calls polysystem theory, which construes literature as a site of several systems that constitute it as a 'champ' to use Pierre Bourdieu's term. Clément Moisan, a member of the team, defines the polysystem as 'cette relation entre les deux systèmes de la *vie textuelle* ... et de la *vie anthropo-sociale*.' As a consequence, *La Vie littéraire au Québec* would appear not to be so much a history as a description of various kinds of interaction between discursive practices. By necessity, however, it constructs history as 'un *campo di tensioni*.'[7] The tensions configure the play of the systems, which, however, become history as they extend over time.

Because the emphasis is upon the *life* of literature, Lemire's history appears to be at once a narrative and an encyclopedia, to use Perkins's distinction. Thus the initial sentence of the *Présentation*, repeated in each subsequent volume, announces that '*La Vie littéraire au Québec* est d'abord conçue comme un outil de référence à caractère scientifique.' It makes the assumption that the reader can then make use of it encyclopedically. Nevertheless, each volume has a narrative that can be traced, and it must be surmised that all the volumes together will carry a larger plot that subsumes the individual parts.[8] As a consequence, 'l'histoire littéraire du Québec devrait se lire non comme un axe continu, allant de la production à la réception, mais plutôt comme une spirale où le mouvement lui-même est facteur de changement.'[9] Like Alberto Aso Rosa's *Letteratura italiana*, however, which is conceived in the same vein, it serves many purposes, and theory, as I have remarked, plays a deep role in both plot construction and design.

Certain terms need explication before an understanding of the theory can be obtained, and these are, notably, 'beginning,' 'margin,' 'field,' 'autonomy,' 'institution,' and 'opposition.' Although these terms are variously raised as part of the spiral of the history's plot, it is more useful to discuss them in the order proposed. As we have observed already, the point of departure is not only decisive, but also determinant of the sense of what follows. The beginning is also profoundly polysemous. It appears to be located in the past, while also being located in the present of the history as it is constructed. Primarily, however, it is a shaping conception of the whole. Edward Said remarks that 'a beginning suggests either *(a)* a time, *(b)* a place, *(c)* an object, *(d)* principle, or *(e)* an act—in short, detachment of the sort that establishes distance and difference between either *a, b, c, d,* or *e,* on the one hand and what came before it on the other.'[10]

In the history of Quebec, the beginning can range from Cartier's sightings in 1534 to nothing at all, if we are to take Lord Durham's assertion concerning Quebec's lack of history seriously. A beginning in the first instance might address the colonizing activities of a foreign power, at least from an Aboriginal perspective. A beginning in the second instance would be a construction *ex nihilo*, which has its transcendental and essentializing attractions to which Garneau in a certain sense succumbed. He chose two beginnings, which ranged from the failed French 'discovery' and settlement of North America (1534–44) to the more permanent creation of New France in 1603. This was the dominant invented tradition as the nineteenth century chose to conceive it, and it endured certainly as long as Louis Hémon's *Maria Chapdelaine* (1914), in which the famous assertion occurs, namely: 'Nous sommes venus il y a trois cent ans, et nous sommes restés.' Its intertextual echo is in Félix-Antoine Savard's *Menaud Maître-Draveur* (1937), beginning as the epigraph to chapter one, and inscribed into one of the more exceptional examples of 'le roman de la fidélité.'[11] A beginning, then, is always somewhere between the imagination of the historian and novelist as a moment and an act in time and space.

The authors of this history chose 1764 as a point of departure. The separation that the beginning constructs makes New France a French responsibility and the Conquest is viewed briefly and at a certain distance through the expression 'la défaite de l'armée française.' If the early documents have any value, one might say it is primarily because they belong to a discourse of difference that separates a *Canadien* from a *Français*.[12] As we have seen already, such a beginning was also chosen notably by both Roy and Baillargeon, and the sense of it resides not only in the difference that can be drawn between colony and nation but also, as I shall indicate, in the manner by which a literary institution acquires self-awareness and develops a history for itself.

Beginning so is a gesture that inscribes itself into the discourse of literary history as post-colonial critique. Thus Durham must be exorcized because of the charge that French Canada is without history, for to be without history is to be without existence. The post-colonial response is to confer existence by appropriating one's own history. A central struggle, then, that must be articulated is the relation of margin to centre, for a discourse in the process of acquiring agency is produced by the sense of itself as a centre. Thus a notion of la Nouvelle-France is retained as national heritage in order to write against the margin that its literature left behind: 'Cet heritage sera donc gardé et progressivement intégré, mais tout le mouvement qui constitue une littérature autonome travaillera à cette transformation d'une littérature marginale en littérature canadienne, puis québécoise.'[13] The first volume, then, is designed to pose a struggle on two fronts, first with France and subsequently with England. Far from exalting the position of France before the Conquest, the text emphasizes the negative characteristics of dependence and poverty a colony endures, which was a situation that did not change immediately after the Treaty of Paris. Indeed, one of the effects of the Conquest was to exaggerate the difference between the remaining French nobility and the francophone Canadian settlers. The former, just as the clergy would later do, were quite ready to manifest their allegiance to British rule.

The argument of colonial domination, furthermore, is the primary situation of the political *champ* developed by each volume. In volume I the argument is developed along several lines beginning with the arrival of the British, and the composite of approaches is designed to clear a space for a literary *champ* that consists of a struggle between the new arrivals (the later *Canadiens*) and the French and English. The field is not, however, an order of historical events; it is, rather, layers of interests that continually intersect, beginning in school curricula, moving through the field of production and reception, and including the changes that occurred in Europe during the seventeenth and eighteenth centuries in respect of the function of literature.[14] The field, then, addresses both the conditions in which literature emerges and those who are responsible for the emergence and the changes it undergoes.

As it is used by Lemire and his associates, the term derives, at least, from Bourdieu. It is what is meant by the term *vie* in the title, which is borrowed from the heritage of Russian Formalism in the expression *literaturnyj byt*.[15] The complexity of the term '*champ*' as Bourdieu uses it cannot be encompassed with either a brief description or quotation, but, as he develops it, for example, in his article, 'The Field of Cultural Production,' we can observe that it is a site of continuous struggle in which the whole notion of literature and its social function is continually assuming different shapes and values. Borrowed from the science of electromagnetism, the metaphor of the field consists of agents who play the role of several lines of interacting forces and tensions that shape cultural products for use.[16] The agents are not only producers (writers), but also all those who are involved in the control, transmission, interpretation, and 're-production,' of the text, that is, to borrow an obvious industrial model, all those from inventors, makers, managers, advertisers, salespeople, and consumers who are involved in the production, let us say, of automobiles. The field of cultural production is an economy which, as it acquires autonomy, that is, the ability to regulate its own modes of behaviour, operates like the larger market, with the exception that the avant-garde ('the field of restricted production') measures success in an inverse ratio to economic profit.[17] The avant-garde produces symbolic capital, rather than economic capital, which belongs to the domain of 'bourgeois art,' that is, bestsellers. The distinction is central to Bourdieu's theory, just as it is to CRELIQ, for it is the avant-garde, for the most part, that produces the historically new.

A fundamental difference, then, between Grandpré's history and this one is that while both derive from sociological theory, *La Vie littéraire au Québec* understands history more broadly by including the frame of economic conditions. The field is traced as a site in which the literature of Quebec accumulates symbolic capital, but, insofar as it does, it can always be summoned as a powerful cultural witness, which is precisely how it is brought to bear in this history. The plot, then, turns upon the question of empowerment, which is at once a post-colonial and national theme. As Bourdieu argues, the primary function of literary history is one of mapping the field, that is, of 'constructing the space of positions and the space of position-takings [*prises-de-position*] in which they are expressed.'[18] '*La Vie littéraire*' is a kind of self-reflexive title that reflects its own operation in taking a position in the field. Autonomy thus becomes both the argument and its demonstration on the level of plot. Finally, the argument began to take shape prior to the history, during its own prehistory so to speak, largely in the work of Lemire, Denis Saint-Jacques, Clément Moisan, and Lucie Robert.

The notion of the autonomous field is developed most clearly in the conference papers of Saint-Jacques, especially in the use made of Bourdieu's work for the research of CRELIQ. Adaptation was necessary because of the limitations in the theory of the literary field, permitting an overture to the notion of institution as developed in Jacques Dubois's *L'Institution de la littérature: Introduction à une sociologie* (1978). The problem with Bourdieu, according to Saint-Jacques, is the centrality of the market and the fact that the notion of the *champ* tends to obscure significant aspects of the institution, notably the role of agents and the function of praxis in literary evolution. In fact, the latter is given a particular emphasis: 'Sans l'habitus [praxis] l'institution reste lettre morte dotée d'un pouvoir tout aussi exorbitant qu'inexplicable. Sans l'habitus, l'institution se fige et l'histoire objectivée en elle se mue en loi transcendente. Sans l'habitus, s'estompent les agents, leurs trajectoires diverses et le marché sur lequel ils sont engagés.' Furthermore, from a literary perspective, the suitability of the institution for literary history is not only unquestionable, but also seems the only appropriate way to contain the unpredictability of the market. Nevertheless, as Saint-Jacques argues, the use of the institution carries a price: 'la forme de définition socio-historique de la littérature qui permet le mieux de tenir comte, *tout en les secondarisant*, de ses marchés et de leur structure spécifique.'[19]

The problem with the institution is that it can be turned more toward 'la stabilité sécuritaire des codes ... plutôt que vers les surprises des accidents des champs.' It is a temptation that any historian, aware of history as an accident-prone field, would wish to avoid, inasmuch as 'nous aimons mieux instituer des textes qu'interroger les lecteurs.' Life would be simpler, in a word, if it could be reduced to a canon. So it is that after appearing to substitute the institution for Bourdieu's field, Saint-Jacques returns to the latter's dynamism through the use of *habitus* which 'met en cause les dispositions acquises des agents, c'est-à-dire, dans le cas de la littérature, la formation scolaire linguistique.' Hence, by the end of his paper, he is able to pose a question, which, as it was responded to by *La Vie littéraire au Québec*, returns to the function of praxis: 'Ne devrions-nous pas plutôt étudier le marché de la littérature restreinte et le sort des habitus qui le détermine et, en contrepartie, nous intéresser à l'institution de la littérature de grande diffusion?' In other words, the sense of the institution depends upon a field constantly in motion through the effect of agents, *habitus*, and market, combining the best of institutional and field theory.[20]

At a conference held a year later, Saint-Jacques raised yet another question: 'Trouve-t-on des situations où la littérature ne joue pas le rôle d'enjeu aussi bien que d'arme dans les luttes pour l'hégémonie de la langue nationale?' Since the answer must be negative, literature can only be understood as partaking in some way of the national, and its history is homologous with the history of the nation in the continuous effort of literature to realize itself at least discursively. Other choices in the uses of literary texts are posed between the limits of writing as propaganda and escapism, and the struggle for control exists somewhere in between. The members of CRELIQ at an early stage chose to find the uniqueness of their research centre in one salient way: 'à établir l'existence d'une littérature et à vérifier le rôle qu'elle joue au plan national.' The first aspect of the plan was realized in the publication of the multi-volume *Dictionnaire des œuvres littéraires du Québec* (1976–). The second was the history of the acquisition of autonomy as manifest in this history. In order to do so, the first move, as we have seen, was toward Bourdieu whose own work, despite overtures toward European culture, is itself profoundly national in character. The major problem with Bourdieu as a guide, however, is not so much his emphasis on the market but the tendency toward understanding France as the centre, an idea which Saint-Jacques ironically repositions: 'Aux métropoles, la raison; aux formations subordonnées, l'exotisme!' It is an opposition which cannot be understood other than in a relation of dominant to dominated. Although he hesitates to accuse Bourdieu of imperialism *tout court*, occasional hints are given, opening the way toward a post-colonial understanding of Quebec's position in the global field of La Francophonie. Hence, the conflict that arranges the field of Québécois literary activity is one in which 'la littérature se fait dans un perpétuel conflit entre le national et le littéraire strict, si par là on entend les valeurs de modélisations venues de France.' The struggle, then, that characterizes the field is a struggle focussed primarily on the acquisition of autonomy, particularly in respect of French literature, recalling similar problems between the literature of English Canada and both Great Britain and the United States.[21]

Autonomy, however, as it is announced in Saint-Jacques's 1989 article, is 'Nationalisation et autonomisation,' a title in which it would be simple, upon first hearing, to substitute *est* for *et*. For Bourdieu, autonomization is the history of culture since the Renaissance, a history 'correlated with the constant growth of a public of potential consumers, of increasing social diversity, which guarantee the producers of symbolic goods minimal conditions of economic independence and, also, a competing principle of legitimacy.' It is a field governed by 'the specifically intellectual or artistic traditions handed down by their predecessors.' In an autonomous field, producers 'are also in a position to liberate their products from all external constraints, whether the moral censure and aesthetic programs of a proselytizing church or the academic controls and directives of political power, inclined to regard art as propaganda.'[22] Saint-Jacques's reference to Lemire's research 'sur l'émergence de l'institution littéraire au Canada français' makes it clear especially that the field as institution in nineteenth-century Quebec was one of continual struggle at the level Bourdieu indicates: 'D'un côté, des libéraux laïques introduisant la littérature au pays suivant l'inspiration de divers examples étrangers anglais et français; de l'autre, le clergé réactionnaire tentant pour maîtriser ce danger de le dresser à l'idéologie ultramontane qui assez curieusement fonctionne alors comme un nationalisme d'importation.'[23] As he concludes, such confrontations continue, they belong to the constitution of Québécois literature, and it would be impossible to write its history without analysing them. As we have seen, the struggle for autonomy in one form or another is the dominant in francophone literary history, and what distinguishes this one is the manner in which it is analysed and thus brought to bear as crucial at every turn. In that sense it also demonstrates the manner in which history is primarily understood as an order of events that can only be known, as Walter Benjamin observes, cited by . Laurent Mailhot at the same colloquium at which Saint-Jacques presented his paper, 'en corrélation avec leur temps, mais bien, *dans le temps où elles sont nées, de présenter le temps qui les connaît* – c'est à dire la nôtre.'[24] The theory of the institution, certainly powerful in Québécois academic milieux in the period when this history was developed, is a sign of the time that knows both the past and the manner in which it is known.

We are now ready to return again to the question of beginnings. The first volume of *La Vie littéraire au Québec* begins with the arrival of the British and then turns immediately to a discussion of the French heritage. Such a decision is taken in light of the use of 'Québec' in the history's title. This is the moment when its literary activity begins, and the decision makes perfect sense. First, the status of writers during the French regime was ambiguous and, second, they belong, in any event, to the French literary system. The primary audience of their writing was the European imaginary, and its central preoccupation was the life of native people. As a consequence, 'cette popularité des indigènes a pour effet premier de mettre en veilleuse l'évolution des Canadiens.'[25] What is significant in this initial phase of the argument is the fact that both the written documents and their content in the colonial period are set within a framework of production and reception, thus constructing a field, addressing their position within a foreign literary system, and thus indicating how field and institution coincide.

As we have seen, moreover, the life of the field is also driven by the role of agents and their *habitus*. The second and third chapters deepen our knowledge of these aspects of the field by analysing both the social and cultural conditions of life after the French regime and those figures active at that moment. The theme that continually recurs in the discussion of social conditions is the question of language and opportunities for education, and how both issues were subject to various sites of power. As the authors aver, literacy is a function of social status, which explains the necessity of addressing the hierarchy of both regimes before and after the Conquest. Both regimes were in their respective ways inimical to an emerging 'Canadianization' on the part of francophone inhabitants, neither French nor British seeing this process as part of their interests. Canadianization or autonomy is constructed as the object primarily at stake and, consequently, the point of departure around which the struggle for possession of field is constructed, and Canadianization, furthermore, 'se manifeste ensuite dans l'édification d'une société rendue cohérente par la langue, la religion et un ensemble d'institutions qui accentuent tout au long du XVIIIe siècle cette autonomie, dans tous les secteurs de la société, notamment dans l'organisation de la vie politique qui conquiert en partie son autonomie nationale et dans l'enseignement où apparaissent les sujets canadiens.'[26] The literary, then, is deeply imbricated in the conditions of its emergence and perforce carries with it the various marks of its birth, so to speak.

Literary activity thus becomes a scene of action, and nothing emphasizes more clearly the role that drama plays in the narrative than the title of the initial subsection of chapter three, namely, 'Les acteurs de la vie littéraire.' The first paragraph, by describing the field of the post-

Conquest period as one of conflict, illustrates succinctly one of the ways that *acteur* is to be understood in the text. They are the immediate source of action, and, as actors, they represent the theme of agency. The drama concerns two opposing representations of the dispensing of public information. One, championed by William Brown, desired a commercial press that would sell anything; the other, championed by Fleury Mesplet (1734–94) and Valentin Jautard (1736–87), desired a periodical of a literary character with a political bias. What is significant about the drama is that the actors are both foreign and designed to indicate the problematic character of the field as it emerged in the late eighteenth century. The point of the story is to illustrate the fact that text and author derive their importance from their *habitus*, thus prompting the question: 'D'après leur profession, leur religion ou formation, les Français et les Britanniques ont-ils une façon d'intervenir qui diffère passablement de celle des coloniaux?' The answer requires analysis of all the agents – French, British, and Canadian – and covers both their general formation and the kinds of texts that were the result. The groups are hardly homogeneous. The French group is divided by those who are for the most part merchants with Huguenot or Masonic tendencies, on the one hand, and men of the church, on the other. The former had a strongly developed sense of their rights and freedom; the latter were pleased to remain complicit in their dealings with the British regime. Both the British and the French together shared, however, a certain sense of superiority in respect of Canadians who both accepted, if grudgingly, this attitude, and were, as a result, 'plus disposés à apprendre qu'à produire.'[27] Nothing could more neatly open a discussion on the effect of the collèges classiques and the reason why such literary periodicals as *La Gazette littéraire* were founded by French émigrés.

Another effect of the Conquest and the role of agents was the change of social order from that of a hierarchy 'stable de statuts finement déterminés, propre à l'ordre féodal' – in other words the *ancien régime* – to one that reflected more the British ideals that encouraged free association, which was the result 'de la poursuite libre et raisonnée des intérêts particuliers.'[28] Needless to say, the British were adept at such associations, but for French Canadians, those associations that came into existence between 1760 and 1805 were both short-lived and often divided by those with clerical ideologies and those with secular interests derived from the Enlightenment. Although efforts were made by the British to draw francophones into their clubs, this usually worked to the advantage of the former. It is a field, then, which is conflicted on more than one level, and while both groups shared the same intent, their models differed sufficiently to keep them apart. The major significance for such organizations among francophones, however, is their role in forming the basis of parliamentary oratory, which is a genre, as we have seen, often given pride of place in the literary histories of French Canada.[29]

The major genre, however, that concludes the chapter on agents is theatre, implying its emergence from clubs or groups, and the conditions of its emergence are, like those of printing, embedded in a conflicted site. The shocked reception of a representation of Molière's *Tartuffe* in 1694 was sufficient to 'faire avorter toute représentation théâtrale au Quebec jusqu'au début du Régime anglais' – and this after a somewhat passionate history beginning with Marc Lescarbot's *Théâtre de Neptune*, produced in 1606.[30] Such were, nevertheless, the beginnings of literature in Canada and, indeed, North America, long before an indigenous production of prose and poetry. Theatre productions were not, of course, all of a kind, and their performances were put on by schools, garrisons, and repertory groups, both amateur and professional. Because, however, of the traditional enmity of the Church toward theatre, it cannot be said that it thrived during this period, and what was produced were for the most part French comedies. British drama was by far more successful, and while its public was both francophone and anglophone, the former was largely a bourgeois elite.

Both those who produced and those who consumed the literature of the period are clearly constructed as composed of heterogeneous groups, and to speak merely of francophone or anglophone writing would obscure the complexity of the emerging institution. Furthermore, the period covered by the first volume, it should be remembered, ranges between the years 1764 and 1805. Such a beginning, as I have indicated, constitutes a distinct departure from earlier histories, which generally prefer a date closer to 1760. The later date is chosen precisely because it was in that year that a press was set up in Quebec City, and the first issue of *La Gazette de Québec / The Quebec Gazette* appeared. It was the first of a series of infrastructural developments without which the emergence of a national literature would have been impossible. The choice of the date, then, clearly distinguishes this history from a primarily literary perspective, no matter how significant the writing of a sense of nation would become as one of its consequences.

It is not enough, therefore, simply to note the establishment of printing presses, for they carry with them interests that carry ideological weight. Although the initial press was established in Quebec City, its initial printers had worked in Philadelphia with Benjamin Franklin, who is represented as the incarnation of the Enlightenment in action. The press later established in Montréal by Mesplet came under the same influence, and it is cautiously suggested that analogies can be seen between Quebec's presses and the independence movement in the former American colonies. Significant as this implication may be from an ideological perspective, even more important is the final shape given to the history of these presses. On the one hand, it has been argued that the primary function of the presses was the work received from the government, the Church, and schools. On the other hand, Camille Roy is cited in support of the argument that at this moment 'la littérature canadienne est donc née.'[31] The consequence of bringing both views to bear continues to confirm the authors' general argument that the constitution of a field of production in Quebec is one of continuous opposition, and in this instance is rendered more complex through its rapport with the emerging American nation.

The subtext of production is the quest for autonomy, which is carefully embedded in the material conditions of making a literature through an analysis of journals and books from several points of view, not the least of which are notes on the size and paper quality, for example, of La Gazette de Québec / The Quebec Gazette. Moreover, while the journal's bilingual character is noted, it is also noted that this was considered 'une façon pratique d'enseigner l'anglais à la population de langue française.' In other words, it carried a mission of assimilation. This assertion is supported by the fact that it often found the task of translating articles from French a nuisance. The journal was also limited in its extracts from foreign newspapers, since those from France were censured. Among all the journals that lived rather ephemeral lives during the period, this was the only one that survived. Besides being the king's printer, it was the source of foreign news (mostly British) and well supported by advertisers. Having fulfilled these conditions, it offered a few literary productions for sale so long as they were 'assez restreintes et non compromettantes.' Such restraints were considered in another light by Mesplet and Jautard, the hapless editors of the short-lived Gazette littéraire, and after a year of promulgating the ideas of the Enlightenment, their journal was closed by the Sepulcians and they were incarcerated. Some eleven years later in 1790 Mesplet resumed its publication, but after his death in 1793 the authorities prevented any further circulation of liberal thinking. By the end of the decade, the British had defeated the French at sea, which had the effect of reinforcing state and ecclesiastical collusion. Clearly, the close rapport between editorial and government policy left little room for the literary institution to operate freely. Libraries were equally affected by the political situation during the final years of the eighteenth century. Although there were books in circulation, the majority were in English. Furthermore, the target-audience for imported books was not only largely British, but also the attitude of the Church was opposed to both 'les imprimés impies, de même que la propagande démocratique et révolutionnaire.'[32] Consequently, the various libraries that were established had only a limited number of books that would have been of interest to a francophone audience. In sum, the conditions for a literary culture to take shape were limited indeed.

Although I have considered at some length what may be thought of as merely the social and economic conditions in which Quebec writing was to take its rise, they belong intimately to that emergence, and this is the first literary history in Canada that has prepared the ground with such care. Without such a ground it would be difficult to explain the place given to sermons, saints' lives, and oratory, which also figure in other histories of French-Canadian writing, no matter how significant they were in the nineteenth century. This is a practice that contrasts with that of English-Canadian literary history, for example, and some readers might want to know what their continued relevance is. They are, if nothing else, the first fruits of the ground that much of volume 1 is devoted to, and as I shall discuss later, fruit and ground is probably a false dichotomy, inasmuch as everything composes the *champ* as ground. Given, then, the construction of the field, it might be said that the literature of French Canada begins with sermons, but their paucity makes it difficult to do more than intimate a notable zone of tension, and greater emphasis is laid upon political oratory, notably, Pierre Du Calvet's *L'Appel à la Justice de l'État*, published in London in 1784. It is a book that is signalled as the 'texte fondateur d'une longue lignée engengrée par la pensée libérale au Canada français.'[33]

Why is Du Calvet's text assigned the role it has in this history, given its somewhat checkered career? First, it serves as an object of contention in a political field, supported, on the one hand, by such liberals as Garneau, Fréchette, and Lareau and neglected, on the other hand, by a sufficient number of conservatives, of whom Camille Roy is one and who omits Du Calvet from his manuals. Second, he was jailed from 1780 to 1783 on suspicion of treason, largely because he was thought to have had dealings with the Americans, although subsequently the charges were dropped. He took his case to London in an effort to have the governor-general recalled and brought to trial. Failing in this, he took his case to the Canadian public, adding an open letter of some 200 pages. In doing so, he placed himself in a tradition that reaches as far back as Blaise Pascal (1623–62) and includes Voltaire (1694–1778) and Rousseau. Beyond its theme – the appeal to justice – its style, rhetorical usage, and intertextuality mark it as a literary text of a very high order, and within the system of genres of the eighteenth century there would be no question of its position as literature. What is most striking, however, is its position in the literary system by which 'le premier monument littéraire du Canada français se révèle, d'une certaine façon, anglais.' As an object in the field, it is hybrid indeed, and as a position in an argument concerning autonomy, equally significant insofar as 'la problématique de l'État' that it inaugurates 'n'a pas fini d'alimenter le discours littéraire au Canada français.'[34] Its role did not have any real effect in the history of French-Canadian writing before the founding of Le Canadien, which inaugurates the period of the second volume.

The final sections of the first volume address respectively the rise of 'imaginative' literature and, to round off the whole understanding of literature as communicative process, its reception. As the authors argue, the emergence of imaginative literature owes its impetus to such periodicals as La Gazette de Québec and La Gazette de Montréal, which provide various models for future development. The periodicals were composed from three sources – American, English, and French – which indicate the heterogeneous character of the field in its beginnings. Certain themes, particularly in the French texts, which dominated, were the reporting of sensational events, tales of pirates and assassins, captivity stories and tales of scalping by 'savages,' and fictions that refer to actual crimes. Such were the narratives (not unlike ancient Greek romance) 'qui ont contribué à former la conscience littéraire et le goût publique lecteur, qui ont façonné l'imaginaire québécois, laissant présager la production d'œuvres narratives caractéristiques de l'âme collective au XIXe siècle.'[35] Not only, then, are periodicals accorded a proleptic role in the formation of a readership, but also they indicate how the development of the literary institution is the necessary condition for the creation of literature and a corresponding public.

The beginnings of drama and poetry are also evident in this period and, for the most part, the two genres evince the qualities of colonial writing. Drama is considered from three perspectives. Noted are 'Les Fétes villageoises,' a one-act comedy produced in 1765 but now lost, some anonymous pieces performed in the collèges classiques, and finally the work of the French émigré, Joseph Quesnel (1749–1809), who was both a poet and playwright. Although his most well-known play was *Colas et Colinette ou le Bailli dupé*, written in France and England and performed initially in Montréal in 1790, it is placed where it belongs in the French literary system of the eighteenth century. A play that is given greater significance – *L'Anglomanie ou le dîner à l'angloise* (1803) – is a satire of excessive loyalism on the part of some Canadians and, if not actually canonized, is considered more representative of the field in the early nineteenth century than the more famous *Colas et Colinette*. Even more significant is the fact that it was not produced because of the political position it took. In any event, Quesnel is generally marginalized because he exemplifies a colonial tendency which 'continue de vivre à la française.'[36] The situation for poetry differed little in this respect.

The dominant system that provided models for much of the poetry of the seventeenth and eighteenth centuries was the classical tradition, and until the Conquest the major themes were drawn from historical events. After the establishment of periodicals, greater place was available for shorter forms, the generality of which were occasional poems, such as New Year's 'étrennes,' first published in 1767, and poems of celebration. Both are marked by their classicism and the recurrent motif of praise for the British Crown. Poems in a lighter vein were provided by Quesnel, who remains 'le seul poète de l'époque dont l'œuvre ait été légitimé.'[37] Despite its uniqueness as satire, Ross Cuthbert's *L'Aréopage* (1803) is signalled for its role as a precursor of similar political poetry later in the century. Finally, two types of songs are considered: traditional folk song and songs composed for the people. Despite the latter's recognition as a minor genre, its political function was quickly perceived and often denounced by the authorities. As the authors remark, 'en lisant la production poétique de l'époque, on est tenté d'affirmer qu'au Canada français ... tout finit par une chanson!' Folk songs were French in their derivation and French-Canadian in their adaptation. With the exception, however, of satirical popular songs, the tendency of the period was conservative and, in fact, a 'littérature de propagande.'[38] The same might be said of the British poetry of the period, for example, Thomas Carey's *Abram's Plains: A Poem* (1789), which was not only written in a style derived from English neoclassicism, but also thematized the superiority of British institutions, displaying a manifest condescension toward French-Canadians.

What is significant are the summary statements made about these *débuts*, which are normally skimmed over by literary historians because of their limited literary value, which does not, as Gérard Tougas is cited as observing, merit survival. If Tougas's judgment is valid, what is to be done with these texts? The response is firm: 'Dans le mouvement qui met progressivement en place la littérature québécoise, ces écrits éclairent la voie par laquelle se constitue son champ propre.' They are necessary in the constitution of an ever-expanding and developing field. The basis for this assertion that follows directly is equally unequivocal: 'Si la soumission au discours de l'opinion publique qui les caracté-rise assure pour longtemps leur spécificité canadienne, le processus d'autonomisation inhérent au développement moderne du champ littéraire se fait alors en décalage par rapport à l'évolution de son homolgue français qui tend ainsi à se poser en référence 'universelle' pour les acteurs qui s'emploient à le promovoir.'[39] The significance of this statement cannot be overlooked: it is central to the argument of the history as a whole and echoes Saint-Jacques's reading of Bourdieu. The institution is to be conceptualized as a field in which tension in its initial stages indicates a gradually growing difference between the local and the general (the French model as universal) and mark the literature as a post-colonial phenomenon. The value of the field lies in its activity and not necessarily in the 'quality' of the literature it produces. Thus, the primary significance of the text lies in its position in the field, in the whole conflicted process that relates production to reception.

The final section returns in some respects, then, to the role of the press as the instrument of production, which creates, to use the language of communication models, a receiver who, in turn, becomes a subsequent producer. 'Ainsi,' it is affirmed, 'se referme un cercle qui peut se répéter presque indéfiniment.'[40] Here lie all the possibilities of the developing field in the metaphor of the circle, announcing the inception of autonomy. If the circle is not closed, such periodicals as *La Gazette de Québec*, which seek primarily to please the social elite with a lit-erature of escapism, no horizon of expectation is created and the public remains a passive recipient. In this respect, the journal differs markedly from the practice of *La Gazette de Montréal*, designed primarily, as we have seen, to awaken its reader to the ideas of the Enlightenment and thus provoke both positive and negative responses. The latter, as we know, were sufficient to have the journal closed and the editors jailed. Nevertheless, its provocation animated a reader who felt prompted to take part or take issue and so become a producer. Even *La Gazette de Québec*, however, may be said to have formed the horizons of its readers, especially after its rival failed for a second time in the early 1790s, after hostilities resumed between France and England in 1793 as a consequence of the Terror. Both the English and French novel were supported by *La Gazette de Québec* but only to the degree that it did not inflame the passions. Furthermore, the second period of publication of *La Gazette de Montréal* made it more and more apparent that the models and perspectives were primarily French, which did not augur well for the formation of a national literature. Between the anodyne, on the one hand, and the foreign, on the other, a French-Canadian reader as producer was not given the best of models.

The example of Quesnel is drawn upon to demonstrate, finally, that the francophone circle of readers was very restricted. His efforts to establish such circles ended in failure, and he was not alone in lamenting the lack of necessary infrastructures that would promote the rise of literature in Quebec. Hence, the conclusion of the initial period in the history of French-Canadian literature is not particularly hopeful. Quesnel's ironically unproduced *L'Anglomanie* is summoned to witness the beginning of a dialogue between the British and their new subjects, the *Canadiens*: 'Ces derniers commencent à se poser des questions sur leur identité, les institutions, leur projet collectif. Le discours porté sur ces sujets n'est pas toujours réflexif, mais la pensée canadienne est sommée de s'interroger pour définir une société nouvelle, sans quoi elle est condamnée à l'assimilation. Le choix se pose alors en ces termes: cette société sera-t-elle anglaise ou bilingue?' Although the Conquest initially appears to be a shift from one colonial situation to another, the field is so constructed that 'malgré les nombreuse tentatives d'assimilation et contre toute prévisibilité, la colonie est demeurée française après la Conquête.' So the final sentence of the first volume is prepared to allow for a hopeful attitude toward a nascent francophone literature: 'Les lettres canadiennes l'attestent, et même, la réalisent.'[41] Thus, the authors avoid the clarity that Perkins would presuppose. The Conquest was not a Fall. Furthermore, it would be difficult to predict a rise, and a decline does not occur, for everything before the beginning belongs to a different literary system. If a literature is to emerge, and we know it did, the first volume places the reader at more or less ground zero in a field that is continually at odds with itself.[39]

The general format of the subsequent volumes follows that of the first, facilitating considerably their use both as narratives and encyclopedias in Perkins's sense. The difference that each possesses is in respect of plot, on the one hand, and the continuous increase of figures active in the field, on the other. The question of the various plots is made apparent in the *Présentation* that precedes each volume. Thus, the first period comprises a field that is contested by Scottish merchants and Canadian *seigneurs*, and, despite the introduction of the press and efforts to 'accorder le droit français aux lois anglais ... les Canadiens, peu familiarisés avec les nouvelles institutions, restent plutôt à l'écart d'une vie littéraire que domine l'imprimé.' The second volume, however, announces that, 'à la suite de la nouvelle Constitution de 1791, un changement radical s'opère.' The consequence is that avenues of empowerment were opened for French Canadians, and 'la création du *Canadien* en 1806 leur donne une voix propre dans la lutte pour l'hégé-monie sur l'opinion publique en servant de creuset à la formation d'un nouveau projet collectif.'[42] As a result, the beginning of volume 2 is again clearly established within the framework of the literary institution. Moreover, the position of the periodical was not always assured and, like other manifestations of the field in the emergence of an autonomous francophone literature, it had to struggle to maintain its position. The choice, finally, to conclude the volume with the year 1839, a year that marked the end of the rebellion and its often crushing consequences, suggests an emplotment that is hardly more, and perhaps less, encouraging than that of the first volume.

The central fact of the new period, at least in Europe, is the presence of romanticism, and its introduction in the discourse of the second volume is designed to command the reader's immediate attention. The initial paragraph that sets the stage of the new age begins by remarking that 'les guerres napoléoniennes et leurs contrecoups dominent les premières années du XIXe siècle en Occident.' The paragraph concludes with the statement: 'Ni la guerre ni la restauration d'un pouvoir traditionnellement hostile à la liberté d'expression ne semblent propices aux lettres. Et pourtant ...' The relation of the sentence and its unfinished reply is a kind of leitmotif of both the developing understanding of the field and of the plot of the volume as a whole. No matter how repressive the state, freedom of speech and its articulation as literature could not be stopped, as a host of major writers from England, France, Germany, Italy, and Russia bear witness. The full force of the romantic movement is summed up in two declarations: 'Sous les augures économiques et politiques apparement les moins favorables, la littérature s'ennoblit du "sacre de l'écrivain," tel que le caractérisé Paul Bénichou. S'y fonde l'acte de naissance de la littérature moderne.'[43] Needless to say, however, this was not a birth without complications, and much of the discussion that forms the general condition addresses particularly the implications of the change of status of the writer.

The key shift affecting the writer, production, and reception was the emergence of the middle class, which had the effect of shifting economic conditions of writing from a system of patronage to one that has all the infrastructures of capitalism. The significant change affects the autonomy of both writer and reader or, in the language of Bourdieu, producer and consumer. No longer dependent upon a patron for economic survival, the writer now bears a contractual relationship with a printer, opening a space between both the writer and virtual reader that 'donne une nouvelle liberté de jeu à l'un et à l'autre.' The operation of the field changes accordingly, and among some of the more important effects of the reshaping of the field is the increase of women as producers of fiction, notably, Jane Austen (1775–1817), Mary Shelley (1797–1851), Madame de Staël (1766–1817), and George Sand (1804–76). Furthermore, because of more efficient modes of printing developed in the early decades of the century, more print-runs were possible and larger audiences were reached by both books and periodicals. Finally, the increase in scope tended to fragment the reading public into several diverse publics and, at the same time, attested to the emergence of national difference: 'De cette façon, les littératures des deux principales ethnies immigrées canadiennes évoluent vers la séparation l'une de l'autre et le renforcement des liens avec leurs mères patries respectives, la Grande-Bretagne et la France.' So it is that an intimate homology is formed between the emergence of a middle class, the modified status of the writer, and a sense of the national. That the changes which occurred did not take place without a struggle is evident, and the argument of the second volume is a record of that struggle. The final paragraph reflecting on the full impact of the Romantic period points to the emergence of autonomy as the central theme: 'S'il faut voir naître alors la modernité dans les lettres, c'est dans cette valorisation paradoxale de l'activité littéraire à la fois habilitée à intervenir pour défendre publiquement des valeurs dans l'ordre du politique et autorisée à ne tirer que d'elle-même la consécration de son statut propre. Position logiquement intenable, mais promise à une grande fécondité historique.'[44]

Although conditions in Quebec cannot be said to correspond in many respects to those in Europe, some matters have echoes and are given highest significance. The first lies in the changing political field that resulted from the Constitutional Act of 1791, opening the door to a new understanding of parliamentary representation. Just as Parliament represented the people, as opposed to the aristocracy, so the sense of the word people (*peuple*), 'dans l'esprit des élus canadiens-français ... se confond très tôt avec "nation."' The connotation aimed in the direction of collective empowerment, and, by arguing that 'leur nationalisme revêt une forme éminemment moderne,' a serious link is forged with the earlier presentation of romanticism and its proleptic force.[45] Such knowledge did not, of course, confer immediate legitimacy, and the Church remained opposed to any emergence of a national middle class, thus allowing for a conflicted field.[46] Its influence in the field of education added a further highly charged element in its especial privileging of Latin at the expense of French, and, just as in the preceding period, the struggle for the survival of French is intimately related to the survival of the nation, which was particularly apparent in parliamentary debate.

Although debate was permitted in the native language of the member and the preponderant language was French, the fact that Parliament was in fact British meant that the generality of speeches were given in French, translated into English, and then retranslated into a French that came late and unfaithfully. French was considered to be merely a 'langue de traduction' and not a 'langue légale.' Hence, one of the guiding threads of the period from the rise of *Le Canadien* to *The Durham Report* was a struggle to legitimize French. Thus, 'loin de favoriser le projet d'assimilation, l'établissement du parlementarisme a, au contraire, permis la formulation d'un projet de société canadien et assuré, dans les conflits politiques qui marquent cette période, la survie de la langue française dans une société qui se prétend bilingue.' Paradoxically and perhaps predictably, the Act of Union in 1840 brought about 'la rupture définitive de la cohésion idéologique qui avait uni les Canadiens autour de ce projet commun.' Some opted for bilingualism; others, for 'particularisme culturel.' The new constitution, however, by proscribing the legal use of French in Parliament only served to motivate French as 'le symbole de la nationalité.'[47]

It is evident that the inauguration of *Le Canadien* in 1806 bode well for the rise of French-Canadian nationalism, but it not only faced immediate competition from the *Courrier de Québec* in 1807 but also fell afoul of the government, which closed it down in 1810 and imprisoned the editors and the printer, enacting the surest form of censorship that worked with equal effectiveness in the previous century. Like the phoenix it rose again in the years 1817 to 1820 and again from 1825 to 1830, folding each time because of financial difficulties. It rose again for a third time in 1831 under the editorship of Étienne Parent, this time taking as its motto the words, 'Nos institutions, notre langue et nos lois,' an expression picked up a year later by the educationist Joseph-François Perrault as part of the effort to legalize the language. In many respects the fitful career of *Le Canadien* is an earnest of the difficulties of the period that is labelled as 'Une période de crises,' echoing an expression used as the structuring principle, for example, of Baillargeon's history.[48] Despite the fact that the periodical was still alive at both the beginning and end of the period, the end of the period, a moment when 'l'avenir ... semble on ne peut plus sombre,' suggests a plot design of slight rise followed by continuous descent, despite moments of light. Because 'un peuple sans littérature est condamné à l'oubli,' as the authors rightly assert, nation, survival, and the literary are inextricably intertwined.[49]

Given this context, there can be no wonder why the genre of history was cultivated so assiduously in the nineteenth century[50] and what its fundamental role should be: historiography is *par excellence* the discourse of legitimation and appropriation. In an interesting use of the present tense, the authors observe that 'en réponse au discours des nouveaux colons britanniques qui disqualifient pour cause d'"ignorance" la population francophone, les Canadiens se forgent une identité commune.' Indeed, as they continue, 'pour fonder leur conscience nationale, les Canadiens doivent se donner des références commune: s'approprier un pays et une mémoire. L'histoire devient l'enjeu ...' Thus, history becomes a discursive field of existential dimensions. It not only memorializes but also, by doing so, writes the historical subject into existence and so recuperates it from Lord Durham's comment that 'there can hardly be conceived a nationality more destitute of all that can invigorate and elevate a people, than that which is exhibited in the descendants of the French in Lower Canada, owing to their retaining their peculiar language and manners.' As he famously goes on to argue, 'with no history, and literature' they have no 'hope of continuing to preserve their nationality.'[51] As a consequence, both literature and history are enjoined to make the nation, an act that, needless to say, literary history is also actively engaged in.

The effort to make a nation has certain side effects, and one of these harks back to a theme announced in the initial chapter on romanticism, namely, the tendency of nations to develop exclusively. The point is sustained in the discussion on the creation of the two periodicals, the *Quebec Mercury* and *Le Canadien*. Both announce a 'tendance à organiser leur vie culturelle indépendamment les uns des autres.' The formation of theatrical groups also indicates the same tendency: 'Si, d'un côté, le regroupement en associations volontaires demeure largement une pratique anglophone, de l'autre, la polarisation du débat idéologique entraîne les Canadiens à limiter leur participation dans ce genre de pratique.' Moreover, in the establishment of libraries, language formed a barrier. The Act of Union, as we saw above, by proscribing French as a legal language, was a sufficient symbol of the necessity for this tendency to continue. The emphasis upon national difference runs parallel to the construction of 'une identité commune' that represents the collective voice, which is articulated in the decision, repeated in each volume, to include a section entitled 'Les acteurs de la vie littéraire,' which gathers individuals active in the field in a variety of ways into a group. In this way a national project is formed. Indeed, at the darkest moment of the period during the Rebellion of 1837–8 and its aftermath, the one way possible to prevent disappearance could only occur 'en sacrifiant l'individu à la collectivité.'[52] That sacrifice, performed under various degrees of compulsion, could be said to be the animating force of the field driven by the necessity to prevent assimilation.

If this is a story that turns on the acquisition of agency, how is it narrated? The first aspect of the narration that faces the reader in each volume is the repeated structure that runs from a discussion of general conditions to varieties of reception. The shape itself is a measure of the didactic intent of this history, an intent present in all literary history, but emphatically a part of this one. The initial effect of such a structure is the implicit reassurance that the repetition provides. Not only is the past built upon in each successive volume, but also the past is expanded upon in ways that fulfil reader expectations derived from the repeated format. Where this history differs, however, from other examples of francophone literary history is in the use of linearity. The volumes are a combination of the synchronic and the diachronic that, in the end, complicate their use as continuous narrative. Nor can they be used entirely as encyclopedias, that is, the 'outil de référence' which the first sentence of each declares. This is because the multiple references to authors and works prevent one from making a synthetic use of them. As I shall argue, however, this is a technique that appropriately and persuasively serves the construction of the field.

If this history is neither a narrative nor an encyclopedia in Perkins's sense, how can it be described? Because of the combined synchronic and diachronic form, it may be considered as a series of micronarratives, some of which are designed to provide information and others to sketch the drama of the conflict that characterizes the field. If we look briefly at François-Xavier Garneau in volume 3, for example, a figure who is an unquestioned founder of French-Canadian writing, we find a large number of references in the index, indicating his recurrent presence throughout the period that runs from 1840 to 1869. Thus, he does not make a single, large appearance that would indicate his commanding role, but he appears in such a way as to dramatize that role, by repeatedly impressing the reader. Although many of the references include him in lists of significant contemporaries, other references, even before an analysis of his work, suggest, for example, the problems of making publication subject to subscriptions. As the authors note later, Garneau is one of very few writers whose work in any way rivals that of authors imported from France. Subsequently, we find his work appropriated by the Church 'à propos d'un enjeu central, celui du sens donner au passé collectif.' As is well known, efforts were also made by the Church to have him repress his more liberal attitudes in later editions, but, as the authors argue in their analysis of his *Histoire*, he modified 'sans renier pour autant ses idées,' which assured him, finally, an unassailable position in the canon, even among conservatives.[53] Not only was his influence on both literature and history profound, as all literary historians attest, he became the 'historien national,' just as Crémazie became the 'poète national,' and they are often paired as such in different contexts. In the final section entitled, *La Réception*, he figures often; attention is drawn to his position in the field as one of opposition to the conservatives who feared his text 'capable de donner naissance au "torrent révolutionnaire."' In a word, Garneau is everywhere and in different positions, and to all of this one should add his role as a poet discussed in volume 2.[54]

The number of citations suggests that Garneau plays a preponderant role in the text, and rightfully so. With the exception of the analysis of his *Histoire*, however, the mentions are frequent, but brief. It is, therefore, easy to see him as one of three, the others being Aubert de Gaspé, père, and Crémazie, canonized by the era, and more especially, as one among the several liberal spirits engaged in the acquisition of agency, which the form of the volume encourages the reader to see. The shared identity conjoins them to a larger sphere of action that transcends their individual levels of performance. They become figures in a common ground, which permits their presence in each successive volume, if only, but significantly, in reminiscence. As figures engaged in a variety of literary activities, they thus represent the interaction of the discursive practices which constitute the field. It might be suggested that being drawn into the narrative in such a manner allows them to demonstrate that history itself is also a discursive field and that one of the higher functions of literary history is to make such a demonstration. As a genre of historiography, then, such a demonstration would place it in many respects at a summit.[55]

The continual turn toward the collective purpose of French Canada argues that the preferred rhetorical mode corresponds to White's Synecdoche, and the repeated structure is reinforcement of such a position. Although the form interferes with a metonymical order, the authors tend to stress, nevertheless, the dynamics of causality less than that of the recurrent struggle for control of the field. Still, the continual inscription of changes in the economic and political base allows room for Metonymy, and in this respect, La Vie littéraire au Québec has affinities with White's understanding of Marx and his interplay of both diachronic levels of causality and synchronic levels of integration. The full realization of autonomous structures in respect of both the collective unfolding of history and the literary field with which it is imbricated suggests that between the two rhetorical modes and the social orders they project Synecdoche is the dominant. Such a preference follows a general movement in francophone literary history, especially as the use of synecdoche is directed toward the realization of autonomy. Tendency and direction implies what we have seen already, which is the sense of telos inscribed in these histories as the aim of the struggle. History in French Canada is agon, but a struggle that contually turns upon the same issues in different guises manifest 'comme une spirale où le mouvement lui-même est facteur de changement.' As we know from elsewhere in the Présentation, 'cette histoire littéraire n'est pas principalement organisé autour des œuvres et auteurs. Elle apparaît plutôt comme celle de la constitution de la littérature québécoise et elle concerne en premier lieu l'étude des conditions d'émergence et du cheminement par lequel la littérature acquiert son autonomie et sa légitimation, c'est-à-dire sa reconnaissance sociale.'[56] Because the struggle is continuous, and because with hindsight it is possible to construct an ever more possible future from successful turns in the past, it could be posited that in histories of this kind both process and telos overlap in the emergence of autonomy, which is why Metonymy and Synecdoche interrelate in the narrative.

As I have argued, a recurrent register of literary history is the didactic. In this instance the tools are provided to understand how the field works and the literature of Quebec is constituted. The meaning of the past, as a result, lies in its usable, prefiguring character. In this respect, the future tense is used at significant moments to serve this function and belongs to the dramatic element of the style that engages the reader in the act of conceptualizing the operation of the field. Thus, referring to a shift in the understanding of history in the 1830s, the authors state: 'en ce domaine comme en celui de l'opinion publique se réunissent et s'organisent les pièces d'un dossier que Garneau, après 1840, réarticulera en une affirmation décisive de la valeur des Canadiens.' Such a sentence is a clear example of how the central themes of the acquisition of autonomy and recognition are discursively realized, and it marks the extent to which this history is perlocutionary in Austin's sense. At other moments there are interesting shifts of narrative level which create at once a dramatic effect and indicate problems with the movement of the field. At the end of volume 3 the question of a national literature is raised as one of the significant debates of the period. Because of a desire to acquire recognition by the French, competition is avoided: 'Aussi les Canadiens s'abstiendront-ils de décrire la vie moderne et se chercheront un créneau qui leur soit exclusif.' Such conservatism inspires the response in the following paragraph with reference to the emerging literature: 'Réclame-t-elle une autonomie entière? Aspire-t-elle une autonomie entière?'[57] The questions direct attention to the limited future that is being chosen and also move the reader to a metanarratological level which suggests by its appeal a desire to intervene in the field. Intervention, of course, is impossible, but the dramatic tension sought in the reader thus interpellated is, nevertheless, heightened. In such a way the reader becomes engaged in both the narrative process and the shaping of an autonomous field.

As I have suggested, literary history cannot help revealing its various practices, and *La Vie littéraire au Québec* is exemplary of such procedures. Drawing upon the most contemporary of theories from Bourdieu to Even-Zohar, its narrative style is wholly appropriate to the task. If, on the one hand, dramatic tension lies at the heart of literary activity, then a style which projects a distanced narratorial position would have limited the effect of the argument. On the other hand, the desire to confer scientific status upon literary research explains the shift from mere narrative story to a form that always places the reader in front of the variety of modes in which the field expresses itself. If history of literature is about the interaction of discursive practices, which is a position difficult to argue against, the interaction requires showing, and this is what occurs. I have implied a certain greatness in such approaches to literary history, and occasionally it can be found, especially in such histories, for example, as that of Francesco de Sanctis, mentioned in the first chapter. In his *Storia della letteratura italiana* the linearity of the story is enhanced by the use of Hegelian dialectic and Viconian notions of growing self-consciousness. In three broad strokes he presents the image of the raw, medieval poet, e.g., Dante, played off against the civilized art of the Renaissance romance writer Ariosto. Italian literature is designed to reveal itself as a search for the ideal synthesis of this opposition found in Alessandro Manzoni's *Inni sacri* (1815). Bound neither by dogma nor classical rules, Manzoni found his way into both the contemporary and the 'forze collettive, il cui complesso costituisce l'individualità di una società o di un secolo.' His work attained its status in De Sanctis's eyes because it was 'un produtto piú o meno inconscio dello spirito del mondo in un dato momento della sua esistenza.' The notion of the spirit of the times carried, of course, immeasurable weight in the nineteenth century, explaining progress and legitimizing national emergence. Relating such a notion to both Vico and Hegel, however, provided an explicating architecture for his history, lifting it from chronicle to vision and so providing a model for the best kinds of literary history.[58] *La Vie littéraire au Québec* may readily be placed among such histories that at once inscribe a vision and demonstrate both its operation and significance.

CHAPTER SEVEN

The Question of Alterity:
Histories of Their Own, 1968–1993

Once you cross the ocean, you'll always be on the wrong side of it.[1]

So.
In the beginning, there was nothing. Just the water.[2]

It is impossible to construct a notion of Canadian culture without bearing in mind that it is not two, but many, cultures. Histories of its literatures are dominated, however, by the notion that there are two literatures, and in practice these histories are written as if there were only one literature and perhaps another. While a national policy on biculturalism was inevitable if the Canadian Federation was to remain viable, it was also inevitable that, once cultural claims had been asserted, to preserve the dominant cultures as exclusive in a pluralistic society would be hypocritical at the very least. Because the *Report of the Royal Commission on Bilingualism and Biculturalism* (1963–9) equated language with culture, it was equally inevitable that an ethnic member of the commission, J.B. Rudnyckyj, would indicate that the loss of a language is the loss of a culture.[3] Despite the subsequent passage of the Multiculturalism Act (1987), provisions are not made for preservation of language other than that of the two charter languages; they are made only for the preservation of other cultures. Taken together, both policies, flawed as they may be, strive to decentre a sense of Canada as embodying a single culture.

They pose, however, certain embarrassments for scholars. The embarrassment is primarily institutional and political. In many respects, both are deeply related, and I have only separated them for purposes of discussion. Although the majority of histories I discuss are treated here as a group, this is because their bearing is primarily upon the anglophone institution. Although Diane Boudreau fits more appropriately with respect to the francophone system, at least as a mode of resistance to the dominant culture in Quebec, inasmuch as she situates her corpus deliberately on the margin of the literary institution,[4] she will be discussed in this chapter. The political position is in some respects more complex. The report of the commission specifically excludes native cultures as ethnic and, as a consequence, inhibits their mutual study.[5] The editors of a special edition of the *Canadian Review of Comparative Literature / Revue canadienne de la littérature comparée* (16:3–4 [1989]) have more prudently opted for the neutral expression, 'literatures of lesser diffusion,' which endeavours only to place the literatures designated within the literary institution, without raising the question of alterity. In a multicultural society, alterity, however, is central and goes much farther than the matter of diffusion. Nevertheless, such an expression has the virtue of permitting the inclusion of studies of both 'ethnic minority'[6] and native writing. Although their relation to the history of Canada is ontologically and politically assymetrical, they have shared concerns. For this reason, I have chosen to treat them together.

In many respects, their relation to each other is an inverse one: both are in a certain measure victims of history. It is not certain that the native peoples of the Americas desired immigration, and, had conditions been better, people of most, if not all, ethnic groups would have preferred not to emigrate. An exception can be made for French Canadians who argue that they are not, in a certain fashion, immigrants, but rather 'native' by virtue of losing the war with the British. Insofar as the British represented imperial expansion, they constitute another exception. Therefore, the cultures considered in this chapter share a history of crisis or catastrophe, which constitutes for them a beginning. The crisis occurs when the fact of alterity becomes the formative energy of consciousness. Beginning is the moment when the Other, the dominant group, causes one's sense of oneself as a subject to lose definition. In the eye of the dominant group one becomes Other. The loss of agency in historiography gives rise to plots in which the beginning is a fall, and whether or not it leads to recovery, it is always one that requires an acculturation or, at least, some modification of the subject.

According to Enoch Padolsky, the crisis of acculturation has four options: integration, assimilation, separation, and marginalization.[7] In each case, the subject relates to the dominant culture in a descending degree of agency, but in every case it is clear that relation is necessary for survival and growth. Nevertheless, while the strongest relation is one of integration, the subject remains in a certain way divided between its own and the dominant culture. Because relation is inescapable, it raises the question of language. Only specialists in the language of the dominant culture take the trouble to learn the language of the Other. Therefore, although acculturation requires that something is always lost in translation, almost everything is lost when one opts to use one's native language, rather than the language of the dominant culture. The Fall, then, is always present in these narratives to some degree.

These histories are narratives, then, of deterritorialization and often depend upon the longing to find a place somewhere in some territory, whether in space or in time. The function of writing in the process of reterritorialization is central, for it allows the subject to articulate its desire, but the process is burdened with layers of ambiguity not necessarily faced by those who have never been aware of themselves as part of what Deleuze and Guattari construct as a minority literature.[8] Those who have been deterritorialized, so to speak, are always defined by a sense of alterity. Like the displaced persons that war creates, they are displaced as subjects. A wonderfully clear example of how the displaced subject finds it necessary to assert itself may be found in Henry Kreisel's (1922–91) opening statement given at a conference on ethnicity held some years ago: 'It was in a large, overcrowded army barracks in the little town of Pontefract, Yorkshire, that I made the deliberate decision to abandon German and express myself in English.' Although not every minority writer needs to make such a decision, even the decision to retain one's own language in a linguistic situation where it is not officially recognized distinguishes the minority writer in Canada from those who grow up in families of largely anglophone or francophone ancestry. What marks Kreisel's sentence is the process by which the speaker articulates himself as initially deterritorialized, beginning with the phrase that has no particular referent ('It was'), then shows himself by implication as displaced both spatially and linguistically, and finally moves toward finding a new place in another language.[9] It is perfect proof, if proof is necessary, that language, culture, and, by implication, the subject are coterminous, as Rudnyckyj asserts. To change a language results in cultural slippage: something is lost as something else is gained. Ambiguity, with all its positive and negative connotations, is always in some way present.

A consequence of deterritorialization is its function as a historical determinant. Kreisel is referring to the year 1940, toward the beginning of the Second World War. The history that his sentence inscribes as a beginning has nothing to do with dates that are normally necessary for the construction of English- or French-Canadian history. While his beginning exists in time, it also exists as a project: 'to abandon German and express myself in English.' Thus it neatly illustrates an aspect of Said's argument about beginnings: 'Once made the focus of attention, the beginning occupies the foreground and is no longer a beginning but has the status of an actuality; and when it cedes its place to that which it has aimed to produce or give rise to, it can exist in the mind as virtuality.' It has the power, then, to shape understanding and so becomes a matrix for forming both the subject and the shape of a world. This, I take it, is how we are to construct a subsequent remark of Said: 'Thus "the beginning," belonging as often to myth as to logic, conceived of as a place in time, and treated as a root as well as an objective, remains a kind of gift inside language.'[10] Kreisel's statement in such a light makes of beginning an ordering trajectory projecting the subject toward another culture and mode of being, while carrying with it the transformed character of a remembered past that is both displaced and replaced. The 'place in time' is chosen and constructed, and the language which forms its syntax is the signifying territory.

Another consequence of beginning as voluntary intervention and transformation is reflected in the narrative stances chosen by the historians of cultures that have suffered intervention. Beginning, as Kreisel articulates it, is invested with governing virtuality. Before and after are marked, on the one hand, and then related dialectically, on the other. Before is both negated and subsumed by after, one giving meaning to the other. Thus although the narrators of these histories place their events in Canada, their Canada is not constructed like those of the anglophone and francophone histories we have been examining. The Canadas of writers like Kreisel are always taken as part of relationship and never something that subsists in itself. Ethnic minority histories assume what official, national literary histories of Canada are incapable of doing: they assume that 'Canada' has no ontological function.[11] The nation that the charter histories construct proceeds from assumptions about, and desires for, the typical, which allows them to be perceived as 'mainstream.' The typical as a sign of the universal, desires closure. In the instance of Canada, national policy prepares a space for anglophone and francophone culture. It permits this to be challenged by the admission of multicultural 'values,' but these values are only encouraged to challenge in the official languages. To follow Padolsky's model, they belong primarily on the level of integration.

The practice of constructing culture, which is the primary role of literary history, rarely follows national policy, as we have seen. It prefers monolingual spaces. The challenge of alterity is constructed as marginal, that is, on the outside of the culture that has the status of being Canadian.[12] The true challenge, which argues implicitly that 'Canada' is not ontologically grounded, is not problematized in anglophone or francophone histories. In the histories we are about to discuss, however, it is always assumed that 'Canada' is a relational term whose semiotic function is without ontological status. By refusing to admit closure, the position of the narrator does not accept beginnings as foundational, but rather as moments of continuous *différance* in which the movement forward is mirrored by retrospection. Meaning comes from the culture that constitutes the point of departure, but it is by necessity a meaning that subjects one to the endless extensions of memory and desire. Once the decision is made to run the risk of alterity, the past becomes, to use L.P. Hartley's expression, 'a foreign country' that can only be visited by the mind.[13] To a greater degree, therefore, than those who are able to construct an ontological status for themselves, the immigrant and the native, whether integrated or not in Padolsky's sense, are at once constrained and permitted to be imaginary. It is a past that dwells in a reified manner in the mind, without a living relationship to a continuously changing present, and therefore may be drawn upon to confirm ideology. Although accessibility to the country of the past is especially limited for those who live in exile, the same is true for those like Italian-Canadians, who are able to return at any time. No one can live in two places at once and, hence, reterritorialization is, as Henri Gobard argues, a mythological discourse.[14] Thus, full admission to either the imaginary or the symbolic in Jacques Lacan's sense is often inhibited.

Transplanting the Nation

So it is that the determination of the status of such writers is inconclusive. As Edward Możejko asks, are these minority writers or do they more appropriately belong to their own nationalities? They are, in fact, both,[15] but being both, they can be exclusively neither one nor the other. As Michael Greenstein neatly asks, 'Frye's question about Canadian identity – where is here? – becomes compounded by a Jewish question – where was there, opening a space between here and now and the past.' These are writers who are as much lost in time as they are in space. Indeed, the true territory is temporality, and the desired territory is in time's transcendence. The role of the narrator is to begin at a place in time that will permit the shift of order and meaning. Thus M.I. Mandryka begins his *History of Ukrainian Literature in Canada* (1968), appropriately enough, in Ukraine.[16] The title already suggests such a possibility, for this is not only a history of Ukrainian-Canadian literature but also one of a national literature transplanted, and so he implicitly anticipates the problem Możejko raises. The beginning of history in Ukraine is dated by the year 862, when 'during the reigns of Volodymyr the Great (980–1015) and his son Yaroslav the Wise (1019–54) Kievan monarchy (called at that time "Rus") reached its zenith, becoming one of the foremost states in Europe.'[17] The monarchy not only lost its title of 'Rus,' but also within less than two centuries was plunged into continuous struggle with Mongols, Hungarians, Poles, Lithuanians, Tartars, Turks, and, finally, Russians. It is a history in which moments of autonomy are indeed rare, and so its plot is one of rise and fall.

The past, then, is not a random series of events, but events ordered to explain and justify the cultural values that the history undertakes to inscribe. Because Ukraine is constructed as a former significant power, which, at the time of writing, was a part of the Soviet Union, the writers that are canonized are meant to be perceived as heroes. This, I assume, is one way of explaining the rather unimaginative method of the history, which is in effect a series of biographical sketches focused on each writer's literary achievement. Canada, as a synecdoche for 'the free world,' is a place where an idea of liberty can be developed, which represents a desire for freedom and a preservation from loss. Thus, although Ukrainian literature dates from 988, the year in which Christianity was adopted, most of it was destroyed in the Tartar invasions that began in 1223. The history of literature is, as a result, made to coincide with national history: the loss of the former is a sign of the loss of the latter. One great text survived, notably the mediaeval *Campaign of Igor.* Its theme is succinctly given as 'the tragic campaign of Prince Ihor against the Polvtsians in 1185.' Such a statement might be compared to a standard modern history of Russian literature, which underlines the theme of 'self-sacrifice for Russia as the noblest of virtues.' The differences are worth some attention, for Russia in D.S. Mirsky's version, which has appeared already to appropriate a Ukrainian text, was, first of all, not yet a nation, nor is there any mention of an enemy until much later in the analysis. Mandryka, in contrast, continuously foregrounds enemies, suggesting that literature is a necessary and salutary aspect of nation. Having reached Canada, especially after the Second World War,

Ukraine's writing community represents 'the free soul and thought of Ukraine, chained by Moscow to silence.'[18] The Ukrainian literature of Canada is the sign of 'national continuity' that relates the past to the present in a way that would not have been possible under the many repressive regimes that have defined Ukrainian history.

Although the microstructure of Mandryka's history is commemorative, enshrining the best and dismissing those who fail to challenge the enemy, the macrostructure consists of a transitional period and two periods that follow that represent literary activity in Canada. The period of transition is designed to distinguish folklore from literature, which first appears in the work of Semen Kovbel (1877–1966), who emigrated to Canada in 1909. The two following periods each follow the two world wars. In order to understand how the biographies are structured, it is useful to give some consideration to the life and work of the man who is proposed as the founder. Kovbel, first of all, is 'the dividing line' in a 'period of distinct advance.' Unlike his predecessors, who 'felt themselves uprooted from their native soil and not planted permanently in the Canadian soil,' Kovbel's mind was made up firmly before he left. Although this appears to contradict my remark that emigrants usually do not leave unless it seems more or less impossible to stay in their country of origin, Kovbel had 'decided not to return under the oppressive domination over Ukrainian people by their enemies.' Such a decision was clearly made under duress. Canada was chosen because it was democratic and would, therefore, provide 'liberty and prosperity.'[19]

Kovbel becomes exemplary because, finding oppression intolerable, he decided to carry the cause of freedom abroad. Unlike his folkloric predecessors, he strove to overcome nostalgia and mere retrospection, becoming '[Ukraine's] free voice before the world.' Although his poetry and short stories were not collected, his plays were frequently performed, addressing themes of patriotism and 'the Ukrainian struggle for independence.' The difference that distinguishes Kovbel's work from folklore and marks it as the true beginning is his willingness to relate to 'heroic deeds and tragic moments' and so continue the spirit of *The Campaign of Igor*. It reflects a moral and political *prise de conscience* rather than an inability to rise from the 'despair, privation, hopelessness and nostalgia' of the earlier song-writers.[20] Kovbel enacts, therefore, the animating ideology of Mandryka's history.

Two other writers of the same generation, Pavlo Krat (1882–1952) and Vera Lysenko (1910–75), published more, but Krat does not fare as well for no other reason, it appears, than that he is not so intimately related to national struggle. In fact, Krat's entry is anticipated by a brief mention in the survey of the early period. Having 'participated in the social-democratic movement before emigrating to Canada (1907),' he failed to 'make any imprint on the Ukrainian Canadian literary process.' He failed because 'the development of the latter followed its logical course, having as its vital force-mobile the insuperable historic traditions of Ukrainian culture and self-denying love of the Ukrainian people.'[21] Despite his subsequent ideological reorientation as a United Church pastor,[22] Krat does not fit with Mandryka's nationalist code, for not only does he have leftist tendencies, but also his stories are 'all radical, even revolutionary.' Vera Lysenko's novel and historical essay written in English are treated even more dismissively. *The Men in Sheepskin Coats* (1947) is disposed of because 'the obvious pro-communist tendencies deprive this book of objectivity.' Consequently, she 'belongs to Ukrainian Canadian literature only by her origin and by the themes from Ukrainian Canadian life in her two books.'[23]

The other criterion of inclusion in the canon is the refusal to espouse the attitudes of modernism. Tetiana Shevchuk (1904–96), for example, 'operates with a new modern form of versification, but not abstract.' Yar Slavutych (1918–), representing the generation that emigrated after the Second World War, exemplifies another aspect of the continuous struggle of being Ukrainian: 'Belonging to the "new" generation of poets, now in their majority in Europe and the New World plunged in a muddy world of illogical nothingness, in which a poet looks like a lunatic, and not a bard of humanity, Slavutych has saved his poetical integrity and taken a firm stand on the great poetic road.' Borys Oleksandriv's (1921–79) poetry is also praised for never swerving 'into the treacherous nihilistic camp of a new fashion,' and Larysa Murovych (1917–) is deemed akin to Emily Dickinson (1830–86), in the sense that both worshipped 'Beauty and Right.' Needless to say, Dickinson did not dwell exclusively in beauty and rectitude, and strong readings of her work, those, say of Oleh Zujewskyj (1920–96), one of the greatest of the modernists in the Ukrainian diaspora, reflect other, more difficult aspects of her work.[24]

Greatness, however, is assigned to Illia Kyriak (1889–1955) and the Ukrainian Catholic priest, Semen Semckuk (1899–1984). The former's novel, *Syny Zemli* (1939–45; translated as *Sons of the Soil*) is praised for its account 'of the process of settlement of Ukrainian pioneers, their social, spiritual and cultural organization, their step by step integration into the Canadian system, and finally the achievement of remarkable success and stability without losing their identity and cultural heritage.' Its realism allows favourable comparison with *War and Peace*, at least on the level of talent, and it is implied that Kyriak's achievement is all the more admirable since he had none of the material advantages of his predecessor. Semchuk's poetry and short stories are particularly singled out for their moral and spiritual vigour, and the stand they take against the 'pessimism and negation of the present day moral looseness.'[25]

Mandryka's history, then inscribes a moral, political, and aesthetic centre whose purpose is to emphasize the struggle for, and preservation of, Ukrainian liberty, which, at the time of writing at least, can only occur in the diaspora. Deviations to the political left or into aesthetic concerns that are deemed nihilistic, that is, which undermine the coherence of the nation, are not constructed as a dynamic activity within the literary system. They are excluded, because they do not belong to the 'force-mobile' of Ukrainian culture. In the same way, anything that opposes it is treated as non-Ukrainian and therefore valorized in a negative fashion. Interaction is not permitted, and the Other is not granted a causal status, impelling certain changes in the internal development of the literature. For this reason, 'the history of Ukrainian literature in Canada cannot be written on the basis of chronological stages.' Rather, 'its history is a logical process.'[26]

What is this process? It is that '*of the wholesome social growth of the Ukrainian society itself.*' This means that Mandryka espouses an organicist understanding of history in which there is natural relationship between literature and the people. It is, as he says, citing Isidore Hlynka, 'the *subjective and objective philosophy of a people at its best.*' Literature, furthermore, does not so much grow in time, but transcends it and carries within itself as a 'force-mobile' 'the immortal Promethean idea of liberation of man and peoples from bondage, of elevating them to spiritual perfection.' Growth and elevation from a central core belong to a semiotic field that recalls Herder's idea of history as a harmonious order that turns upon a Synecdochic centre whose aspirations are Comic.[27] Comedy is what Canada provides as an answer to the continuous tragedy of Ukrainian history. Comedy is only possible, however, as long as there is no Ukrainian-Canadian literature, but only a Ukrainian literature in Canada. Thus, despite Kyriak and Lysenko, integration in Padolsky's sense is not desired, and he is correct to place 'Ukrainian-Canadian Ukrainian [*sic*] language writing in the voluntary separation category.' While it is true that Mandryka belonged 'to the nationalist camp,[28] it is a nation without ontological possibility. Nor is it capable of having an effect upon the dominant literatures of the Canadian system, having chosen exclusivity as its role, driven by its own 'force-mobile.'

Being Written

As I have suggested, the situation of Native peoples is the inverse of that of immigrants. The fundamental difference, of course, is that they had no decision in the matter and therefore may be said to have lost agency entirely, while immigrants, often choosing the lesser of two undesired objects, have lost agency while, paradoxically, exercising it. They share, however, the sense of necessity and catastrophe that is so often a part of necessity. Hence, beginning for both may be understood as akin to a seismic fault which is felt at both personal and cultural levels, and as a beginning all over again. In both instances, the beginnings are ambivalent and may be construed as either disastrous or carrying some possibilities. But division is always present at the centre of the subject and the subject's world, and the cultural history that it encourages must address both the loss of beginning as origin somewhere in the past and the acquisition of a beginning which drives the subject to carry loss forward into the future as a necessary legacy and defining presence.[29]

Thus Robin McGrath's *Canadian Inuit Literature: The Development of a Tradition* (1984) begins appropriately enough with this defining condition, using it to entitle her first chapter 'European Contact as It Affected Literacy.' Clearly, in a literary history of this kind, literacy is the significant issue, the issue that had the power to change a particular culture radically enough to force a (new) beginning. Implicit in the notion of European contact, however, are the initial efforts made to construct the Inuit as Other in exploration journals, but what is more significant were the efforts made to present Inuit writing in both syllabics and European languages. It was a process that engendered, however, 'Eskimo Europeanization' either through trade, religion, or government, the latter almost destroying Inuit culture by means of residential schools.[30]

Crucial, however, in the formation of the new culture was the presence and accessibility of European writing. A significant element of the beginning was elsewhere, as well as non-indigenous. McGrath appropriately draws an analogy between the rise of literacy and the formation of Christian culture in medieval Europe, and provides a number of reasons to explain its usefulness. Certainly the desire to record and preserve a dying way of life, as well as the transmitting of Christian doctrine to 'pagan countrymen,' would count as strong, motivating elements among the Inuit. It should be noted, however, that a central sign of contact between Inuit and European was the text, and it was also the sign of both ending and beginning. The first syllabic alphabet was developed by the beginning of the eighteenth century, which means that its understanding and usage was rapidly acquired compared to medieval Europe, which did not become accustomed to the written text until the beginning of the fifteenth century, during a period of slow gestation indeed.[31] What could well have been a cultural catastrophe was, however, according to McGrath, averted because Inuit 'culture was one which was already predisposed to literacy.' They already made use of pictographic traditions, as well as showing a 'fondness for words and pictures.' Syllabics seemed to come easily, but one still wonders to what extent 'written Inuit literature [was] a normal and desirable development in their history.' Scholars are often inclined to look benignly upon the technologies which they themselves use and serve, and the difference that McGrath notes between traditional Inuit society and European culture suggests almost radically opposed world-views. In the former

> every person was a singer, and to some extent a poet, just as every person was a craftsperson, and to some extent an artist. It was necessary to work on language just as it was necessary to work on skins or ivory, in order to produce the requirements of life. In European culture it was, and is, possible to grow from adolescence to old age without ever having to sing or create a poem, but in Inuit culture you had to sing and compose in order to catch a seal, break a fever, obtain justice, control the universe.

The gradual acquisition of literacy in Europe, then, did not change the relationship of people to the universe to the extent that it must have done in American First Nations cultures, and that change may testify to a crisis that McGrath does not consider at length, but refers to briefly at the end as 'the pain and frustration caused by the trauma of European contact.'[32]

According to McGrath's argument, alterity came as a function of literacy: it was the cultural act that had the most radical of effects. It is for this reason that her history is divided into a large structure embracing oral and written literature, and this division is further distinguished generically. Thus, by structuring the book into sections which address respectively oral and written poetry, and then oral and written prose, one cannot escape the impression that the incursion of literacy, if it did not happen twice, happened at least emphatically and became the single most important aspect of their development. Literacy divided Inuit society from its past by dividing its understanding of its cultural practices and their effects. Oral poetry is performative to a degree that surpasses anything of which written literature is capable. Part of its vitality inheres in the word itself for poetry which, according to Edward Carpenter, derives from '*anerca*, the soul, that which is eternal, the breath of life.' How much this differs from our word, which derives from the Greek *poiēin*, which, meaning 'to make,' emphasizes poetry as craftsmanship. A closer sense of the Inuit notion of poetry occurs if we were to think of it as a form of animation and derive 'poetry' from *anima*, which refers both to breath and soul. Thus the subgenres of Inuit oral poetry, namely, 'songs of mood, hunting songs, charms, and songs of derision,' are kinds that establish a direct rapport between speaker, language, content, and audience, which is conveyed especially through the music.[33]

The fact that sympathetic anthropologists have been gathering these traditional songs since 1913 is clear evidence that the Inuit past 'belongs,' as a result, as much to European as it does to Inuit culture.[34] Traditional songs exist as a function of the process of acculturation which acquires its full force as the oral is transformed by the written as much as by the general impact of European civilization in the North. The 'mood poems' are now inspired by a nostalgia that is also apparent in ethnic minority poetry, the old hunting songs have now been replaced by political issues, the incantations are now accessible as hymns, and songs of derision have acquired more contemporary themes. The new subgenre that has followed in the wake of literacy is the love poem, which, McGrath argues, is a result of a loss of 'control of their own destinies.' Such a development is the exact contrary of the earlier poems, and it reflects a serious sociological change: 'The right to choose a mate and to develop close personal relationships outside the family was not considered to be very important in traditional times, but it has accrued considerable importance in post-contact life.'[35]

McGrath has already drawn attention in a general way to a shift from oral to written in the European Middle Ages as analogous to what has happened among the Inuit, and the most powerful effect of this shift may be described as the emergence of the Inuit subject as a function of the acquisition of literacy. Ivan Illich has argued in his reading of Hugh of St Victor's *Didascalion* that the beginnings of such an event occurred in Europe during the twelfth century, and he finds in this text 'a special correspondence between the emergence of selfhood understood as a person and the emergence of "the" text from the page.' Thus, it is not surprising that in written prose the dominant subgenre is autobiography. It is a sign of acculturation because it is often the result of both non-Inuit encouragement and the fact that this is what the writer knows best.[36] Moreover, in unwitting corroboration of Illich's argument, McGrath observes that 'the oral tradition does not favour individualism, but the book isolates the reader from the living situation and promotes a close relationship between author and individual reader.' The other subgenre, which McGrath considers 'the greatest departure from the old cultural tradition,' is the political and cultural essay. The recurring theme 'is that of self-determination.'[37] Needless to say, such essays construct a somewhat different 'self' from that of autobiography, but it is clear that these are texts that are designed to effect a dialogue between Inuit and European Canadians and, in the process, to explain an Inuit subject which in this instance is more social, more politically defined, than the autobiographical subject.

As part of her conclusion, McGrath reiterates the Inuit predisposition to literacy, based partly on the relationship between the written and the illustrated. This provides a significant structure to her plot as a cultural intervention that at once separates and fulfils. As I have suggested, its significance lies in its role of facilitating the construction of a subject, as if the same act that colonizes also prepares for post-colonial gestures. Thus, political dates are not marked in McGrath's texts, but the moment of *prise de conscience* is. This means that the making of alterity implies the possible making of the subject, and so the implied history that McGrath constructs is that of the emerging subject. Its autonomy, however, is always mediated, insofar as the construction of the subject is a result of continued contact with the Other, whose presence has the effect of construing Inuit culture as an alterity, thus inhibiting the full *épanouissent* of its subjectivity. History, however, is to be perceived as an interior event, an unfolding of the spirit.

Splitting the Subject

The Americas, needless to say, were not discovered, but invaded, and this is a condition that its Native inhabitants share with other peoples of the world. Thus, as I have argued, they bear a symmetrical relationship with many of the ethnic groups who have chosen to leave *their* native lands for other countries such as Canada. We have seen that this was the *leitmotif* of Mandryka's history, and it is drawn upon by George Bisztray in his *Hungarian-Canadian Literature* (1987).[38] The beginning is clearly marked as 1956, the year in which the Soviet Union invaded Hungary. Unlike Mandryka, however, Bisztray does not situate his history in the fate of a single nation as the victim of continuous incursion by hostile armies, but places it rather in a larger context of the general and massive diaspora that has occurred since the Second World War, which he terms 'a new age of great migration.' A consequence of such demographic shifts is that 'the concept of nation, as well as the definitions of national culture and literature, will soon be radically reinterpreted.' Such a statement anticipates Joseph Pugliese's thesis about the ontology of nation and argues against Herder's notion that language and nation are coterminous.[39] Although it serves as a general justification for Bisztray's project, his main purpose is the presentation of Hungarian-Canadian literature, especially since 1956, offering the hope that it will both serve as a useful method for future histories of literature in the non-official languages of Canada and lead eventually to 'a synthetic, integrated multicultural literary history of Canada.'[40]

One aspect of his method is a function of the distinction he draws between his history and that, for example, of Mandryka, which he castigates for the lack of both genre and aesthetic criteria. Literary history requires, he argues, a canon, and care must be taken to exclude non-literary texts, such as those of a 'religious, journalistic, [and] popularizing-scientific' character. This is a curious assertion, especially when read in light of one his later definitions of literary history that 'integrates the history of authors, written works, readers or audience, and the institutions which make the publication, distribution, and preservation of literature possible.' As Lemire and his colleagues eloquently indicate, the kinds of texts Bisztray would exclude could readily serve his purpose. It might even be argued, however, that he, like Mandryka, denigrates folklore for being 'aesthetically unambitious and genetically anonymous, usually unrecorded social products which almost always served certain institutions such as religion, law, and collective production without forming an autonomous institution.' The significant expression is 'collective production,' and it is possible that Mandryka and Bisztray share a mutual suspicion of the function of folklore during the Soviet regime in Eastern and Central Europe as a means of promoting the *Volk*. To be fair, however, Bisztray goes on to assert that folklore is not literature as he defines it and, consequently, incapable 'of establishing any historical continuity and interactional patterns' with, one assumes, Canadian literature.[41] Thus, Hungarian-Canadian literature has two phases, namely, a prehistory as folklore and a history as literature.

The poetry that constitutes the first phase is prehistorical primarily because it is without a history and, therefore, 'truly ethnic in character.' Such was the Hungarian literature written in Canada between the two wars. Differences between it and Hungarian poetry consisted in only minor shifts of address. For example, 'the *délibáb* ("mirage"), a frequent poetic motif inspired by the familiar natural phenomenon of the Hungarian Great Plains, is replaced by the northern lights in several poems.' But the theme of nostalgia – common enough in immigrant writing – takes on a special meaning by virtue of which this poetry reflected 'a subtle propaganda campaign [which] was directed from Hungary ... to make the emigrants accept the old country as the centre of their emotional existence.' The change that occurred in the 1950s, especially after the Soviet invasion, was of such a kind that one can no longer speak of 'Hungarian literature written in Canada – it is Hungarian-Canadian literature.'[42]

Although a complete structural analogy cannot be drawn between the Inuit and Hungarian-Canadian literatures, they both share the order of before and after whose cardinal point is a crisis characterized by invasion. Needless to say, the technological changes that the shift from an oral to a written culture entails did not occur in the development of Hungarian-Canadian literature, Bisztray's use of folk song has a parallel with McGrath's use of orality: crisis precipitates history and permits a move from the timeless to the historical.[43] One might say, moreover, that the effect upon the subject was of a similar character, suggesting a kind of metonymical relationship between social and political events, on the one hand, and self-awareness, on the other. The inescapable presence of the Other engenders the subject. Had Bisztray, for example, chosen to situate Hungarian-Canadian literature within a larger context of Hungarian literature than that which folk song represents, the kind of analogy I am drawing would not be valid. It differs in this respect from Mandryka's structure, which not only makes use of folk song but also places his literature within the context of a diaspora and makes of it an extension of Ukrainian literature proper. It belongs, nevertheless, to the continuous crisis of Ukrainian culture which began in the Middle Ages.

To enter history, then, to borrow an Old Testament motif that occurs often in Canadian literary history, is to fall into consciousness. What happened before, whether as oral literature or folklore, between which there is little formal difference, belongs to the order of myth and often to origins of a mysterious kind; what happened after belongs to time, to beginnings that can often be given precise dates, and to the end of ano-nymity in which the subject, as the example from Kreisel suggests, begins to assert itself. History for Hungarian-Canadian literature begins in 1956, and individual lives replace 'collective production.' The move into history is also witnessed by the fact that after this date, writers belong to a generation that is capable of being further divided into three phases, namely, older, middle, and younger, and each of which has differing, but related, aspects that allow them to share the same life in time.

Of the three moments of this generation, the first is marked by the fact that none of its representatives had returned to Hungary at the time of Bisztray's writing. Furthermore, their work began in Hungary, is governed by dispositions developed there, and, as a result, marked by an inability to find a home. Part of the pessimism with which their work is imbued belongs to their general generation in Europe and is, therefore, difficult to place in respect of Canadian writing of the period. As Bisz-tray puts it, they all found 'it difficult or impossible to accept the reali-ties of the New World.' Being younger, the middle group appear to have adapted more readily to these realities and to have substituted irony for the despair of their elders. Hence, they are perceived as more 'inte-grated,' if not in the sense used by Padolsky, who would find that their persistent use of Hungarian places them between the levels of assimila-tion and maginalization. Suspended, however, somewhere between these two levels, their ability 'to reinterpret their Hungarian heritage from a physical and intellectual distance, thereby avoiding the illusions, ideologies, and fetishes prevailing in the poetry of the older generation' marks the double register of their work to the extent that it is neither Hungarian nor Canadian.[44] Perhaps it is more apt to say that it is Cana-dian expressed in the Hungarian language and through Hungarian cul-ture as it is remembered and transformed. If this is a valid assertion, then Padolsky's categories require certain qualifications to admit the Other – at the level of the subject – in a non-official language. Certainly the policy of multiculturalism does not permit such admissions but this, it seems to me, at least, is what cultural interaction in Canada is in some respects striving to accomplish. Part of McGrath's conclusion appeals for such a possibility, and it is implied in Bisztray's argument. Its pur-pose, however, poses a clear threat to the idea of the homogenous nation, already weakened by a policy of biculturalism and asks: Why does Canada need to have the illusion of a common centre when such a centre does not, in any case, exist already? Neither of the two official cultures constructs its history in an entirely similar manner, nor do the Inuit and other Aboriginal people.

Precisely such a lack of centre anywhere is what seems to unite the youngest of these poets who share 'the same amorphous and ambivalent attitude towards Canadian existence.' Thus Bisztray constructs the relationship between each phase of the whole generation by drawing upon gardening metaphors. The older members were 'transplanted from Hungary or Europe,' and, indeed, 'uprooted.' The middle group were 'replanted,' suggesting a somewhat easier passage.[45] The youngest poets are simply 'rootless, as they probably would also be in Hungary.' All of them are plants in various positions of movement between two plots of land, and the younger the plant is, the lesser amount of previous soil clings to its roots. Although the metaphor lends coherence to Bisztray's argument, the way the organicist metaphor is used appears to weaken the argument. On the face of it, all the poets appear to be merely extensions of Hungarian literature itself, but the play of the middle group of poets, for instance, with 'the emigrant psyche and consciousness' echoes Możejko's point mentioned earlier: once having entered the diaspora, they are partly minority and partly national. Thus, it is not entirely valid, as Bisztray would have it, that by the middle period it was 'possible to establish an autonomous nationality literature.' It is apparent from the chapter devoted to drawing a socio-psychological profile of the Hungarian-Canadian writer that their situation is perhaps too ambivalent to achieve autonomy. Bisztray sums up their use of themes as follows: 'their attachment to a primarily Hungarian and secondarily European heritage definitely indicates that Hungarian-Canadian literature is rooted in the Old rather than the New World.' This statement is sufficiently qualified, however, to underscore a certain ambivalence. Indeed, the Hungarian writer 'finds himself alone between two cultural iron curtains: one shutting off communication with ten million Hungarians, the other ... closing the vista of the large anglophone and francophone Canada.'[46]

The choice of separation, that is, to continue with the use of the Hungarian language, appears motivated by the fear that if one abandoned the language, one might 'be written off as a *Hungarian* writer.' The price for such a choice is 'the greater than average isolation of Hungarian-Canadian literature in the multicultural context of the nation.'[47] Where, then, is the Hungarian-Canadian writer in respect of Hungary, on the one hand, and Canada, on the other? To pose such a question is to draw a crucial difference between the immigrant writer and the Aboriginal writer. Yet, significantly, both immigrant and Native histories inscribe statements about the status of language because their histories face the problem of continuous linguistic erosion in a predominantly bilingual society. Language and history constitute the subject, and all three share the continuous presence of a state of crisis in which first language, then history, and finally the subject may disappear. Thus, while the crisis may be initiated in a metonymical manner through invasion, as I have suggested, it is transmuted into a mode of integrated meaning represented by White's Synecdoche. Everything in such histories or cultures turns upon a central idea, in this instance the division caused by invasion, which then ramifies everywhere. If the division is not closed, the historian appears drawn toward inscribing futures that would do so, appealing to the necessity of preserving a language. The future, then, is implicated into the whole plot. Texts, finally, that can be positioned on both sides if the divide become canonical, and in so doing preserve the historically split subject, whose history is the repetition of division.

History as Dissemination

Language, however, is not always at issue, as Michael Greenstein implies in *Third Solitudes* (1989). The title alludes to Hugh MacLennan's novel *Two Solitudes* (1945), which is meant to embrace anglophone and francophone cultures. It is evident, however, that all writing that emerges from the minority languages and cultures of Canada constitutes its own solitude, and a history of Canadian culture is perforce a history of many solitudes. The subtitle of Greenstein's book – *Tradition and Discontinuity in Jewish-Canadian Literature* – embraces the issue all the minority cultures share. Its tradition is, in fact, one of discontinuity, which is a condition it shares, at least, with the Ukrainian and Hungarian literatures of Canada. It is a history that turns upon the notion of diaspora, which prevents a conceptualization of history in a linear, chronological sense. The general meaning of 'diaspora' is caught in Greenstein's expression, 'a continual process of walking abroad,' even back and forth, and being always in a 'hyphenated "in-between" state.' Such a view of diaspora argues, furthermore, with both the cyclical and dialectical notions of history; and the work of A.M. Klein, which is taken as a model of the existential situation of diaspora, 'breaks circles [and] negates dialectical synthesis.'[48] His 'second scroll,' for example, is not second after a first, but the second after a second, illustrating the validity of Jacques Derrida's theory that there is no origin from which everything proceeds and that texts are places where meaning constantly modifies as a consequence of dissemination. What else, however, is diaspora but dissemination, both words sharing the meanings of 'sowing seed' and 'scattering abroad'? These meanings adapt themselves metaphorically not only to the experience of emigration but also to the role texts play in endeavouring to find meaning only to become the seeds of differing meaning through the efforts of other (second) texts.

Thus, it is perfectly apt that the full intellectual matrix of Greenstein's work is to be found in a number of European and American Jewish thinkers who range from Sigmund Freud to Martin Buber, T.W. Adorno, Jacques Derrida, Harold Bloom, and Geoffrey Hartman, all of whom are embarrassed by closure and certainty, and so manifest their own debts to the Talmud and kabbalistic thought. All of them, furthermore, are practitioners of what one might call the art of diaspora in their practice of a 'Jewish heretical hermeneutics.' As Susan Handelman argues, 'We may now read Jesus, Paul, Freud, and Freud's most recent interpreters, Derrida, Lacan, and Bloom as all sharing in a particular mode of Jewish interpretive heresy: a distorted displacement, an aspect of which is the conversion of metonymy into metaphor, or displacement pretending to substitution.' And, as she notes elsewhere, 'Displacement ... is both the *condition* of and *answer* to exile.'[49] In other words, the only way to live with diaspora is to practise the full meaning of displacement. To perceive diaspora not simply as a cause, which is included in the notion of metonymy, but to understand it as a meaning that pervades one's vision of the world is at the heart of Greenstein's method, and thus his history corresponds to White's use of Synecdoche. That place is everywhere and nowhere, that meanings are multiple – this constitutes the design that integrates the writers that constitute his corpus.

As a consequence, Klein, who stands at the beginning of Jewish-Canadian writing in Canada, also constitutes a centre, and while time moves forward and younger writers emerge, these writers are marked by a reversion to Klein and their texts become reversions and re-inscriptions of perennial preoccupations. One might call this centre an origin in Said's sense, who distinguishes origin and beginning by noting that 'origin is a condition or state that permits beginning.' Klein becomes an origin by assuming in his poetry and prose the full sense of diaspora, and his novel, *The Second Scroll* (1951), according to Greenstein, serves as 'an archi-text through which gleams the untravelled world and fading margin of Jewish-Canadian literature.'[50] It does so, however, through a process of interpretive displacement derived from the talmudic tradition that asserts that writing is always re-writing, all scrolls are always second scrolls. This means that even the notion of archi-text suffers from displacement and becomes metatext, a text which is both tied to, and dissociated from, another.

Greenstein's method, having once established Klein as a matrix, is to address his writers in separate chapters, with the exception of a general chapter on poetry. The Holocaust is the central theme of Jewish-Canadian poetry, and it constitutes a kind of second start to Greenstein's history, which quotes Robert Mirashi in epigraph, referring to it as '*This past beginning.*' The expression may be neatly interpreted as 'after Klein' or, more appropriately, as an event which opened an unbridgeable gulf between the present and the world before the Holocaust. One of the consequences is that the Holocaust appears as a loss of those primal referents that would permit one to acquire self-knowledge. This lack precipitates a more perplexing problem: it casts doubt on who the Other – in this case, the enemy – might be. For Irving Layton and Leonard Cohen (1934–), both victim and victimizer share identities, and Eli Mandel (1922–92), suspended between past and present, prairie childhood and Toronto, barely able to pronounce the word 'Auschwitz,' is impelled toward 'fragments, disguise, indirection, dislocation, and almost meetings between event and expression.' The Holocaust becomes a sign that corresponds to, and, in this instance, activates the unrecoverable loss that lies at the centre of the histories that we have been discussing. Indeed, as these three poets suggest, the Holocaust confirms the validity of a 'heretic hermeneutic [which] is a complex dialectic of identification and displacement,'[51] and in its repetition in their texts its meaning plays forever into the meaning of diaspora as dissemination. It is always present and always confusing the relationship between sign and referent.

For Greenstein, this is a primary heritage of Klein, that reaches through these poets to its confirmation in Henry Kreisel in which nothing fits, closure does not occur, and 'answers falsify the fiction.' Clearly, as Greenstein argues, all these writers and those who follow – Norman Levine (1923–), Jack Ludwig (1922–), Adele Wiseman (1928–92), Mordecai Richler (1931–2001), Monique Bosco (1927–), Naim Kattan (1928–) and Matt Cohen (1942–99) – all construct texts that enact Derrida's notion of *différance*, that is, texts that in their rewriting of other texts transmute the world into a scene of eternal diaspora in which connections between origins and process are broken, and meaning can only be construed as a patchwork of trajectories going nowhere. Thus identities merge in Richler, origins disappear in Leonard Cohen and Richler, and in Ludwig, Levine, and Leonard Cohen 'dissemination, unanswerable questions,' are preferable to semantic closure.[52] Wiseman decentres, and borders lose their function everywhere in Levine, Richler, and Kattan. Bosco, who alone was a direct victim of the Holocaust, enacts the displacement of diaspora and is, like Leonard Cohen 'distrustful of master narratives,' whose power she dissipates through obsessive repetition' and dissemination. Nothing is capable of perfect reconciliation; metaphor, which Handelman finds 'characteristic ... of Christian thought,' is not a semantic or narrative dominant.[53]

Such an analysis makes of Jewish-Canadian literature a postmodern corpus, which Greenstein's opening and closing overtures to Robert Kroetsch underscore. He implies that history, to be made relevant to these writers, must be construed in the same way. Thus the beginning is not a moment in time, but a text which is both archi-text and metatext. In rhetorical terms, beginning is a metonymy, a chain of signifiers, a process which may be seen in the reading above of Kreisel's opening sentence. Such an implication has an ironic bearing on Canadian literary history when viewed from an ontological perspective. Where in the labyrinth of language will Being be found, and, if it is found, what will guarantee that it would not be reduced to a play of signifiers? In what temporal register, furthermore, does history occur? Inasmuch as the construction of minority ethnic writing in Canada is, with the exception of Mandryka, a phenomenon of the 1980s and 1990s and, with the exception of First Nations and Inuit histories, focused primarily upon writing of the twentieth century, the respective historical frames of francophone and anglophone history are not useful and, in fact, ignored, nor is their function as a master-narrative given recognition. Nothing unfolds from past to future. The characteristics of minority ethnic writing are (always) already given, becoming the object of continuous qualification and reinterpretation.

Greenstein implies that the reason for such understanding is to be found in the confirmation of the heretical hermeneutics in the Holocaust. The combination serves as the catastrophe that marks the kind of histories we have been explicating. History provides the event that permits the loss of historical certitude. While other historians are thus prompted to project a future that otherwise runs the risk of being lost, Greenstein suggests that the future is a tense that is not available because of the loss of a clearly signifying past. Thus, while both the historical and the literary text depend upon metonymical linearity, the semantic reliability of linearity that suggest connections of one thing leading to, perhaps causing, another, is lost as texts either render obscure or misconstrue their points of departure. Futures also imply a certain kind of closure and suggest that an ethnic group can continue to be what it is, for example, if it can retain the language that preserves its culture. The question that Greenstein poses, however, is: What are we if language can keep redefining us? To modify one of Leonard Cohen's titles, Greenstein is asking us to compare ontologies and, in so doing, to discover their role as mythologies. History is a fiction that we try to make real through the use of events and dates whose meanings are, however, so open to modification of meaning that we can only find history in the labyrinth of fiction.

Alternative Agencies

Penny Petrone's history, *Native Literature in Canada*, which carries the subtitle, *From the Oral Tradition to the Present* (1990), invites, as we shall see, immediate comparison with Diane Boudreau's *Histoire de la littérature amérindienne au Québec*, the subtitle of which is simply *oralité et littérature*. As we observed with McGrath, although Petrone's history does not announce its intent in the title, its structure follows the same binary pattern that these terms imply. The correlation between writing and European settlement among First Nations, with the exception to a certain degree of the Inuit, is highly marked. Indeed, for Petrone history and writing appear to coincide, and she suggests this by entitling her first chapter 'Oral Literatures' and her second '1820–1850.' Prior to this period, Native texts were recorded in English or French primarily by missionaries. It was both Native and appropriated. After 1812 and the failure of Tecumseh's efforts to organize a confederacy, Native writers began to record their experiences directly without recourse to mythology.[54] So anglophone Native writers entered history. Unlike Boudreau, Petrone does not question the significance of how performative the structure of her history is. The structure clearly implies that First Nations had no history before 1812 but lived in a kind of mythological space that is the function of oral literature to create and enact. Petrone's text asserts that Native history is not a history unless it coincides with European dates, which may be attributed to the fact that she is not a Native writer herself. Such a move has the virtue of underscoring a significant aspect of Native and ethnic minority cultures and makes the inverse relationship that we have called attention to more evident. Emigrants in a certain sense give up a history; Natives have a history forced upon them. Neither have a history that is manifestly their own, and both are defined historically with respect to histories of the Other. The radical alteration of history that emigration and immigration produce cannot help but structure the turn from myth to time as a Fall. That the model is almost always that of Genesis belies a certain ideology that may be different from a Native perspective, but 'Native' is not in itself a term of a homogeneous character.

In fact, the initial alterations in Native culture are profoundly implicated in Judaeo-Christian ideologies and thoroughly an effect of missionary activity.[55] The first Native texts reflect the influence of the Bible, particularly in the translations of books of the Old and New Testaments by Native missionaries into Ojibwa. Another genre in which the biblical intertext and paradigm is present is the sermon literature of the period. It is, of course, difficult to measure the full impact of these and other kinds of writing practised by Native missionaries and preachers, since they appear to be the only texts collected, implying that oral literature and the ideologies that it inscribed were not as present. As Petrone observes, 'the force and effectiveness of Indian speech – once heard around the council fires and in orations among kinsmen and in negotiations with enemies – was now heard most often in the pulpit, and in negotiations with the white government.' Judging by William Wilson's verse, it would be hard to find any trace in the poetry of the period of the techniques and purposes of oral poetry:

A solemn voice is heard from ev'ry shore,
That now the Indian nations are no more, –
A remnant scarce remain to tell their wrongs,
But soon will fade to live in poets' songs.[56]

To be so derivative of Oliver Goldsmith, as Petrone remarks, is to be assimilated with a vengeance. It is to be a mimic of a mimic, which is the worst effect of colonizing.

Where the theme of dispossession shows to best advantage is not in Wilson's flagging verse, but in the protest literature of the period, which constitutes a new genre. But, surely, if this literature is like sermons of Native eloquence, this is a new genre based at least stylistically in the older oral literature and recalls a tradition of council oratory. The genres that are more 'unfamiliar' are 'the letter, autobiography, travel-ogue, diary, and journal,' inasmuch as they testify to 'a break with the oral tradition.' Although Petrone is cautious about being too explicit in the definition of oral narrative, referring to it as 'traditional' and 'oral,' rather than as 'myth' and 'legend,' her examples fall into two large kinds, namely, 'trickster/transformer/culture-hero stories' and 'Origin, Creation, and Migration tales.' These dominant modes imply by their themes how central they are to Native oral literature: they belong to collective memory and history and they provide models of behaviour and action for the community. In short, they are exemplary narratives. Furthermore, they may be seen, if the contrast is not to sharply drawn, as inscriptions of a cosmic, rather than anthropomorphic, vision. Although the 'new genres,' notably, autobiography, would seem to sug-gest a break because of the emergence of the subject within a collective story, the evidence bears more upon a hybridization. As she remarks of autobiography at a later stage when it became more generally used, 'the narrators invariably conform to the native autobiographical tradition that blends personal, tribal, and mythological history, and moves back and forth among them.'[57] The same observation is confirmed by Bou-dreau and McGrath.[58]

Writing, then, is not so much the sign of a rupture and a new start, but rather is the sign of invasion that, as a consequence, memorializes catastrophe along with traces of a pre-catastrophic past. It is the present sign of dispossession. It is the one means that a people that finds itself in a dominated position possesses in order to seek agency, and in various ways, all the peoples of Canada, with the exception of English Canadi-ans, where they sense themselves as dominant,[59] make use of writing so.[60] The paradox for First Nations people, Inuit, and immigrants whose native language is not English, is that if access to agency appears offered by English, it carries a high cultural price. If some immigrant writers continue to write in their national languages, such as Ukrainian and Hungarian, their presence in Canada and their bearing on the literary system of anglophone writing is limited, inasmuch as they have chosen separation or marginalization. If they choose English or French, as First Nations people, Inuit, and most immigrants have done, they acquire, in many cases, the insights of integration, but run the risk of being read without full understanding by the people of other cultures of their dif-ference and their challenge.[61]

Because, however, of their relation to the federal government, it is difficult for First Nations people and the Inuit not to make use of

English, which in fact facilitated communication between the several indigenous languages. The major turning-point in their post-conquest history, the *Statement of the Government of Canada on Indian Policy*, enunciated in 1969, in conjunction with the impact in Canada of the American Indian Movement, made such use imperative, and Native writing has displayed itself in a variety of forms. Besides those mentioned, tribal stories, short stories, children's stories, and drama have become more apparent since the 1970s as dominant genres. Poetry is produced, but not to the same extent. The form that relates them and which is continuously present from the nineteenth century is the literature of protest, for 'the literature of Canada's native peoples has always been quintessentially political, addressing their persecutions and betrayals and summoning their resources for resistance.'[62]

Literature and its history, then, are inseparable from a political dimension. The political as it relates to fiction, however, takes a particular form, and one might say that there are two beginnings to Petrone's history. The first we have mentioned, and it derives from the simultaneous impact of European invasion and writing. This much she shares with McGrath and Boudreau. The other is raised as a matter of fiction, as opposed to 'the real.' The Introduction raises immediately the question of the neglect and ignorance of Native literature. The reason for this is that the Native has a history in the European imaginary that begins with a state of bewilderment: Columbus had stumbled on Indians who were not Indians. This paradox appeared to free the North American Indian into a zone of replaceable images that ranged from the 'bon sauvage' and Caliban to 'the Hollywood image of the silent Indian.'[63] In other words, the Native has always been Other, at least in European discourse, speaking either French or English, or nothing at all. In all these instances, Natives are figures without agency. The beginning, then, is in a fictional zone of alterity that is akin to the inauthentic. Their history, as Petrone constructs it, is a process that is designed to separate the authentic from the fictional. As a result, history becomes political allegory,[64] which is a not uncommon way of making post-colonial history, and it uses the beginning as a moment that separates the true from the false. History acquires, therefore, both moral and epistemological force. In the first instance, to remain possessed of the old imagery is to manifest morally prejudicial attitudes. To remain possessed of the second is to be a victim of false knowledge. The historian is consequently constructed as more than someone recounting events; the historian is, rather, a spiritual mentor.

Outside the Literary Institution

Besides the successive volumes of *La Vie littéraire au Québec*, the most recent francophone literary history to appear is Diane Boudreau's *Histoire de la littérature amérindienne au Québec* (1993). It is not a little ironic that the method that is in many respects highly effective for the elucidation of the process of emergence for one literature, and especially so in addressing such issues as marginality and colonization, is peremptorily rejected by Boudreau. Aboriginal writing is understood as 'une culture qui se situe en marge de l'institution de la littérature.'[65] By implication, the institution constitutes a centre with all the power that centres can deploy. In both histories the centre is construed in political terms as exercising certain prerogatives. The statement also suggests that only fully matured literary cultures possess institutional structures. If they belong to fields of power that paradoxically include, but deny, the possibility of taking a position in Pierre Bourdieu's sense, those fields carry a negative ethical image, and both anglophone and francophone histories of literature in Canada are shown as possessing such an image. Their refusal or decision not to include is generally mutual, however, and native writing in Quebec at least does not seek its legitimation within the Québécois literary institution.

While it is asserted that institutionalization at any price is not the motivation of Native writing, the essentialist expression of 'l'indianité' is. The reason for this desire is made clear by both the history's argument and the structure it is given. It consists of an introduction, in which a familiar English-Canadian query into eligibility is raised, and two large following sections. The first is devoted to oral literature; the second, to written. The book is structured so that the encounter between the European and Native peoples is marked by the emergence of writing. In other words, a radical change in Native culture coincides with radical technological change. History, then, is constructed as both a catastrophe and an effort toward a recovery with the very tools that ironically both represent and symbolize the catastrophe. Although limited to Quebec, the history draws upon the larger North American context of which the several nations that inhabit Quebec serve as examples. Thus the first section is for the most part theoretical and taxonomic, explaining and categorizing kinds of oral literature. Several types of creation and etiological myths are described, as well as the roles of animals, tricksters, and heroes. The central significance of these narratives is didactic and moral. The telling of tales in such societies is designed to reinforce 'les structures et l'harmonie sociales.'[66] No matter how humorous the antics of tricksters may be, these tales are entertaining only at a secondary level. They move somewhere between the zones of propaganda and pure pleasure. They, therefore, construct social identity, and the examples that are chosen serve the larger design of the history, which is to reinforce notions of group survival and difference. They narrate the memory and history of collective concerns in a society that continually subordinates the individual to the group. In contrast to European cosmologies, humans are primarily neither rational nor intelligent and must make every effort to find harmony with nature. This is the larger understanding with which native oral literature is invested, and it was precisely this understanding which opposed that of the Europeans, throwing both into sharper relief.[67]

Cosmocentricity, however, is the *leitmotif* of Boudreau's argument, suggesting that the canon is dominated by what White refers to as Organicist principles, which in turn prompt a dominance of Synecdoche, the trope according to which the parts must be integrated with the whole.[68] The organic informs the plot and structure of her history, and all the texts collaborate to support it. Thus writing, the magic instrument of the Europeans, enters the history pivotally, separating the culture from itself and spreading confusion in respect of organic order. Although the commitment of Native languages to forms of writing was initially for the use of missionaries and considered dangerous for Natives to understand, it became in the end a primary means of empowerment shaped to recover the sense of wholeness that the conquest of the Americans endeavoured to destroy.

The conquest began by a process of deterritorialization and only stopped as Native people began to 'write back.' Certainly, in a sense that Boudreau does not investigate, the history of the literature she is constructing is minor in the sense that Deleuze and Guattari use the word when they remark that 'the three characteristics of minor literature are the deterritorialization of language, the connection of the individual to a political immediacy, and the collective assemblage of enunciation.' Aboriginal culture remains more organicist than that of Franz Kafka only insofar as it derives directly from the earth of which they have been deprived, the soil of their orality. Just as Kafka's writing, moreover, is 'at a border,'[69] so too is the literature that Boudreau constructs, in which the oral element always appears present through a métissage on the level of enunciation. It is also unremittingly political, developing in stages from statements of resistance, through a special form of autobiography to ethnology and historiography, and, finally, to a literature in which the culture appears reterritorialized.[70] Every mode employed turns upon the single theme of dispossession, the loss, in other words, of the plenitude that Synecdoche implies.

Most of the written literature by Natives of Quebec that is available was prompted by reactions to the federal White Paper (1969), which was designed primarily to remove the special status that the treaties had created. The threat of assimilation is the conclusion that conquest is driven by. In many ways such a threat prompted Natives to 'speak white,' to use the Québécoise poet Michèle Lalonde's (1973–) poignant expression, to save their culture by creating a new one inside another, by becoming 'a collective machine of expression.' To do this, the narrator becomes less important than the events in autobiography and may even become coterminous with the nation itself. Predominant is the theme of survival or the dream of reterritorialization, all of which is illustrated in An Antane Kapesh's (1926–) *Qu'as-tu fait de mon pays?* (1979), the story of a Native child who comes to the revelation that she has been stripped of her land, her language, and her culture. The text follows a pattern that is constructed to make it exemplary of the history Boudreau is writing: the first part is territorially whole, imbued with traditional practices; the second describes the coming of the Europeans and the exploitation of the land; the third and fourth parts address the creation of reserves and the efforts to assimilate the Natives; the last part describes the child's revolt and efforts to establish a dialogue.

It is difficult not to recall in this child's parable the opening sentence of Anne Hébert's 'Le Torrent,' namely, 'J'étais un enfant dépossédé du monde.'[71] An infant, it should be remembered, is so named because, to translate the Latin *infans*, it is a creature incapable of speech. In these two instances the infant is dispossessed by a traumatic experience that represents, respectively, kinds of conquest. The presence of conquest, which English-Canadian literary historians tend to ignore, plays a continuous, defining role in any history written from the persepctive of Quebec. Paradoxically, it both conjoins and separates representations made by Natives and francophone Quebeckers. It permits them both to construct histories that have characteristics in common with minority and post-colonial literary discourses. Although the theme is shared, it is deployed differently in the two examples we have examined. One consequence is that its use conjoins the two groups in a tragic manner, and this may be attributed to a certain extent to what appears to be the contemporary francophone attitude toward the Conquest. *La Vie littéraire au*

Québec, as we have seen, begins, with clearly defined literary reasons, the day after the Conquest. Thus, the colonizing role of the French is not assumed as part of the whole history, but the fact that the French lost the war to the British still allows anglophone culture to be perceived as an interference in the stable evolution of an otherwise stable literary field. In this sense the Conquest may be construed, as I have already mentioned, as a Fortunate Fall because it can stimulate a sense of ethnic difference. Nevertheless, there can be no persuasive way of overlooking the general effect of European migration in the Americas, and those of European ancestry cannot entirely escape the opprobrium of the first and larger invasion to which Native writers refer. Because that remains to a certain extent unacknowledged by the majority of European inhabitants of Canada, the impasses that appear to stand in the way of autonomous evolutions remain unresolved.

Ironically, however, the relationship that the two most recent histories of literature in Quebec bear to each other shares many common concerns. The first, obviously, is the sense of dispossession, which prompts the idea that colonization and possible assimilation will destroy distinct cultures. Thus the general French-Canadian motif of collective survival is shared, and a sense of the past is assiduously cultivated. The provincial motto, *je me souviens*, could be applied to both Native and Québécois histories, despite differences of manner. The latter steadfastly cultivate linearity, despite its recursive rhythm, while the former, having developed a more cyclical cosmology, find memory in recurrence. The past, however, is always shaped to bear upon a desired future. For the sense of not being fully integrated with the past promotes a sense of 'la difficulté d'être Amérindien dans la société actuelle,'[72] a phrase which, as we have seen in chapter 4, Anthony Purdy has found particularly significant for describing contemporary Québécois culture. Nevertheless, the difference in power that each history manifests is apparent. Despite repeated obstacles, *La Vie littéraire au Québec* inscribes a continuous narrative of growing autonomy in both the richness of the volumes and the number envisioned. It is about both reterritorialization and sovereignty, and it may be said to have achieved these ends, at least from a Native perspective. In this respect, at least, it is difficult to distinguish between either of the two charter cultures, whose dispute is often at the expense of a third and generally unheard culture. Despite the eloquence of its writing, it is a culture still treated as if it were *enfans* by both anglophone and francophone culture.

It is here that literary history, particularly of those literatures that are endeavouring to affirm collective identity, which is inevitable among smaller cultures, reaches the anguish that lies at the root of its ideological burden. These are histories that are written to foster a future by practising modes of legitimization and memorialization. A sense of loss, therefore, cannot help but be present. History is writing against loss or, as it is frequently thematized, dispossession. When one bears in mind Bourdieu's notion of the field as a field of conflict, one is urged to remember more than one's own loss, for one person's success may readily be at the expense of someone else. As I will discuss in the conclusion, is it possible to conceive of literary history in countries that cultivate policies of cultural inclusion in such a way as to construct a collective that shares, rather than disputes, the field?

Women and Literary History

The three histories that address First Nations and Inuit writing pose a simple yet intriguing question, namely, how are they to be read? Unlike all the other histories we have considred, these are not authored by representatives of their respective cultures. The three authors are of European descent, despite the various kinds of support they have received from the communities they have spoken for,[73] and thus raise the issue of cultural appropriation. Since the histories are not auto-representative, in that way, one might ask, do they constitute constructions of Canada? Before answering this question, it might be useful to consider their limits as cultural enquiries.

Among the more serious issues they raise is the extent to which they are marked as signs of colonization. As I have indicated, a minimal use of history is made. It is drawn upon in a 'European,' manner, to the extent that it follows a dating system common to Western histories.[74] Such a practice certainly places Native writing within the contexts of the dominant cultures. Nevertheless, the general emphasis in each of the histories falls upon the effect of, and recovery from, European contact, which is an inevitable aspect of all Amerindian and Inuit experience. Furthermore, in a gesture entirely appropriate for a consideration of such literary histories, contact means the eventual impact of writing in both its negative and positive aspects. At the same time, great care is made to locate the impact writing had within the assumptions of an oral culture. To that extent, it would be difficult to argue that these histories have a colonizing agenda. They can in no way be compared, for example, to the design of assimilation that lay behind the residential school policy. It may be said that certain aspects of the Native sense of the sacred are revealed in the notion of cosmocentricity as Boudreau discusses it, but this is not exactly new knowledge. To be fully persuasive, however, arguments against these histories would have to argue with Edward Said, for example, that they 'operate as representations usually do, for a purpose, according to a tendency, in a specified historical, intellectual, and even economic setting.' So far, no one to my knowledge has stepped forward from Native communities to identify such a tendency. The nub of Said's argument is that all representations 'are embedded first in the languages and then in the culture, institutions, and political ambience of the representer.'[75] Thus 'truth' is not the object of the representation.

While such an argument would be valid for all the histories we have examined, its significance in these instances should not be overlooked. Nevertheless, these three histories should not be ignored, as indeed they are not, but rather understood as pioneering (another European metaphor) efforts to mediate between cultures. Boudreau's history sets a fine example in this regard by consciously placing her text outside the dominant discourse of the literary system, thus locating her text close to her material. Although there are no histories prepared as yet by Native critics, it might be remarked that they too would have to face the issue of cultural mediation depending upon the intended audience and whether or not a large publishing house produced the book.

As I have already intimated, cultural mediation is equally, if not so radically, an issue with histories of ethnic minority writing. But given the fact that these three histories have been prepared by critics of European descent, it may be for this reason that their representations, although similar in many ways, also appear, as a result of their emphasis upon catastrophe as governing principle, at least inversely related to the other histories discussed in this chapter. Although this might suggest that awareness of suffering and loss is European, which could not be demonstrated, it may be that the use made of it is a European 'tendency,' as Said would say. To imply as much, however, begs one to ask, finally, whether it is possible to essentialize 'European' and 'Native.' We can no more do this than essentialize 'Québécois.' Therefore, the best we can do is bear Said's restrictions in mind and remember that all the histories of literature in Canada and Quebec are simply formations. Nevertheless, grouped in the way that I have placed them, they appear to possess sufficient characteristics which allow for significant distinctions to be made, which give shape to the groups.

To suggest that a history may not be culturally appropriate, may be, however, an unspoken purpose of indigenous histories, all of which are significantly written by women. The implication is clear, I think, that these women have been drawn toward peoples who have, in many ways, been denied histories of their own by the dominant cultures in Canada. Their theme is dispossession and 'disappropriation,' and their plots are designed to show how appropriation and agency are sought. They are, then, analogous, at least, to a history of women's cultures in their effort to indicate difference, domination, stereotyping, and what Boudreau calls 'la difficulté d'être Amérindien' under such circumstances. Both Petrone and Boudreau, wherever possible, foreground women, and one of the reasons, I would argue, is to destabilize a frequent image of the Native as male. Furthermore, the emphasis upon writing is significantly shared with historians and theorists of women writers.[76] Significantly, at issue is the sense of 'invasion,' to which Shirley Neuman, citing Daphne Marlatt (1942–) draws attention in her essay 'Life Writing,' and Helen Buss insists that far from 'defining the separate self,' women in constructing themselves as subjects are more likely to be involved in an 'act of separation/merging,'[77] which manifests in a tendency to make autobiography, for example, a generically complex speech act that conjoins more than one mode. Learning to read such texts, which is the burden of Buss's argument, is an exercise in discovering a story hidden by dominant discourses. Finding their history would mean writing against the assumptions of 'national' histories of Canada, which are not in doubt about certain structures of time, the character of beginnings, the mode of emplotment, assured as they are that all of this is in their possession and need only be declared to be valid. These certainties are not shared by peoples who know themselves to be marginalized by other discourses.

CHAPTER EIGHT

Canada as Alterity: The View from Europe, 1895–1961

A ca nada

The literary histories of anglophone and francophone Canada as they are prepared primarily for European audiences constitute a kind of epiphany of what we have observed already. As epiphanies, they revisit the same sites from the late nineteenth century until the present day. The difference lies in the point of view adopted: they are more assiduous, at least in some instances, in situating texts in historical contexts that are considered unknown by their respective readers, and French readers are often permitted to see a number of parallels in historical development between Quebec and other former francophone colonies and regions, such as we have seen in Lortie. In other words, Quebec especially is placed in the world as more a part of Francophonie than Canada, and the English histories belong to series that evoke, at least, the Commonwealth. Canada, therefore, is constructed in such a way that the implied reader will see them as more international than Canadian practice usually endeavours to develop. As with the original epiphany, then, our perspective is summoned to view familiar events from a somewhat higher and broader perspective.

There is a rapport, furthermore, between audience and point of view, which becomes more apparent as the more intimate nexus of nation, narrative, and participating reader is relaxed, and the objects of interest are correspondingly modified. Hence it is clear that just as a subject is interpellated, that is, constructed through the operation of the text,[1] so too is an idea of the nation interpellated and given a desired shape. All of the European historians treat Canada as foreign or Other, and the Canadian historians, as they respond to the various demands of audiences that may include, but go beyond, those in Canada, become less grounded in the immediacies of literary history as the construction of a nation, with the possible exception of Jules Léger. The consequences of changing positions vary, but in every case the literatures of Canada and Quebec are drawn into situations that mark either their similarities to other colonial and post-colonial nations or their characteristics from various ideological perspectives. The two exceptions to this general statement would be Heinz Kloos's sketchy introduction to his anthology of German-Canadian poetry and René Dionne's eclectic collection of essays, *Le Québécois et sa littérature.*

Quebec and *Weltliteratur*

Virgile Rossel's *Histoire de littérature hors de France* (1895) appeared some two decades after Edmond Lareau's text. Although it relies upon the latter for some, if not all, of its specific insights, its general perspective, as one might surmise from the title, differs from it profoundly. Rossel shares little of Lareau's romanticism and none of the concomitant sense of progress and organicism. The formation of the new Dominion is not a central theme, nor are the ideas of nation that would arise from it. Rossel's interest is not, therefore, Canadian, but rather Swiss, and the literatures that fall within his purview are those of Europe, primarily those of Switzerland and Belgium. The reader who is interpellated is precisely the one who would feel bound to the countries invoked by the opening sentence: 'Petits pays, petites ressources, petites gloires, n'est-ce pas?' Rossel's beginning raises a question about relative position, which, corresponding to gestures made by historians of ethnic minority literatures, challenge a notion of national essentialism. The intent is to shift emphasis away from France – 'le foyer central' – to countries outside France – 'ces modestes foyers régionaux.' And yet, far from establishing borders between nations in the characteristic manner of nineteenth-century historians, Rossel appeals for a certain sympathy among French readers: 'Que les barrières s'abaissent donc, que les frontières disparaissent entre des littératures qui sont, malgré leur importance fort inégale, les diverse parties d'un tout.' Such a free circulation of ideas is a theme that is not encountered in the other histories we have examined, and if it were to have any source, a likely, but unacknowledged, place would be Goethe's notion of *Weltliteratur,* which derives part of its significance from the recognition of apparently insignificant peoples and nations.[2] The proposal has risks, of course, inasmuch as the general direction of

Rossel's argument is to assert that 'l'usage d'une même langue crée entre des peuples séparés à d'autres égards, une patrie commune d'intelligence et d'idéal, les associe, pour le rôle civilisateur, par une sorte de lien mystique et puissant.' The larger country would only have sense if it were a federation of equal powers, which was a notion that could not even have been conceptualized in Europe a hundred years ago. Each of the countries discussed would constitute in themselves a little France and be part of a family, which would hardly have avoided the problem of France itself being the parent. The point, however, would be to find a forum in which 'leur autonomie intellectuelle et jusqu'à leurs originalités locales' would be preserved.[3]

Always subordinate to a Goethean ideal, Rossel's aim in the first instance is didactic: the persistent value of French culture is its apparent ability to enlarge one's intellectual horizons, an intent implicit in Goethe's own admonishment of his parochial fellow-citizens.[4] Clearly, nothing can be lost but a certain mediocrity; the very lack of an accomplished culture provides a useful stimulus, and the means by which it can be acquired is through the language that France has given to the world. Thus, the framework within which Rossel's history is written rests upon the problem of language, particularly its neglect and corruption under the pressure of the other languages that surround and infiltrate French as it is used outside France. Not surprisingly, then, Belgium, la Suisse romande, and Canada are all summoned, referring to the French Revolution, 'à préparer une sorte de quatre-vingt-neuf du français littéraire.'[5] Such an interpellation of the reader not only departs, of course, from the spirit of Goethe but also modifies trenchantly the general sense of the national literature as constructed in Quebec: the borders are open and the sense of beginning in a changed international context is fully evident.

The appeal to revolution is most relevant to the francophone literature of Canada, which is defined as 'la longue protestation d'une race conquise.' As a result of the indifference of the French public, isolation, and legislative obstacles, the literature of Quebec could only be described as provincial. Whatever can be gathered to constitute a corpus lacks all pretension to art, and more than anything else, a fresh sympathy arriving from France would be sufficient to revive its moribund character. The policy of France toward its North American possession, we discover, in what forms the beginning of literary history in Canada, was anything but consistent, and its loss to England, despite the 'glorieuse folie de patriotisme' displayed on the Plains of Abraham, appears inevitable. The sustaining element from 1763 to 1867, even more powerful than religion, was language. Consistent then with Rossel's general thesis, the initial hero of the Canadian enterprise is Arthur Buies (1840–1901), who first enters his history as a response to Lord Durham and dominates the whole of section 3 of the first chapter entitled 'Les Canadiens-Français.' He dominates primarily because of his didactic function. He is a schoolmaster whose task was to salvage the French as spoken in his native province, and whose example garnered him the praise of being the best writer of his time.[6] Such a use of Buies confirms the fact that for Rossel, history, while it might arise from a series of political acts, takes its meaning from an idea of purity – the preservation of correct French. Any other activity, whether political or literary, derives from this position. Thus, Buies stands structurally outside history, and his function is to intervene between political and literary phenomena in order to give them their significance.

The second chapter, 'La Littérature canadienne,' begins with a peroration on the problems of creating a literature in a pioneer country. Rossel agrees readily enough with Lareau's assessment that the conditions of life in Quebec for a number of generations was simply too demanding to foster a true literature. What the colony and the province needed was 'le libre épanouissement du génie nationale dans un milieu favorable,'[7] by which he seems to imply a less religiously repressive society with greater general access to French culture. Such an implication would explain the central position of Buies, whose liberal politics were not in sympathy with an ultramontanist ideology. What matters, however, beyond all consideration of French-Canadian distinctiveness, is the style that French culture incarnates. Lacking for the most part the latter, the primary object of French Canada's cultivation has been a historiography in which its native distinction shows to clearest advantage. Thus Garneau, needless to say, is given a central position in Rossel's history, and no small emphasis is given to the repression of the first edition by the Church in Quebec. The cultural milieu of Quebec was clearly unfavourably disposed toward the liberalism that Rossel represents, and without it the style that he admires could flourish. Nevertheless, he is fair to Ferland, whose Cours d'histoire au Canada is recognized as superior in style to that of Garneau, who is considered closer, however, to the soul of the people.

In the wake of historiography, political oratory and journalism follow.[8] His admiration for Papineau is inevitable, especially when one notes Rossel's apparent lack of interest in every other major political figure of the nineteenth century. Among Catholic journalists, Parent is admired, but no one reaches the heights of Buies, who is allowed to enter history, temporally removed from his early position as the centre of significance. As Rossel succinctly puts it: 'Dans une littérature un peu fade, en somme, et fort timide, M. Buies a l'air d'un capitan [*sic*] égaré en un troupeau de pensionnaires.'[9] His significance is two-fold: he provides the general view by which Rossel's history is to be understood, and as a journalist his influence shared in the decisive bearing journals took in respect of literature.

The final two sections of the chapter are devoted to works of imagination, and it is not a happy picture. While the Swiss and the Belgians take their inspiration from France, 'les Canadiens restent Canadien.' In other words, 'Le nouveau, voilà l'ennemi.' What is worse, 'l'invention ni l'expression littéraires excitent leur esprit. Ils arrangent des souvenirs et des légendes; leurs livres ne sont guère que des relations coloriées de faits empruntés aux traditions et aux annales du pays. C'est extraordinairement simple, un peu traînant; la matière est intéressante, par bonheur.'[10] The unsympathetic character of Rossel's judgment derives precisely from the ideological premises of his history, which hold that the aesthetic finish of a text is primary and that such a finish can only be acquired from France itself in a francophone world. The pretensions that French-Canadians may have that would urge them toward nationhood are not considered sufficient to save the generality of imaginative fiction produced in the nineteenth century and hence, Garneau's role, which is constructed as seminal in Québec, is here given short shrift as being but one of the unnamed sources of memories, legends, and traditions.

Although the novel is presented as the preferred literary genre, its beginnings are nothing if not hesitant and uncertain. Philippe Aubert de Gaspé, fils, (1814–41) is ignored entirely, and Joseph Doutre's *Les Fiancés de 1812* is credited as being the first French-Canadian novel, perhaps on the unstated, but implicit, grounds that Doutre was otherwise a well-known liberal. The novel is, however, dismissed as merely 'un bon travail d'écolier,' and Chauveau's *Charles Guérin* is praised for its stylistic and psychological effort. Only Georges de Boucherville and Joseph-Charles Taché emerge relatively unscathed; the former, perhaps, because one of his characters is modelled on Molière's Tartuffe, and the latter because he evokes the French Romatic poet Alfred de Vigny (1797–1863). Rossel does not share Lareau's opinion that Aubert de Gaspé, père, is the Jean-Paul Richter (1763–1825) of Canada on the ground that he lacks his flights of fancy and the sense of the beyond. Indeed, he is, in his own words, 'tout canadien par le style,' that is, too ingenuous, insistent, and conscientious to merit Rossel's praise.[11] Despite what many consider as rather dull in the style of Antoine Gérin-Lajoie's *Jean Rivard*, Rossel finds it a piece of honest workmanship and is prepared to overlook the conventionality of its idealism.

It is evident that Rossel prefers the pleasures of style to the burdens of the past and projections of the future, which characterize respectively the novels of Aubert de Gaspé and Gérin-Lajoie. But style has certain limits, as he indicates in his critical treatment of Abbé Casgrain, whose efforts to adorn his prose for the sake of softening his didacticism do not meet with Rossel's entire approval. In fact, all of Rossel's critical judgments are tempered according to notions of French neoclassicism, seeking a balanced use of language and form. Thus, despite apologies, Rossel summarily dismisses most of the poets of the second half of the nineteenth century: 'Cette poésie retarde sur celle de la France; elle imite, sans même mêler une petite note originale à ses imitations; elle n'a que la valeur d'un modeste produit local, et ce serait vraiment peine perdue d'insister.' The model of France, then, is insufficient without the leaven of difference that being *hors France* can provide. Crémazie, despite the accomplishment of 'La Promenade des trois morts,' suffers from uncertainty, 'ballotté entre l'art ancien et le nouveau, [il] n'a su choisir ou s'émanciper.' Le May is praised for perseverance and then reminded that once Rossel advised him to give up poetry and return to prose. Thus Fréchette is the one poet who can be called 'le poète le plus remarquable du Canada,' and he merits this title on the ground that he transcends the efforts of other poems to make rhymes, as he neatly observes, of 'les petites affaires de leur "moi."'[12] He succeeds because he has remained French and because his poetry is brought to life by means of his ardent conviction and invincible hope. His poetry is historical, but it celebrates both his homeland and progress. He becomes, then, the most illustrative model of Rossel's thesis.

Rossel's history ends, without reflection, with Fréchette. One can only infer what his sense of the historical might be. Certainly that sense does not turn upon significant moments and events in French-Canadian history to demonstrate any palpable structure of progress toward autonomy, for instance. Progress is of a spiritual, intellectual, and aesthetic character, and accomplishment depends how adept one is at making use of the 'universal' French model for local purposes. Canonization depends solely upon neoclassical criteria as they are adapted to the 'change of the times.' Although the only direction of such a history is upward, it does so at the expense of the continual fall of the mediocre and the derivative. Only a few writers survive in an Arnoldian manner, which suggests that one can only progress toward the timeless nation of the great stylists – the ambition of all classicism – to become 'un prolongement lumineux des vieilles lettres classiques.'[13] History, then, is a threshold that must be transcended, and it can only be transcended through a particular conception of art. In such a sphere, the national is of no consequence.

Unchanging Quebec

One history of some scope intervenes between Rossel and the end of the Second World War, namely, Jules Léger's infrequently cited *Le Canada français et son expression littéraire*, which appeared near the end of the thirties.[14] By his own admission it was in the shade of Camille Roy, his admiration for whom he expresses firmly and clearly, and both he and Léger's mentor Émile Chartier stand as evident ideological foundations in his work. Nevertheless, the text is his doctoral thesis, written under the direction of Paul Van Tieghem, a leading French scholar and comparatist of the period. Despite his supervision, the thesis remains resolutely in the tracks set out by Roy and possesses a certain value as a fairly accurate reflection of French-Canadian attitudes toward literature and French Canada before the revisions of the Quiet Revolution. It seeks to discover the manner in which the literature of French Canada differs from that of France and where its originality lies. 'Autonomy' is not a word that appears as the continuous goal in his text: Léger's French Canada acquired it through the British North America Act. Finally, like many of his contemporaries in English Canada, nothing seems to irritate him more than the continual comparison of French-Canadian writers with a superior French model.

Despite his best efforts, Léger does not always follow the prompting of his heart, particularly in respect of French models. As he observes at the very outset of his thesis, such comparison is inevitable wherever French is written. Without citing him, he echoes Rossel: all francophone texts, he observes: 'ont leurs racines, leurs modèles dans la littérature française ... Politiquement, la Suisse, la Belgique ou le Canada ne sont pas des pays français; pour la littérature, ils le sont et la politique n'a rien à voir là-dedans.'[15] Try as he may, Léger finds it often close to impossible to find an escape from the ambivalence of a colonial condition in his effort to find the distinctiveness of French Canada. Unlike other 'settler colonies,'[16] French Canada is constructed as beneath the dominion of both British imperial rule and French culture. The problem of having two masters is that, while a measure of political autonomy was achieved in respect of the British, the instrument for securing it was the French language and the culture that it dispensed; in Léger's argument, the true colonial problem for French Canada, which made it at once distinctive and provincial, was French culture.

Unlike most French-Canadian literary historians, his decision to include the period of New France as necessary and foundational may be understood, then, as a kind of self-colonizing project that governs the direction that Léger's argument takes. All the early figures, from Jacques Cartier to the Jesuit historian Pierre-François-Xavier de Charlevoix (1682–1761), are grouped under the larger heading of 'Les Œuvres,' a disconcerting procedure that is used throughout. The works are not quite as significant as their authors, who are to be construed, in a manner reminiscent of Roy, as agents in a larger drama. Their significance for the argument is the manner in which they form a bridge from Europe to North America, and with the exception of the Baron Lahontan, they possess suitable ideologies. Lahontan's work is castigated as 'faussée par une vision révolutionnaire et dont les idées subversives affecteront plus d'un esprit du XVIIIme siècle.' Thus New France is constructed along the conservative lines that would appeal to a majority of francophone readers in the 1930s.[17] By contrast, the *Histoire de la Nouvelle France* (1744) by the Charlevoix, steeped stylistically in the seventeenth-century classicism of Racine and Molière, is given as the model to follow and is made particularly foundational to the degree that his love of nature anticipates that of François-René Chateaubriand (1768–1848). Taken together, however, both Lahontan and Charlevoix represent at this early stage an aspect of the contradictory impulses in French-Canadian culture that Léger is at pains to resolve.

According to the structure of his argument, the French foundation is temporally set aside because of the impact of British occupation. The moment of the Conquest is not employed as is usually done, that is, to underline the true beginning of French-Canadian culture, for the beginning was already established by Cartier. The plot of the text is presented, rather, through the organic image of a temporarily uprooted tree whose roots, however, 'étaient si fort ancrées dans le sol qu'il s'est repris à vivre.'[18] Although such an image suggests a plot structure of fall and rise, the plot is complicated by the fact that the movement, simplistic as it may be, is a dialectical one that never entirely desires to give up a certain image of New France, particularly that represented by Jesuit ideals and French attitudes as they were before the Enlightenment. The past, then, must be cultivated in every sense, and the argument intimates strongly that the implied reader is one who is content not simply to remain in some ways a part of a French colony, but even the colony of a colony.

For such, it would seem, was the effect of British policy, which was resolved 'de nous faire perdre le souvenir même de nos origines.'[19] The response was to remain French while being British subjects. To do otherwise would be to betray these very origins, and hence *la survivance française* is an act of fetishization of which the result is that 'les Canadiens-français ressemblent plus aux Français que furent leurs aïeux qu'aux Français actuels.' Such an admission, designed to justify the beginning in 1534, is, however, fraught with burdens and gives other assertions an air of contradiction. For if the imitation of French literary practices can be condemned frequently as derivative and reactionary, what is the French-Canadian writer to do given 'la large part faite à l'imitation de la littérature française'?[20] The answer is to reify a France that can only be encountered through the imagination, that is, that of seventeenth-century France, which coincide with what is even referred to as French Canada's glorious epoch. In many respects, the Revolution and anticlericalism make such reification possible and permits Léger to both have and not have France simultaneously, which appears to resolve the problem with the mother country.

It is almost with a sigh of relief, then, that Léger reaches the year 1867 – a year not normally dwelt upon in francophone literary history – because it permitted French Canadians to become, in a phrase full of long echoes, 'maîtres chez nous.'[21] What the date signifies on the symbolic level of Léger's plot is that the problem of political colonialism has been resolved and the more fascinating issue of France can be addressed again. Confederation occurred near the beginning of French Canada's period of major resurgence during the years 1860 to 1900. It is grouped with two other causes to explain the resurgence. The first was the impact of Garneau's *Histoire* and the second was the resumption of relations with France, both of which testify to the French connection in the past and the present and which together assist in the construction of a future. The future is clearly linked to a reified past in Garneau, and, according to the way the present is treated, it is evident that the present is received in such a way as to build upon that past.

In fact, the past is constructed in order to explain not only the present of the late nineteenth century, but also that of the period in which Léger's thesis was written. Just as he indicates two tendencies manifest in the history of French Canada, namely, a liberal, secular position and a conservative, ecclesiastical position, the same tendencies were noticeable in the 1930s. Furthermore, the economic crisis favoured the latter.[22] Thus the emergence of the École Patriotique, which is often taken as the moment of romanticism in Quebec, is considered but the appearance of romantic, revolutionary impulses, contrary, as we shall see, to Gérard Tougas's argument in *Histoire de la littérature canadienne-française*.[23] Romanticism is defined as a revolutionary gesture, and J.C. Taché is cited with some satisfaction as he explains that French Canadians are not 'fils de la révolution,' having no need for the 'expédiants du romantisme moderne.' Hence, Taché continues: 'Notre langue doit donc être comme un écho de la saine littérature d'autrefois,' referring again to that period of classicism, ecclesiastical control, and monarchical order that preceded the Enlightenment, the Revolution, and Romanticism. What was valid in 1864 remains valid in 1938. The liberalism and anticlerical spirit of Léger's romanticism is roundly constrained by the vigilance of the Church, and 'aussi, aujourd'hui encore, le catholicisme fait-il partie intégrante de l'âme canadienne.' So it is that the present, the formative years from 1860 to 1900, and 'la saine littérature d'autrefois' are drawn into one trajectory. Hence, for example, the illustrative conflict been the Institut Canadien and the Church, which concluded in the demise of the former, is readily disposed of: 'On sait que, en 1851, se fondait à Montréal l'*Institut Canadien,* une sorte de club jacobin qui se développa avec succès, puisqu'il comptait sept cents adhérents en 1857. Mais le seul fait que, l'Église ayant excommunié le journal l'*Avenir,* organe de ce club, l'association dut se dissoudre, prouve assez la force dont elle dispose.'[24] The irony of citing a journal that represented an alternative future is, of course, not commented upon, for Léger's future, as I have been arguing, is directed by a reified vision of the past.

In such a context, the general and rather late emergence of the novel after 1850 is considered from two perspectives. The first is that francophone literature in the first half of the century was primarily politically engaged. It was, in an expression echoing Charles ab der Halden, a 'littérature d'action.'[25] Ironically enough, there was a strong liberal ideology supporting such a literature, notably in Garneau, but such an ideology is countenanced primarily because of its anti-British stance. The other reason raised is that the Church took a repressive view of the novel, a view which Léger swiftly condemns. He cites Casgrain, who was at once a romantic and a priest, as favourably disposed toward the novel, as well as other members of the laity, who were not. He concludes, however, that the Church protested 'contre le libéralisme trop avancé de Hugo ou la légèrté libertine de Musset, mais, en tout cela, il ne fait que réfléter l'esprit de son temps.' Such condemnation, however, is not a question of a certain moment in time. It reaches deeper into something more archetypal. Contemporary novels, themselves too deeply inscribed with a pernicious French influence, are also judged as an offence against 'l'âme canadienne.' The expression was used before in the context of a semiotic field that includes the Church and the atemporal past of New France, and it is a clear instance of how the literary institution, in this instance Léger's history, colludes easily with dominant ideological forces, and is made to seem to be a natural part of 'nos esprits conformistes.'[26]

In a manner that anticipates at least superficially that of Auguste Viatte, Léger gives his history five periods, which correspond to the structure of a French classical play, such as one by Racine. The five acts cover Canadian literature under the French, the terrible years from 1760 to 1840, the two precursors (Garneau and Crémazie), L'École Patriotique (1860–1900), and the modern movement. Although the structure of the argument suggests, as I have remarked, a fall and recovery, it more closely resembles the kind of intricate dance around the same centre that is characteristic of the well-made classical drama.[27] The dance occurs in time, but the centre, which controls and directs the dance, is eternal. Thus, to speak of a rise in the common, progressive sense would be inappropriate. Becoming yields to Being in the same way that the organic character of romanticism yields to the inorganic structure of classicism. Such a sense of plot does not fit any of White's categories, but the conservative ideology of Léger's argument should imply that he should have a comic sense. Yet despite Léger's use of the image of a tree that almost dies and returns to life – an image fraught, ironically, with romantic echoes – Léger not only argues strongly against the romantic, but also more than once refers to Quebec as suffering a tragic destiny (another echo of Racine). It is tragic because French Canada is always placed in the dilemma of either being French *tout court* or hopelessly provincial. This dilemma comes to a climax in the final chapter in the discussion of the differences between L'École littéraire de Montréal and L'École du terroir. The only solution to such a tragic dilemma is provided by the model of Hémon's *Maria Chapdelaine* and the nationalism of Lionel Groulx, Thomas Chapais, and Camille Roy. Although the nationalist project is constructed as taking the best of native and French schools, its inscription through these two historians, critic, and novelist suggests something less dialectical than may at first appear. Hémon's novel is not analysed at length because it is already well enough known, but a significant use is made of it in the Introduction. There he cites the unforgettable sentence: 'Au pays du Québec, rien n'est changé, parce que nous sommes un témoinage.' Nothing has changed because 'les Canadiens-français ressemblent plus aux Français que furent leurs aïeux qu'aux Français actuels.'[28]

While it seems possible that the French-Canadian 'soul' might continue unchanged, the world around Léger seemed at such loggerheads that from his perspective tragedy seemed to be its inevitable fate. Both the French school and the more local one were active in a historical world, the former corresponding to developments in contemporary France and the latter discovering and preserving a place that marked Quebec's distinctiveness. Neither gesture was as enamoured of the unalterable as Léger, and one is tempted to remark that the aspect of French Canada's destiny that appeared tragic was, ironically, the privileging of a world that could only be perceived in the imagination. It was a world that had long ago faded away and which, therefore, lent itself readily to acts of essentialization that are not uncommon in literary history. And so at the conclusion of his thesis, it is not surprising that Léger prefers *Dichtung* to *Wahrheit* to make his point that the best of French Canada is to be found in the unalterable. Without mentioning Hémon directly, he asserts that 'd'autres hommes sont venus, d'autres générations ont poussé qui ont accepté le lourd héritage de leurs pères.'[29] Such a sentence and the peroration of which it is a part would, needless to say, have appealed to the generation of Savard's *Menaud Maître-Draveur,* which makes lavish intertextual use of *Maria Chapdelaine* and whose canonization process began in the year Léger's thesis appeared. Its rhetoric buries, however, whatever role that women might have played in the formation of French Canada and consecrates exclusively a conservative, ecclesiastical tradition that was not far from becoming an inaccessible past. Nor does it dwell in any way upon the effect the French regime had upon Aboriginals; rather, it transmutes what could be called an imperial, colonizing past into an ideal model that serves as a guide to recovery, masking what appears to be a desire to recover colonial status in a paradoxically autonomous fashion. The true colonizer, however, was not England, but a constructed New France.

One is tempted to see more than nostalgia in this use of the past. No French-Canadian literary historian has made such use of New France, and this may be attributed partly to the thesis being developed in France and partly from a desire to distinguish French Canada not just relatively but essentially from France, to find a way both to have France and to consume it. France is both a dream and a nightmare for him, which is part of the colonial conundrum and also distinguishes his perspective from the Swiss historian Rossel, who is capable of admiring without fetishizing France. Auguste Viatte, who follows Rossel's lead, also manifests certain misgivings about France's place in the cultural life of the West following the Second World War and, therefore, has a certain stake in its future, which can be perceived in the possible futures and fading pasts of North American francophone peoples.

French America

Viatte's *Histoire littéraire de l'Amérique française des origines à 1950* (1954) contains a general introduction, a section devoted to Canada, and a conclusion that draws the threads of his argument together. Although at no point is the reader permitted to lose sight of France, Viatte's France includes both its literary and larger cultural functions. Unlike Rossel's timeless France and Léger's equally timeless New France, Viatte's is a religious and political colonizer that intervened in North America at a certain place and time, and it is evident that from the beginning the literature such an intervention produced was both French and 'American.' Primarily, however, the writing of the colonial period was written for a French audience, and serves as a means to translate cultures, creating, for example a 'style "sauvage"' for a number of writers from Montaigne (1533–92) to Chateaubriand.[30] Canada does not, in any event, become known as such until after the Conquest, which is the true beginning of Viatte's history of this region.

The beginning is defined as the absence of a French presence, an absence which is felt everywhere in the years following the Conquest until 1830, the period which constitutes the first act of the five that compose Viatte's history. Like any other classical comedy of the seventeenth-century manner, the first act establishes the themes, forecasts the conflicts, and announces the possibility of renewal in youthful self-assertion. And, as comedies require, the beginning is full of foreboding, the Church and the English serving as complicit blocking figures, and Fleury Mesplet, the editor of the *Gazette*, responding with texts from his contemporaries, Voltaire and Rousseau.[31] The central conflict between ultramontanism and liberalism that continued for well over a century became the dominant ideological focus around which the culture of French Canada was to move. Viatte, unlike Léger, takes the secular position, which allows him to see forecasts of the new at the turn of the century, notably in the establishment of a number of colleges and the first publication of the journal *Le Canadien* (1806).

The first true moment of recovery begins as part of the 'souffle de 1830,' the inspring breath of revolution passing over from Europe, bearing the news of freedom, liberal thought, nationalism, and anticlericalism. And so France enters delicately but clearly as an ideological guide for Papineau, the figure who is an incarnation of the period, and Garneau, who is paradoxically both romantic and Voltairian, finding   his true subject in the people.[32] The collective emphasis, an almost unavoidable theme of literary historical narrative, despite the organization around major writers, is, however, almost inconceivable without the presence of Herder and his idea of the *Volk* as primary hero. Thus, Viatte's reading of Garneau, derived from the romantic historian of the French Revolution, Jules Michelet, and confirmed by Camille Roy, is one that makes his subject not simply New France, and 'faisant prendre conscience d'elle-même à une nation, c'est lui qui a mis en branle ses facultés créatrices.'[33]

The beginnings of the novel follow upon Garneau, but move in two directions, one toward the past that Garneau had opened, and the other toward the present, but both within the shade of French romanticism. The novel, however, was not the preferred genre of the period. It was poetry, particularly that of Crémazie, which is its better representative, and it suffers from the worst of French neoclassicism and romanticism. Crémazie's romanticism, however, is only one side of the continuous conflict between the liberals and the Church, which still forms the centre of the intrigue of Viatte's Quebec, conducted on the several levels of the university, the church, the periodicals, and the novel. The figure who represents the triumph of clericalism was Casgrain, also a romantic in a manner derived from Alphonse Lamartine and Chateaubriand. Thus francophone Canada is made to act out in many respects the French shifts in its understanding of the romantic movement from liberal to conservative, and at the end of the second chapter or – to use the metaphor of drama, act – Buies appears. His wit, however, so strongly emphasized by Rossel, is insufficient; in Viatte's words, he 'vient trop tard,' echoing, perhaps unconsciously, by the whole tone of the concluding pages, Alfred de Musset's (1810–57) famous line: 'Je suis venu trop tard dans un monde trop vieux.'[35]

By the opening of third chapter, 'Repli,' it would seem that the conflict has come to an end, coincidentally enough, in the same decade that seemed to bring the constitutional problems of British North America to a conclusion. At the same time, Viatte intervenes in his history to comment that he does not intend to give much weight to the conflict: 'L'histoire littéraire n'en relève qu'indirectement.'[35] This astonishing statement comes near the end of a general argument that gives the impression that his history cannot be understood without such knowledge, and indeed it cannot, for the debate dominated – one might even say held captive – the literary institution. Furthermore, it prevented the rise of a national literature, which is precisely Viatte's theme, and prevented it primarily by the repression of French culture.[36] Both prose and poetry suffered as a result. None of the astonishing eruption of Charles Baudelaire (1821–67) and Arthur Rimbaud (1854–91) was available, and it is not surprising that Fréchette, considered the one poet of merit in the final decades of the century 'évoluera jusq'au romantisme de Hugo mûri, sans le dépasser.'[37] Yet he moved from strength to strength, just like his older contemporary Le May, a fact which Viatte accounts for by suggesting that in the early years of the twentieth century signs of cultural change were appearing in French Canada, even as they were elsewhere in Europe and the Americas. The change ushers in the fourth moment of the drama of literary life in Quebec, intimating a wakening and rising of fortunes.

About the year 1890, it appeared that the debate between conservatives and liberals had ended to the advantage of the former and that cultural life could not recover. The change began, as one might expect, under a French influence exercised by both the Sulpician order and the Université de Montréal, filtering down to literary journals. Its first effect in literature was manifest in the discovery by 'École littéraire de Montréal' of Baudelaire, Rimbaud, and the Parnassians, evident in Émile Nelligan and his circle, and reaching its densest point of saturation in the poet of Paul Morin and René Chopin (1885–1953), who went directly to Paris to take in the full effect of modernity. As a consequence, the conflict between ultramontanism and liberalism that had occupied the previous century began to shift in emphasis and showed itself as a conflict between those who espoused the regional or national and those who preferred a more cosmopolitan culture, a conflict which, as we have already observed, became central to A.J.M. Smith's presentation of English-Canadian poetry.[38] Unlike the previous debate, which was based on a deliberate effort to prevent the influence of secular French culture from having a deep effect in French Canada, this one brought Quebec powerfully into a French circle of ideas. Viatte asks: 'Mais qu'est-ce que un nationalisme littéraire canadien-français? où mettre l'accent, sur le mot *canadien* ou sur le mot *français*?' The ambiguity rests on the fact that much of the inspiration was both parallel to, and influenced by, the work of such conservative thinkers as Charles Maurras (1868–1952), Maurice Barrès (1862–1923), and Charles Péguy (1875–1914), whose ideas were readily adapted to the French-Canadian scene by such writers as Lionel Groulx. The awakening, then, only appears to have changed the character and terms of the debate, primarily by bringing French Canada more openly into its relation with France. Thus, Camille Roy is strategically placed at the end of the chapter on the conservative and national side, but displaying all the ambiguities of being both French and Canadian. His literary values are shared with all the French neoclassicists of the nineteenth century, and his desire is to create a 'littérature aussi national que possible,' which would be 'le prolongement des vertus de notre langue française.'[39]

Nothing could more persuasively set the scene for the final movement of the French-Canadian drama than the reference to Hémon's declaration, 'Au pays de Québec rien n'a changé.' In some respects, however, the reference is somewhat maladroitly placed and chosen more for dramatic, than historic, validity. As Viatte had already remarked, Hémon's novel 'influencera profondément ce qui va suivre,' and so it must be taken as a Janus-faced text, rooted deeply in the *terroir*, but preparing ineluctably its own demise that owed as much to the moment of its publication (1914) as to the social changes that occurred following the First World War. Although the tendency of the period that extends from 1914 to 1950 is categorized as one that breaks the frame, the frame remains part of the continuing debate between liberals and conservatives. The frame breaks only in the sense that its limits are both negated and transposed. In Marxist terms they are sublated. Hence, the literary journal *Nigog* (1918), which promulgated the views of Paul Morin and represented the position of Parisian modernism, not to mention a number of novelists, critics, and historians, was readily denounced by those who preferred a more traditional Quebec. France was continually invoked by both sides, however, which allows Viatte to prepare for his final argument, that the francophone literatures of North and Central America moved more or less together and at a pace that was by the end of the Second World War simultaneous. As a result, no French-Canadian writer of any repute can fail to be Canadian and French, which means that even the protectionism of nineteenth-century

conservatism remained French in its preference for certain pre-
revolutionary writers. French Canada, as the term suggests, can only
break the frame to the degree that ultramontanism is given up, as it was
given up in France where 'aucun interdit ne pèse sur aucun genre.'[40]
Quebec's ambivalence, however, is the enduring mark of its culture:
'Les poètes, avec et non après ceux de France, prospectent les secrets de
la vie intérieure, les romanciers avec ceux de France approfondissent les
grands problèmes humains.' The theatre of French Canada, which did
not come into its own before the twentieth century, 'débute, comme en
France, par la mise en scène,' and under the auspices of the Church. It
was a Church, however, that learned the technique in France. Father
Gustave Lamarche (1895–1987) 'donne au théâtre son œuvre la plus
copieuse et la plus originale,'[41] and his debt to Henri Ghéon (1875–
1944) and Paul Claudel (1868–1955) is not left to pass unnoticed. Gratien Gélinas's *Tit-Coq* (1948), which is generally considered 'a landmark
in the artistic evolution of Gélinas and Quebec theatre'[42] is dismissed,
along with Félix Leclerc's *Le Théâtre du village* (1951), despite the efforts
of both playwrights to create a national and popular theatre, as trying to
reach 'un public enfantin.'[43]

So it is that Viatte's canon is shaped by his general thesis, which is
given shape by a plot that begins in doubt, rises slightly around the year
1839, then sinks almost beyond hope after Confederation, only to be
revived after 1900 through contacts with France. It is a comic plot, but
more complex than the designs that Perkins proposes. From a rhetorical perspective, it is dominated by the notion of Synecdoche 'in which
all struggle, strife, and conflict are dissolved in the realization of a perfect harmony.' As we have seen, this is not an uncommon structure and
trope in Canadian literary histories, but its significance is at variance
with others because of the desire to draw francophone literatures into
an intimate orbit with France. It is, however, a history of triumph: 'les
obstacles ont été surmontés.' But if the patrimony of these literatures
was inherited, it shortened their first efforts, and the most recent generations 'comptent bon nombre d'écrivains qui se comparent très hono-
rablement avec la moyenne de ceux dont retentissent nos libraires,' and
not to be familiar with them would be to lack a full knowledge 'de notre
littérature française.'[44]

The larger view of Viatte's history is one that expressly removes distinction from the literatures of the Americas. The sense of harmony that
White discerns as a general tendency in histories of this kind is disturbed by the fact that the theme of autonomy, so often repeated since

Roy, here yields to the purposes of la Francophonie. In many respects, Quebec's relation with anglophone North America is only a subtext, and autonomy itself is only an issue relative to France, whose role as a variable model tends to diminish the role of autonomy as the desired state of harmony. The idea of the nation cannot, under such conditions, be essentialized, and Quebec becomes an example among others of how literary history can make parallel moves, despite a lack of mutual awareness. Quebec is constructed to illustrate a thesis.[45]

Autonomy, but Not Necessarily Autonomy

Gérard Tougas, at the time a professor of French at the University of British Columbia, began, in the *Avant-propos* of his *Histoire de la littérature canadienne-française* (1960) with a series of rejections. The first is his dismissal of those critical approaches that used to be called 'extrinsic,' that is, the use of methods borrowed from sociology and psychology. Tougas will only admit a structuralist approach, on the ground that it remains most faithful to the text. The second is that the literature that appeared during the long century that concluded in the 1920s is limited by its provincial character and requires biographical sketches, paraphrase, and sociological commentary. In other words, it is not responsive to textual analysis, and, therefore, his major focus is the literature of the modern and contemporary periods. Finally, despite their best efforts, Roy and his successors are dismissed, Viatte is the only historian considered worthy of Tougas's respect, and the only flaw of the latter's history was its brevity.[46] As a consequence, everything from 1534 to 1845 is dispensed with in some ten pages, and the true beginning is Garneau's *Histoire*.

Such a rapid entry into the first work of significance means that the issue of the French presence in North America until 1759 is for the most part passed over as an extension of French literature. The Conquest itself, however, is put into a positive focus. It was 'une grande chance,' for, in effect, it forced the former French colony to depend on its own resources and made them 'conscients de leur nationalité.' Perhaps for this reason, the transfer of power is simply referred to as 'ce moment où le Canada devient anglais.'[47] Neither 'cession'[48] nor 'conquête' is used to describe the change, and only the condition of isolation is drawn upon as motivating the new consciousness. From the early period, the poetry of Michel Bibaud is presented both as an inauguration of French-Canada's literature and an affirmation of 'son immense désir d'accéder à une vie spirituelle autonome.' Cultural autonomy becomes, then, the principal subtext of Tougas's history, and its full sense is raised when he distinguishes French Canada's subsequent turn toward romanticism – thus distinguishing itself from the French predilection for the classical – but in such a way as to mark the progress toward autonomy as a conflicted site: 'Le romantisme semble correspondre à quelque secrète exigence du tempérament canadien-français tel que le continent américain l'a façonné. Les poètes, les historiens et les romanciers canadiens du dix-neuvième siècle auront fait plus qu'imiter des modèles français: ils se sont trouvés en eux.'[49] One is reminded of Mackenzie King's famous assertion on conscription. Tougas's autonomy denotes autonomy, but not necessarily autonomy, and it is precisely this ambivalence, related as it is to romanticism, that provides the tension of his argument.[50]

The foundation, as I have remarked, is Garneau, Canada's first true writer – romantic, liberal, and capable of understanding the British notion of freedom at the same as he praised both the heroism and weakness of the French administration. To a more marked degree, Crémazie is constructed as at once Canadian and French, and the double nature of his personality was, so long as he remained in Canada, the source of his strengths as a poet. The burden of France, however, was not his alone, and he is but one of many examples of the problems that give rise to the second level of Tougas's discussion of the question of autonomy. Taking his cue from the fate of Crémazie, he observes that the fate of the French-Canadian intellectual is to be so overwhelmed by Anglo-Saxon culture that only by means of internal struggle is it possible for him to acquire an adequate knowledge of French. The effort to be protected from the moral and intellectual limitations of such a culture is of such a character that 'en un mot être tendu est son destin,'[51] and it is this tension that provides a general form for Tougas's history. It should not be understood as a dialectical relationship, for the simple reason that the tension does not move by a process of negation to further levels of affirmation. It is a Synecdoche, a field of energy within which the French-Canadian writer works, and in a certain sense it is the only autonomy that is desired.[52]

As a consequence, the major moments of Tougas's history, namely, 'The Creation of a Tradition (1865–1899),' 'Modernity (1900–1939),' and 'The Contemporary Period,' are to be seen as phases or aspects of the central tension, rather than a certain rise toward a clear autonomy, which is more characteristic of histories written by Québécois historians.

True enough, the mark of the contemporary period is its ability to move the perennial French-Canadian themes of the eunuch and the virgin to one side, but this is only part of its broader, twofold scope which is of a double character: 'élargissement du fond et épuration de la forme.' Taken together, they work toward the 'déprovincialisation' of French-Canadian literature. In order to move in such a direction, there was needed, so to speak, a basis in the provincial, which, in its formative years, consisted of 'deux pôles d'attraction: patriotisme et religion.'[53] Certainly, these poles have not faded away. The former continues to be exemplified in the historiography of Guy Frégault; the latter, in the poetry of Rina Lasnier. They are, rather, subsumed, in a widening field which is always constructed, however, in pairs or – and this reveals the governing function of structuralism in Tougas – binary oppositions. His structuralism goes no further than this, but the fondness of antinomy is where his greatest debt to Viatte lies.

Tougas's history has, nevertheless, a direction and, consistent with role that French culture plays in the argument, it is toward a certain linguistic freedom from the interference of English in the development of style. Among modern poets who pointed the way, both Nelligan and Morin are mentioned, but the problem with the latter, as with Crémazie, was that he was too much under the spell of French. As we have already noted, 'French' and 'Canadian' are semiological indications of another opposition, namely, that of classicism and romanticism, which implies, then, the greater purity of language and the greater virtues of classicism, which is why, for example, the influence of Camille Roy is considered salutary. His only peer is his contemporary, Louis Dantin (1866–1945), who shared all of Roy's admiration for French culture without the moral intent. The indigenous does not appear to make its way into the novel in some inevitable manner before Roger Lemelin (1919–92), despite the best efforts of the French-Canadian elite, and the French-Canadian nationalism that appears in his novels is considered essentially American. Thus, the structure of French and Canadian is broadened to make way for the particular (or regional) and the universal. Yet if the novel tends in this direction, the best Canadian poets after 1945 'ressemblent certes à leurs homologues de France.'[54] As Tougas goes on immediately to remark, this is the sign of their being contemporary.

Needless to say, the directions taken by the novel and poetry in Tougas cannot be understood as other than generalizations that are determined by his argument. It is governed by a transcendent semiotic design that at once controls history and determines meaning. History is controlled because its fundamental object is not to rise and fall in Perkins's sense, but rather to dilate and deepen. It is given a kind of classical stasis, which is evident especially in the balance that every judgment bears. No matter, for example, how inimical Lionel Groulx is to Tougas as an historian, it is still possible for him to remark: 'Son influence s'explique en partie par le rayonnement d'une âme d'une absolue sincérité, capable de susciter des disciples et de remuer les cœurs.'[55]

The form of the whole follows that of Viatte; and while it is divided into five chapters, it would be difficult to find in it the same sense of drama as Viatte's history, although the use of oppositions might have suggested this to him. Part of an answer resides in a final, sixth chapter, which is separate from the history and which is a meditation on the relationship of French-Canadian literature and the culture of France. Even this paraphrase of the title indicates a certain bias. How is a small literature to be favourably compared with a larger culture, particularly one of the scope and magnitude of that of France?[56] It is a chapter that might have served as an introduction, as way of leading into the argument, but Tougas prefers to use it, it would appear, to put the final cap upon suggestions made in the course of his history. The mark of French-Canadian literature is that 'ses écrivains ont filtré les éléments étrangers qui, avec le temps, sont venus greffer sur la sensibilité nationale.' Despite the best efforts of the province's elite to cultivate French culture, the people have gravitated more toward that of the United States, and speaking of the contemporary period, Tougas notes: 'c'est l'idéal américain qu'il comprend d'instinct.' Nevertheless, in concluding the same paragraph, Tougas hastens to declare that 'quels que soient les futurs avatars du peuple canadien-français, les écrivains, dont la situation en Amérique est si exceptionelle, constitueront longtemps encore un trait d'union vivant entre la France et le Canada.' Tougas wavers again when addressing the perennial question of language, and in what might appear to be a paradoxical reversal of perspective, he asserts that the Anglo-Saxon presence in North America is simply an excuse: 'L'obstacle n'est pas tant l'anglais omniprésent qu'un français mal appris.' Thus the language question is a false dilemma, and the real issue is the relation of language to life. One set of oppositions is drawn upon to counter another, which then allows him to return to the virtue of clarté, which is the true character of French culture, especially as transmitted by Roy and Dantin. It is a virtue followed by some contemporary novelists, if not by others (poetry is not raised at this juncture, perhaps because it does not possess the same tension), and it is they –

contemporary novelists – who allow a glimpse into the future: 'Dans son ensemble, la littérature canadienne semble destiné à trouvé son équilibre et sa véritable originalité par un dosage inédit des esprits français et anglo-saxon.'[57] Whether or not such a conclusion would find favour in Quebec, the desire to find an equilibrium, which belongs to the semiotic field of traditional classicism, may be considered the dominant trait of Tougas's text. In its perfected state, it is a condition of inertia and, as such, argues against a notion of history that addresses events in time. It is, like the classical ideal, more at home in spatial, rather than temporal, dimension, and, to that extent at least, Tougas's sensibility comes closer to that of the literary historians of English Canada.

Canada and the German Presence

Heinz Kloss's '*Einleitung*' to his *Ahornblätter: Deutsche Dichtung aus Kanada* (1961), an anthology of German-Canadian poetry, serves, if nothing else, as a curious interlude between the texts of the first half of this century and those that follow.[58] The title plays upon the maple leaf, a symbol appropriate to evoke both Canada and the function of nature imagery in lyric poetry, both of which are the themes of the two poems that stand as prefaces to the book. Although the suitability of the symbol may be questioned for both the brief history and the poetry, it is, nevertheless, what makes Kloss stand clearly apart from ethnic historians living in Canada. His text allows us to see, moreover, the extent to which cultural histories are often profoundly influenced by experience, which, in the instance of ethnic writing, is intent upon either irrevocable moments – patterns that intimate myth – or existential vision. These aspects are absent from Kloss's history, partially because the perspective is European, and partially because the poems anthologized do not represent the experience of a homogeneous nation or group, for example, Hungarians, Jews, Ukrainians. The anthology represents German-speaking peoples who range from Mennonites from Ukraine to Canadians of German descent. The only unifying element is language.

Thus, although German-speaking people constitute the largest ethnic community in Canada after francophones and anglophones, they are difficult to present in a cohesive literary history. They do not represent a single nation. As a consequence, according to Kloss, German-Canadian literature can boast of no internationally great poets, such as the Icelander Stephan Stephansson (1853–1927), nor a continuous developing tradition. Stephansson's immigration to Canada was rather unusual, and certainly a lack of tradition is significant, but the disparate character of the community, which is not dwelt upon sufficiently,[59] is the major problem. It is a problem that might have formed an argument if the introduction were a full history, rather than an outline. Nevertheless, Kloss endeavours to provide his history with a conventional structure, consisting of an early period, a second section devoted to traditionalists, another to Modernists, and finally a miscellany of sections on Mennonites, German-speakers born in Ontario, drama and folk poetry (both produced by Mennonites), and various kinds of prose.

The major genres of German writing in Canada since its beginnings in the late eighteenth century were either religious or poetic texts. The former played a vital role in forming and preserving a sense of community among both Lutherans and Mennonites, but the community, unlike those communities that represent nations, was perforce spiritual. Unlike the Mennonites, members of the Lutheran faith are not bound by language, and therefore the claims for maintaining the language from generation to generation are seriously weakened. Poetry depends profoundly upon the language of its expression, but with the exception of traditionalist verse, is as much intent upon the individual as the community. Given, then, the variety of audiences and intents, can there be a history? Is it not, rather, an accumulation? Kloss remarks in his conclusion:

> Wir haben ein Schrifttum kennen gelernt, das sich aufgliedern läßt in die problemreiche, hochindividualistische Dichtung der Deutschen aus Mitteleuropa, die ebenso problemgeladene, aber noch stärker im Gruppenbewußtsein webende Dichtung der Mennoniten und die ganz gemüthaftproblemlose Dichtung kanadabürtigen Ontariodeutschen – meist in pensilfaanischer Sprache – die noch so verpersönlich ist, daß man sie als Volksdichtung bezeichnen möchte – eine wesenhafte anonyme Dichtung.

A common thread, however, appears to enter the poetry and that is a penchant of the poets for 'Themen aus seiner fernen Heimat.'[60] In other words, they stand somewhere in Padolsky's model between separation and marginalization. Given the variety of countries that serve as origins, it is a thread with so many different meanings that the common character is dispersed.

Thus Kloss's history has only the appearance of history. It occurs in time and space, and it moves from one moment in the past to another. Yet these are simply the structural elements that make it a narrative. It

stands apart from all the histories that compose this book in its inability
to find a common origin and even a shared development. It suggests,
moreover, that language and culture are not in themselves coterminous,
as some historians would have us believe. Various communities may
share a language without sharing either a tradition or a culture. Such a
fact also problematizes the whole notion implicit in the expression 'German-Canadian,' inasmuch as 'German' operates in a different semantic
field from Canadian.' The latter refers to a country of immigration; the
former, a language composed of dialects and regional differences. Such
a history can only trace an evolution in time, when aspects of the language appeared in Canada, but always bids one to ask: from whence,
and within what communities? The two subtitles of the book reflect,
in fact, the problem the book poses. On the cover we find *Anthologie
deutschkanadischer Dichtung* and on the title page we read *Deutsche Dichtung aus Kanada*. The latter comes nearest to describing the kinds of
texts it contains, since the relation between the country and the language, with few exceptions, is that of a kind of writing located in space
but in no particular way part of the culture of the host country and thus
cut off from the historical possibility of the development of any culture,
as attested in Walter Bauer's (1904–76) lines: 'Ungenossene Frucht ist
der Mann in Exil, sich sehnend zum Baum, von dem er sich selber
abriß, / Wie käme sie je zurück?'[61] Because his work continued to be
published in Germany, his poems are, as the title pages declare, closer
to dispatches from Canada, rather than an integral part of the literatures of Canada.

The lack of integration may, however, be an inevitable function of a
text on Canada written primarily for a non-Canadian audience. The
necessity to find a vital rapport with a continuously changing culture is
not required. Needless to say, both Rossel and Viatte diffuse the distinctive by finding it in more than one literature. 'Canada' derives its significance mostly by being part of France and its extension among
francophone countries. Yet neither Léger nor Tougas construct cultures
with a future. The former constructs the 'Canadian soul' by reifying
New France, and the latter would prefer to remove French Canada in a
certain measure from historical evolution. The significance of 'Canada'
is not clear in Kloss's text other than as a place from which texts in German come. The histories written in the latter half of the century – all
written by Canadians for primarily non-Canadian audiences – pose
somewhat different problems, but for each of them Canada assumes a
definite didactic role.

CHAPTER NINE

Canada by Canadians for Europeans, 1974–1989

I am constantly assured that Canadians no longer know what they are, or what to be Canadian should mean; for want of a satisfactory definition, a national identity has been mislaid.[1]

The four histories considered in this chapter, while written by Canadians, were contracted for series that are designed for readers outside Canada. Significantly, the two anglophone histories are those most widely in use as narrative histories, and one of them can only be acquired from its English publisher, thus inhibiting its use in Canada. Both these histories and that of Laurent Mailhot were also written at times when the histories of Grandpré and Klinck would have been in general use, which may have been the reason why they were published by foreign publishers. Alternatively, they may all have suited the needs of the French and English publishers and the series responsible for them. In any event, the large, collaborative works of both Grandpré and Klinck would certainly have posed challenges of scope and conception that would have required either different teams or changed understandings to form viable alternatives. Of the four, only René Dionne's is collaborative, and it is sufficiently distant in time and conception from that of Grandpré to be considered apart from it.

Waiting for the Future

Laurant Mailhot's *Littérature québécoise* (1974) was prepared for the *Que sais je?* Series published by the Presses Universitaires de France. It is a series of limited format, designed primarily for student use and meant to be a distillation of the most reliable of recent scholarship. At their best these texts reflect the moment of their publication, and so Maihot's text should be placed in a certain historical context. First, it should be remembered that the final volume of Grandpré's history appeared in 1969, a year before the October Crisis. Mailhot's history, therefore, was conceived during the aftermath of that event and also during a period of gradual, but intense polarization between federalism and nationalism in Quebec. Tension between government and unions increased, and the women's movement acquired greater strength. Perhaps the most significant activity, however, turned upon anxiety over the continued viability of French culture in respect of the perceived threat of immigrants and the use of English in the province.[2] The optimism so evident in Grandpré could be said to be contested by the events that followed October 1970. Mailhot's history reflects a more tempered optimism and constructs a culture that has yet to reach an assured future.

It is not surprising, then, that Maihot's 'Introduction' is organized by a series of questions whose frequency suggests that they are not entirely rhetorical or designed simply to excite interest among French students in his project. The questions are also designed to provide occasions for assertion, and so to place literature somewhere in time. 'La littérature québécoise,' writes Mailhot, 'est un avenir, un projet, dont on trouve des signes au XIXe siècle, et qu'on retrace jusqu'au XVIe. Est-ce une tradition? C'est une tradition "à inventer," des lectures à faire, des relectures, à mesure que se' développent (surtout depuis 1945 et 1960) la curiosité et les appétits.' Such statements insert the author into the text as the one who both questions and answers a corpus in its relation to a particular society, and so provide the reader with a way of interpreting such a sentence as, the literature of French Canada 'sera longtemps nationaliste avant d'être nationale, individualiste avant d'être personnelle.' We are to understand this declaration to mean, I think, that Quebec for many generations had a distinctive character which preceded its acquisition of subjectivity. While the latter may be too recent to be certain of it, the idea of subjectivity provides the author with a special insight. If francophone literature is a tradition to be discovered and then assumed, one supposes, then the author's function in the text is to demonstrate the process of discovery. Such a process begins 'depuis que Groulx lit Garneau; Savard, Cartier; Ducharme, Nelligan; Aquin, les Patriotes. Depuis que révolution et tradition se reconnaissent, s'articulent.' Process, then, is a series of articulated interrelationships that is only made possible through the personal intervention of re-reading.[3]

The assumptions of the early 1970s are clearly inscribed as interplay, confrontation, and a will to re-orient.

Such is the role of the Conquest. It is not a defeat as it was for many, not exactly a chance as it is Tougas, but an obligation for the French of North America 'à chercher chez eux ... une voie originale.' But even before the Conquest Cartier is allowed to be a beginning: he provided 'un mouvement, un style, une vision encore sensibles, quatre siècles plus tard, chez un Savard, un Perrault, un Vigneault ...'[4] Thus, history does not merely unfold through time; rather, it is the place of moments of conjunction that encourage discovery. The period of New France is neither dismissed as fundamentally French nor hypostasized as the primary moment of significance. It is necessary as a locus and an articulation of discovery. It also plays a double role that not only conjoins authors, but also serves as the first half of the whole period of origins that extends from 1534 to 1837. It belongs, then, to a process of complementarity that serves as the primary structural principle of the history. The origin is a period before and after the Conquest, the latter seeming to depend upon the former to acquire its sense. The next period (1837–1918) is one of 'Cheminements et reflets.' Both the conjunction and the word 'reflets' are important in the title; they belong to the whole syntax of coordination that motivates the construction of history. The following period (1918–48) is characterized as 'Entre la campagne et la ville.' The emphasis is upon suspension ('entre') and combination. Country and city are used less in opposition than in relationship, one informing the other. Finally, the contemporary period (1948–73) redefines relationship as process in the title 'De la province au pays.'

Conjunction does not, however, deny the possibility of tension and conflict. Quebec's own long nineteenth century is one indeed of ambiguity, compromise, and interaction between opposing parties that are neatly drawn together beneath the rubric '1860: le mouvement immobile.' While history was its dominant discourse and genre, thus partly justifying the term 'reflets,' it was a history that could not always form an ideological whole, and Garneau's desire to compromise is a notable example. Yet even the informing style of romanticism, contrary to Tougas's argument, is never indigenous and integrated with the constructed will of the country. The twentieth century, as it emerged from the First World War, is characterized by a demographic shift to urban centres, but the population 'habite les faubourgs comme elle habite les rangs et les villages: en famille, en paroisse, avec la nostalgie de l'érablière, de la jument grise et de la croix de chemin.'[5] Nevertheless, tensions that were articulated in the nineteenth century continue in the twentieth. The poets who published the periodical *Nigog* (1918) were resolutely opposed to the more indigenous poets of an earlier periodical, *Terroir* (1909), thus intimating that the conjunction of city and country was not always a happy one, for what could be more urban and urbane than *Nigog*'s adoration of Paris? Moreover, Groulx and his disciples were intent upon addressing other, analogous tensions in Quebec that would hinder the formation of a more unified, autonomous state.

The tensions that mark the decades of the first half of the twentieth century are now given a change in structure. They are more anticipatory, and syntactical relationships are more frequently articulated with the preposition *à* in order to orient them toward a future. Thus we find rubrics such as, 'De "La Relève" à "Refus global"' and 'De "Maria Chapdelaine" à "Bonheur d'occasion"' alongside others that use the conjunction *et*. The use of the preposition indicates a shift in emphasis on the author's part from empirical description to assertions of a future. There is a shift from the declarative to the subjective mood, and nothing more clearly testifies to the shift than the relationship between the title of the last chapter ('De la province au pays') and its initial section, 'L'âge de la parole.' 'Parole' is to be understood, on the one hand, in contrast with 'langue' in the Saussurean sense, that is, in the contrast of a collective and individual use of language. What is the individual but 'le sujet parlant,' a subject, one might say, whose agency is displayed in the use of language. On the other hand, 'parole' can also to be understood is the collective voice given agency. It is the central conjunction that Mailhot's tradition desires to discover, and the agent of its occasion was primarily the publishing house l'Hexagone, which perceived its function as follows: 'Agir par la poésie, agir la poésie – lui donner une "patrie," une conscience collective, un contexte.' The catalyst, of course, was Borduas's *Refus global*, which is constructed as a primal act of agency by taking '"responsabilité entière."' It is also noted for having accorded 'la première importance au geste, à l'objet, aux "relations sensibles de la matière employé."'[6] Of first importance, then, to draw a literary historical analogy, is relation and not the corpus itself. Borduas's project, then, as it is for Grandpré, is the symbolic crucible through which Québécois culture must pass so that the acts of conjunction that compose a tradition can be perceived and articulated.

It is precisely to this point and no farther, however, that Mailhot wishes the tradition to go. Because it is a tradition to be discovered ('à inventer'), the literary culture of Quebec can only be a process that is the duty of the historian, taking his cue from Borduas the artist, to make palpable. By definition, it can possess agency, but it can never arrive. It is always oriented toward an unfulfilled future in a Faustian quest of discovery. Curiously enough, what appears as revolution in Borduas and the literature that followed in his wake, and what especially seems to announce itself fully in Anne Hébert's unforgettable sentence, 'notre pays est à l'âge des premiers jours du monde,'[7] is not, in the end, to be so understood. The primal is not the perfect moment of genesis to which poetry summons us to return but rather the ineluctability of temporality itself. Thus he avoids Léger's trap of transferring the past into the future and prefers to define literary history as a threshold experience. To belong is not to belong to a tradition but to what it can be made to prefigure. Citing the title of Hubert Aquin's (1929–77) first novel as support, Mailhot sees history as an 'appartenance à un futur, à un "prochain épisode."'[8] The theme of conjunction, then, is to be understood as temporal and anticipatory, and to this extent, at least, Mailhot takes the preoccupation of French-Canadian literary historians with time and makes it the informing spirit of his own history.

An Archaeology of le Québécois

The purpose of the collection of essays edited by René Dionne, *Le Québécois et sa littérature* (1984), a title that makes an odd echo of Jean-Charles Falardeau's book, *Notre société et son roman* (1972), targets an audience which consists of the 'diverses communautés de la Francophonie' and endeavours to provide 'une synthèse de l'état actuel de la recherche (jusqu'en 1978–79).' It is a history of two kinds. The first is general, providing 'le visage historique de la nation à travers l'esquisse d'un portrait du Québécois.' Such a decision necessitated another, namely: not to treat of francophone writers *hors Québec* inasmuch as 'pours maints d'entre eux, il existe même une sorte d'impérialisme québécois, qu'ils abhorrent comme naguère les Québécois exécrèrent le colonialisme français.'[9] Such an admission is rare in francophone literary history. In fact, the assumption is normally made that there is little writing in French beyond the borders of the province. The other history is of genres. Several genres ranging from the novel to comic strips are given individual histories that have several concurrent, but distinct lines of development. Following in a certain respect the pattern set by Grandpré, each section was prepared by a different person, but the effect of unity of purpose is missing. Indeed, the intent appears to seek unity in diversity, which is announced with elaborate care in the initial essay designed to define the character of the Québécois.

Following a pattern we have seen before, especially in Baillargeon, Dionne defines the Québécois as an historical type which is known according to the steps of its formation. It is a type that is at once an evolution and a condition that begins with the French foundation and concludes by becoming Québécois. It is characterized by fifteen different discursive traits, each of which acquires different names with different ideological trajectories. For example, it is 'Canadien' from 1672 to 1713. A shift occurs during the next period, which extends to the Conquest, as a more conscious national identity is produced. In the early decades of the British régime, these acquired characteristics are modified as the necessity of resistance is assumed. For reasons of survival, more radical changes occur at the time of the American Revolution and the discourse of the loyal British subject is adopted. This discourse yields to a more nationalist stance from 1812 to 1840. After subsequent metamorphoses, the type is redefined as British from 1867 to 1921 and American from 1921 to the end of the Second World War. Following the war, a more multinational perspective pervades in Quebec and the *points de repère* with other countries becoming independent assume a central interest. Since 1958, the rubric of Québécois is adopted.

Each of these categories, as I have remarked, carries different discursive possibilities. They constitute something more than a history, which, like many other francophone histories, is shaped around a certain unified theme. Dionne's history is, rather, an archaeology, and in that sense the type that finally acquires the name *Québécois* is not solely composed of that discourse which was generated in seminal fashion by Séguin and the Montréal School of history. Its theme is independence, which, needless to say, requires the rejection of both the words *canadien* and *français*. Thus he concludes the essay by asking: 'Comment définir le Québécois autrement que comme un être complexe, "torturé," mais bien constitué, original, qui emprunte aux différentes périodes de sa vie collective ses traits les plus accusés?'[10] Although Dionne puts most of his effort into stressing the desire for national independence as the unifying element of the Québécois, he does so by both glossing over the history he constructs and taking the central contradiction between federalists and sovereigntists as two sides of the same coin. It is an argument that works against the archaeological character of his history. For, as Dionne himself remarks, the initial phase in the constitution of the type he desires to construct is a 'pré-texte' of what follows,[11] and, indeed, what follows is a series of other texts and their logical construction, following Foucault, would assert that 'les diverses modalités d'énonciation au lieu de renvoyer à *la* synthèse ou à *la* fonction unifiante d'*un* sujet, manifeste sa dispersion.'[12] The subject, as Dionne's argument trenchantly states, is multiple, unless we are to believe that all the discursive positions adopted by the Québécois over 350 years were simply masks of a unified subject that was always what it would become in the years after 1958. Even Séguin does not attribute so much foresight to *his* Québécois,[13] which, after all, was part of a larger debate in French Canada in the 1940s that grew out of the publication of Arthur Maheux's lectures at Laval entitled *Ton Histoire est une épopé* (1941). Maheux's position of moderation and conciliation was attacked as racial treachery,[14] but for this reason it need not be considered invalid. It represents, rather, one of the several discursive trajectories produced by the history of the province.

What is of highest significance in Dionne's introductory essay, however, is the emphasis on history: the Québécois is a composite of its several pasts. It may, at the present time, be dominated by a desire for autonomy, but the present is not the end of history, only another aspect of it. The same tendency toward archaeological reconstruction is apparent throughout the rest of the collection of essays. In a sense, the book is structured as a continuous effort to resume a diachronic process designed to foreground moments of difference, all of which seem to be subsumed in the contemporary. Although gestures toward autonomy are frequent, the sense of autonomy is not always consistent. The comic strip has no politically autonomous ambitions, while the chapter on the folk song strives to finds its authenticity in its ability to reflect 'la collectivité québécoise.'[15] Robert Vigneault's chapter on the essay takes serious issue with the construction of tradition, characteristic of most francophone literary histories; and the chapter on orality, while providing the collective as a context, is a discussion of the discursive practices that distinguish the tale and the legend. Finally, and as a primary mode of orientation, the reader is offered both a brief history of literature and a twofold examination of the question of origins. The continual *recherche* of more than one corpus, as well as their situation in history, can only prompt a deep sense of anxiety concerning origin, difference, contradiction, context, direction, and meaning, but these are the anxieties of archaeology.

Preceding the histories of various genres are three histories. The first is a brief historical sketch by Dionne from the beginning to the present;

the second and third are discussions of two different moments of origin that extend the problem raised by the first sketch. The matter of the beginnings of French-Canadian literature will never, perhaps, be resolved, as it is not, for example, in Mailhot. In this scenario, it has two: one French, the other Canadian. Dionne begins by conceding that the first moment of origin is generally considered an event in French history. Nevertheless, they have become 'progressivement canadianisés,' especially by contemporary writers. Therefore, it is only a convention to refer to the period from 1534 to 1760 as 'French,' because 'l'on ne doute plus que la littérature canadienne-française commence en 1534.' Leaving to one side the premptory and moot aspect of this assertion, what is clear is that there are two origins, which provide two perspectives on the larger issue of beginnings and French-Canadian writing. Its history is to be considered one, but interrupted by the Conquest. In this way the possible imperial aspect of the French beginning is elided when it is 'Canadianized.' The Canadian beginning announces both a defeat and a new start in an unforeseen direction. From an archaeological perspective, however, the decision to retain both as beginnings admits a rift and a difference which determines the whole physiognomy of the history. To modify the title of one of Luce Irigaray's books, this is a 'histoire qui n'en est plus une.'[16] It means that the first beginning informs the efforts of nation-building that follow, for had the colony not been lost, as it were, there would have been no need to restore the idea of a 'patrie littéraire' which is the intent of the rise of French-Canadian nationalism. The first beginning is strongly reified in order to provide significance both to the idea of nation and the role of literature in shaping a nation. Thus while the period of Canadian origins is barely aware of that of New France, 'c'est quand même celle où s'ébauchent ... les premières tentatives de créer en Canada une littérature nationale de langue française; c'est aussi celle qui voit naître le nationalisme canadien-française, et nationalisme va ériger la patrie littéraire.' Needless to say, the text that draws the two beginnings together is Garneau's *Histoire*, a text whose significance as *literature* is never forgotten in the history of francophone literature; for, while one might question its status as literature, it remains a seminal fount of literature and nationalism. At the same time, its own ideologically conflicted condition is well known,[17] if not treated by Dionne. Nevertheless, French-Canadian nationalism, as Dionne's comments on the late nineteenth century make clear, is not a harmonious discursive site. For if the path of a national literature is to be found in Casgrain, how recognizable is it today in a Quebec still *à la recherche* of its true country? Dionne cites his famous declaration that French-Canadian literature 'sera grave, méditative, spiritualiste, religieuse, évangélatrice comme nos missionaires, généreuse comme nos martyres.' He also indicates that the statement was valid, at least from 1866 to 1895. It constituted a discursive practice for the nation as narrative for some three decades, at least. The secularization of Quebec, which now appears irreversible, constitutes another discursive practice, neither of which consort well together, and both of which have differing ideological trajectories. Hence, it is fair to say that, just as there are differing nationalisms, so the expression 'patrie littéraire' does not always evoke the same space. Where contemporary Quebec is heading is not clear, especially in the face of opposition between 'le nationalisme bourgeois et le socialisme populaire,' which in turn are threatened by a conservative resistance.[18]

The conclusion of Dionne's sketch, when read against his profile of *le québécois* makes even more evident the extent to which his history is archaeological, and where difference is not easilt resolved. The resumption of the quest for origins in Léopold LeBlanc's essay adds more detail but does not change the function of the French period, for it is then that 'se constituent quelques-uns de grands types humains qui traversent toute notre littérature, que se forme notre propre sensibilité au temps et à l'espace, que débute notre propre relation à la langue française et aux formes littéraires.'[19] In other words, it is the foundation of one of several discursive practices. The second moment, which follows the Conquest, is marked by a number of events that constitute another ideological direction. First to be mentioned is the establishment of a printing press; second, the circulation of French books; third, the creation of a library by Governor Haldimand, consisting of 2,400 books, half of which were in French; and finally, the arrival of Republican ideas in French Canada during the American Revolution. The introductory paragraph does not so much as mention the Conquest; rather, its emphasis is on access to liberal ideology, which forms the direction of Quebec's history until 1830. It draws upon the discourse of neither New France nor that of Father Casgrain. So it is that with this large and conflicted register of what are, in effect, discursive origins, the history of various genres is established.

The consequence of distinguishing genres and providing successive moments of their history is that the question of beginnings[20] is continually re-opened. Because the histories are treated by more than one essayist, each history is cut into sections, each of which stresses different themes and different discursive strategies, thus reinforcing the archaeo-logical mode. What is of even greater significance is that the gesture toward constructing a nation becomes more muted. For example, the final period of the development of the novel, from 1958 to 1979, is marked first as 'le règne de l'anarchie.' In order to provide some struc-ture in the discussion, however, two novels, both published in 1958 – Anne Hébert's *Les Chambres de bois* and Gérard Bessette's *La Bagarre* – are given as two discursive models, both of which bring to a conclusion the 'traditional' novel in its structure and contents. Hébert's model is that of the 'roman-poème,' which 'provient d'une crise d'identité qui cherche sa résolution dans la création de formes inédits qui soient le reflet d'une conscience en devenir.' Less introspective than Hébert, the discursive practice clustered around Bessette is more public and used to challenge a dying tradition. Its central themes are 'l'aliénation et la pos-sibilité objective de son dépassement.'[21] In the early years of the 1960s, as 'la conscience nationaliste' grew sharper, 'l'appelation "canadienne-française" cède la place, au Québec du moins, à celle, autonomatiste, pour ne pas dire séparatiste, de québécoise.' This neatly phrased sen-tence is the limit to which the narrative of a Quebec nation is taken, and, moreover, following the demise of the periodical *Parti pris* in 1968, 'l'aventure romanesque, à la recherche d'un centre absent, est devenue obsessive, hallucinée et hallucinante.'[22]

The history of poetry represents in even lesser involvement in national consciousness, and this is true especially after 1958, despite the possibilities it offers to the contrary.[23] One might assume from the fol-lowing sentences, which open the discussion on the period 1830 to 1895, that the orientation of the genre will be toward autonomy if not more: 'Le millésime 1830 marque en France le triumphe de la révolution de juillet et la victoire des romantiques dans la bataille d'*Hernani*. Au Bas-Canada, cette date signale l'éclosion d'une littérature autonome.' It is autonomous because of the discontinuity with France, rather than a ges-ture toward revolution. Nevertheless, the same period indicates the large degree to which 'le Canada français était tributaire de la France dans le domaine des lettres,'[24] and the same remains true in large mea-sure for the following period. Even the *Terroir* poets, whose work is char-acterized by its regionalism, still show, if more rarely, signs of French influence. The poets who follow – Saint-Denys Garneau, Hébert, Grand-bois, and Lasnier – are all constructed inevitably as founders of the mod-ern and the future, which is owed to their enormous talent and, therefore, their ability to overcome the derivative. Their poetry, as a consequence, 'pose désormais comme condition préalable à son exercice une solitude fondamentale qui devient à son tour le lieu d'une quête.'[25] Neither they nor the poets who followed, notably those published by Héxagone, are characterized as nationalist. The most that could be remarked of them, despite differences of style, tone, and theme is that they are autonomous, which is anodyne in the extreme, for they are hardly constructed as a reflection or voice of a collectivity.

Contemporary drama, like the contemporary novel, is dominated by two discourses, that of Gratien Gélinas (1909–99) and Claude Gauvreau (1925–71). While the former's work is dominated by the national and popular, the latter is drawn more toward the libertarian and occult. Neither, however, is characterized as wholly 'autonomous.'[26] Gélinas is indebted to the work of the French theatre as practised by the Théatre National Populaire, and Gauvreau followed attentively such playwrights as Samuel Beckett (1906–89), Antonin Artaud (1896–1948), and Bertolt Brecht (1898–1956). Although such influences do not preclude the cultivation of the national, they are presented more within the history of Québécois theatre and its relations with the world, thus following the lines of the other essay on theatre from its beginnings to 1930.

A significant effort to return to a collective voice is made in the chapter on the essay in the twentieth century, which, despite its title, reaches also into the nineteenth century. In order to control the corpus, a distinction is drawn between *écrivant* and *écrivain*. The latter is deemed the true essayist, who, in a manner that recalls Montaigne, is characterized by the intimate relation between the writer and language. Moreover, 'l'essai ... pourrait même se définir par cette dialecte vivante, jamais achevée, entre le *je* de l'essayiste et le *référent*, c'est-à-dire, le milieu historique, social, culturel auquel ce *je* tente, plus ou mois labourieusement, de s'intégrer.' Thus, as the essayist suffers for the collective, so s/he becomes a voice or witness. To simplify the corpus yet further, three essayists are chosen as discursive models, notably, Edmond de Nevers (1862–1906), Jules Fournier (1884–1918), and Pierre Vadeboncœur (1920–). The former is chosen not only for his style but also because of his representation of the weakness of the late nineteenth century where one finds 'les traits essentiels de la mentalité québécoise de son temps: attitude fâcheusement anti-politique, mythe de notre mission spiritualiste et civilisatrice en Amérique, bizarrement jumelée à une vocation agricole non moins exigente.' If de Nevers is a victim of his contradictions, Fournier is a steady castigator of Quebec's weaknesses as an aspiring nation. Pride of place, however, is reserved for Vadeboncœur whose achievement as an essayist is based upon his desire to undertake 'le difficile voyage vers le centre de soi-même.' The referent of his essays ranges from an opposition to reactionary nationalism, to a neonationalism along Groulx's lines, to a further point which answers 'un besoin d'affranchissement, de décantation du *je*, qui est le terme entrevu de la recherche de l'essayiste.'[27] As a discursive model, Vadeboncœur's prose reaches a point where the relation of the 'I' to its referent is transparent, and he considered the best archaeological witness of the post-war period through the 1970s.

Vadeboncœur's example bears witness, however, to a recurrent preoccupation of the entire book. We are reminded in the Avant-propos that the book represents 'une synthèse de l'état actual de la recherche.' *Recherche*, in the French sense of continually returning to examine a problem implicitly from various perspectives, is clearly an archaeological activity. Although there is general agreement on the dates that mark certain periods with only some exceptions, they are repeatedly reopened from fresh vantages. Thus, no particular theme dominates. Nevertheless, to control the canon in its relation to history, developments are organized around a variety of thematic and ideological interests, which may be understood as discursive practices. The structure and implied argument of the book cast a kind of ironic light, therefore, over the final sentence of Dionne's historical introduction, which follows his emphasis upon national, popular, and conservative tendencies in the formation of contemporary Quebec: 'Une fois la patrie réelle rétrouvée, la patrie littéraire n'aura plus son raison d'être, mais la littérature seule.'[28] The first level of irony concerns the phrase, 'la patrie réelle rétrouvée.' How can it be found again, if it never existed and is constantly subjected to renewed construction? Moreover, if the 'la patrie littéraire' is more a theme that belongs to a discursive practice than a dominant preoccupation in the book, it is apparent already that the desire for 'la littérature seule' is realized already in the essays that follow.

Canada and the Arnoldian Ideal

W.J. Keith's *Canadian Literature in English* (1985) is part of the Longman Literature in English Series, a series decidedly in the vein of histories of anglophone writing. By far the largest share of its texts are or will be devoted to aspects of writing in England. When Keith's book was published, six volumes were planned on the United States, and single volumes were being prepared for 'Other Literatures.' Unlike Dionne's collection of essays, Keith has a theme that unifies the history. The theme is developed, however, in a format rather similar to that of Dionne, that is, it rests upon a history of literature from the beginnings to various other times whose significance is determined by genre. It is, then, primarily a history of genres, whose treatment, however, varies according to specific needs. His intent is to trace a 'cultural tradition, the way in which literature written in Canada began as a continuation of what was being produced in Great Britain, had to define itself against the American tradition as it developed in the United States, and eventually evolved as a distinctive literature related to but independent of both parent and neighbour.'[29] It has, then, the appearance of a clear plot that moves from dependence to autonomy, a plot we have seen often in francophone histories of literature.

Keith's history unfolds beneath three epigraphs which turn upon notions of difference, tradition, and aesthetic judgment, and, given the attention to 'cultural tradition' in the Preface, it is difficult to avoid the sense that F.R. Leavis's notion of a great tradition that lies behind the English character of the history. Even more cogent, however, is Matthew Arnold (1822–88), whose presence both dominates the rise of English Studies in the twentieth century, particularly at Cambridge University,[30] and supports Keith's own approach to his history as developed in a paper whose title is a pointed echo of one of Arnold's essays, namely, 'The Function of Canadian Criticism at the Present Time.' Reviewing the situation of Canadian criticism in 1983, he agrees with John Metcalf's assertion that 'there is no critical consensus in Canada about Canadian writing and very little critical writing is worth the paper it's written on.' Critical standards are deemed unsatisfactory compared with those employed in English Studies, and the critical approaches are at best wanting. After discussing his dissatisfaction with 'the overuse of the adjectives "colonial," "puritan," and "genteel,"' he moves directly to his discomfort with 'structuralist, deconstructionist, and post-modernist criticisms,' which appear misguided, as he asserts, because they have been imported from the United States.[31] They reflect Canada's colonialism. What Canada needs is, first of all, a new emphasis on '*historical* continuities' to overcome the problems of treating texts autonomously. Second – and here he draws upon Arnold's essay, 'The Function of Criticism at the Present Time,' for support – he argues against any 'retreat into an intense inane of abstract theorizing.' The role of the critic is be a 'mediator between writer and reader, one who explains trends, transmits relevant information, clarifies difficulties, and, yes, offers considered value-judgements.' In order to be even more clear, he adds: 'This is not the time to be talking about interesting patterns or semiotic subtleties.'[32] Keith's history proceeds directly from these assumptions, which, no matter how relevant he suggests they may be for the present time, are clearly those that held sway in departments of English in the 1950s. True enough, no critical consensus currently obtains in Canada about Canadian literature, but the assumption that there should be one is the point behind the articulation of cultural tradition in the history. It means, among other things, clearly separating anglophone and francophone writing, and defining, in an expression that evokes another of Leavis's expressions, 'the common pursuit.'[33]

His history begins with orientations we have seen before. Canada is defined primarily as a space that needs to be filled and surrounded by boundaries to be understood. The problem of defining 'Canada' (surely a semiotic exercise of some magnitude) is compounded by the fact that the dates that mark its history, as he warns the reader early, bestow upon it a frequently shifting character. The size of the country did not encourage rapid settlement, and until the American Revolution 'consisted of a series of (more or less) loyal communities.' The Revolution, not French Canada, is implicitly constructed as a threat to what had been largely British territory. The threat was met by the decision to remain loyal to the Crown on the part of both settlers and immigrants from the United States. The beginning was the assertion of the British connection, a connection which defined the space of Canada in a significant and proleptic fashion. Because of the size of the country, it is marked by regional struggles in respect of the centre, and, as a result, 'ambiguous compromise' became its governing principle. The enduring threat remained the United States, and it was responded to by a desire 'to produce an alternative and distinctive literature in English.'[34] Size also tended to vitiate the possibility of developing a tradition, as well as the general acceptance by critics and literary historians of Canada's colonialism, puritanism, dullness, and 'the lack of an authentic history,' all of which Keith rejects as a 'myth.' Citing only Klinck as the one literary history before his own of any value, whose usefulness lies in its role as a reference rather than as a narrative history, Keith asserts his intent to provide Canadian literature with a 'consistent historical continuity.' It has a tradition, that has been 'but rarely traced with any care,' which suggests that it was present all the time but invisible to other observers. The tradition that is traced is the enactment of the tendency to compromise between 'British assumptions' and 'modern American attitudes' through which Canadian culture steers a middle course that embodies 'a scattered and elusive people's communal vision.'[35]

Nothing could be less archaeological than such a notion of historical development, which seeks unity at all costs. Inasmuch, however, as Canada is a shifting ground in its political history, a tradition offers the possibility of something enduring. The tradition is to be found in the emergence of a certain, admired style, and it is controlled and articulated by structuring the book according to genre. The 'early stages' address prose, poetry and fiction, and the following sections are respectively devoted to poetry, fiction, and other kinds. The question of beginnings in every case has little to do with a common understanding of historical moments and everything to do with the characteristics of various genres and their apparent internal evolution. Thus, after having discussed poetry in the first chapter through the Confederation poets, the discussion is later resumed by beginning with E.J. Pratt as the figure who serves as a transition, as he usually does, connecting the Victorian with the modern. For Keith, however, he is seminal because he represents the 'middle way.'[36] The section on 'The Beginnings in Fiction' concludes with Sara Jeannette Duncan in the early years of the twentieth century, and fiction later resumes in the same period.[37] Transition in this genre is less apparent than continuity. Yet the history of both genres shares a tendency toward unravelling the common thread that each genre possesses. Connections are established by 'evolution rather revolution,' and thus the challenge of the new is continuously accommodated if not always overcome. As a consequence, history as the zone that provides opportunities for change is not constructed as such. History enters Keith's text as hardly much more than the dates that place a text of poetry or fiction in time. It is the *mise-en-scène* for space which is understood to provide order. Indeed, as the example of Pratt indicates, he 'can be understood in geographical as well as historical terms,'[38] and perhaps more effectively from a geographical perspective, inasmuch as the historical terms are presented as a blurred binary opposition between 'Victorian' and 'modern.'

The durable, however, is what transcends the accidents of time. Being as classical in his formation as Arnold, Keith's notion of the 'historical' is such that it is never allowed to affect his judgment of excellence, which is what constitutes tradition. Thus at the very beginning of 'The Beginnings in Prose,' little effort is made to situate Alexander Henry (1739–1824) historically. His significance lies, first of all, 'in his ready adaptability to new ways,' which is reflected in 'a clear, unostentatious, flowing prose' (a model of the eighteenth-century norm), whose ability to communicate plainly and without ostentation is later praised by Anna Jameson (1794–1860). The three things are established at the beginning, suggesting Mailhot's method, which form the deep structure of the history: first, he praises writers for stylistic traits of which Arnold would have approved; second, these are supportively related to those of a later writers, thus facilitating the tracing of a tradition; and third, taken together, they lay the foundation for Keith's construction of a history. History is the assertion and maintenance of the values of appropriateness, consistency, balance, order, and clarity, which distinguish and relate writers, no matter what their genre may be. Thus, Isabella Crawford, whose poems 'are remarkable not for any profundity of insight but for the consistency and clarity of their imagined world,' is salvaged. D.C. Scott (1962–1947) is memorialized not only because of his ability to establish 'effective lines of poetic continuity' but also because he is thoroughly Arnoldian.[39] Commenting on a typical stanza, Keith observes: 'We notice here Scott's characteristic blending of a Victorian traditionalism (he is close to the cadences of Arnold's "Rugby Chapel") with a modern avoidance of the verbally ornate and an equally modern concern (again via Arnold) for honest precision, "seeing the object as it really is."' Such a Rankean vision is the mark of balance and, for Arnold, is among the most precious aspects of the Hellenic cast of mind, a mind, it is superfluous to add, inured against history in the sense of development. History is preservation and, therefore, appropriate to 'the conservative character of the Canadian experiment.'[40]

The 'modern,' however, is not the same as 'modernism,' and, consequently, the latter is taken to task, apparently because it was not part of the 'tradition,' but rather 'international,' and an aspect of Canada's 'deferential colonialism.' Although it is presented as a challenge, Keith's modernists, paradoxically, have no difficult meeting and subduing modernism, thereby manifesting a Canadian manner in adopting a balanced response. Moreover, no matter how much Michael Ondaatje (1943–), Robert Kroetsch (1927–), and Stephen Scobie (1943–), for example, may reveal 'a determination to challenge traditional modes of perception' and so take Canadian poetry into the post-modern, Keith argues in every case that they all acquire that 'poised balance,' which he qualifies as 'quintessentially Canadian.' All are concerned with 'the relation between the past and the present and a preference for direct language as the dominating features of modern [read: "modern" and "postmodern"] Canadian poetry.'[41] They are, then, valorized for espousing, in effect, the same values that Keith shares with Arnold, which makes them, it might noted, neither Canadian nor true to their own intent. Thus, Keith, despite his discontent with the semiotic, powerfully charges 'Canadian' with a number of binary oppositions and connotations in such a way as to create a tradition which appears more Victorian and British than the fine balance he would like to draw between English and American.

Fiction suffers a corresponding fate. During its foundational period in the early years of this century, F.P. Grove, despite his German origin, 'is pre-eminent among early Canadian novelists for many reasons,' not the least of which is 'the deeply considered criticism of life.[42] The remark is made in a context that would explain the purpose of Grove's didacticism, a trait he shares with MacLennan, who is credited with being 'the first to articulate a tradition in fictional terms,' in such a way as to link him both to Grove and, subsequently, to Kroetsch.[43] Such relationships are established in the instance of fiction not so much through aspects of style as through the inscription of a Canadian fictional world, which draws Margaret Laurence, for example, to Sinclair Ross, and Rudy Wiebe, among many others, to Sheila Watson. Among later writers relationships become more frequent and more intimate, and thus a tradition becomes more evident. Alice Munro (1931–), for example, conjoins both Laurence and Mavis Gallant (1922–) in content and form, but one recurring quality emerges in the formation of the whole canon Keith is intent upon establishing. To attain Arnoldian status they must transcend the local and the idiosyncratic. Although Canada may be 'a loose confederation,' it possesses 'a common purpose.' Charles Bruce's *The Channel Shore* (1954) suffers from being too regional, while Munro achieves her stature because 'the universal is always incarnate in the local and particular.' Margaret Atwood's (1939–) fiction is 'as a whole unsurpassed' because of its 'poised artistry.'[44] These are classical virtues, and they are perhaps best attained through an understanding of Arnold's Hellenism, which is the pursuit 'to use Plato's words, of things as they are,' which implies 'a balance and regulation of the mind.' These prized Victorian values are those that subtend a tradition of nineteenth-century realism. Balance allows the admission of everything so long as it does not transgress the classical notion of *nequid nimis* – nothing in excess. Margaret Laurence's Hagar as she speaks in *The Stone Angel* (1964), then, will be both 'individually distinctive yet representative and wholly credible.' Kroetsch, despite the fact that he flouts realism, 'depends on what he denies; his effects rely upon the shock to our

sensibilities that would not work without our attachment to realistic conventions and a literary tradition implying continuity.' Balance overcomes the difference of the particular in order to achieve the universal,
which is certainly a Platonic ideal, allowing Austin Clarke (1934–), for
example, to overcome the limitations of his 'ethnic boundaries' and
Robertson Davies (1913–95) to transcend the national. Balance, finally,
removes a certain edge, particularly from contemporary writers, by
bringing them, through the process of continuous accommodation that
appears the mark of 'a typically Canadian cautiousness,'[45] into a world
of order and security. No challenge seems too large to overcome.[46]

Not wholly surprisingly, Keith concludes his text with a paean for
George Grant, a descendant of the Loyalist tradition, who defends 'the
good, the sacred, the moral, order, restraint, justice, reverence, perfection,' most, if not all, of which Arnold would have approved. All these
values are brought to bear against North American liberalism, which are,
for the most part, generated in the United States. Indeed, it would be difficult to misconstrue the British bias of Grant's thought, which moves
the best of Canadian thought in a direction away from the American,
despite Keith's effort to hold everything in balance.[47] The return, however, to the Loyalist role in the making of Canada is strategically
designed to intimate that Arnoldian values belong to a tradition   in
Canada that appears, to use a phrase perhaps abhorrent to Keith, 'always
already' there. The phrase, however, can only be used with a certain measure of irony: it is an invented tradition, whose invention is only enforced
by the reflexive structure of the book. Yet the appearance of something
'always already,' particularly if it aspires to the universal, has an ability to
overcome contingency. Time loses its grittiness, and, as a result, history
appears illusory. Plot, which appears so necessary to a historical imagination, is subordinate to a recurrent order in which even the challenge of
binary oppositions is dissolved, as in the instance of Irving Layton,
through the defence of 'the best of human ideals that have come down
to him from the past.'[48] Thus Layton's poetry is brought into phase with
Arnold's notion of criticism, which is exclusively concerned with 'the
best that is known and thought in the world.' Thus, Layton becomes
exemplary of the Hellenic in Arnold's sense and an example of how 'to
adopt a real, not a historic, estimate of poetry.' Representing the Canadian in such a manner, Keith attains Arnold's notion of culture, which is
the real 'in its origin as the love of perfection.'[49] As such, the historical
and the transitory is merely a hindrance to its attainment.[50]

If Arnold and Keith, however, are beset by a predominant obsession, it would be with the idea of unity. In 'The Study of Poetry' Arnold cites the *Imitation of Christ* to argue that no matter how much one reads or knows, it is necessary to return '*ad unum ... principium*,' which is 'the real,' that is, 'the truly classic. He had already raised the same principle in *Culture and Anarchy,* finding it in human perfection.[51] It is the key to the argument for order and balance in Keith. Nevertheless, it raises a serious issue in a culture that professes to have at least two cultures and into which some would wish to admit still others. None of these cultures at the time Keith wrote possessed any desire, as we have seen, to be pressed into a necessary unity. Culture in Canada, in fact, is not encouraged even at the federal level to do so, a point which forms the basis for W.H. New's *A History of Canadian Literature* (1989).

Dissemination of the Nation

In many respects, faced with the same facts of continuous change in Canadian history that Keith draws upon, New comes to a conclusion opposed to Keith's. The tradition is not the formation of a unified culture of an Arnoldian cast; it is, rather, something to be found in change itself. His first sentence argues immediately against the unified: 'Snow, North, Wilderness: these stereotypes of Canada suggest a fierce uniformity – but even from the earliest times, such generalizations have been inaccurate.' Indeed, the central fact of Canadian culture is its diversity, and 'definitions of a single Canadian identity are suspect.' Canada is marked by a 'cultural plurality,' which forms the basis for New's construction of the Canadian literatures. Plurality is illustrated by the difficulty of determining the derivation of the name of the country; the several meanings of the word 'also suggest the ambivalent position that the native peoples occupy in Canada.' The beginning, then, of New's history is marked by a meditation on difference, uncertainty, and illusion, which leads directly to an attempt to locate Aboriginal cultures. He begins by arguing that 'the notion of a uniform "Red Indian" culture is a false one,'[52] and he then places it in the larger context of 'mythmakers,' thus making it in many ways foundational of his history's larger design, which is to organize each section according to a different mode of narrating. Thus the four large chapters that follow are graded from 'reporters' to 'tale-tellers' and from narrators to 'encoders.' It is a structure that is shaped to emphasize literature as diverse kinds of fictions, each of which narrate in varying degrees of sophistication; through these narrations an idea of a polymorphous nation is constructed.

Lest one imagine, however, that the literary text in some way reflects history, New reminds us that we are 'to think along two political planes: one observing writers sequentially against a set of events, the other observing written works as formal embodiments of separate attitudes and expectations.'[53] Perhaps because New's text was written for the Macmillan History of Literature Series, published in England and consisting of histories of literatures of anglophone countries, his attention to historical sets of events is more careful than most historians of English-Canadian literature.[54] Details that most Canadian readers would find superfluous, such as reminding one that York University is in Toronto, is another indication of attentiveness to a non-Canadian audience. The 'set of events' is explicitly treated in the second chapter as a background against which texts are placed. The same method is followed in subsequent chapters, without the rubric 'Backgrounds,' but the desire to situate the unfamiliar reader is always evident. Nevertheless, historical information is provided as a thematically related context. Thus, the early period, from 'the putative visits to North America by Chinese sailors' to 1867, is marked by the legacy of the Renaissance 'desire for political control,' that is, 'political tensions' in matters of trade and 'government rivalries' for the sake of overseas possessions.[55] As a consequence, on the cultural plane North America in the eighteenth century became a site of pluralism, which became particularly evident in the differences in colonial settlements, thus laying the foundations for New's Canada.

The relation between the history of settlement and literature is marked by the variety of the responses. The two that dominate are those of exile, on the one hand, and a growing sense of rootedness, on the other. Exploration journals are equally conflicted, torn between fantasy and reason. Of greater significance than themes that indicate a desire to undermine a uniform vision of Canada is New's reading of these texts as literary artifacts; he places them stylistically next to European texts and indicates how literature problematizes the idea of nation, even in its nascent stages.[56] Texts cannot help but construct – and in literary histories they are frequently used to construct nations – yet for New they are of particular value to the degree that they make the nation pluralistic, implicitly desiring to change the American national motto from *e pluribus unum* to *e pluribus plures*. In those texts that emerged from 1830 to 1860, considered more properly literary, the dominant styles were either satiric or romantic, and they are used to draw together both anglophone and francophone writing.

The effort to combine the literatures of French and English Canada is always rare in Canadian literary history, and in the light of Keith's refusal to do so is worth some consideration.[57] New has consciously taken all the Canadian literatures into his purview as a means of arguing cultural plurality. Francophone and anglophone writings are combined variously. For example, when Élisabeth Bégon (1696–1755) is discussed, she is easily combined with Frances Brooke through a common interest in the epistolary form. Haliburton and Crémazie are later conjoined in the shared problem of a generation trying 'to root its culture locally, and its difficulties in doing so [which] stemmed in part from being unable to identify with what seemed a raw local culture or a sophisticated imperial one.' The difference between them is one of context since Crémazie's poems emerged from 'a growing sense of French-Canadian nationalism.' The implications of this comment are not, however, developed, especially the extent to which the national was a fiercely debated issue in Lower Canada at the time. More significant, however, is the fact that francophone writing is clearly an adjunct to anglophone writing. Its style, unlike the writing of English Canada, is not examined, and Crémazie alone is discussed from a list of several others. Later in the chapter, Aubert de Gaspé's *Les anciens canadiens* is discussed, but mostly in the context of its English-Canadian response, and the names of Boucher de Boucherville and Gérin-Lajoie are raised in the context of patriotism and 'cultural sovereignty.'[58]

The difference between the narrator as reporter (the dominant of literature up to 1967) and taleteller (the dominant up to 1922) is not entirely clear: the 'signal feature' of the latter was 'the expectation ... that an orderly sequence would lead to a definite resolution.' Surely such an expectation governs a reading, for example, of Gérin-Lajoie's novel, but perhaps the distinction is based on the fact that much early Canadian writing, exemplified in journals and reports, was designed to create by a process of naming. The effort of taletellers to achieve a definite resolution occurred in a changed context of tension of a regional, ethnic, and religious character, so that 'challenges to the orderly sequence' shifted after 1910 from fixed to ambivalent conclusions. The major opposition to national order was regional difference, largely illustrated by Louis Riel and the hostile reaction of the West to a bicultural model for the nation.[59] Indeed, challenges of every kind moved through Canada in the post-Confederation period, undermining what appeared to be the fascination for imperial conservatism, so that regional sentimentality yielded to comedy and satire; this is finely illustrated in the work of Sara Jeannette Duncan, who used it in her efforts to support the women's movement for 'independence and recognition.' It was a period during which 'at one extreme, then, the cult of sentimentality simply perpetuated stereotypes; at the other, when it coupled with didactic satire, it invited its own demise.'[60]

Much of the social change of the period may be attributed to the awareness of technological change and the necessity to address the implications of Darwinism, which had effects upon both nature stories and, especially, Confederation poetry, which 'struggled with many Canadian dilemmas, especially those created by imperial conservatism, by the contrast between urban life and the values attached to rural poetic imagery, and by the disparities between literary landscape conventions and empirical landscapes.' Although these poets are treated at some length, French-Canadian poets are, with the exception of Nelligan, passed over quickly. Nelligan, however, is dwelt upon because he is a 'poet in conflict with the material world and his own soul,' thus illustrating the dominant theme of the chapter in a way which Arthur de Buissières (1877–1913) and Nerée Beauchemin (1850–1931), for example, cannot. Appropriately, much of the conclusion of the chapter is devoted to Stephen Leacock, who symbolizes both the preoccupation with the empire and its weakening hold on the anglo-Protestant imagination, for, while 'championing empire, Leacock did not at the same time champion colonial status.'[61] It is a statement that puts English Canada, at least, on the threshold of its awareness of nationhood.

It is, perhaps, no coincidence that nations depend on narrators, since myth, reportage, and mere telling are insufficient vehicles for the political implications of a nation-state. Evidently, the term 'narrator' is meant to carry more significance than these other terms and to suggest an analogy of a hierarchical kind: just as Canada moved from colony to nation, so its fictional style acquired a greater density and importance. The dominant speaker of the final chapter, the 'encoder,' also suggests that, as Canada moves into its contemporary phase, the emphasis upon its formation as story and history is to be understood as a question of discourse. This means that myth, which carries the dual significance of shamanic speech and various inaccurate ways of constructing Aboriginals for a European audience; reportage, which implies aspects of observation; and taletelling, which contains modes of amusement conjoined with moral instruction, are progressive steps toward narration. None of them, however, is a mode of discourse that adequately bears the weight that 'nation' implies. Encoding, however, by emphasizing discursive practice as to a degree more significant than its content, implies that it would not be appropriate for addressing the notion of 'nation.' It also implies that Canada had a period in which it constructed itself as a nation, and that period is now in the past.

As a condition for plotting, however, New's structure is of some interest indeed, for it implies that history is a function of more complicated discursive practices that move with varying emphasis from those that are more recognizable by their content to those that are more recognizable by their formal qualities. The moment when discourse and a public seem most in balance is the moment of the nation. The structure of the plot is governed, in any event, by fictional practice rather than by the extraliterary 'set of events,' no matter how judiciously they may be shown to correspond with each other. So it is that while literature and history interrelate, history is understood as a function of fictional modes, and each period has a dominant mode of narration by which the culture of the past is organized. There are many implications that emerge from such an understanding of culture and history.

One of the implications, however, of this method of relating literature to history is that through literature history is given its significance. New raises this in an aside to Archibald MacMechan in which he argues against the latter's 'emphasis on Canadian history and setting [which] confirmed a belief in the empirical basis of literature.' Compared to the French-Canadian use of history, MacMechan's is mild indeed, but from a particular perspective the observation is important. The issue is the extent to which the extraliterary series becomes a determining principle in reading, that is, the manner in which history is drawn upon to derive meaning. Despite the abundance of historical information in New – which in itself is unusual among anglophone historians of literature – history is being read through New's construction of literary texts. It is drawn upon sufficiently, but selectively, in order to guide the reader toward a clear understanding of how, despite every effort to provide symbols of nationhood, the nation does not seem to cohere, in the same way that its literature does not seem capable of homogenization. Thus in the same chapter The Group of Seven are part 'of the new wave of nationalism' and also an aspect of Irving Layton's objection to 'the now conventional definition of Canada in Group of Seven terms.'[62] Although the norm of cultural institutions is to redefine value on a regular basis, New's argument implies that change and conflict are the only constants in Canadian literature and art, and what is true for culture is, consequently, true for the extraliterary series.

Thus, assuming that the first section of chapter 4, 'National Romance and the Land,' is constructed to inaugurate the emergence of the nation (and surely the dates 1922 to 1959 would confirm such an assumption), it is of interest that the momentum of change seems to accelerate from that time on. Although conservative readings such as Keith's argue against such a perspective, it is evident that Mackenzie King's challenges to empire were widely supported. King's political cleverness, prevarication, opportunism, and other political skills, however, are not given any consideration, despite his being the dominant political figure of the time. He is not, therefore, a guide but, rather, a character who makes a cameo appearance to emphasize the larger point about culture as a conflicted site that may be seen in the use of language, the decline of omniscient narrators, the use of lyrical structure and discursive practice as a political gesture, the manipulation of voice and point of view that undermine conventional realism, and the rise of poetry in both francophone and anglophone as 'the openness of passion in the public world.'[63]

All these issues taken together proceed to the final sections entitled respectively, 'National Presumptions' and 'Sources of Change.' They are presumptions, one assumes, because the contemporary efforts to produce a summary of the achievements of the period in the 1950s resulted in 'the Protestant hierarchy of taste and culture.' Accordingly, 'the novel was considered superior to the short story, poetry superior to both; epic was deemed a greater accomplishment than lyric; and the tenets of "realism" (however romantic in execution) were more readily approved than those of discontinuous narrative.'[64] Despite New's frequent references to French-Canadian writing in this chapter, it is revealing that the national presumption is summed up as Protestant. It suggests the limits of what has been called 'the national dream,' and, measured against all the varieties of change, dissolution, and undermining that New signals as characteristic of the period, it implies that the dream of the nation was only a dream. The Protestant position does not take into its purview the subtext of Canadian culture, in preparation since the earliest contact between Europeans and Aboriginals, which are now understood as the conflicted issues of race, gender, region.

The present, then, shapes the past, and it is the intent of the final chapter on the narrator as encoder to argue that language redefines 'the parameters of power and the character of available history.' From 1960 on 'nation' can only be defined as a figure of 'multiple identity,' and all of New's considerable skill as an interpreter is brought to bear in the construction of a secular and 'pentecostal' (that is, speaking many tongues) Canada, in which writers would 'reinterpret their culture, free it from the definitions of the "Other," so to speak, and hence encode a new authenticity of self.'[65] The initial section of the chapter refers to the 'state,' rather than the nation; when nation is discussed, it appears in quotation marks, implying semantic difficulties;[66] and Pierre Trudeau and René Lévesque are given motivational roles that focus the central debate on plural and unified cultures. One of the consequences of New's preference for the former is that references to francophone writers are less frequent unless they are Acadian or can be conjoined to such issues as race, gender, fantasy, and parody, in other words, conflicted relationships.

The various codes discussed begin with that of myth and conclude with that of parody, moving from the more public to the more private. By beginning with myth, he recovers the beginning of his history and modifies its meaning, insofar as myth as, for example, James Reaney (1926–) employs it, is not an effort 'to repeat history but to reinterpret it, celebrating not the Europeanness of the archetype but the archetypal fascination of one's own history and experience, and [so engage] the power of myth to reconstruct it in terms that carry contemporary meaning.' It could also be said that this not an Aboriginal use of myth, which is more of a collective story. In the development of the code of history, repetition itself is finally rejected, and 'systems of language became a more accurate measure of truth than systems of social continuity, historical reference or referentiality.' The force of history depends, in the instance of Joy Kogawa (1935–) and, by implication several other novelists, upon the degree to which it can be 'translated into personal experience and translated by it, turning silence into speech.' Thus, a number of texts, particularly those that claim some bearing upon the past, 'do not interest themselves in what historians have received as "fact" so much as they seek to reinterpret or reclaim the past from one particular interpretation of it, with an eye on some present tension.' Such a perspective implies, particularly for writers intent upon exploring the boundaries of gender and its representation, that 'various forms of division ... focus on the alienation embodied in language'[67] and the intertextual relationships of parody.

With the exception of occasional references to the political situation in Quebec, references to Canada become rarer and rarer as the history reaches its conclusion. Consistent with his argument, the historical referent becomes a function of discourse. Moreover, there is no summary conclusion reflecting upon the whole text, merely a brief 'Epilogue' with an emphasis on the plural and the temporal, forecasting nothing but continued change: 'Because "definitions" of inheritance and culture remain in flux, change will likely take several simultaneous forms.' The concluding sentence, which follows upon this announcement, is perfectly logical, but, within the context of the history of anglophone literary history, nevertheless, remarkable: 'Given the context of the closing chapter, it is well to regard this entire book as history-in-process.' In many respects, such an assertion takes an entirely different course from the tendency to monumentalize the past that we have seen in francophone literary history, including Mailhot, whose history constructs a culture about which 'il s'agit toujours d'entrer dans l'Histoire.' The one exception to this would be *La Vie littéraire au Québec*, which along with New, constitutes the only highly significant undertaking in its culture both to address history as the place of change and to explain its interrelation with literature. In an extraordinary gesture for an anglophone literary historian, however, New projects his text into history as history, exposing it to all the conditions of 'fracture, discontinuity, uncertainty, and disorder' that place it within orders of discourse made familiar by Foucault.[68]

No effort is made to transcend time, an anglophone norm still apparent in Keith, and this constitutes the most remarkable aspect of New's history. The ease, however, with which discursive practices overtake, indeed, eclipse the referential in the concluding chapter, to the point where the discourse of his own text assumes the role of 'history-in-process,' may be said to empty, at least in some respects, history of history itself, for is there any sequential extraliterary series, any diachronic 'set of events' left in the end? Although there are no overtures to any theorist of discourse or history,[69] the implications are fairly evident; part of the consequence of alluding to Foucault is that it is possible to see in the allusion Foucault's desire to 'se passer des "choses,"' which does not mean that the 'thing' is so much abolished as rendered 'irréductible à la langue et à la parole.' The point, then, when literary history enters upon a history of discursive practice and formation – and this, I take it, is the sense of the reference to 'a network of connections between forms and themes, between writers, their society and the language they use' – is the moment when something that appeared in the past to be an embarrassment to anglophone literary historians, that is, history itself, is paradoxically overcome by assuming the immanence of the cultural ideas of instability, the indeterminate, and difference as the only catalyst of change. At such a moment a notion of a diachronic series is of little use. For the point of 'observing writers sequentially against a set of events,'[70] is to provide for them a context of operation that would explain, if nothing else, why this a history of *Canadian* literature, rather than a history of writing of a post-structuralist character that occurs in a place called Canada.

Thus, history, at least a historicist view of history, redeems anglophone writing from the burden of history. It is the final effort among many to achieve this end in English Canada, and it helps explain, perhaps, why it is so difficult for anglophone literary historians to find the nation within their narratives. In this instance, the nation is simply a moment that has passed, that is, if it ever got beyond a certain 'presumption,' to use New's word. For the nation is not what is desired by the text. What is desired is the realization of discontinuity as, paradoxically, Synecdoche, that is, an integrative structure, for this is the beginning of a plot that is initiated by the mutual misprision of Aboriginal and European and that reaches fulfilment in the fissures of discursive practice. If an idea of nation is to survive the challenge of multiple contexts, it is not clear in what way, for as the multicultural society espoused by the text is at odds with what is constructed as the more unified society of Quebec, another nation in itself, not to speak of burgeoning Aboriginal nations. Or, it means that the idea of nation that literary history struggles with has not yet been fully invented as an articulated entity. More disturbing, however, is the fact that whether or not history is overcome in New, his text represents the culmination of the problem of writing English and French Canada, as well as ethnic, Aboriginal, and Inuit cultures, into the same mentality. Adjacent though they may be geographically, they do not appear to know each other, to encounter each other, in any significant way even when they, as in New, accept the framework of history. For histories as articulated through various literatures differ in both use and function, and appear capable only of carrying all the cultures 'madly off in all directions,' as one might say.

Afterthoughts, Models, Possibilities

La mémoire se fait plurielle.

Literary History, Literature, History

I have suggested in my introduction that the genre of literary history may be understood as akin to the German tradition of the *Bildungsroman*. Texts familiar to most readers would be Thomas Mann's *The Magic Mountain* (1914) and, possibly, Hermann Hesse's *The Glass Bead Game* (1943). I made this suggestion for a number of reasons. First, it relates literary history to a great international genre. Furthermore, it relates literary history to a genre of some consequence, which is noted for the rare, indeed, rarified depths in its searching examinations of certain characters. Finally, I wanted to emphasize the condition of unresolved tension that most theorists and critics of literary history have remarked upon. The significance of each of these contextual aspects of literary history is designed particularly to lift the understanding of literary history as it prevails in this country, not to speak of elsewhere, from its norm of self-preoccupation, a norm that implicitly insists upon the exclusive or distinctive character of the culture examined. To relate it to the *Bildungsroman*, as I have in the introduction, does not exactly relieve it, however, of such a burden. Characters like Mann's Hans Castorp are not exactly free of such a charge; in fact, they make it more obvious, which was part of my purpose.

It may be that such an analogy is not the most appropriate. One of the many charges brought against the *Bildungsroman* is that there is hardly any tension, as Swales argues, but rather in the German tradition, at least, an overweening emphasis on the poetic life of the protagonist; and 'at times it runs the risk of esteeming actualities only insofar as they are validated and underwritten by the hero's inwardness.' Moreover, the emphasis on inwardness is so great that it 'celebrates the imagination of the hero as the faculty which allows him to transcend the limitations of everyday, practical reality.' As a consequence, the simple act, complicated as it may appear, of the protagonist's self-realization is what the narrative is 'about': 'neither "consciousness" nor "activity" are separate realms which man can choose to enter or leave. Rather he inhabits both in their interdependence.' Because the poetry (the protagonist's inner life) and the prose (the socio-economic world) are coterminous, it is difficult, finally, to distinguish process from goal. The goal is contained by the process, and the reader is always catching more significant glimpses of it. Hans Castorp may choose to immolate himself at the end in the First World War, but that is only the conclusion, not the telos, of the narrative. Telos, the means by which significance is oriented, is always present. Thus, the narrative unfolding of these novels has a static character, and charges such as, 'vagueness and bloodlessness,' are, as Swales indicates, 'hardly original responses.'[1]

The difference, of course, between literary history and this subgenre of the novel is that the former is history and the latter, fiction. One wonders, however, how firmly the line between the two can be drawn, particularly in light of the fact that both are narratives and, therefore, make use of plot, shared rhetorical strategies, and ideological perspectives that provide a certain telos in the sense I have provided. If it is proposed that history is research designed to bring a certain knowledge to light,[2] one may reply that certain novels – particularly those with didactic proclivities like the *Bildungsroman* – are of the same character, and they differ only in the material they draw upon. History draws upon experiences of wide and general verification; the novel validates experiences that can acquire wide and general verification, and in the obvious instance of the historical novel, often draws upon the same experiences as history. The difference lies in the use of the nation as the protagonist of literary history. One of the questions literary histories of Canada pose inevitably is: whose history? Clearly there is no agreement on the history, so that a sense of a whole history, no matter how unattainable, is rarely sought. The history is always partial, by necessity and design. The same is true for the nation as protagonist. The nation emerges – it always emerges, following the pattern of the *Bildungsroman* – as it relates to the texts that form its basis. Literary texts are the signs of the inner life of the protagonist, and the semantic weight that is placed upon them forms in their narrative ordering the telos of the history. A nation as protagonist is only formally different from a character as protagonist: Hans Castorp can readily be constructed as a culture hero of pre-war Germany, as well as post-war reconsiderations of it.[3] He is not, however, and cannot be everyone's culture-hero of that generation. He belongs to a certain class, and he reflects the ideology of a specific, highly refined imagination. Yet, he represents the nation in a some measure. The representation may be more in respect of deeply drawn characters (the *Nebeneinander* of possible selves), in contrast to the manner in which history is constructed, particularly the social and political history of German in this generation, which would be more metonymical or *Nacheinander*.[4] At a certain point, both representations converge, and there the line between history and fiction loses its acuteness.

In literary history both representations, on the one hand, and fiction and history, on the other hand, converge somewhere in the problem of the nation, especially when the nation is construed less as law, symbol, and shared events and more as a character that possesses possibilities that are continually deepened and given nuance, that is, when, through the use of literary texts and the agency with which they are endowed, the nation acquires a role as protagonist. The nation, under such circumstances then, finds itself on the same two planes of being as the character in the *Bildungsroman*. The nation is given both inwardness, as reflected in literary texts in their various of horizons of significance, and an outer dimension based upon the equally careful selection of moments of self-awareness as they appear to unfold in time. In rhetorical terms, the nation is provided with both a metaphorical and a metonymical range that coincide according to the narrator's design. As we have seen, narratives vary from the most metonymical (Quebec literary history) to the least (ethnic minority, First Nations, and Inuit). Narrative decisions are a consequence of semantic disposition.

Nation: Remembering and Forgetting

It might be inferred that the possibility of realizing some sort of a nation is function of this disposition. Clearly, ethnic minority writers are not part of an effort to make a new nation, but to modify an existing one. First Nations people and Inuit writers have other agendas, and while it is apparent that part of their desire is to recover lost ground in many senses of the term, it is increasingly more evident that their idea of nation does not mean creating new countries. Because English-Canadians have been relatively confident in the durability of their nation, their cultural histories rarely foreground struggle, but rather a range of values. Quebec literary historians cannot help but locate struggle as central, particularly over time, and the effort to locate is based upon a notion of history that has deep roots in a French and Roman Catholic past. In every case, however, kinds of autonomy and interrelation are implicit in every proposal. The multicultural model appears the most inclusive but it, nevertheless, poses serious problems, paradoxically, for ethnic-minority cultures, all of which, with the exception of the Jewish-Canadian, desire to function in varying degrees in the language that preserves their culture. Their choice is limited to English and French and, as a consequence, full *épanouissement* of their cultures cannot occur.

Is it possible for Canadians to agree on what their nation is capable of? This may seem to be a mere Canadian question, but given the massive *Volkerwanderungen* that are now taking place in the world, and which make those of the early centuries of Christian Europe appear simply regional events in retrospect, it is a question of general, international significance. In this respect, what is happening in Canada is microcosmic and relevant to countries everywhere across the globe. Ernest Renan's seminal article, 'Qu'est-ce que une nation?' (1882) has raised a number of issues which pertain still to problems that nations face in the contemporary world.[5] Each of the issues is prefaced by the comment that 'nation' is a term clear in appearance only and, indeed, fraught with the most dangerous misunderstandings. He develops the term into a number of connotations, namely, race, language, religion, a community of interests, geography, and military necessity. His method is in keeping with the fashion of the day, and both the metaphor of vivisection that he employs and the desire to be impartial echo the discourse of naturalism dominant in France at the time. Paradoxically, however, the rhetoric of naturalism is then drawn upon to undermine various determinisms.[6] But if these often generally accepted notions of the nation are discarded, what is left? All that is left is the spiritual dimension that most consistent naturalists choose to deny. For Renan, however, 'une nation est une âme, un principe spirituel.' The principle functions on two temporal levels that articulate two converging desires: 'L'une est la possession en commun d'un riche legs de souvenirs; l'autre est le consentement actuel, le désir de vivre ensemble, la volonté de continuer à faire valoir l'héritage qu'on a reçus indivis.' Common possession is not the same as a community of interests, which Renan defines simply as a *Zollverein* or, as we would say, a free-trade agreement. And so, many things are asked to be transcended and put in the most positive light possible. The notion of transcendence forms the basis of the central position of Renan's argument, which is that 'l'essence d'une nation est que tous les individus aient beaucoup de choses en commun, et aussi que tous aient oublié bien des choses.' This remarkable statement, the validity of which cannot escape anyone of a Machivellian cast of mind, is the climax of a section which begins with the observation that 'l'oubli, et je dirai même l'erreur historique, sont un facteur essentiel de la création de la nation, et c'est ainsi que le progrès des études historiques est souvent pour la nationalité un danger.' For a historian, such a statement, made under the rubric of scientific dispassion, is shocking in the extreme, for what he is arguing for is the use of historiography to gloss over, as he goes on to assert, the violence and brutality of the past. Transcendence comes at a price which then, as part of the duty of the historian, must be written over. The example that is given is that of the crusade against the Cathars in the thirteenth century, which added the territory of what is now southern France to that of the North. According to Renan's argument, however, this is not an example of territorial expansion, since neither race nor land constitute a nation. Despite the fact that the South was taken as a result of 'une extermination et d'une terreur continuée pendant un siècle,' it may be forgotten because the king, Philippe-Auguste, was 'le type idéal d'un civilisateur séculaire.'[7] Inasmuch, however, as kings are not the sole founders of nations, nations must have some other reason for coming into being and continuing to exist, and this is the exercise of will. Needless to say, it would be naive to imagine that Canada does not practise history by omission, especially at federal levels. One of the more curious examples among many is the RCMP's acceding to a request originating from a Métis leader to Stéphane Dion, the National Unity Minister, to remove the rope which may have been used to hang Louis Riel from the RCMP Centennial Museum in Regina.[8] It is curious because suppression, at least in Renan's thinking, comes from those who wield power, rather than those who feel that power has been removed from them. When both sides choose omission, it is no longer clear what purpose is served.

Martin Thom's argument that Renan's definition of nation is 'irrationalist, anti-Jacobin,' and opposed to 'the unmasking of power by reason' is unquestionably valid, but it leaves undecided the question of the nation, and certainly permits one to select the arguments, at least, of race, language, and religion, which continue to find sufficient contemporary support to provide justification not to bind nations together so much as to destroy them internally. They have not proved particularly beneficent for nations; nor has the proposal of rewriting the past in favour of a particular ideology, as Renan proposes. The other option, as Václav Havel proposes in his brilliant essay, 'The Power of the Powerless,' is 'living within the truth,' a phrase he repeats often. Not to do so, he argues, leads to a '*deep moral crisis in society*' in which all responsibility for the state of particular society is abandoned for personal interests: 'Living within the truth, as humanity's revolt against an enforced position, is, on the contrary, an attempt to regain control over one's own sense of responsibility. In other words, it is clearly a moral act, not only because one must pay so dearly for it, but principally because it is not self-serving.'[9]

What, it would be fair to ask, do truth, morality, and responsibility have to do with the history of literary history? To the extent that they turn unfailingly upon a sense of the nation, everything. John Ralston Saul observes, commenting on Renan, that 'our duty is to remember everything,' but he demonstrates at some length that 'we choose that which is remembered versus that which is forgotten.'[10] This choice is necessary not because nations are in any way sacrosanct, but because the uses to which their cultural histories are put can often lead to disaster. Canada is not a major offender in this respect, but, as I have argued, the manner in which cultural achievement is imbricated with ideas of nation is at best partial for the most part, and at worst, Canada practises kinds of forgetting that Renan would approve of. Once having examined the various ways in which literary history are practised in this country, it would be impossible for the historian to propose forgetting as a viable way of considering and constructing the nation in Canada. It would also be impossible to construct it along lines that Renan proposes because, among other things, 'la possession en commun d'un riche legs de souvenirs' does not appear available, even desirable, everywhere, and to everyone. Where it is, it assumes often opposing perspectives.

Saul's proposal is to continue to 'choose that which is remembered,' and the choice is a return to the sense of equality developed in the first half of the nineteenth century between William Lyon Mackenzie (1795–1861) and Louis-Joseph Papineau (1786–1871), and later between Robert Baldwin (1804–58) and Louis-Hippolyte LaFontaine (1807–64). To do so requires certain exclusions, which he is prepared to make in the name of a centralized federation. It means establishing the existence of a 'triangular reality,' 'constructed upon three, deeply rooted pillars, three experiences' – the Aboriginal, the francophone, and the anglophone. But later he has second thoughts, which not only weaken the Aboriginal pillar, but also raise serious doubts about whether the notion of country as 'a confusion of minorities major and minor' is viable. Despite the fact that Saul's study is among the more searching of contemporary meditations on the relations between the various cultural communities of Canada and the myths that sustain them, the beginning of Saul's Canada is invariably based upon franco-phone and anglo-phone accord: 'The coalition which Mackenzie-Pap-ineau attempted and LaFontaine-Baldwin achieved is the key to the Canadian sensibility.' From a political perspective there is a certain validity in Saul's position which forms the anatomy of his book. To assent to it fully, however, requires that the 'triangular reality,' which includes Aboriginals, and the larger meaning of minorities, which would include immigrants, be subordinate to what amounts to identity politics in a larger (central) Canadian design. Despite the fact that the Aboriginal 'contribution' is often mentioned in Saul's argument, it is difficult to see in what way it functions, and there appears to be a cer-tain apprehensiveness in a concluding chapter on nationalism with regard to immigrants: 'The idea of belonging to multiple communities makes practical sense in a decentralized federation built upon three cultural foundations. But it has also distressed some people.'[11] Although the rhetorical strategy of the latter sentence implies that Saul is not among the distressed, his subsequent argument does not give much space for immigrants in the triangle. This is because 'the social reality of our diversity – the reality we all live – has never had much to do with the formal politics of multiculturalism.' Such a statement may provide a measure of comfort for those to whom 'we' refers, but it seems to imply that immigrants do not inhabit 'our reality.' Reality, however, as Saul well knows, is not a simple notion, and as he later remarks, 'history is reality. But it is also the product of how we imagine reality.' Multiculturalism is imagined as no more than a formal, not lived reality, and the consequence is that 'the immigrants who come here and stay do so because in the long run they want to become some-thing called Canadian.'[12] If they have difficulty doing so, it is primarily because 'we' have failed in our public and civic duty to see that immi-grants are educated, whether in French or English, adequately. If there is any destabilization in the smooth admission of immigrants into Cana-dian society, the onus rests primarily with provincial governments.

The argument Saul makes here is one that implies that immigration can be a source of distress and destabilization, but this not the fault of immigrants but rather of those who establish immigration policy and invite them. To shape the argument in this manner works to Saul's advantage in two ways. On the one hand, it allows him to manifest liberal sympathy toward immigrants, and, on the other, it can allow him to return easily to a position well elaborated in his Massey Lectures, *The Unconscious Civilization* (1995). Admiration for that book, however, should not cloud one's view of what happens to the notion of diverse communities in this book. Immigrants are the responsibility, finally, of provincial governments whose duty it is to find them places in another, triangular reality. Such an argument seriously weakens the larger position of *Reflections of a Siamese Twin*, which supports a notion of Canada as a community of communities. To make such an argument against multicultural communities returns one to a modified view of a bipolar construction of Canada (a Siamese twin) that has a regard, but merely a regard, for Aboriginal cultures. This may be a viable reality, but in some ways it falls short of a fully imagined Canada.

Multiple Memories

If Canada is not a monolithic state based on European models, nor two states in a kind of static tension, is there a way to imagine multiculuralism in a manner that would support Saul's premise? It is evident that Balkanization is at the root of fears concerning decentralization. But Balkanization implies a number of small states federated against their will. Such a model, however, is not the same as multiculturalism, especially under the terms of a policy that discourages the fostering of the various languages that immigrants bring with them. One of the problems that multiculturalism raises may be seen in the privileging of mere 'difference,' which can lead to negative destabilization. Autonomies which are unmindful of the Other are autonomies, however, which would propagate, as a kind of categorical imperative, a general, public state of unmindfulness. If there has been a metahistorical purpose in my bringing the literary histories of Canada into a common compass, it has been to demonstrate the limits of autonomous perspectives, no matter how valid in themselves. To step beyond the limits, one has to recognize the legitimate claims of other autonomies, which is one of the meanings, I suggest, of the epigraph taken from Nicole Brossard (1943–), namely, 'la mémoire se fait plurielle.'[13] We share a plurality of memories or, at least, have the possibility of doing so, and the possibility extends beyond political arrangements.

Among the more deeply thought responses to the problem of autonomy as simply difference is Ian Angus's discussion in *A Border Within*, which develops the philosophical implications of multiculturalism within a context of English-Canadian thought concerning civil polity. Multiculturalism is seized upon because it 'evinces a key feature that characterizes the attempt to bring particularities into the public domain: in emerging from the private, particularities are articulated as "rights"; that is to say, they are put a universalizing form.' The universal is central to Angus's argument, at least insofar as it supports a notion of something held in common (if not exactly in Renan's manner), rather than something that evades the common through difference. It is an argument shaped to overcome the objections that emphasis upon regional and ethnic difference can only end in unmanageable fragmentation and that multiculturalism leads to indifferent tolerance of difference without the possibility of a shared vision, and certainly both of these perspectives could be conclusions available after such a study as I have made. As Angus argues, however, Canada shares with other postcolonial, immigrant societies a problem, which its cultural history, as I have represented it, bears out. As he puts the matter:

> If we can define a tradition hemeneutically as a historical continuity constructed as a synthesis of past and future through an active interpretation in the present, then immigration shatters this threefold temporal structure with a dualism of before and after. The immigrant society is a *layered periodization* of such dualisms – for example, the difference between the Jews or Ukrainians who came before the Russian Revolution and those who came after.[14]

As we have seen, in the instance of the Hungarians who came after 1956, such layering may be even somewhat more complex. Because, however, Canada's concept of the nation remains weak, the conditions for successful integration are attenuated,[15] a reason which I would take as stronger than that of the fiscal inhibitions of provincial governments being at fault. Weak national identity from a central Canadian perspective is certainly a reason why multiculturalism has made less of an impact in Quebec, and where it may well be perceived as menacingly moving into '*the same domain of relevance*,' as the dominant domain. Multiculturalism's justification, then, would have be seen as not carrying so much of a threat to the nation as understood in Quebec or among Aboriginals, and, indeed, Angus places both in an ontological domain external to, and distinct from, that of English Canada. Under such circumstances, the social ideal in Angus's sense is to be understood as '*the universalization of a right to particularity within a pluri-cultural, unilingual framework*, and it is in such a formulation that multiculturalism as a social ideal in English Canada may make a contribution to the extension of democratic theory to include the public recognition of particularities.'[16] As a consequence, the implications of Saul's 'triangular reality' are not only retained but given the leaven of a philosophical basis for the recognition of immigrant communities within the tradition of English-Canadian political theory.

The full implication of Angus's definition of multiculturalism may be seen in the distinction he draws between civic nationalism, which 'eliminates differences from within public life' and ethnic nationalism, which 'places them outside.' To make such a claim implies that an individual can only enjoy the possibility of being an individual when his/her identity can be shared. This is in turn only possible when respect for the Other springs not from the impossible 'knowledge of all cultures' but 'from a reflexive sense of one's own limitation.'[17] What makes the situation of immigrants instructive in such countries as Canada is that it forces recognition of the distinctive fact that s/he can only inhabit a '*sub*culture.' Thus, the immigrant can never possess clarity about position and belonging either in respect of the former or the subsequent culture, and this condition pluralizes the reference of 'us' and 'we' for the immigrant, not to speak of 'them.' For Angus, then, 'the key issue for multicultural understanding is an us/we relation, not an us/them one. By this I mean the "us" to refer to one's ethno-cultural group and the "we" to refer to the multicultural civic context of English Canada.'[18]

There are two aspects of Angus's subsequent argument that are of profound significance because they respond to the anxieties of those who see the disappearance of older (English) Canadian ideals in the possible confusions of the multicultural and, at the same time, place the nation in a history that extends into the future. They are based upon the assumption that particularity is without meaning if is not shared and if it does not, by virtue of being shared, assert larger ambitions. A multiculturalism that does not fold in upon itself and remain ignorant of the Other requires 'a *justification* of particularity, which must of necessity be retrospective, and the *formulation* of a universality inclusive of differences, which is projective and anticipatory.' It is a social ideal, then, that transcends the static metaphor of the mosaic by always dynamically shaping the numerous relationships it constructs. The process insists, however, on mutual respect that requires the retention of one's own culture. Because Angus's notion of the dominant culture is that of English Canada, particularly one that emerges from George Grant's conservative Loyalism, the shape multiculturalism takes in his argument is one that, paradoxical as it may appear, at once defends that culture and lifts it to a larger zone of significance than that of simply Loyalism. The larger zone is perceived as a dialogue through which both partners are themselves (particulars) and tending toward a mutually articulated universality, and 'the relation may be stated this way: I *feel* my own belonging; I *know* the other's difference; I *justify* my own belonging; I *justify* the other's belonging; we *understand* that human life is about identities; we *engage* each other in the construction of a common culture that illuminates human universality.'[19]

I have dwelt upon Angus's argument at some length because of its strong relevance to the emerging social world of contemporary Canada. It also provides an important context for some of the issues raised by the history I have been engaged in writing. It is evident that, to use Angus's language, literary history in Canada normally means, with some few exceptions such as that of New, cultivation of particularity. One might say, furthermore, that it represents multiculturalism in its negative aspect, that is, the pursuit of difference that does not give proper recognition of the Other. These are histories that operate as if fruitful, continuous, and creative engagement between participants that would share a culture composed of cultures is doomed from the start, and I would argue that for this reason constructions of the nation appear to be so often static in character like the *Bildungsroman*. Saul, at least, supports a partly multicultural nation and provides a model that might have been employed before the rise of immigration of non-charter cultures toward the end of the nineteenth century that began to leave their mark in the 1920s. Efforts, however, even for francophones and anglophones, to engage in mutually constructive dialogue through their literary life have not been better than sporadic.

The easy solution, and the one most readily pursued, is the way of mutual tolerance, at best, and indifference, at worst. Such a solution prompts two kinds of excesses in the study of literature and history. The first is to abandon any pretense of order beyond what multiculturalism dictates; the other is found in the aggressive promotion of 'national values.' I have not put this last expression in quotation marks in order to be ironic, but to say more directly what I have been saying indirectly, and that is that such interests often can be construed as parochial and lacking in what Angus would call universalizing. The national values in the generality of literary histories are to be found in the memorializing and justification of particularities, *tout court*. Before elaborating upon this point, let me situate myself in respect of the multicultural as a sole justification. Its excesses have been rather thoroughly documented in John M. Ellis's *Literature Lost*, a text which excoriates the excess of theory based on the agendas of race, class, and gender. For someone whose own approach to the Canadian literatures is derived from a long and affectionate relationship with classical and European literatures, it is not difficult for me to feel a twinge of sympathy for Ellis's polemic. Nevertheless, that same relationship, despite the respect it has prompted toward traditions, has also prompted a greater respect toward the diversity they possess. As a consequence, the contemporary is largely significant for me in its relation with the past, and I am apt to view the great emphasis placed upon contemporary social issues by scholars of literature as operating in a context that is made to appear larger than it may, in fact, be. Although I am in not in a position to judge competence in every case, it is not difficult to feel some uneasiness at the facility with which literary critics move about in several other fields. Because of the lack of competence to judge, however, I leave that matter aside. In the end, however, arguments such as Ellis's testify to the deep anxiety that may be felt in the face of what, on the one hand, appears to be the loss of unifying threads in a discipline (or, by extension, a 'nation') and, on the other, the advancement of positions that in many respects appear pre-emptory.

The very pluralistic character, however, of what is now taking place in the humanities is, as I have suggested, a small reflection of what is happening in the world. Its bearing upon the past and future of Canadian social theory as painstakingly analysed by Angus is an earnest of the relevance of these changes as they affect Canada. Another, perhaps more frequently heard response to such changes are those articulated in J.L. Granatstein's polemic, provocatively entitled *Who Killed Canadian History?* Although it does not hesitate to list state-appointed perpetrators of the crime, the burden of his argument falls upon 'Canadian history,' and he means *history*, not historiography. Like many scholars who remain perfectly assured of their knowledge, which is a condition that remains true for participants on both sides of this debate, Granatstein has a perfectly clear idea of the Canadian past, how the nation came to be, and what its significance, based upon these factors, is. His point of departure is that 'we have chosen not to remember it.' This is a position that appears to differ from Renan's, which prefers to remember in a certain way by refusing to investigate certain actions too closely. We are to accept, rather, that some kings, notably Philip Augustus, act from the highest of motivations, and therefore denigrating scrutiny must be not be allowed. Granatstein's data support his contention: Canadian history is not only not taught extensively, but when it is, it is somehow reduced to litanies of error. These litanies are produced by those who promote other cultures at the expense of the Canadian past. His answer is 'to think of Canada as a nation, as a whole, as a society, and not simply as a collection of races, genders, regions, and classes.' All of these amount to a 'trend away from the particular.' The particular would be recovered by providing 'a history that puts Canada up front, that points to the success and failures of past policies, and that gives due weight to contributions made by non-charter-group Canadians.' In other words, he would provide 'a history that puts Canada firmly in the context of Western civilization, but gives full weight to the non-Western world.'[20]

This is history which offers unity, a national idea, and a sense of proportion that would seem to answer the excesses of multicultural agendas. This is because 'history happened. The object is not to undo it, distort it, or to make it fit our present political attitudes.'[21] A second reading of these remarks makes them appear perilously close to Renan's model. It makes the historian appear powerless in respect of the past. It may be that the past cannot change, but such a condition need not determine our response to it. Because Granatstein does not wish to remake the past but to allow its imperfections, he creates a new level of the ideal within Renan's model. Renan's Philip Augustus is to be cherished as perfection; Granatstein's argument would allow him to be cherished as imperfection. After that, the forgetting of historiography may continue. Such forgetting provides the past – tarnished or untarnished – but it does not help in the making of futures.

Or does it? One of problems with Granatstein's model is that it can lead to a hegemony of a certain past, just as the excesses of multiculturalism can lead to a hegemony of the future. They are not sufficient guides, however, to the uncertainties of the present. Nietzsche remarked that 'we need history, for the past pours through us in a hundred streams, and we are in fact nothing else but what we experience every moment of this pouring through.' It could also be remarked that the past is not only in constant rapport with the present, but also the present is in constant rapport with the past, that is, every moment in the past was also once in its present. That present cannot afford to be reified any more than whatever present we may like to think the future will possess. It is at such junctures that literary history's significance may be derived, for the texts upon which it draws to compose a history arc always steeped in their own actuality, constructing a past, desiring a future, and putting both into a discourse that makes a present. As Walter Benjamin aphoristically observed, 'history is the subject of a structure whose site is not homogeneous, empty time, but time filled by the presence of the now [*Jetzzeit*].' The present, then, of cultural arti- facts, such as literary texts, is at once in the middle of time pouring through and in a situation of dialogue. They assume, even interpellate, some audiences and ignore, even dismiss, others. In the contexts of 'new worlds' their culture is never as closed as it may appear or is con- structed; it is always in some way implicated with at least one other. These are, for literary history in such contexts, inevitable moments of origin. Because they are at minimum dialogic, the placing of literary texts into a canonic order tends to falsify their historical function, for they are, no matter how accomplished in themselves, tentative projects whose sequence and design depends upon the historian. The desire to compose narratives, which most literary historians still find a suitable mode, is the design probably least apt to convey the often purposeless gestures that literary texts make. Thus much of the effort that goes into canonization is a work of salvaging, and what is salvaged, in order to be useful to a history, seems best when its dialogic character is made to yield to the design of its redeeming context, so to speak. The canon may redeem us, as Lecker argues, by imagining a future community,[22] but everything depends upon how the community is said to have con- versed.

It seems, therefore, impossible not construct literary history in Can- ada as a condition that is continually directed toward the recognition of the Other, whether it fails to do so or not, inasmuch as the Other is present from the beginning in the shape of one ghost or another. One might in fact argue that the Other is at once beginning and origin, an inescapable presence that hovers in all 'new world' discourse as reality and myth. Thus, although one might assent to the implication in Granatstein that the impact of non-charter-groups is relatively recent (whenever that might be), one cannot escape the fact that First Nations and Inuit people have always been part of the Canadian social contract, forgotten, neglected, and abused as they may have been. Furthermore, as their literary histories suggest, they bear an inverse relation to ethnic minorities, and thus they may be said to anticipate the latter's role and equally marginalized presence in Canadian cultural history. Nevertheless, so long as the Other remains excluded from the contract, the realization of a 'Canadian identity' will always be thwarted. I refer to such an identity in quotation marks because, as Angus argues, such an identity is not fixed and therefore eludes definition. Such an identity is, however, the not yet uncovered core of whatever texts constitute a Canadian canon, the history that can never be definitive.

Notes

Introduction

1 Sheppard, 'It's Time for an Unreality Check.'
2 This text is only mentioned because of its title. If an argument against Fuku-yama's thesis were necessary, it is provided amply in Niethammer's *Posthis-toire: Has History Come to an End?*
3 Jauß, 'Literaturgeschichte als Provokation,' 144.
4 Nietzsche, 'Vom Nutzen und Nachteil des Historie für das Lebcn,' *Werke in drei Bänden*, I: 251; Perkins, *Is Literary History Possible?* 39, 37.
5 Bourdieu, *The Field of Cultural Production*, 125; White, *Metahistory*, 430.
6 Richard A. Etlin, for example, argues that the theory of tropology is too reductive and deterministic and leads to a predominance of theory in respect of history. See *In Defense of Humanism*, 127–9.
7 White, *Metahistory*, 427.
8 Ibid., 177, 190.
9 Ibid., 16.
10 Frow, *Marxism and Literary History*, 92; Moisan, *Qu'est-ce que l'histoire littéraire?* 196.
11 See Lacan, *The Language of Self*, 160.
12 Baillargeon, *Littérature canadienne-française*. See below, chapter 3.
13 Jones, *Butterfly on Rock*, 183. See also below, chapter 5.
14 New, *A History of Canadian Literature*, 296.
15 Perkins, *Is Literary History Possible?* 39. In a rather well-known article, 'Liter-ary History and Literary Modernity' (1969), Paul de Man wittily plays with an antinomy between modernity and history as they bear upon literature in such a way that they both become interdependent: 'modernity, which is fun-damentally a falling away from literature and a rejection of history, also acts

as the principle that gives literature duration and historical existence' (162). His insights may be generally valid, but they do not take into account the practice of a great number of literary historians.

16 Cf. Brennan, 'The National Longing for Form,' 50–2.
17 David Galloway, 'The Voyagers,' ed. Carl F. Klinck, *Literary History of Canada* (1965), 3; Keith, *Canadian Literature in English*, 1.
18 Marshall, *Harsh and Lovely Land*, xi; Frye, 'Conclusion,' 826.
19 New, *A History of Canadian Literature*, 2.
20 Gagnon, *Quebec and Its Historians*, 10–11.
21 Gray, *Mrs. King*, 13.
22 Pivato, *Echo*, 33.
23 The complexities of cartography as discursive formations have been widely discussed. See *inter alia* Harley, 'Maps, Knowledge, and Power,' and Huggan, 'Decolonizing the Map.'
24 Jones, *Butterfly on Rock*, 11; Frye, Conclusion, 830. A fascinating example of such distancing of subject and object in contemporary Canadian film is to be found in Atom Egoyan's *Calendar*, Zeitgeist Films, 1993. See Monique Tschofen's discussion, 'Anagrams of the Body,' 219–25.
25 Ian Angus remarks that 'geography becomes important for identity [in English Canada] where history has failed to provide it.' See *A Border Within*, 114.
26 Swales, *The German Bildungsroman*, 14, 17, 29.
27 Jakobson and Halle, 'Two Aspects of Language'; Mudge, 'The Man with Two Brains,' 100; cf. Patterson, 'Literary History,' 250; and De Man, 'Literary History and Literary Modernity.'
28 Saul, *Reflections of a Siamese Twin*, 111, 110, 129.
29 Atwood, *Survival*; Frye, *Anatomy of Criticism*, 169.

Chapter One. Writing Boundaries, 1874–1920

1 Halden, *Études de littérature canadienne française*, 14.
2 Wellek, *The Rise of English Literary History*, 1, 94. Language as a major determinant of nation was 'invented' in precisely the period we are about to consider. See Hobsbawm, *The Age of Empire 1875–1914*, 146.
3 Coopman and Scharpé, *Geschiedenis der vlaamsche Letterkunde*, 1, 10, 11, 11–12. Unless otherwise noted, all translations are mine.
4 Not the least of those who have noted the problems that De Sanctis had in finding a beginning, Benedetto Croce observes that the selection of Ciullo was part of an effort to avoid the abstractions of language and race for the sake of concrete poetic forms. See *Teoria e Storia della Storiografia*, 145.

5 De Sanctis, *Storia della letteratura italiana*, 1: 20, 24, 32.

6 Cf. Croce, 'La critica letteraria italiana dal de Sanctis ai giorni nostri,' 1: 208.

7 De Sanctis, *Storia della letteratura italiana*, 2: 441, 463–4.

8 Ibid., 1: 9.

9 Novák and Novák, *Přehledné dějiny literatury české*, 90. I am indebted to my wife, Irena, for assistance with the subtleties of Czech.

10 Nautet, *Histoire des lettres belges d'expression française*, 2: 26, 27, 29, 32, 35.

11 Ibid., 1: 30–1, 100. That this was no idle gesture to give the Flemish writer De Coster such a commanding position as a founder of francophone Belgian literature may be seen in his subsequent role in the formation of its history. See Hanse, *Naissance d'une littérature*, vii–xi.

12 Lareau, *Histoire*, iii.

13 Ibid., 10, 15, 16.

14 See his moving description of a personally witnessed discourse of one of Arthur Buies's (1840–1901) speeches to the Institut, ibid., 464; on Lareau's anticlericalism, see Gagnon, *Le Québec et ses historiens*, 348.

15 Lareau, *Histoire*, 130. The distinctions between the radical and moderate liberals are succinctly developed in Monière, *Le Développement des idéologies*, 172–84. For a general summary of Lareau's ideological position based upon his *Histoire du droit canadien* (1888), see also Gagnon, *Le Québec et ses historiens*, 223.

16 Lareau, 37.

17 The importance of 'print-as-commodity' forms the crux of Benedict Anderson's argument in respect of the rise of a national consciousness. See *Imagined Communities*, 37.

18 Lareau, *Histoire*, 57; cf. Anderson, *Imagined Communities*, 154.

19 Lareau, *Histoire*, 57–8.

20 Ibid., 57.

21 Ibid., 136, 88, 80.

22 Ibid., 114, 130.

23 Ibid., 140, 140, 137.

24 White, *Metahistory*, 164.

25 Lareau, *Histoire*, 161–2; cf., Gagnon, *Le Québec et ses historiens*, 320, 289n8.

26 Lareau, *Histoire*, 190.

27 Ibid., 255; cf. Gagnon, *Le Québec et ses historiens*, 343–4.

28 Lareau, *Histoire*, 172.

29 Ibid., 171, 204.

30 Née Rosanna Eleanora Mullins, her marriage to a French-Canadian doctor and the choice of French-Canadian themes has made Leprohon as much a bridge of the two central cultures of Canada as Gabrielle Roy.

31 Lareau, *Histoire*, 306–7, 276 (emphasis added).

32 Ibid., 275.

33 Ibid., 278, 292, 293.

34 Ibid., 293, (cf. 334), 294, 335.

35 Ibid., 128.

36 Cf. Boileau, *Œuvres complètes*, 160. François de Malherbe (1555–1628) was a poet and critic of the French language who, according to Boileau, 'reduisit la Muse aux regles du devoir' (ibid.).

37 Cf. Ballstadt, *The Search for English-Canadian Literature*, xv.

38 Dewart, *Selections from Canadian Poets*, ix, xiii.

39 Reading, *The University in Ruins*, 76.

40 Although Lighthall's *Songs of the Great Dominion* was published by a London printer, a fact which goes a long way in explaining its implied audience, I have placed my discussion of it here, rather than in chapter 8 where it more appropriately belongs, because of the anthology's equally appropriate place in British North America at the end of the century.

41 Ibid., xxii, xxiv, xxxii.

42 Ibid., xxiv.

43 In a sense, the space devoted to either life or works is an implicit value judgment, and it is worth comparing the respective entries, for example, for Thomas Chandler Haliburton (1796–1865) and Samuel Strickland (1804–67). See MacMurchy, *Handbook of Canadian Literature (English)*, 13–17 and 31–2.

44 See Robert, *Le Manuel d'histoire*, 13–19.

45 Roy, *Nos Origines littéraires*, 14, 49.

46 Ibid., 38.

47 Cf. Frow, *Marxism and Literary History*, 103.

48 Roy, *Nos Origines littéraires*, 55, 111.

49 Roy, *French Canadian Literature*, 436, 450.

50 Robert, *Le Manuel d'histoire*, 17.

51 Roy, *French Canadian Literature*, 450.

52 Ibid., 456, 458, 461, 468.

53 Ibid., 472, 473, 474; on the Lacanian aspect of Conan's novel, see Blodgett, 'The Father's Seduction.'

54 Cf. Gagnon, *Le Québec et ses historiens*, 320.

55 Marquis, 'English Canadian Literature,' 495. Ironically, the expression 'birds of passage' had already been applied to British settlers as early as 1830 by the French-Canadian historian Pierre-Jean de Sales Laterrière in his *Political and Historical Account of Lower Canada*. See Taylor, *Promoters, Patriots, and Partisans*, 102.

56 Marquis, 'English Canadian Literature,' 548.

57 Ibid., see 534.

58 Ibid., 535, 539, 542.

59 Ibid., 539, 541.

60 Ibid., 553, 555, 564, 562.

61 Ibid., 566, 562.

62 Ibid., 571.

63 Ibid., 584–5.

64 Ibid., 587, 588.

65 Ibid., 589.

66 See Taylor, *Promoters, Patriots, and Partisans*, chapter 4; Marquis, 'English Canadian Literature,' 588, 493.

67 Brief and astringent as Edgar's article is, it deserves consideration for no other reason than that, as no less a critic than E.K. Brown remarked during the Second World War, he 'has done more to foster Canadian literature than any other academic figure' (*On Canadian Poetry*, 147). Despite the fact that Edgar's article was published in *The Cambridge History of English Literature*, he can hardly be considered part of the British literary system. In fact, he was deeply involved in the shaping of English-Canadian letters as Head of the Department of English at Victoria College, University of Toronto. See Edgar, *Across My Path*. That he was chosen to write for this history is a sign of the general esteem in which he was held.

68 Edgar, 'English-Canadian Literature,' 345.

69 Ibid., 346, 348, 354, 350; on Canada and circumstances, cf. Hutcheon, *As Canadian as ... possible ... under the circumstances!* 9.

70 Edgar, 'English-Canadian Literature,' 355, 344–5.

71 Ibid., 358, 359.

72 Craig, *Lord Durham's Report*, 150.

73 Of the three authors published outside Canada that are discussed in this chapter, Baker is the only one for which a case might be made, perhaps, for consideration in chapter 8. A Maritimer whose *History* was originally a dissertation defended at Harvard University, his work is in some ways an anomaly here. Nevertheless, his argument is not an anomaly, agreeing in many ways with such continentalists as Goldwin Smith, despite his disparaging remarks about Smith's scholarship and the premises of his thesis. See Baker, *A History of English-Canadian Literature*, 4. One might assume that much of Baker's thinking matched that of his thesis director, but he had the opportunity, if he had so wished, to modify his argument upon publishing it.

74 Baker, *History of English-Canadian Literature*, 183.

75 Ibid., 17–23; cf. 83.

76 Ibid., 69.

77 Ibid., 68, 84, 97.
78 Ibid., 178, 125, 132, 158, 182.
79 Ibid., 153, 139.
80 To a certain extent, however, Leprohon fits because she belongs to those writers whose work is 'closely connected with the literature of the United States' (ibid., 182).
81 Ibid., 122, 124.
82 Ibid., 185–6, 187, 188.
83 Ibid., 191.

Chapter Two. The Nation as Discourse, 1924–1946

1 Foucault, *L'Archéologie du savoir,* 83.
2 Robert, *Le Manuel d'histoire,* 77–99.
3 MacMechan, *Headwaters of Canadian Literature,* vii; E.K. Brown, *On Canadian Poetry,* 118.
4 Cf. Pierce's comment in his *An Outline of Canadian Literature (French and English),* 134: 'His judgements are conservative, always leading back to the golden mile-post at the centre of the forum.'
5 Marquis, 'English Canadian Literature,' 495; MacMechan, *Headwaters of Canadian Literature,* 100, x.
6 Ibid., 18.
7 This is a subsequent editor's name for De Quincey's distinction. See De Quincey, 'Letters to a Young Man,' 151–4.
8 MacMechan, *Headwaters of Canadian Literature,* 17, 97–8, 58.
9 Ibid., 58, 97, 98.
10 Ibid., 97, 98, 98–9.
11 Ibid., 145, 146, 157, 185.
12 Ibid., 191, 194.
13 Ibid., 191, 237.
14 Ibid., 199; White, *Metahistory,* 36; cf. MacMechan, *Headwaters of Canadian Literature,* 229.
15 Stevenson, *Appraisals of Canadian Literature,* vii, 10, viii.
16 Ibid., 12, 11.
17 While Emerson and Thoreau are mentioned in passing, more could have been made of the pantheistic element in Emerson, ibid., 51.
18 Ibid., 41, 56.
19 Ibid., 65.
20 Frye, 'Conclusion,' 830.
21 Pratt's first collection, *Newfoundland Verse* appeared in 1923, and an analysis

of the full impact of his poetry, which subsequent historians had to address, would not have been possible for Stevenson. For his impact on the young Northrop Frye, see Frye's eloquent testimony, 'Silence in the Sea,' *The Bush Garden*, 181–97.

22 Frye, 'Preface to an Uncollected Anthology' (1956), ibid., 171.

23 Pacey, 'The Course of Canadian Criticism,' in Klinck, *Literary History of Canada*, 2nd ed., 3: 19.

24 Indeed, Frye, as I shall discuss further in the next chapter, is able to entertain both positions as 'complementary.' See his 'Conclusion,' 845.

25 Stevenson, *Appraisals of Canadian Literature*, 78, 79, 98, 99.

26 Ibid., v (italics added).

27 Ibid., 64–5, xii, 130.

28 Ibid., 131, 134.

29 Giguère, *Exile, Révolte et Dissidence*, 3. It should be noted that inasmuch as Giguère's text is exemplary as a comparative study, the exclusive focus on Montreal (13) limits its usefulness to a study of the kind undertaken here.

30 Pierce, *Outline*, Foreword (n.p.); Pacey, 'The Course of Canadian Criticism,' 3: 19; Pierce, *Outline*, Letter of Dedication (n.p.); Foreword (n.p.).

31 Cf. White, *Metahistory*, 35.

32 Pierce, *Outline*, 237; Letter of Dedication.

33 Ibid., 3–4, 10.

34 Ibid., 8.

35 Ibid., 11, 12, 13, 88.

36 Ibid., 18, 9, 23–4, 62.

37 Ibid., 238; Roy, *Manuel d'histoire*, 116–19.

38 Pierce, *Outline*, 239, 243.

39 See Davies, 'J.D. Logan and the Great Feud,' 113–28.

40 Logan and French, *Highways of Canadian Literature*, 15, 28–9.

41 Ibid., 26.

42 Their poetry is judged as 'aesthetically bad through and through' on the ground that it is not ' "real," ' that is, it does not manifest 'chaste speech, lovely imagery, dulcet music, and exquisite emotion' (ibid., 278).

43 Pierce, *Outline*, 95; on plot structure, see Perkins, *Is Literary History Possible?* 39

44 Logan and French, *Highways of Canadian Literature*, 21.

45 Ibid., 106, 6.

46 Grove's first novel, *Settlers of the Marsh*, appeared in 1926, exciting some moral indignation on the part of his reviewers, following two earlier publications. Uncertainty about Grove's position in the literary system may have caused the omission.

47 Logan and French, *Highways of Canadian Literature*, 25, 130, 131, 133, 154.
48 Ibid., 131, 133, 154.
49 Ibid., 230, 279; Marquis, 'English-Canadian Literature,' 496.
50 The absence of any serious location in chapter 30 (mentioned only in respect of Roberts and Pauline Johnson [Logan and French, *Highway of Canadian Literature*, 110, 199]) of *The Week*, Canada's *fin de siècle* periodical that, as Alfred G. Bailey noted, 'embodied an impulse reflective of the new nationality,' gives the impression of the same tendency. See Klinck, ed., *Literary History of Canada*, 1st ed., 64.
51 Logan and French, *Highways of Canadian Literature*, 395.
52 Cf. Roy, *Histoire*, 13–18.
53 Ibid., 265–6; cf. Robert, *Le Manuel d'histoire*, 39, 118.
54 Robert, *Le Manuel d'histoire*, 40.
55 Ibid., 120, 126.
56 Ibid., 122; Pierce, *Outline*, 83 (italics added).
57 Pierce, Foreword; see Robert, *Le Manuel d'histoire*, 118–19. Maurice Duplessis was the premier of Quebec during the years 1936–9 and 1944–59. Because of his highly conservative policies, his regime was known as the period of *la grande noirceur*. See Quinn, *The Union Nationale*, chapter 5.
58 Given the importance of this adjective in Logan and French (*Highways of Canadian Literature*, 21), it may be assumed that this is an implicit response to their more dismissive attitude. Since Logan taught a course in Canadian literature at Acadia University with Rhodenizer, it is very possible that this response was explicit. On their teaching together, see Davies, 'J.D. Logan and the Great Feud,' 118.
59 Rhodenizer, *A Handbook of Canadian Literature*, 12, 13.
60 Ibid., 144, 223.
61 Unforgivably but still interestingly enough, it is here that he places Sara Jeannette Duncan, who 'has never been surpassed by any Canadian humorist' (ibid., 141). Witty as *The Imperialist* is, it finds no position among novels.
62 Despite Rhodenizer's recognition of Grove's significance (ibid., 262), one may wonder about his judgment as a reader of his contemporaries' poetry when he signals Lloyd Roberts, Louise Morey Bowman, and Marian Osborne as the future of Canadian verse.
63 Ibid., 265, 266.
64 Dandurand, *La Poésie canadienne-française*, 230. Cf. Dandurand, *Le Roman canadien-français*, 246.
65 Dandurand, *La Poésie canadienne-française*, 231, 234, 231. It is difficult to state precisely the relation that Dandurand's argument bears to Émile Chartier's

doctoral thesis, defended in 1932, and later developed in his *Au Canada français*. 1941. The similarities are striking indeed. Chartier proposes three periods for poetry, the first from 1800–55 (pseudo-classical), 1855–90 (L'Ecole de Québec), and 1890–1920 (two movements, respectively Parnassian and symbolist). See ibid., 255–7. Each one bears the signature of French style. In summary, 'les vers de nos poètes sont un écho, poussée jusqu'à décalque, disons même au plagiat parfois des procédés chers aux Ecoles françaises' (ibid., 164). The grafting was necessary as a protection against English culture, but the process was complicated by the fact that after the reestablishment of relations with France, Quebec became saturated with French texts. Francophone self-realization was a struggle on two fronts, in which the language was at once the necessary instrument and paradoxical trap (ibid., 241–2).

66 Klink, *Literary History of Canada*, 1st ed., 487; cf. Germaine Warkentin's Introduction to *The White Savannahs*, xi, xxxv.

67 Collin, *The White Savannahs*, 147, 14, 52–3. The distinction Collin draws between Le Franc and 'other Rousseauists' is certainly valid, but the adjective 'other' still places her in their ideological camp. The distinction is part of the nuanced gradualism with which he rises from Lampman toward Pratt. On Hulme and the Nordic, see Warkentine's Introduction, xv–xvi.

68 Collin, *The White Savannahs*, 144, 256. Inasmuch as Collin was a professor of French, it is likely that he knew Villiers de l'Isle Adam's play *Axel* (1890) through his normal reading; nevertheless, he may also have come across this description of Axel's behaviour in Edmund Wilson's widely read *Axel's Castle*, 263.

69 Collin, *The White Savannahs*, 137, 144.

70 Ibid., 144, 263.

71 Ibid., 150, 172.

72 Ibid. 172, 33, 281, 253 (citing T.S. Eliot).

73 Ibid., 189, 208.

74 Ibid., 263; see 240.

75 Ibid., 257, 188, 197, 203, 198, 197.

76 White, *Metahistory*, 371–2; cf. Collin, *The White Savannahs*, 179 et passim, 172; Pierce, *Outline*, 83.

77 Collin, *The White Savannahs*, 173.

78 As I shall indicate in the following chapter, this is also a necessary aspect of Samuel Baillargeon's construction of Quebec in its literature.

79 Turnbull, *Essential Traits*, 3, 10; Taine, *L'Histoire*, 1: xxii, v.

80 Turnbull, *Essential Traits*, 9.

81 Ibid., 19; Hémon, *Maria Chapdelaine*, 198; cf. Savard, *Menaud maître-draveur*, 32.

82 Turnbull, *Essential Traits*, 83; cf. Dandurand, *La Poésie canadienne-française*, 75.
83 Turnbull, *Essential Traits*, 90.
84 Ibid., 15.
85 Cited 116.
86 Ibid., 116, 134, 199.
87 Smith, *The Book of Canadian Poetry*, 3, 5.
88 Ibid., 5, 7, 10, 14–15, 14, 28. As he is for most historians, Pratt is considered simply too unique to place except as the end of the old and the threshold of the new, and for Smith's generation 'the very expansiveness of his good nature and the exuberance of his energy serve as something of a barrier' (28).
89 Bloom, *The Anxiety of Influence*, 91; Smith, *The Book of Canadian Poetry*, 28.
90 Smith, *The Oxford Anthology of Canadian Verse*, li. Smith, *Modern Canadian Verse*, xviii; Smith, *The Book of Canadian Poetry*, 31.
91 Frye, 'Canada and Its Poetry,' (1943) *The Bush Garden*, 136; *Anatomy of Criticism*, 351; Frye, 'Canada and Its Poetry,' 138; Smith, *The Book of Canadian Poetry*, 29; cf. Tynjanov, 'On Literary Evolution,' 72–3.
92 A.J.M. Smith, 'Eclectic Detachment: Aspects of Identity in Canadian Poetry' (1961), *Towards a View of Canadian Letters*, 24–5; 'Poet' (1956), ibid., 191.
93 Collin, 'The Stream and the Master' (1943–4), *The White Savannahs*, 298, 300; Mandel, Introduction, *Contexts of Canadian Criticism*, 6.
94 Brown, *On Canadian Poetry*, vii, 21, 23, 27.
95 Ibid., 28, 29, 42, 44, 48.
96 Ibid., 56, 67; cf. Frow, *Marxism and Literary History*, 94.
97 Brown, *On Canadian Poetry*, 67, 74, 82, 85, 86.
98 Ibid., 92, 117; cf. Gwyn, *The Private Capital*.
99 Brown, *On Canadian Poetry*, 113, 107, 111.
100 Ibid., 119–20, 123, 139.
101 Brown, *On Canadian Poetry*, 139; Collin, 'The Stream and the Master,' *The White Savannahs*, 296.
102 Brown, *On Canadian Poetry*, 143, 162.
103 Ibid., 48, 86.
104 Robert, *Le Manuel d'histoire*, 132.
105 Brunet, *Histoire de la littérature canadienne française*, 177; Baillargeon, *Littérature canadienne-française*, 482.
106 Brunet, *Histoire de la littérature canadienne-française*, 7.
107 Ibid., 10, 34, 40, 34.
108 Ibid., 107–8, 108, 178.
109 Robert, *Le Manuel d'histoire*, 131; cited in Brunet, *Histoire de la littérature canadienne française*, 26.

Chapter Three. The Search for Agency, 1948–1965

1 Jean Chrétien, CBC Interview, 26 January 1995.
2 Cardin and Couture, *Histoire du Canada*, 270–4; Rioux, 'Borduas, our eternal contemporary,' 30.
3 Cf. the penultimate paragraph: 'Au terme imaginable, nous entrevoyons l'homme libéré de ses chaînes inutiles, réaliser dans l'ordre imprévu, nécessaire de la spontanéité, dans l'anarchie resplendissante, la plénitude de ses dons individuels.' See Borduas, *Écrits*, 1, 349. Although we, at the end of the twentieth century, might find such a statement quixotic or cant or both, the immediate censure incurred by Borduas was harsh, and its gradual impact deeply animating.
4 Cook, *Canada, Québec, and the Uses of Nationalism*, 99.
5 The many kinds of support it received and the history of its development is discussed in Klinck, *Giving Canada a Literary History*, chapter 8.
6 Brunet, *Canadians et Canadiens*, 55, 58.
7 McCourt, *The Canadian West in Fiction*, 110–11.
8 Connor's best-seller *The Doctor* appeared in 1906, Niven's trilogy was published between the years 1935 and 1944, and Grove's first novel came out in 1925.
9 McCourt, *The Canadian West in Fiction*, 70.
10 Ibid., 55–6, 97.
11 Ibid., 111, 113, 117.
12 In that sense, odd as it may appear, McCourt's West is Lacanian in the sense that it is akin to the history of a subject that has not yet acquired speech of its own kind (*parole*), but soon will have, at which point it will be able to grow to adulthood and into the symbolic beside the nation, represented by the province of Ontario, as parent.
13 Pacey, *Creative Writing in Canada*, 1–3.
14 Ibid., 32, 38, 41, 45.
15 Cf. Gwyn, *The Private Capital*, 441.
16 Paccy, *Creative Writing in Canada*, 70.
17 Ibid., 82; despite Fréchette's prefatory blessing extended to the first collection of Drummond's *habitant* poems, neither preface nor poetry can be said to be significant responses to ideological difference in Canada at that time.
18 Ibid., 95 (in view of Collin's critique of Pickthall, it is not clear how she moves the clock forward, and no reference to Collin is provided), 91.
19 Ibid., 101, 109.
20 Ibid., 111, 114, 110, 139. Pratt and Birney do not exhaust Pacey's canon,

which makes room for A.J.M. Smith, A.M. Klein, Dorothy Livesay, and P.K. Page ([1916–] ibid., 156), but they stand as exemplary.

21 Ibid., 122, 123, 139.

22 Ibid., 181, 187, 176.

23 Although Pacey admires *Two Solitudes* with appropriate reservations (ibid., 188), the issue of French and English unity the novel addresses is not mentioned as a contemporary (1920–50) historical problem.

24 Ibid., 189.

25 Ibid., 167, 168, 170.

26 Ibid., 7; in our relativizing age, it could be argued that such a historical construction was perhaps a widely shared view in the 1950s. It was repeated without change in the second edition of 1961 and not altered in the 1967 reissue.

27 Ibid., 202.

28 White, *Metahistory*, 27; cf. 29. The Sœurs de Sainte-Anne, *Histoire des littératures française et canadienne*, 369. Some confusion within the metaphor occurs with the term 'essais,' inasmuch as the sisters also refer to this period as *'littérature embryonnaire.'*

29 As I have suggested in discussing McCourt, such an understanding of the growth of a literature may be understood within the framework of Lacanian psychology, which argues that the autonomy of the child depends upon the acquisition of self-empowering discourse. It can only do this through a process of separation from the mother.

30 It might be thought that the highly didactic characteristics of this text limit its usefulness to a history of literary history. On the contrary, it is extremely useful because of its intimate place in the evolution of the literary system in French Canada.

31 Sœurs de Sainte-Anne, *Histoire des littératures française et canadienne*, 376, 434.

32 Ibid., 369, 419, 393.

33 Ibid., 384–5, 389, 397.

34 Ibid., 436, 437, 365.

35 The provincial motto, 'Je me souviens,' is ubiquitously appropriate in Quebec culture.

36 O'Leary, *Le Roman canadien-français*, 18.

37 It should be remembered that official relations with France were not permitted after the Treaty of Paris (1763) until 1860.

38 O'Leary, *Le Roman canadien-français*, 21, 28; it is perhaps only in this context of survival that one can understand the fact that O'Leary had published before the war a polemic in favour of separation in which he desired to see 'sur le sol américain un peuple, catholique de religion, français de langue et culture, devenir le centre d'attraction de la pensée française, le centre des

minoritaires françaises éparpillées sur le continent, que les Français ont été les premier à conquérir et à coloniser' (see O'Leary, *Séparatisme*, 215. In his history of the novel the powerful emphasis on French culture remains without the ecclesiastical and separatist subtexts.

39 Ibid., 41, 42, 44. Accessibility is not the same as familiarity. Balzac was known almost as soon as he was published in France, but, as Yves Dostaler remarks, 'de Stendhal, de Benjamin Constant, de Flaubert, de Gautier, on peut à peine noter, vers la fin de siècle.' See *Les Infortunes du roman dans le Québec du XIXe siècle*, 24.

40 O'Leary, *Le Roman canadien-français*, 45.

41 Ibid., 46, 47.

42 Ibid., 195.

43 Baillargeon, *Littérature canadienne-française*, ix; Groulx, *Préface*, ibid., viii.

44 Baillargeon, *Littérature canadienne-francaise*, 448.

45 Ibid., 45.

46 Ibid., 63.

47 Such a structure is reinforced visibly by biographies simplified and transposed into large arrows.

48 Baillargeon, *Littérature canadienne-française*, 2nd ed., 350.

49 Ibid., 61–3.

50 Cited in ibid., 167

51 Ibid., 303.

52 Ibid., 313.

53 The influence of Georg Lukács is possible here. On the typical as characteristic of Lukács's aesthetics, see Kiralyfalvi, *The Aesthetics of György Lukács*, 78–83.

54 Rashley, *Poetry in Canada*, xiv.

55 Ibid., xiv, xvi.

56 Ibid., 69, 97, cited 98.

57 Ibid., 125, 138.

58 Jameson, *Marxism and Form*, 307; Cf. Rashley, *Poetry in Canada*, 83–7. Lukács, *History and Class Consciousness*, 176. By 'objective developments' we are to understand the events of history.

59 Cited in Rashley, *Poetry in Canada*, 70, 72.

60 Lukács, *History and Class Consciousness*, 155. The metaphor of the poet as vehicle aligns itself easily with the Marxist tendency to formalize human activity as metonymy. See White, *Metahistory*, 286.

61 Rashley, *Poetry in Canada*, 150, 151, 160; Fischer, *The Necessity of Art*, 224.

62 Klinck, *Giving Canada a Literary History*, 111–12; Klinck, *Literary History of Canada*, 1st ed., xi; David Galloway, ibid., 3.

63 Indeed, as Galloway notes, the Native was more or less elided from Canada in

English literature before the seventeenth century, and 'in the work of several English writers the Spanish conqueror becomes a symbol of the corrupt civilization which degraded natural man' (Galloway, ibid., 17).

64 Klinck, Introduction, *Literary History of Canada*, 1st ed., x, xi.
65 Galloway, ibid., 4; Dante, *The Divine Comedy*, 26: 117; Ovid *Metamorphoseon*, I. 107.
66 See Friedrich, *Dante's Fame Abroad, 1350–1850*, 190; Galloway in Klinck, *Literary History of Canada*, 18.
67 Victor G. Hopwood, in Klinck, *Literary History of Canada*, 2nd ed., 1: 19. (In this instance I have used the later edition because of Hopwood's additions.)
68 The validity of the distinction I leave untested. For the author of this chapter it is a way of making an origin, just as Friedrich Schiller's distinction was for him. See Schiller, *Über naive und sentimentalische Dichtung*. That European epic arose from myth is open to doubt, and the Spanish scholar Ramon Menéndez-Pidal argues that the Old French *La Chanson de Roland* manifests many kinds of intertextual imbrications that locate the song first in history from which the myth is composed. See Menéndez-Pidal, *La Chanson de Roland*.
69 Victor G. Hopwood, in Klinck, *Literary History of Canada*, 2nd ed., 1: 19; Alfred G. Bailey, ibid., 56, 57, 59, 61, 65, 67.
70 Fred Cogswell, ibid., 69.
71 James and Ruth Talman, ibid., 85.
72 Cogswell, ibid., 92, 92.
73 Cogswell, ibid., 98, 102.
74 Cogswell, ibid., 118.
75 Klinck, ibid., 136, 145, 146
76 H. Pearson Gundy, ibid., 188.
77 Roy Daniells, ibid., 191, 193, 194, 194, 198, 205.
78 Gordon Roper, ibid., 273.
79 Brandon Conron, ibid., 338.
80 Daniells, ibid., 426.
81 Frank W. Watt, ibid., 472.
82 Ibid., 457.
83 Desmond Pacey, ibid., 495.
84 Millar MacLure, ibid., 529, 537, 550, 539.
85 Munroe Beattie, ibid., 765, 773.
86 Frye, 'Conclusion,' 821, 822; Frye, *Anatomy of Criticism*, 351; Frye, 'Conclusion,' 823, 824, 825, 828, 829.
87 Frye, 'Conclusion,' 830, 832, 834, 835, 836. It is in this sense that Frye's notion of 'obstacle' converges with Marquis's intuition that to be Canadian

is to live with a 'handicapped' condition (see Marquis, *English Canadian Literature*, 588).

88 Frye, 'Conclusion,' 838, 839–40.

89 Ibid., 842, 847, 848; Frye, *Anatomy of Criticism*, 17.

90 Geoffrey H. Hartman, 'Ghostlier Demarcations: The Sweet Science of Northrop Frye,' *Beyond Formalism*, 33.

91 Frye, 'Conclusion,' 826. Elsewhere Frye observes that 'the past of Canada ... is like the past of a psychiatric patient.' See 'National Consciousness in Canadian Culture,' *Divisions on a Ground*, 48. It is comments like these that give a certain credibility to Linda Hutcheon's argument that Frye, when addressing Canadian literature, has 'perhaps postmodern moments,' and among these would be the ability to suggest, on the one hand, that literature in its autonomy has a history and, on the other, that English-Canadian culture seeks a deliverance from the temporal and contingent. Both notions seem capable of being held simultaneously in suspension, just as all statements in Frye about English Canada pertain to French Canada either through their contrast or similarity. Getting it both ways, as Hutcheon proposes, releases Frye from the oppositional mark of modernism. See 'Frye Recoded,' 111.

92 Frye, 'Conclusion,' 826.

93 Hartman, 'Ghostlier Demarcations,' 33.

94 See Kushner, 'Frye and the Historicity of Literature,' 296–303.

95 Frye, 'Conclusion,' 838; Frye, *The Secular Scripture*, 167.

96 See *The Secular Scripture*, 168–9.

97 Frye, ibid., 824.

98 See Lecker, *Making It Real*, 201.

99 McCourt, *The Canadian West in Fiction*, 55.

100 Sœurs de Sainte-Anne, *Histoire des littératures française et canadienne*, 436–37.

101 White, *Metahistory*, 35.

102 Ibid., 281 286.

103 Turnbull, *Essential Traits of French Poetry*, 19.

Chapter Four. *Notre Maître le Passé*, 1967–1969

1 Merleau-Ponty, *Phénomenologie de la perception*, 229.

2 Cardin, and Couture, *Histoire du Canada*, 275–80; see also Cook, *Canada, Québec, and the Uses of Nationalism*, chapter 8.

3 I say 'modest' primarily because its first edition appeared in a periodical and a second edition esd later republished by HMH (1969).

4 Jean-Charles Falardeau, Introduction to Gay, *Survol de la littérature canadienne-française*, 176–8.

5 Cf. Calvet, *Linguistique et colonialisme*, 51–4, and Cook, *Canada, Québec, and the Uses of Nationalism*, 150–8.

6 A view supported, for example, by Duff Roblin, while premier of Manitoba. See Gagnon, *Quebec and Its Historians*, 29; cf. Baillargeon, *Littérature canadienne-française*, who remarks that the long separation from France resulted in *'l'infantillisme littéraire'* (177).

7 Garneau, cited in Gay, *Survol de la littérature canadienne-française*, 180.

8 Ibid., 180. The full quotation is: 'What though the field be lost? / All is not lost; the unconquerable will, / And study of revenge, immortal hate, / And courage never to submit or yield: / And what is else not to be overcome?' The lines constitute a central parainesis in Satan's first speech (*Paradise Lost* I.105–9).

9 Gay, *Survol de la littérature canadienne-française*, 184, 187.

10 Ibid., 186, 189.

11 Ibid., 191. See Jean Le Moyne, *Convergences*, 89.

12 Gay, *Survol de la littérature canadienne-française*, 193–5.

13 Cook, *Canada, Québec, and the Uses of Nationalism*, 92.

14 Gay, *Survol de la littérature canadienne-française*, 197; Cf. Saul, *Reflections of a Siamese Twin*, 19–23.

15 Gay, *Survol de la littérature canadienne-française*, 203, 205.

16 Ibid., 208, 209.

17 A structuralist argument against the ideological reading that Gay makes of Hémon may be found in Boynard-Frot, *Un Matriarcat en procès*. Hémon's novel is not mentioned as frequently as it might have been; see 98–9.

18 Gay, *Survol de la littérature canadienne-française*, 209, 211.

19 Ibid., 214.

20 Ibid., 11.

21 Ibid., 213.

22 Ibid., 219–20.

23 Ibid., 226.

24 Gay is aware that some themes overlap with others, particularly the first and second. It is also worth noting that in the 1969 edition he modifies his terms, while retaining all the categories but the last.

25 Ibid., 227.

26 The coupling of these two adjectives is revealing, to say the least.

27 Ibid., 230, 231.

28 Ibid., 242.

29 Ibid., 212.

30 Ibid., 262. The quotation comes from an essay first published in 1960 entitled 'Eléments et influences,' in which Le Moyne pays his cultural debt to his
father and the pedagogical formation of the collège classique of which he
was a superb example (Le Moyne, *Convergences*, 17).

31 Prudently, Gay changed the rubric 'L'ENVAHISSEMENT DU ROMAN PAR LA PROSE
ÉTRANGÈRE' to the more acceptable one of 'Les courants mondiaux' in the
next edition, *Notre Littérature*, (1969) 174. The use of italics, which is rare in
Gay, suggests a certain warning, if not a state of alarm.

32 Gay, *Survol de la littérature canadienne-française*, 252, 264.

33 Since Tougas's text was published in Paris, it is examined in chapter 9.

34 Gay, *Survol de la littérature canadienne-française*, 174, 240.

35 Nepveu, *L'Écologie du réel*, 50.

36 Of some interest is the fact that Grandpré identifies himself as 'Directeur
général des Arts et des Lettres au ministère des affaires culturelles du
Quebec.'

37 Grandpré, *Histoire de la littérature française du Québec*, 1: 12.

38 Robidoux and Renaud, *Le Roman canadien-français*, 169–70. It might be
argued that this text is a deliberate dissolution of history designed to structure the evolution of the novel in Quebec as a movement in four steps from
the novel of traditional themes to the *roman de moeurs* and thence to the interior, and finally the poetic novel, as if the genre almost inevitably moved
toward poetry, that is, a semiotic play of signification whose meaning can
only be determined through textual auto-determination.

39 Jauß, *Literaturgeschichte als Provokation*, 144.

40 Grandpré, *Histoire de la littérature française du Québec*, 1: 17, 15, 23, 24.

41 Needless to say, there are as many voices in Klinck as there are authors,
and doubts are also expressed about whether the literature is French
Canadian in the early years, and if it is, whether it amounts to more than
sociology.

42 Vachon, *Histoire de la littérature française du Québec*, 1: 27.

43 Cf. Ricoeur, *Hermeneutics and the Human Sciences* 116: 'Phenomenology begins
when, not content to "live" or "relive," we interrupt lived experience in order
to signify it.'

44 Vachon, *Histoire de la littérature française du Québec*, 1: 31, 31–2, 33.

45 Of these political figures, Papineau is passionately described as a man 'de
stature imposante, d'allure et de comportement aristocratiques' (Arsène
Lauzière and Grandpré, ibid., 1: 150–1) and valorized as the most radical; his
grandson Bourassa is presented as a brilliant orator who dominated provincial nationalist politics from the 1890s until the Second World War (Pierre
Savard and Grandpré, ibid., 2: 150; and Laurier, despite his support of Con-

federation and British imperialism, celebrated as 'un héros pour tout le Canada français' (Savard, ibid., 1: 283). Cf. Falardeau's remarks (ibid., 2: 21).

46 Vachon, *Histoire de la littérature française du Québec*, 1: 41, 35, 36, 40, 41, 42.

47 Vachon and Léopold LeBlanc, ibid., 1: 32, 63–5.

48 Rioux, ibid., 1: 79, 82.

49 Like other histories of French-Canadian literature, although Canada has its foundational moment as a French colony, and in this instance the missionaries are given the fullest credit (LeBlanc, ibid., 1: 57), French Canada as a distinct ethnic culture required a shock of consciousness as an origin. It is not understood merely to happen, as in English Canada; it is in fact self-created. Thus the first chapter under the heading 'Le Romanticisme libéral' is entitled 'Une Affirmation de soi,' ibid., 1: 133.

50 Michel Tétu, ibid., 1: 100. Interestingly, the phrase is ('la formation d'une littérature "canadienne"' (1: 133).

51 Ibid., 1: 137; Lauzière, ibid., 1: 143.

52 Lauzière and Grandpré, ibid., 1: 149.

53 Lauzière, ibid., 1: 143.

54 Lauzière, ibid., 1: 179. This emphasis accounts for the manner in which Conan's *L'Angéline de Montbrun* is canonized as 'le roman le plus littéraire du siècle.' This is because the author's central preoccupation is 'la vie intérieure' (Lauzière, ibid., 1: 251, 252), a criterion unnoticed by Gay but in accord with the discovery of personal intimacy in Canada during the twentieth century and cherished by Robidoux and Renaud, for example.

55 Gay, *Survol de la littérature canadienne-française*, 214.

56 Savard, *Histoire de la littérature française du Québec*, 1: 199, 283.

57 Lauzière, ibid., 1: 244. The use of the definite article with 'avenir' is understandable but still revealing. It is *the* future realized as future in the text that this history completes for the novel.

58 Grandpré, ibid., 2: 7–9.

59 Rioux, ibid., 1: 81. It should be noted that this effected a 'prise de conscience' (ibid., 1: 80).

60 Grandpré, ibid., 2: 8, 10, 12–13. Frégault's significance as a historian of the Montreal School is discussed by Gagnon, *Quebec and Its Historians*, 9–12 et passim.

61 Falardeau, *Histoire de la littérature française du Québec*, 2: 33, 19, 189, 198, 194. As a narrative strategy, one is reminded of the technique of free indirect discourse in the last-cited sentences, if we take Groulx as a character whom Falardeau narrates. The narrator's voice at moments becomes more prominent than that of the character and also draws upon it to empower his own narration.

62 Ibid., 2: 195.

63 Cf. White, *Metahistory*, 285–6.

64 Cited in Savard and Grandpré, ibid., 2: 143.

65 Cf. Baillargeon, *Littérature canadienne-française*, 169.

66 See Jean Éthier-Blais and Grandpré, *Histoire de la littérature française du Québec*, 2: 42.

67 André Renaud and Grandpré, ibid., 2: 121.

68 Georges-Henri d'Auteuil and Grandpré, ibid., 2: 128.

69 Grandpré and Éthier-Blais, ibid., 2: 217, 226.

70 Baillargeon, *Littérature canadienne-française*, 354.

71 Grandpré and Éthier-Blais, *Histoire de la littérature française du Québec*, 2: 230, 236.

72 Robidoux, Renaud, Roger Duhamel, Grandpré, ibid., 2: 250.

73 See Fernand Dumont, ibid., 3: 11. This argument is raised some four years before Harold Bloom's *The Anxiety of Influence* (1973). Lacan's argument concerning the acquisition of the discourse of the symbolic, 'Le Stade du miroir comme formateur du fonction du Je,' appeared in 1936, expanded more than once, and reached its final form in 1951. It has been reprinted in *Écrits*, 93–100. See Introduction, 7–8.

74 Dumont, *Histoire de la littérature française du Québec*, 3: 13, 20, 21, 22.

75 Ricoeur, *Hermeneutics*, 116; Dumont, *Histoire de la littérature française du Québec*, 3: 22.

76 René Garneau, Éthier-Blais, and Grandpré, *Histoire de la littérature française du Québec*, 3: 25, 51, 60.

77 Cited in Grandpré and Michel Van Schendel, ibid., 3: 208.

78 Grandpré and Schendel, ibid., 3: 203, 204.

79 Cited in Grandpré and Schendel, ibid., 3: 214.

80 Cited in Grandpré and Schendel, ibid., 3: 219.

81 Fernand Ouellette (1930–), cited in Grandpré and Schendel, ibid., 3: 252.

82 Grandpré and Schendel, ibid., 3: 205; Grandpré and René Garneau, ibid., 3: 288.

83 'The difficulty of being' is an expression taken by Hubert Aquin from the eighteenth-century philosopher Fontenelle and used in his brilliant essay 'La Fatigue culturelle du Canada français' (1962). The sentence reads: 'Le Canada français, comme Fontenelle sur son lit de mort, ressent "une certaine difficulté d'être."' It has been reprinted in *Blocs erratiques*, 96. It forms a central, if unspoken, theme of Grandpré's history and has been used more explicitly in Purdy's *A Certain Difficulty of Being*.

84 Pilon cited in Grandpré and Garneau, *Histoire de la littérature française du Québec*, 3: 295.

85 Grandpré and Garneau, ibid., 3: 295.
86 Jean-Louis Major and Grandpré, ibid., 4: 129.
87 Merleau-Ponty, *Phénoménologie de la perception*, 506.
88 I use this term with the variety of connotations acquired in New Testament Greek. Although 'time' is its only equivalent in English, it refers to time in certain specificities, that is, the present moment, the right time, a time of crisis, the time of apocalypse, all of which at various moments are appropriate for the sense of time in Grandpré.
89 Merleau-Ponty, *Phénoménologie de la perception*, 74, 75–6.
90 Ibid., 489, 519, 473–4.
91 Ibid., 510–11, 513, 515; cf. 510.
92 Grandpré, *Histoire de la littérature française du Québec* 4: 'Avant-Propos,' n.p. Cf. Vachon, *Histoire de la littérature française du Québec*, I: 33.
93 Baillargeon, *Littérature canadienne-française*, 313.
94 Merleau-Ponty, *Phénoménologie de la perception*, 476, 506.
95 Ibid., 446.
96 I use this rather cumbersome neologism as a way of expressing the manner in which texts in this history compose a kind of syntax of which they are actants.
97 Merleau-Ponty, *Phénoménologie de la perception*, 450.
98 Ibid., 229, 484–5.

Chapter Five. Literary History as *Heilsgeschichte*, 1973–1883

1 Puech, 'Gnosis and Time,' 52.
2 Jones, *Butterfly on Rock*, 3, 6, 183, 184.
3 Ibid., 4. It might be remarked that while Jones's point of departure is to be found in Northrop Frye's 'Conclusion' to the first edition of Klinck's history, and therefore marked by a preoccupation with the thematic of space, there are curious coincidences with the tendency toward apocalypse found in Frye and the quest for origin that marks the Hexagone poets.
4 *Butterfly on Rock* is primarily a critical, not an historical, text, and for this reason I have not included it in this study. His argument addresses the 'transition from a garrison culture to one in which the Canadian feels at home in his world' (7), as exemplified in contemporary prose and poetry.
5 Ibid., 184.
6 O'Donovan, *George Grant and the Twilight of Justice*, 162 et passim.
7 Waterston, *Survey*, 1–3.
8 Ibid., 5. Needless to say, this is a misreading of Sheila Watson's use of the metaphor of the double hook. For her, no choice is possible: even if glory is

caught, so is darkness. See Watson, *The Double Hook*, 55. Therefore, the binary opposition of interior and exterior space cannot be so neatly posed.

9 Waterston, *Survey*, 3, 26, 30.

10 Ibid., 3, 172; cf. 177.

11 Ibid., 177. Lortie, *La Poésie nationaliste*, 12, 16–17, 23; cf. 32.

12 Ibid., 1.

13 Ibid., 11n6.

14 Ibid., 70. The appeal to a collective, as we observed in the last chapter, is a necessary performative gesture of the literary history of a nation.

15 Ibid., 71.

16 Ibid., 50, 51.

17 Ibid., 67, 89, 119, 52.

18 Ibid., 15, 22, cited 90n29.

19 Ibid., 173.

20 Cited ibid., 69.

21 Ibid., 169.

22 Ibid., 270, 245.

23 Ibid., 273, 267; cf. 364.

24 *La Capricieuse* was the first French ship to arrive in Quebec after the Conquest. Its arrival was part of the entente in Anglo-French relations established in 1854.

25 Lortie, *La Poésie nationaliste*, 463.

26 Ibid.; cf. 14.

27 The British response, Durham's Report, and the Act of Union, are presented as tantamount to a death knell, condemning the nation to silence (ibid., 222–7).

28 Harrison does not, however, exclude American fiction as a reference and in fact draws upon it to make useful distinctions. Cf. Harrison, *Unnamed Country*, 76–8. He also wishes to distinguish prairie fiction from British, Western American, and Eastern Canadian literature (xiv).

29 Owram, *Promise of Eden*, 126, 134.

30 For example, Frederick Turner, *Beyond Geography: The Western Spirit against the Wilderness* (1980), and Tzvetan Todorov, *La Conquête de l'Amérique: La Question de l'autre* (1982) are contemporaneous.

31 Cf. Ashcroft, Griffiths, and Tiffin, *The Empire Writes Back*, 17–18.

32 Harrison, *Unnamed Country*, xiii; Ashcroft, Griffiths, and Tiffin, *The Empire Writes Back*, 23–7.

33 Harrison, *Unnamed Country*, 30.

34 Ibid.; cf. 38 et passim.

35 Ibid., 45.

36 See ibid., 156 and 164.

37 Ibid., 213. Although Kroetsch's German background and Wiebe's Menno-
nite background are sometimes overlooked, their ethnic position is still a
matter of fact. Needless to say, the use of First Nations people in the work of
Laurence, Mitchell, Kroetsch, and Wiebe expose them to general charges of
cultural appropriation, a point not taken up in Harrison.

38 Ibid., 6, 14, 152, 153. I do not wish to imply that a sense of natural cycle is
absent from French-Canadian writing. The structure of Ringuet's *Trente
Arpents* is notable in this respect. Nature, however, is not an informing structure of French-Canadian literary history.

39 Ibid., 181.

40 Ibid., 205. Time and history as myth in the Western imaginary is well attested
in two cultural critics who preceded Harrison. Stegner, *Wolf Willow*, Kreisel,
'The Prairie: A State of Mind,' Ricou, *Vertical Man / Horizontal World*, followed him. See especially Woodcock, *The Meeting of Time and Space*, 33.

41 Cited in Harrison, *Unnamed Country*, 189, 190.

42 Ibid., 190, 199.

43 Ibid., 200.

44 Ibid., 209.

45 Frye, *Anatomy of Criticism*, 239; Harrison, *Unnamed Country*, 213.

46 See, for example, Sutherland, *Second Image*, 60.

47 Cf. Frye, *Divisions on a Ground*, 47–52.

48 Austin defines these terms as follows: 'We also perform *illocutionary* acts such
as informing, ordering, warning, undertaking ... we may also perform *perlu-
tionary* acts: what we bring about or achieve *by* saying something.' See *How to
Do Things with Words*, 109.

49 Collingwood, *The Idea of History*, 50–2.

50 Kroetsch, *The Lovely Treachery of Words*, 58.

51 Ibid., 63. I know that in the article I am drawing upon, Kroetsch remarks that
when Canadians are 'offered the consolation and pride of the old names ...
[they] will "decline to be Christened"' (ibid., 63). Nevertheless, they will
make a move from the old to the new, which can be construed as a Pauline
perlocution in another guise.

52 Craig, *Lord Durham's Report*, 150.

53 Cf. Purdy, *A Certain Difficulty of Being*, 104.

54 Cf. Ashcroft, Griffiths, and Tiffin, *The Empire Writes Back*, 41. Although they
cite the same article from Kroetsch as I as an example of such abrogation, I
am placing a similar desire into different discursive and epistemological contexts.

55 Harrison, *Unnamed Country*, xii, xiii–xiv.

56 Cited in O'Flaherty, *The Rock Observed*, 15.

57 Ibid., ix.

58 Ibid., 31, 171, 180, 125, 166.

59 Ibid., 125, 125.

60 Ibid., 57, 60, 66, 67, 68–9.

61 Ibid., 185, 186, 187.

62 Cited in Collingwood, *The Idea of History*, 130.

63 O'Flaherty, *The Rock Observed*, 26, 91.

64 Dante, *The Divine Comedy*, XXX, 94–9.

65 O'Flaherty, *The Rock Observed*, 5, 87; Frye, *Anatomy of Criticism*, 169.

66 White, *Metahistory*, 190.

67 O'Flaherty, *The Rock Observed*, 42.

68 Ibid., 3.

69 Marshall, *Harsh and Lovely Land*, xii; White, *Metahistory*, 177.

70 Marshall, *Harsh and Lovely Land*, xiii–xiv.

71 Ibid., xi, 43, 55 et passim.

72 Ibid., 125.

73 Ibid., 126, 125, 91.

74 Ibid., 89, 90.

75 On Heraclitus, see Kirk, Raven, and Schofield, *The Presocratic Philosophers*, 185–6, 190–1.

76 Marshall, *Harsh and Lovely Land*, 178.

77 Cf. Kirk, Raven, and Schofield, *The Presocratic Philosophers*, Frag. 54, 192.

78 Marshall, *Harsh and Lovely Land*, 178.

79 The expression is John Glassco's and used as the title of a useful introduction to this aspect of the wider Canadian problem in an article by Kathy Mezei entitled, 'A Bridge of Sorts: The Translation of Quebec Literature into English.'

80 Cf. Russell Brown, *Borderlines and Borderlands in English Canada*; McLuhan, 'Canada: The Borderline Case.'

81 Moisan, *Poésie des frontières*, 7–8.

82 Ibid., 26.

83 Ibid., 93, 131, 148, 56.

84 Ibid., 287; Jones, *Butterfly on Rock*, 183; Moisan, *Poésie des frontières*, 277, 279. As Moisan observes, echoing this not infrequent phrase in Québécois literary history, the ability to overcome the impossibility of living may be attributed to a 'prise de conscience' (278).

85 Moisan, *Poésie des frontières*, 179. Not surprisingly, the English translation of Moisan's text elides the emphasis on 'History.' See *A Poetry of Frontiers*, 177.

86 Jones, *Butterfly on Rock*, 137.

87 White, *Metahistory,* 119; Moisan, *Poésie des frontières,* 8, 287.

88 Marshall, *Harsh and Lovely Land,* 4, 5; cf. Austin, *How to Do Things with Words,* 98.

89 Lortie, *La Poésie nationaliste,* 273.

90 Maillet, *Histoire de la littérature acadienne,* 176. It is not particularly clear why Maillet locates 1957 as the significant year that closes the period of memory, when her text eloquently suggests that the earlier (1955) is more significant. It is implied that 1958 is the proper year to *begin* the final section, inasmuch as in that year novelist and playwright Antonine Maillet (1929–) began her project which would 'récuperer la petite histoire de son pays et fixer les traditions populaires acadiennes trop longtemps délaissées au profit de l'événement de 1755 et des traditions dites nationales' (182).

91 Maillet, *Histoire de la littérature acadienne,* 16, 17.

92 Ibid., 36, 10; Perkins, *Is Literary History Possible?* 39.

93 Cf. Maillet, *Histoire de la littérature acadienne,* 183 et passim.

94 Ibid., 49; Blodgett, 'Translated Literature and the Polysystem,' 157–68; Martin, *L'Évangéline de Longfellow,* 218.

95 I have called attention to the verb because literary history is primarily auto-representation: it shows itself as it functions and, as a consequence, represents texts in a certain semantic relationship. Literary history is frequently 'about' the way it makes itself work.

96 Cited in Maillet, *Histoire de la littérature acadienne,* 196, 58.

97 White, *Metahistory,* 335–6.

98 Maillet, *Histoire de la littérature acadienne,* 196.

99 White, *Metahistory,* 67, 72; Frye, *Anatomy of Criticism,* 238.

100 See Maillet, *Histoire de la littérature acadienne,* 186, 191.

101 One must assume that the name was used to indicate a place of classical splendour, a *locus amoenus* in its fullest sense. When one considers Maillet's reflections on her Acadia, which began as Arcadia, through the lens of Panofsky's essay, '*Et in Arcadia ego:* On the Conception of Transience in Poussin and Watteau,' new irony is added to her treatment of nation and literature as dream and, indeed, elegy.

102 Morison, *Samuel de Champlain,* 35; Craig Brown, *The Illustrated History of Canada,* 124.

103 Maillet, *Histoire de la littérature acadienne,* 197.

104 Roey-Roux, *La Littérature intime du Québec,* 14; cf. Neuman, 'Life Writing,' 334.

105 Roey-Roux, *La Littérature intime du Québec,* 17, 18, 15, 8.

106 The question of authorship is also implicitly problematized the moment the personal speaks for a collective,

107 See ibid., 18. No mention is made of either St Augustine's *Confessions* or Petrarch's *Secretum meum.*
108 Roey-Roux, *La Littérature intime du Québec*, 29, 16.
109 See ibid., 61.
110 Ibid., 144.
111 See ibid., 147, 148.
112 Cf. Fowler, *Kinds of Literature*, chapter 12.
113 Roey-Roux, *La Littérature intime du Québec*, 147, 209–10.
114 Maillet, *Histoire de la litterature acadienne*, 10.

Chapter Six. Autonomy, Literature, and the National, 1991–

1 Gabrielle Poulin in Dionne, *Le Québécois et sa littérature*, 121.
2 The Accord was reached by the provincial premiers and the federal government in 1987. It failed to achieve unanimous agreement in 1990. Section 2 dealt with recognition of Quebec as a distinct society, which would allow the province to develop in French as a self-defining culture with reference to anglophone Canada. The implicit complications of the section are discussed in Cook, *Canada, Québec, and the Uses of Nationalism*, chapter 11.
3 For a discussion of its appeal to Quebec, see McRoberts, *Misconceiving Canada*, 195–6.
4 The point is made specifically about Stanley Fish. See Hohendahl, *Building a National Literature*, 13.
5 Ibid., 34.
6 Although to simplify matters I refer to *La Vie littéraire au Québec* as 'Lemire's history,' it should be borne in mind that, unlike those edited by Klinck and Grandpré, this is a genuinely collaborative text in which one style is achieved by a team of scholars who do not leave their signatures on individual sections.
7 Moisan, *Qu'est-ce que l'histoire littéraire?* 231; Maria Corti cited in Rosa, *Letteratura italiana*, 1:18.
8 Lemire et al., *La Vie littéraire au Québec*, 1: vii. To date, four volumes have been published, the last of which covers the years 1870–94. It appeared while this book was being prepared for publication and therefore too late to give it the attention it deserves.
9 Ibid., xii.
10 Said, *Beginnings*, 42.
11 Lemire et al., *La Vie littéraire au Québec*, 2: 463; Hémon, *Maria Chapdelaine*, 197; cf. Robidoux and Renaud, *Le Roman canadien-français*, 30–43.
12 Lemire et al., *La Vie littéraire au Québec*, 1: 68; cf. 1:73.

13 Ibid., 1: 2.

14 Ibid., 1: 9–23.

15 However the title was decided upon, it is more effective than, for example, *Le Champ littéraire au Québec*, and certainly better than the working title, which was *Constitution de la littérature québécoise: Histoire des processus de légitimation et d'autonomisation de la littérature dans sa production, son discours et sa réception.* See Saint-Jacques, 'Nationalisation et autonomisation,' 243.

16 Cf. Moisan, 'L'Histoire littéraire comme discours scientifique,' 27.

17 Bourdieu, *The Field of Cultural Production*, 54.

18 Ibid., 30.

19 Denis Saint-Jacques, 'L'Envers de l'institution' in Lemire, *L'Institution littéraire*, 44.

20 Ibid., 45, 47,

21 Denis Saint-Jacques, 'Nationalisation et autonomisation,' in Moisan, *Histoire littéraire*, 242, 243, 244, 245; cf. Lemire, *La Littérature québécoise*, chapter 9.

22 Bourdieu, *The Field of Cultural Production*, 112, 112, 113.

23 Saint-Jacques, 'Nationalisation et autonomisation,' 245–6; cf. Lemire et al., *La Vie littéraire au Québec*, 1: ix.

24 Mailhot, 'Problèmes de périodisation,' 112.

25 Lemire et al., *La Vie littéraire au Québec*, 1: 73.

26 Ibid., 1: 122.

27 Ibid., 1: 130, 159.

28 Ibid., 1: 162.

29 See ibid., 1: 161–80.

30 Ibid., 1: 181.

31 Ibid., 1: 224 (citing *Nos Origines littéraires*, 87).

32 Ibid., 1: 228, 234, 253.

33 Ibid., 1: 290.

34 Ibid., 1: 294, 295.

35 Ibid., 1: 309.

36 Ibid., 1: 320.

37 Ibid., 1: 336.

38 Ibid., 1: 341, 345.

39 Ibid., 1: 351.

40 Ibid., 1: 356.

41 Ibid., 1: 389, 390, 390.

42 Ibid., 2: xii.

43 Ibid., 2: 7.

44 Ibid., 2: 11, 13–14, 20.

45 Ibid., 2: 35, 35; cf. ibid., 3, ed. Lemire and Saint-Jacques, 258.

46 With rare exceptions – Camille Roy comes to mind – the Church in Quebec
was not often on the side of an emerging middle-class nationalism. As Yvan
Lamonde argues, 'Au Canada, par un curieux retour de choses, il appert que
la religion devient un moyen de marginaliser une langue, une culture'
(*Allégeances et Dépendances: L'Histoire d'une ambivalence identitaire* [Québec:
Éditions Nota Bene, 2001], 221). This was the result of a policy, supported by
the Vatican, that encouraged English as the dominant North American language. It constitutes an interesting exception to the argument developed by
Adrian Hastings in *The Construction of Nationhood*. I have elaborated on this
question at greater length in 'Literary History in Canada and National Identity Formation.'

47 Lemire et al., *La Vie littéraire au Québec*, 2: 51, 52.

48 Ibid., 2: 60. Although Baillargeon's history turns upon, and is motivated by,
crisis, the same could not be said for *La Vie littéraire au Québec* in which crises
do not possess the same sense of trauma. They are drawn into the field in a
far less disarming fashion.

49 Lemire et al., *La Vie littéraire au Québec*, 2: 75, 475.

50 In fact for Benedetto Croce the nineteenth century 'era per eccellenza il
secolo della storia.' See his *Storia della storiographia italiana*, 18.

51 Lemire et al., *La Vie littéraire au Québec*, 2: 223, 224; Craig, *Lord Durham's
Report*, 150, 151.

52 Lemire et al., *La Vie littéraire au Québec*, 2: 107, 154, 204, 475.

53 Ibid., 3, Lemire and Saint-Jacques, 249 (cf. 338), 266; for a historian's discussion of the subsequent editions, see Gagnon, *Le Québec et ses historiens*, 321–4,
which makes fewer references to actual emendations.

54 Ibid., 3: 345 (cf. 263), 345, 488; 2: 87 et passim.

55 See the discussion, ibid., 3: 529; cf. the *Présentation* 3: x–xi.

56 Ibid., 1: vii.

57 Ibid., 2: 317; ibid., 3: 526.

58 De Sanctis, *Storia della letteratura italiana*, 2: 438, 446; on Vico, see 2: 334; as
Croce affirms, Hegel predominates. See his *Æsthetic as Science of Expression
and General Linguistic*, 359–60.

Chapter Seven. The Question of Alterity

1 A saying among South Slavic immigrants, which I owe to Srdja Pavlović, an
associate editor of the British periodical, *Stone Soup*.

2 King, *Green Grass, Running Water*, 1.

3 *Report of the Royal Commission on Bilingualism and Biculturalism*, 1: xxxiv.

4 See Boudreau, *Histoire de la littérature amérindienne au Québec*, 15.

5 *Report of the Royal Commission on Bilingualism and Biculturalism*, 1: 26.

6 The expression may be attributed to Enoch Padolsky, and a brief critique of its implications has been made by Pivato, *Echo*, 47.

7 Padolsky, 'Canadian Minority Writing,' 608.

8 Deleuze and Guattari, *Kafka*, chapter 3; Cf. Blodgett, 'Towards an Ethnic Style,' 623–6.

9 Kreisel, 'The "Ethnic" Writer in Canada,' 1; cf. Blodgett, 'Ethnic Writing in Canada as Paratext,' 19–20.

10 Said, *Beginnings*, 42, 43.

11 I am indebted to Joseph Pugliese's discussion of Australian literary history in 'Literary Histories and the Ontologies of Nation.'

12 An exception to this is W.H. New's history, for example, which is considered in the following chapter.

13 Cited in Lowenthal, *The Past Is a Foreign Country*, xvi.

14 Gobard, *L'Aliénation linguistique*, 26–7.

15 Możejko, 'Ethnic or National (?): Polish Literature in Canada,' 810.

16 Greenstein, *Third Solitudes*, 12; This origin may also be attributed to the fact that Mandryka was born in Ukraine and, as Jars Balan notes, 'was dispatched to Canada in 1928 by the Ukrainian Party of Socialist Revolutionaries.' Evidently his sense of the revolution changed considerably in the forty years between his immigration and the history, and only his nationalism remained. See Balan's article, 'Ukrainian-Canadian Literature' in *The Oxford Companion to Canadian Literature*, 1146.

17 Mandryka, *History of Ukrainian Literature in Canada*, 14.

18 Mandryka, *History of Ukrainian Literature in Canada*, 17, 19; Mirsky, *A History of Russian Literature*, 16; Mandryka, *History of Ukrainian Literature in Canada*, 24.

19 Mandryka, *History of Ukrainian Literature in Canada*, 50.

20 Ibid., 33, 51, 54, 31.

21 Ibid., 45.

22 See Balan, 'Ukrainian-Canadian Literature,' *Oxford Companion to Canadian Literature*, 1144.

23 Mandryka, *History of Ukrainian Literature in Canada*, 58, 111.

24 Ibid., 71, 167–8, 181, 185. Zujewskyj's absence from Mandryka's history is not surprising, inasmuch as his modernist poetics and antipathy to nationalism were so vigorous that Mandryka chose (and I must assume he knew of his work, despite the fact that he did not immigrate to Canada until 1966) to be indifferent. His towering eminence in Ukrainian-Canadian literature is now thoroughly assured (see Nazarenko, 'To Pass through on One's Wings'), as well as Grabowicz, 'Ukrainian Poetry,' where he is replaced in

the Ukrainian literary system and considered 'outstanding among a range of poets of the middle generation' (1337).

25 Mandryka, *History of Ukrainian Literature in Canada*, 72, 94.

26 Ibid., 240.

27 Ibid., 240, 239; White, *Metahistory*, 70–9.

28 Padolsky, 'Canadian Minority Writing,' 609; cf. Balan, 'Some Notes toward the Writing of the Ukrainian Literary Institution in Canada,' 752.

29 As I have already argued, beginnings in catastrophe place both native and immigrant writing on a shared plane of perception. Needless to say, the shared cultural origins of all European settlers, no matter when they arrived, creates stronger cultural bonds and allows for more rapid assimilation or integration when desired. Nevertheless, the construction of history is closer between native people and immigrant writers, especially to the extent that language, which is the steward of culture, is always at risk in Canada outside French and English. Finally, as a Polish journalist, Wojciech Węcław, once remarked to me on this matter, it seemed to him that native writers were exiled just as much as immigrants, such that 'they are in a sense immigrants.'

30 McGrath, *Canadian Inuit Literature*, 9.

31 Ibid., 15; see Zumthor, *La Lettre et la voix*, 107–9.

32 McGrath, *Canadian Inuit Literature*, 16, 19, 24, 44, 117.

33 Cited in ibid., 43; cf. 44.

34 Unfortunately, as McGrath notes, it is more the property of the transcribers and 'not yet easily available to Inuit' (116).

35 Ibid., 59, 65.

36 Illich, *In the Vineyard of the Text*, 25; cf. McGrath, *Canadian Inuit Literature*, 84.

37 McGrath, *Canadian Inuit Literature*, 92, 96, 95.

38 Two histories of Hungarian-Canadian literature have recently been written. The other by Miska (*Literature of Hungarian Canadians*) provides a brief introduction to the major genres and themes but is mostly useful for its abundant bibliography. That there are two is noteworthy since the number of Hungarian immigrants to Canada, relative to other European nationalities, is not large enough to find a place in the Table of Ethnic Origins provided by New in *A History of Canadian Literature*, 220.

39 Bisztray, *Hungarian-Canadian Literature*, 3; cf. Blodgett, 'Ethnic Writing in Canada as Paratext,' 26n2.

40 Bisztray, *Hungarian-Canadian Literature*, 8.

41 Ibid., 5, 13, 14.

42 Ibid., 18, 20, 22, 24.

43 Cf. ibid., 14.

44 Ibid., 40, 41, 41.

45 Ibid., 54, 37, 50.

46 Ibid., 43, 49, 68, 72.

47 Ibid., 74, 74.

48 Greenstein, *Third Solitudes*, 199, 91, 18.

49 See ibid., 8–9; Handelman, *The Slayers of Moses*, 137, 137, 223.

50 Said, *Beginnings*, 316; Greenstein, *Third Solitudes*, 34.

51 Greenstein, *Third Solitudes*, 35, 48; Handelman, *The Slayers of Moses*, 138.

52 Greenstein, *Third Solitudes*, 67, 86.

53 Ibid., 171, 164; Handelman, *The Slayers of Moses*, 137.

54 See Petrone, *Native Literature in Canada*, 35; needless to say, writing occurred somewhat earlier among francophone natives. See Boudreau, *Histoire de la littérature amérindienne au Québec*, 75–7.

55 Cf. Boudreau, *Histoire de la littérature amérindienne au Québec*, 88.

56 Petrone, *Native Literature in Canada*, 69; Wilson's poem, cited 68, was published in the *The Christian Guardian*, 23 May 1838.

57 Ibid., 69, 12, 16, 114; part of Petrone's own ambivalence on the significance of autobiography for native writers is that she argues that it is at once 'alien to an oral heritage where the communal and collective were celebrated' and designed to accommodate these same values (70).

58 Boudreau, *Histoire de la littérature amérindienne au Québec*, 134; McGrath, *Canadian Inuit Literature*, 91.

59 English Canadian is an expression, as I have been at pains to argue, that has no fixed denotation. English is the language of domination in Canada, as well as the United States, but not all who use it are in a dominant position.

60 Cf. Boudreau, *Histoire de la littérature amérindienne au Québec*, 91.

61 Cf. for example, King, 'Godzilla vs. Post-Colonial,' 10–16.

62 Petrone, *Native Literature in Canada*, 182.

63 Ibid., 3; as Leslie Monkman argues in *A Native Heritage*, the tradition was kept alive in English-Canadian writing.

64 Cf. Ashcroft, Griffiths, and Tiffin, *The Empire Writes Back*, 28.

65 Boudreau, *Histoire de la littérature amérindienne au Québec*, 180.

66 Ibid., 15, 45.

67 Like most generalizations, this one has its weaknesses. It would not be difficult to marshal a number of European mystical discourses from St Bonaventure (e.g., the *Itinerarium Mentis in Deum*) to Cabeza de Vaca (see Long, *The Marvellous Adventure of Cabeza de Vaca*) as exceptions, but Europe did not send such exceptions to North America in large numbers.

68 White, *Metahistory*, 36.

69 Deleuze and Guattari, *Kafka*, 18, 82.

70 Cf. Boudreau, *Histoire de la littérature amérindienne au Québec*, 100, 139; the sig-

nificance of 'hybridity' as a significant aspect of colonial conditions is carefully discussed in Loomba, *Colonialism/Postcolonialism*, 173–83.

71 Hébert, *Le Torrent*, 9.

72 Boudreau, *Histoire de la littérature amérindienne au Québec*, 111.

73 Penny Petrone has been made an honorary chief of the Ojibwa First Nation, and a number of native representatives supported Diane Boudreau's research.

74 I say this with certain reservations. Clearly Petrone depends upon periodization to a greater extent than McGrath and Boudreau, and Boudreau argues against it (*Histoire de la littérature amérindienne au Québec*, 98). She too, however, makes use of significant dates that affect native culture in Quebec, notably, education policies (1952) and the White Paper (1969).

75 Said, *Orientalism*, 273, 272.

76 See, for example, Gilbert and Gubar, *The Madwoman in the Attic*.

77 Neuman, 'Life Writing, 333; Buss, *Mapping Our Selves*, 17.

Chapter Eight. Canada as Alterity

1 Cf. John Frow, *Marxism and Literary History*, 76–7.

2 Rossel, *Histoire de la littérature française hors de France*, 1, 2; cf. Schrimpf, *Goethes Begriff der Weltliteratur*, 29–30. A more general discussion of the implications of Goethe's term may be found in Brunel and Chevrel, *Précis de la littérature comparée*, 24–6.

3 Rossel, *Histoire de la littérature française hors de France*, 2, 3; cf. Schrimpf, *Goethes Begriff der Weltliteratur*, 29.

4 Rossel, *Histoire de la littérature française hors de France*, 5; Eckermann, *Gespräche mit Goethe*, 198.

5 Rossel, *Histoire de la littérature française hors de France*, 7–8.

6 Ibid., 18, 285; cf. Dionne, *Le Québécois et sa littérature*, 39, and *La Vie littéraire au Québec*, ed. Lemire and Saint-Jacques, 4: 276.

7 Rossel, *Histoire de la littérature française hors de France*, 303.

8 The absence of an interest in sermons that is otherwise evident in French-Canadian literary history cannot be overlooked.

9 Rossel, *Histoire de la littérature française hors de France*, 329.

10 Ibid., 332, 333.

11 Ibid., 334, 337.

12 Ibid., 346, 348, 351, 354.

13 Ibid., 3.

14 Unlike most literary historians, Léger did not lead a quiet, academic life. He was a well-known diplomat whose career was crowned by becoming the Gov-

ernor General from 1974 to 1979. His brother was the eminent cardinal Paul-Émile Léger.

15 Léger, *Le Canada français*, 5.

16 Cf. Ashcroft, Griffiths, and Tiffin, *The Empire Writes Back*, 133.

17 Léger, *Le Canada français*, 36; see Monière, *Le Développement des idéologies au Québec*, 289.

18 Léger, *Le Canada français*, 43.

19 Ibid., 49.

20 Ibid., 10, 191; cf. 145 et passim.

21 Ibid., 91.

22 Cf. Cardin and Couture, *Histoire du Canada*, 266.

23 Unfortunately, Tougas does not mention Léger.

24 Léger, *Le Canada français*, 95, 94.

25 Ibid., 117; cf. 306n1.

26 Léger, *Le Canada français*, 118, 180, 96.

27 See Fergusson's chapter on Racine's *Bérénice* in his *The Idea of a Theater*, 42–67.

28 Léger, *Le Canada français*, 9. The full quotation has been elided, especially the future clause, alleviating some its force. It should read: 'Au pays de Québec rien n'a changé. Rien ne changera, parce que nous sommes un témoinage' (Hémon, *Maria Chapdelaine*, 198); Léger, *Le Canada français*, 10.

29 Léger, *Le Canada français*, 195.

30 Viatte, *Histoire littéraire de l'Amérique française*, 29.

31 Ibid., 54; cf. Lemire et al., *La Vie littéraire au Québec*, 1: 133, discussed in chapter 6.

32 See Viatte, *Histoire littéraire de l'Amérique française*, 71–2. Is Garneau, however, typical of a what might be called Canada's Biedermeyer period? The apparently paradoxical mingling of Voltaire and the romantic are noted in Nemoianu, *The Taming of Romanticism*, 207.

33 Viatte, *Histoire littéraire de l'Amérique française*, 74.

34 Ibid., 97.

35 Ibid., 102.

36 The kinds of texts available to the interested French-Canadian reader in the nineteenth century are discussed by Dostaler, *Les Infortunes du roman dans le Québec du XIXe siècle*, 11–42.

37 Viatte, *Histoire littéraire de l'Amérique française*, 125.

38 Cf. ibid., 137–8; see 313n87.

39 Ibid., 160, cited 172.

40 Ibid., 159, 215.

41 Ibid., 215, 202, 203.

42 *The Oxford Companion to Canadian Theatre*, 228.

43 Viatte, *Histoire littéraire de l'Amérique française*, 205.

44 White, *Metahistory*, 190; Viatte, *Histoire littéraire de l'Amérique française*, 516, 517.

45 A similar thesis is developed in Viatte's subsequent study, *Histoire comparée des littératures francophones*, which includes the francophone literatures of Africa and the Orient. The theme of autonomy is pursued, but the structure of the argument prevents a clear discernment of difference because of the synchronic treatment of the several literatures and the sense of parallelism which it produces.

46 See Tougas, *Histoire de la littérature canadienne française*, 13. Tougas later extended his full respect in *Les Écrivains d'expression française et la France*, 196.

47 Tougas, *Histoire de la littérature canadienne française*, 16.

48 The term is used in passing much later in the book (172).

49 Ibid., 21, 25.

50 Tougas prefers to ignore Léger's assertions that autonomy, as we discussed it earlier, is not of significance.

51 Ibid., 35.

52 My reading of the notion of struggle differs somewhat from that of Clément Moisan only because I place it in a different context. See Moisan, 'L'Histoire littéraire comme texte,' 87.

53 Tougas, *Histoire de la littérature canadienne française*, 168, 66. The measure of how much has changed in Quebec since the book was published is one of Tougas's summary remarks that the survival of French-Canadian culture is assured by the presence of religious feeling (ibid., 266).

54 Ibid., 225.

55 Ibid., 125.

56 The many issues surrounding the 'small' in literature are raised in Paré's searching text, *Les littératures de l'exiguité*.

57 Tougas, *Histoire de la littérature canadienne française*, 251, 256, 262, 266.

58 It could be argued that the introduction is too slight to be worthy of consideration. We have already made use, however, of English-Canadian anthologies from the nineteenth century, which bear as much upon the English-Canadian literary institution as Kloss's text does upon that of ethnic minority writing.

59 Kloss, *Ahornblätter*. The notion of community is given as the seventh and eighth items in his summary of the literature as a whole (40).

60 Ibid., 38, 39.

61 Cited in ibid., 55.

Chapter Nine. Canada by Canadians for Europeans, 1974–1989

1 Gallant, *Home Truths*, xiii.
2 Cf. Cardin and Couture, *Histoire du Canada*, 282.
3 Mailhot, *La Littérature québécoise*, 5, 5, 7.
4 Ibid., 7, 10.
5 Ibid., 27, 43. The First World War, passed over in a phrase, did not seem to have the same impact as it did upon English-Canadian culture other than to condense living space. Its importance in the creation of an English-Canadian sense of identity is developed admirably in Vance, *Death So Noble.*
6 Saussure, *Cours de linguistic général,* 30; Mailhot, *La Littérature québécoise,* 73, cited 51.
7 It is so unforgettable that Mailhot casually draws upon it without citing an author, giving it a kind of gnomic validity. See Hébert, *Poèmes,* 71; cited in Mailhot, *La Littérature québécoise,* 71.
8 Mailhot, *La Littérature québécoise,* 121.
9 Dionne, *Le Québécois et sa littérature,* 9, 10.
10 Ibid., 30.
11 Ibid., 12.
12 Foucault, *L'Archéologie du savoir,* 74.
13 Nevertheless, he emphatically asserts that 1840 was a watershed that divided the federalist from the sovereigntist position. See Séguin, *L'Idée d'indépendance au Québec,* 9.
14 Cf. Gagnon, *Quebec and its Historians,* 7.
15 Robert Saint-Amour, in Dionne, *Le Québécois et sa littérature,* 341.
16 Dionne, *Le Québécois et sa littérature,* 33, 33; I refer to Irigaray, *Ce Sexe qui n'en est pas un.*
17 Dionne, *Le Québécois et sa littérature,* 35, 35; see Gagnon, *Le Québec et ses historiens,* 320.
18 Cited in Dionne, *Le Québécois et sa littérature,* 38, 45.
19 Léopold Leblanc, ibid., 60.
20 The decisive year chosen for literature, as opposed to its anticipation in periodicals, is 1839.
21 Gabrielle Poulin, ibid., 117, 121, 126.
22 Poulin, ibid., 126, 127.
23 On the role of poetry and the 'destin collectif de la nation,' cf. Paré, *Les Littératures de l'exiguité,* 101.
24 David Hayne, in Dionne, *Le Québécois et sa littérature,* 134, 151.

25 Gérard-Claude Fournier, ibid., 195.

26 André-G. Bourassa, ibid., 259.

27 Robert Vigneault, ibid., 280, 282, 292, 293.

28 Dionne, ibid., 9, 45.

29 Keith, *Canadian Literature in English*, x.

30 See Eagleton, *Literary Theory*, 27–30.

31 Cited in Keith, 'The Function of Canadian Criticism at the Present Time,' 2, 7 (cf. Keith, *Canadian Literature in English*, 6), Keith, 'The Function of Canadian Criticism at the Present Time,' 10.

32 Keith, 'The Function of Criticism at the Present Time,' 12, 13, 14.

33 Keith, *Canadian Literature in English*, 8.

34 Ibid., xi, 1, 2, 3.

35 Ibid., 3, 4, 5, 9.

36 Ibid., 5.

37 Ibid., 121; the distinction between 'transition' and 'continuity' is shown, in fact, to be gratuitous, inasmuch as D.C. Scott is also both transitional and the end of an earlier period (ibid., 53).

38 Ibid., 53.

39 Ibid., 13, 14, 31, 40.

40 Ibid., 40, 3.

41 Ibid., 60, 111, 116, 102.

42 Ibid., 127; the expression is used more than once in various ways in Arnold's 'The Study of Poetry, 237 et passim, an essay which serves as on of many models for Keith's history.

43 Keith, *Canadian Literature in English*, 133. Although Kroetsch tends, for example, toward the idiosyncratic, it is balanced by the 'authentic' (ibid., 165).

44 Ibid., 8, 162, 164.

45 Arnold, *Culture and Anarchy*, 140; cf. 44; Keith, *Canadian Literature in English*, 160, 165, 170, 157.

46 For a resistant reading, especially of the post-modern, see Hutcheon, *The Canadian Postmodern*, 183.

47 See Keith, *Canadian Literature in English*, 207; Grant can, of course, be read in another way. See Blodgett, 'George Grant, the Uncertain Nation and Diversity of Being,' 107–23.

48 Keith, *Canadian Literature in English*, 93.

49 Arnold, 'The Function Criticism at the Present Time,' 32; 'The Study of Poetry,' 249; *Culture and Anarchy*, 44–5.

50 Cf. Collingwood, *The Idea of History*, 20–1.

51 Arnold, 'The Study of Poetry,' 240; Cf. *Culture and Anarchy*, 150.

52 New, *A History of Canadian Literature*, 1, 2, 3.

53 Ibid., 24. This is the nearest New comes to referring to Jurij Tynjanov's theory of literary evolution as expressed in 'On Literary Evolution.' See Tynjanov, 'The Literary Evolution,' 66–78.

54 To insist, as I have, on the English series of which this history is a part may appear otiose, but it is not distributed by any publisher in Canada, which limits its accessibility considerably.

55 New, *A History of Canadian Literature*, 24, 26, 27.

56 See ibid., 38–46.

57 Cf. Hutcheon's decision, based on 'an unwillingness ... to obscure ... the important differences between French- and English-Canadian culture and literary history.' See her *The Canadian Postmodern*, ix.

58 New, *A History of Canadian Literature*, 67–8, 66, 78. It should be said, however, that a comparative history of literatures of Canada is practically impossible for a single author. Furthermore, it would seem to exceed the series format, and for that reason alone New's efforts are laudable. The fundamental value for the excursions into francophone writing, which is not given proportionately as much space as anglophone writing, would be its role as a sign of difference, in a predominantly English-Canadian cultural context.

59 Ibid., 81, 82–4. These are among the several indications in the text that indicate New's difference, perhaps due to personal allegiance to the West, with a centralized notion of Canada. Cf., for example, Sandford Fleming's proposal, arising from a trip to the West, for Standard Time Zones that were eventually accepted by the world. It is selected as an example of 'the simultaneity of difference' (ibid., 88).

60 Ibid., 107, 102.

61 Ibid., 120, 128, 131.

62 Ibid., 138, 146, 198.

63 Ibid., 194.

64 Ibid., 198.

65 Ibid., 214, 240, 212.

66 Ibid., specifically 'nationhood' (214) and 'national' (215).

67 Ibid., 233, 252, 242, 252–3, 267.

68 Ibid., 296; Mailhot, *La Littérature québécoise*, 121; New, *A History of Canadian Literature*, 296.

69 If only in respect of the use of archaeology, New world appear in many respects nearest the sense of history developed in Dionne.

70 Foucault, *L'Archéologie du savoir*, 65, 67; New, *A History of Canadian Literature*, 295, 24.

Afterthoughts, Models, Possibilities

1 Swales, *The German Bildungsroman*, 23, 29, 35–6, 35.
2 The Greek verb 'historeo' means primarily to inquire into something, and the account of such an inquiry was, consequently, known as a 'historia.'
3 See Swales, *The German Bildungsroman*, 26–8.
4 On these two terms see ibid., 29 et passim, and my discussion in the Introduction, 17.
5 It may be, of course, that modernism is behind 'us' and that 'the nation-state is withering,' implying that many of these issues are no longer actual. See Reading, *The University in Ruins*, 47.
6 See Renan, 'Qu'est-ce qu'une nation?' 887, 888; cf. Ernest Gellner, cited in Thom, 'Tribes within Nations,' 23.
7 Renan, 'Qu'est-ce qu'une nation?' 903, 903–4, 892, 891, 903, 891.
8 See Cosh, 'The Demise of History,' 33.
9 Thom, 'Tribes within Nations,' 31; Havel, 'The Power of the Powerless,' 62.
10 Saul, *Reflections of a Siamese Twin*, 30.
11 Ibid., 81, 129, 66, 439.
12 Ibid., 439, 504, 439.
13 Brossard, *La Lettre aérienne*, 43.
14 Angus, *A Border Within*, 137, 142.
15 Ibid., 142–3; cf. Bercovitch, 'Fusion and Identity,' 26.
16 Angus, *A Border Within*, 143, 146.
17 Ibid., 149, 153.
18 Ibid., 153, 153–4.
19 Ibid., 155, 161.
20 Granatstein, *Who Killed Canadian History?* xvii, 77, 103.
21 Ibid., 105.
22 Friedrich Nietzsche, *Menschliches, Allzumenschliches: Ein Buch für freier Geiste, Werke in drei Bänden*, 1: 823 (my translation); Benjamin, 'Theses on the Philosophy of History,' *Illuminations*, 261; Lecker, *Making It Real*, 68.

Bibliography

Anderson, Benedict. *Imagined Communities*. 1983. Rev. ed. London: Verso, 1991.

Angus, Ian. *A Border Within: National Identity, Cultural Plurality, and Wilderness*. Montreal: McGill-Queen's University Press, 1997.

Aquin, Hubert. *Blocs erratiques: Textes (1948–1977)*. Montreal: Quinze, 1977.

Arnold, Matthew. *Culture and Anarchy*. 1869. Ed. J. Dover Wilson. Cambridge: Cambridge University Press, 1963.

– 'The Function of Criticism at the Present Time.' 1864. *Essays in Criticism: First and Second Series*. 1865, 1888. Ed. G.K. Chesterton, 9–34. London: Dent and Dutton, 1964.

– 'The Study of Poetry.' 1880. *Essays in Criticism: First and Second Series*. 1865, 1888. Ed. G.K. Chesterton, 235–60. London: Dent and Dutton, 1964.

Ashcroft, Bill, Gareth Griffeths, and Helen Tiffin. *The Empire Writes Back: Theory and Practice in Post-Colonial Literatures*. London: Routledge, 1989.

Atwood, Margaret. *Survival: A Thematic Guide to Canadian Literature*. Toronto: House of Anansi Press, 1972.

Austin, J.L. *How to Do Things with Words*. Ed. J.O. Urmson and Marina Sbisà. 2nd ed. Cambridge: Harvard University Press, 1975.

Baillargeon, Samuel. *Littérature canadienne-française*. Montréal: Fides, 1957.

– *Littérature canadienne-française*. 2nd ed. Montreal: Fides, 1967.

Baker, Ray Palmer. *A History of English-Canadian Literature to the Confederation*. Cambridge: Harvard University Press, and London: Oxford University Press, 1920.

Bakhtin, M.M. *The Dialogic Imagination*. Trans. Caryl Emerson and Michael Holquist. Austin: University of Texas Press, 1981.

Balan, Jars. 'Some Notes toward the Writing of Ukrainian Literary Institution in Canada.' *Canadian Review of Comparative Literature / Revue canadienne de littérature comparée* 16.3–4 (1989): 745–62.

Ballstadt, Carl, ed. *The Search for English-Canadian Literature: An Anthology of Critical Articles from the Nineteenth and Early Twentieth Centuries.* Toronto: University of Toronto Press, 1975.

Benjamin, Walter. *Iluminations.* Trans. Harry Zohn. Ed. Hannah Arendt. 1955. New York: Schoken Books, 1969.

Bercovitch, Sacvan. 'Fusion and Identity: The American Identity.' *The American Identity: Fusion and Fragmentation.* Ed. Rob Kroes, 19–45. European Contributions to American Studies. Amsterdam: Amerika Institut, 1980.

Bisztray, George. *Hungarian-Canadian Literature.* Toronto: University of Toronto Press, 1987.

Blodgett, E.D. 'Ethnic Writing in Canada as Paratext.' *Signature* 1.3 (1990): 13–27.

– 'The Father's Seduction: The Example of Angéline de Montbrun.' *A Mazing Space: Writing Canadian Women Writing.* Ed. Shirley Neuman and Smaro Kamboureli, 17–30. Edmonton: NeWest and Longspoon Press, 1986.

– 'George Grant, the Uncertain Nation and Diversity of Being.' *Canadian Literature* 152.3 (1997): 107–23.

– 'Literary History in Canada and National Identity Formation.' 1.3 (2001). *Spaces of Identity.* University of Vienna, Department of History: www. spacesofidentity.net.

– 'Towards an Ethnic Style.' *Canadian Review of Comparative Literature / Revue canadienne de littérature comparée* 22.3–4 (1995): 623–38.

– 'Translated Literature and the Polysystem: The Example of Le May's *Évangéline.*' *Meta* 34 (1989): 157–68.

Bloom, Harold. *The Anxiety of Influence: A Theory of Poetry.* New York: Oxford University Press, 1973.

Boileau, Nicolas. *Œuvres complètes.* Ed. Françoise Escal. Bibliothèque de la Pléiade. Paris: Éditions Gallimard, 1966.

Borduas, Paul-Émile. *Écrits.* Vol. 1. Bibliothèque du nouveau monde. Ed. André-G. Bourassa, Jean Fisette, Gilles Lapointe. Montreal: Les Presses de l'Université de Montréal, 1987.

Boudreau, Diane. *Histoire de la littérature amérindienne au Québec: Oralité et littérature.* Montreal: Hexagone, 1993.

Bourdieu, Pierre. *The Field of Cultural Production.* Ed. Randal Johnson. New York: Columbia University Press, 1993.

Boynard-Frot, Janine. *Un Matriarcat en procès: Analyse systématique de romans canadiens-français 1860–1960.* Montreal: Les Presses de l'Université de Montréal, 1982.

Brennan, Timothy. 'The National Longing for Form.' *Nation and Narration.* Ed. Homi K. Bhabha, 44–70. London: Routledge, 1990.

Brossard, Nicole. *La Lettre aérienne.* Montreal: Les Éditions du remue-ménage, 1988.

Brown, Craig, ed. *The Illustrated History of Canada.* Toronto: Lester and Orpen Dennys, 1987.

Brown, E.K. *On Canadian Poetry.* 1943. Ottawa: Tecumseh Press, 1973.

Brown, Marshall, ed. *The Uses of Literary History.* Durham, NC: Duke University Press, 1995.

Brown, Russell. *Borderlines and Borderlands in English Canada: The Written Line.* Borderlands Monograph Series 4. Orono, ME: Borderlands Project, 1990.

Brunel, Pierre, and Yves Chevrel. *Précis de la littérature comparée.* Paris: Presses Universitaires de France, 1989.

Brunet, Berthelot. *Histoire de la littérature canadienne française.* Montreal: L'Arbre, 1946.

Brunet, Michel. *Canadians et Canadiens.* Montreal: Fides, 1954.

Buss, Helen M. *Mapping Our Selves: Canadian Women's Autobiography in English.* Montreal: McGill-Queen's University Press, 1993.

Calvet, Louis-Jean. *Linguistique et colonialisme: Petit traité de glottophagie.* 1974. Paris: Payot, 1979.

Cardin, Jean-François, and Claude Couture. *Histoire du Canada: Espace et différences.* Sainte-Foy, QC: Les Presses de l'Université Laval, 1995.

Chartier, Émile. *Au Canada français: La Vie de l'esprit.* Montreal: Bernard Valiquette, 1941.

Collin, W.E. *The White Savannahs.* 1936. Toronto: University of Toronto Press, 1975.

Collingwood, R.G. *The Idea of History.* 1946. New York: Oxford University Press, 1956.

Cook, Ramsay. *Canada, Québec, and the Uses of Nationalism.* 2nd ed. Toronto: McClelland and Stewart, 1995.

Coopman, Theophiel, and Lodewijk Scharpé. *Geschiedenis der vlaamsche Letterkunde.* Antwerp: De Nederlandische Boekhandel, 1910.

Cosh, Colby. 'The Demise of History.' *Alberta Report.* 23 June 1998, 33.

Craig, Gerald M., ed. *Lord Durham's Report: An Abridgement of the Report on the Affairs of British North America.* Toronto: McClelland and Stewart, 1963.

Croce, Benedetto. *Æsthetic as Science of Expression and General Linguistic.* Trans. Douglas Ainslie. Rev. ed. New York: Noonday Press, 1953.

– 'La critica letteraria italiana dal de Sanctis ai giorni nostri.' 2nd ed. *Nuovi Pagini Sparse.* Vol. 1. Bari: Laterza, 1966: 205–16.

– *Storia della storiographia italiana nel secolo decimonono.* 2 vols. 1921. Bari: Laterza, 1964.

– *Teoria e Storia della Storiografia.* Ed. Giuseppe Galasso. Classici 53. Milan: Adelphi, 1989.

Dandurand, Albert. *La Poésie canadienne-française.* Montreal: Editions Albert Lévesque, 1933.

– *Littérature canadienne-française: la prose.* Montreal: Devoir, 1935

– *Le Roman canadien-français.* Montreal: Editions Albert Lévesque, 1937.

Dante Alighieri. *The Divine Comedy.* Trans. Charles S. Singleton. Vol. 1. Bollingen Series 80. Princeton, NJ: Princeton University Press, 1970.

Davies, Gwendolyn. 'J.D. Logan and the Great Feud for Canadian Literature: 1915–1923.' *Canadian Studies at Home and Abroad: Selected Proceedings of the 21st Annual Conference of the Association for Canadian Studies.* Ed. James de Finney, 113–28. Montreal: Association for Canadian Studies/Association d'études canadiennes, 1995.

Deleuze Gilles, and Félix Guattari. *Kafka: Toward a Minor Literature.* 1975. Trans. Dana Polán. Theory and History of Literature 30. Minneapolis: University of Minnesota Press, 1986.

De Man, Paul. 'Literary History and Literary Modernity.' *Blindness and Insight: Essays in the Rhetoric of Contemporary Criticism.* 2nd ed. Theory and History of Literature, vol. 7. Minneapolis: University of Minnesota Press, 1983.

De Quincey, Thomas. 'Letters to a Young Man Whose Education Has Been Neglected.' 1823. *De Quincey's Literary Criticism.* Ed. H. Darbishire, 151–4. London: Henry Frowde, 1909.

De Sanctis, Francesco. *Storia della letteratura italiana.* 1871–9. Ed. Luigi Rossi. 2 vols. Milan: Feltrinelli, 1956.

Dewart, Edward Hartley. *Selections from Canadian Poets with Occasional Critical and Biographical Notes and an Introductory Essay on Canadian Poetry.* 1964. Toronto: University of Toronto Press, 1973.

Dionne, René, ed. *Le Québécois et sa littérature.* Paris: Agence de Coopération Culturelle et Technique; Sherbrooke: Namaan, 1984.

Dostaler, Yves. *Les Infortunes du roman dans le Québec du XIXe siècle.* Cahiers du Québec. Montreal: Hurtubise, 1977.

Ducrocq-Poirier, M. *Le Roman canadien de langue française de 1860 à 1958.* Paris: Nizet, 1978.

Eagleton, Terry. *Literary Theory: An Introduction.* Minneapolis: University of Minnesota Press, 1983.

Eckermann, Johann Peter. *Gespräche mit Goethe in den letzten Jahren seines Lebens.* Ed. Regine Otto. 1982. Munich: Verlag C.H. Beck, 1988.

Edgar, Pelham. *Across My Path.* Ed. Northrop Frye. Toronto: Ryerson Press, 1952.

– 'English-Canadian Literature.' *The Cambridge History of English Literature: The*

Nineteenth Century. Vol. 14. Ed. A.W. Ward and A.R. Waller, 343–60. Cambridge: Cambridge University Press, 1916.

Ellis, John M. *Literature Lost: Social Agendas and the Corruption of the Humanities.* New Haven, CT: Yale University Press, 1997.

Etlin, Richard A. *In Defense of Humanism: Value in the Arts and Letters.* Cambridge: Cambridge University Press, 1996.

Even-Zohar, Itamar. *Polysystem Studies. Poetics Today* 11 (1990).

Fergusson, Francis. *The Idea of a Theater.* Princeton, NJ: Princeton University Press, 1949.

Fischer, Ernst. *The Necessity of Art.* 1959. Trans. Anna Bostock. Harmondsworth: Penguin, 1978.

Foucault, Michel. *L'Archéologie du savoir.* Bibliothèque des sciences humaines. Paris: Gallimard, 1969.

Fowler, Alastair. *Kinds of Literature: An Introduction to the Theory of Genres and Modes.* Cambridge: Harvard University Press, 1982.

Friedrich, Werner P. *Dante's Fame Abroad; 1350–1850.* Studies in Comparative Literature 2. Chapel Hill: University of North Carolina Press, 1950.

Frow, John. *Marxism and Literary History.* Cambridge: Harvard University Press, 1986.

Frye, Northrop. *Anatomy of Criticism: Four Essays.* Princeton: Princeton University Press, 1957.

– *The Bush Garden: Essays on the Canadian Imagination.* Toronto: Anansi, 1971.

– 'Conclusion.' *Literary History of Canada: Canadian Literature in Canada.* Ed. Carl F. Klinck, 821–49. Toronto: University of Toronto Press, 1965.

– *Divisions on a Ground: Essays on Canadian Culture.* Ed. James Polk. Toronto: Anansi, 1982.

– *The Great Code: The Bible and Literature.* Toronto: Academic Press Canada, 1982.

– *The Secular Scripture: A Study of the Structure of Romance.* Cambridge: Harvard University Press, 1976.

Fukuyama, Francis. *The End of History and the Last Man.* New York: Free Press, Toronto: Macmillan, 1992.

Gallant, Mavis. *Home Truths.* Toronto: Macmillan, 1981.

Gagnon, Serge. *Le Québec et ses historiens de 1840 à 1920: La Nouvelle-France, de Garneau à Groulx.* Les Cahiers d'histoire de l'Université Laval. Quebec: Les Presses de l'Université Laval, 1978.

– *Quebec and Its Historians: The Twentieth Century.* Trans. Jane Brierly. Montreal: Harvest House, 1985.

Gay, Paul. *Notre Littérature: Guide littéraire du Canada français à l'usage des niveaux secondaire et collégial.* Montreal: HMH, 1969.

– *Survol de la littérature canadienne-française. L'Enseignement secondaire* 44.4 (1967): 173–268.

Giguère, Richard. *Exil, révolte et dissidence: Étude comparée des poésies québécoise et canadienne (1925–1955).* Centre de Recherche en Littérature Québécoise. Quebec: Les Presses de l'Université Laval, 1984.

Gilbert, Sandra, and Susan Gubar. *The Madwoman in the Attic: The Woman Writer and the Nineteenth Century.* New Haven: Yale University Press, 1979.

Gobard, Henri. *L'Aliénation linguistique.* Paris: Flammarion, 1976.

Grabowicz, George. 'Ukrainian Poetry.' *The New Princeton Encyclopedia of Poetry and Poetics.* Ed. Alex Preminger and T.V.F. Brogan, 1334–7. Princeton, NJ: Princeton University Press, 1993.

Granatstein, J.L. *Who Killed Canadian History?* Toronto: HarperCollins, 1998.

Grandpré, Pierre de, ed. *Histoire de la littérature française du Québec.* 1967–9. 4 vols. Ottawa: Librairie Beauchemin, 1971.

Gray, Charlotte. *Mrs. King: The Life and Times of Isabel Mackenzie King.* Toronto: Viking, 1997.

Greenstein, Michael. *Third Solitudes: Tradition and Discontinuity in Jewish Canadian Literature.* Montreal: McGill-Queen's University Press, 1989.

Groulx, Lionel. *Histoire du Canada français.* 2 vols. 4th ed. Montreal: Fides, 1960.

Gwyn, Sandra. *The Private Capital: Ambition and Love in the Age of Macdonald and Laurier.* Toronto: McClelland and Stewart, 1984.

Halden, Charles ab der. *Études de littérature canadienne française.* Paris: Rudeval, 1904.

Handelman, Susan A. *The Slayers of Moses: The Emergence of Rabbinic Interpretation in Modern Literary Theory.* Albany: State University of New York Press, 1982.

Hanse, Joseph. *Naissance d'une littérature.* Archives du Futur. Brussels: Labor, 1992.

Harley, J.B. 'Maps, Knowledge, and Power.' *The Iconography of Landscape: Essays on the Symbolic Representation, Design and Use of Past Environments.* Ed. Denis Cosgrove and Stephen Daniels. Cambridge: Cambridge University Press, 1988.

Harrison, Dick. *Unnamed Country: The Struggle for a Canadian Prairie Fiction.* Edmonton: University of Alberta Press, 1977.

Hartman, Geoffrey H. *Beyond Formalism: Literary Essays, 1958–1970.* New Haven, CT: Yale University Press, 1970.

Hastings, Adrian. *The Construction of Nationhood: Ethnicity, Religion and Nationalism.* Cambridge: Cambridge University Press, 1997.

Havel, Václav. 'The Power of the Powerless.' *Living in Truth.* Trans. P. Wilson. Ed. Jan Vladislav, 36–122. London: Faber and Faber, 1980.

Hébert, Anne. *Poèmes.* Paris: Seuil, 1960.

– *Le Torrent.* 1950. Montreal: HMH, 1974.

Hémon, Louis. *Maria Chapdelaine: Récit du Canada français.* 1914. Ed. Nicole Deschamps. Montreal: Boréal Express, 1980.

Hobsbawm, E.J. *The Age of Empire, 1875–1914.* London: Weidenfeld and Nicolson, 1987.

Hohendahl, Peter Uwe. *Building a National Literature: The Case of Germany 1830–1870.* 1985. Trans. Renate Baron Franciscono. Ithaca, NY: Cornell University Press, 1989.

Huggan, Graham. 'Decolonizing the Map: Post-Colonialism, Post-Structuralism and the Cartographic Connection.' *Ariel* 20.4 (1989): 115–31.

Hutcheon, Linda. *As Canadian as ... possible ... under the circumstances! Reason over Passion.* Toronto: ECW Press, and North York: York University, 1990.

– 'Frye Recoded: Postmodernity and the Conclusions.' *The Legacy of Northrop Frye.* Ed. Alvin A. Lee and Robert D. Denham, 105–21. Toronto: University of Toronto Press, 1994.

– *The Canadian Postmodern: A Study of Contemporary English-Canadian Fiction.* Studies in Canadian Literature. Toronto: Oxford University Press, 1988.

Illich, Ivan. *In the Vineyard of the Text: A Commentary to Hugh's Didascalion.* Chicago: University of Chicago Press, 1993.

Iragaray, Luce. *Ce Sexe n'en est pas un.* Collection 'Critique.' Paris: Minuit, 1977.

Jakobson, Roman. *Selected Writings.* Ed. Stephen Rudy. Vol. 3. The Hague: Mouton, 1981.

Jakobson, Roman, and Morris Halle. 'Two Aspects of Language and Two Types of Aphasic Disturbances.' *Fundamentals of Language.* 2nd ed., 69–96. The Hague: Mouton, 1971.

Jameson, Fredric. *Marxism and Form: Twentieth-Century Dialectical Theories of Literature.* Princeton, NJ: Princeton University Press, 1971.

Jauß, Hans Robert. 'Literaturgeschichte als Provokation der Literaturwissenschaft.' *Literaturgeschichte als Provokation.* 144–207. Frankfurt am Main: Suhrkamp, 1970.

Jenkins, Richard. *The Victorians and Ancient Greece.* Cambridge: Harvard University Press, 1980.

Jones, D.G. *Butterfly on Rock: A Study of Themes and Images in Canadian Literature.* Toronto: University of Toronto Press, 1970.

Keith, William J. *Canadian Literature in English.* London: Longman, 1985.

– 'The Function of Canadian Criticism at the Present Time.' *Essays on Canadian Writing* 30 (1984–5): 1–16.

King, Thomas. 'Godzilla vs. Post-Colonial.' *World Literature Written in English* 30.2 (1990): 10–16.

- *Green Grass, Running Water.* Toronto: HarperCollins, 1993.

Kiralyfalvi, Bela. *The Aesthetics of György Lukács.* Princeton, NJ: Princeton University Press, 1975.

Kirk, G.S., J.E. Raven, and M. Schofield. *The Presocratic Philosophers.* 2nd ed. Cambridge: Cambridge University Press, 1983.

Klinck, Carl F. *Giving Canada a Literary History.* Ed. Sandra Djwa. Ottawa: Carleton University Press, 1991.

- ed. *Literary History of Canada: Canadian Literature in English.* Toronto: University of Toronto Press, 1965.

- ed. *Literary History of Canada: Canadian Literature in English.* 2nd ed. 3 vols. Toronto: University of Toronto Press, 1976.

Kloss, Heinz. *Ahornblätter: Deutsche Dichtung aus Kanada.* Würzburg: Auslieferung Holzner-Verlag, 1961.

Kreisel, Henry. 'The "Ethnic" Writer in Canada.' *Identifications: Ethnicity and the Writer in Canada.* Ed. Jars Balan, 1–13. Edmonton: Canadian Institute of Ukrainian Studies and University of Alberta, 1989.

- 'The Prairie: A State of Mind.' *Transactions of the Royal Society of Canada.* 4th ser., vol. 6, sec. 2 (1968): 171–80.

Kroetsch, Robert. *The Lovely Treachery of Words: Essays Selected and New.* Toronto: Oxford University Press, 1989.

Kushner, Eva. 'Frye and the Historicity of Literature.' *The Legacy of Northrop Frye.* Ed. Alvin A. Lee and Robert D. Denham, 296–334. Toronto: University of Toronto Press, 1994.

Lacan. Jacques. *Écrits.* Le champ freudien. Paris: Éditions du Seuil, 1966.

- *The Language of Self: The Function of Language in Psycho-analysis.* Trans. Anthony Wilden. Baltimore: Johns Hopkins University Press, 1968.

Lareau, Edmond. *Histoire de la littérature canadienne.* Montreal: John Lovell, 1874.

Lecker, Robert. *Making It Real: The Canonization of English-Canadian Literature.* Concord, ON: Anansi, 1995.

Léger, Jules. *Le Canada français et son expression littéraire.* Paris: Librairie Nizet et Bastard, 1938.

Lemire, Maurice. *Formation de l'imaginaire littéraire au Québec (1764–1867).* Collection Essais Littéraires. Montreal: Hexagone, 1993.

- 'L'Instance critique.' *L'Histoire littéraire. Théories, méthodes practiques.* Ed. Clément Moisan, 249–70. Quebec: Les Presses de l'Université Laval, 1989.

- ed. *L'Institution litteraire.* Quebec: CRELIQ, 1986.

- *La Littérature québécoise en projet au milieu du XIXe siècle.* Saint-Laurent, QC: Fides, 1993.

- et al., eds. *La Vie littéraire au Québec.* Vols. 1–2. Sainte-Foy, QC: Les Presses de l'Université Laval, 1991–2.

Lemire, Maurice, and Denis Saint-Jacques. *La Vie littéraire au Québec.* Vols. 3–4. Sainte-Foy, QC: Les Presses de l'Université Laval, 1996, 1999.

Le Moyne, Jean. *Convergences.* 1966. Montreal: Hurtubise HMH, 1977.

Lighthall, William Douw. *Songs of the Great Dominion: Voices from the Forests and Waters, the Settlements and Cities of Canada.* London: Walter Scott, 1889.

Logan, J.D., and Donald G. French. *Highways of Canadian Literature: A Synoptic Introduction to the Literary History of Canada (English) from 1760–1924.* 1924. Toronto: McClelland and Stewart, 1928.

Long, Haniel. *The Marvellous Adventure of Cabeza de Vaca.* 1939. London: Souvenir Press, and Toronto: J.M. Dent & Son, 1972.

Loomba, Ania. *Colonialism/Postcolonialism.* New Critical Idiom Series. London: Routledge, 1998.

Lortie, Jeanne d'Arc. *La Poésie nationaliste au Canada français, 1606–1867.* Quebec: Les Presses de l'Université Laval, 1975.

Lowenthal, David. *The Past Is a Foreign Country.* Cambridge: Cambridge University Press, 1985.

Lucas, C.P., ed. *Lord Durham's Report on the Affairs of North America.* 3 vols. London: Oxford University Press, 1912.

Lukács, Georg. *History and Class Consciousness: Studies in Marxist Dialectics.* Trans. Rodney Livingstone. 1971. Cambridge: MIT Press, 1972.

MacMechan, Archibald. *Headwaters of Canadian Literature.* 1924. Toronto: McClelland and Stewart, 1974.

MacMurchy, Archibald. *Handbook of Canadian Literature (English).* Toronto: William Briggs, 1906.

McCourt, Edward A. *The Canadian West in Fiction.* Toronto: Ryerson Press, 1949.

McGrath, Robin. *Canadian Inuit Literature: The Development of a Tradition.* National Museum of Man Series / Musée nationale de L'Homme collection Mercure. Canadian Ethnology Service Paper No. 94 / Le Service canadien d'Ethnologie dossier No. 94. Ottawa: National Museums of Canada / Musées nationaux du Canada, 1984.

McLuhan, Marshall. 'Canada: The Borderline Case.' *The Canadian Imagination: Dimensions of a Literary Culture.* Ed. David Staines, 226–48. Cambridge: Harvard University Press, 1977.

McRoberts, Kenneth. *Misconceiving Canada: The Struggle for National Unity.* Toronto: Oxford University Press, 1997.

Mailhot, Laurent. *La Littérature québécoise.* Que sais-je? Paris: Presses Universitaires de France, 1974.

– 'Problèmes de périodisation en histoire littéraire du Québec.' *L'Histoire littéraire: Théories, méthodes practiques.* Ed. Clement Moisan, 105–24. Quebec: Les Presses de l'Université Laval, 1989.

Maillet, Marguerite. *Histoire de la littérature acadienne: De Rêve en rêve.* Ottawa: Les Editions d'Acadie, 1983.

Mandel, Eli, ed. *Contexts of Canadian Criticism.* Patterns of Literary Criticism 9. Chicago: University of Chicago Press, 1971.

Mandryka, M.I. *History of Ukrainian Literature in Canada.* Winnipeg: Ukrainian Free Academy of Sciences, 1968.

Marquis, Thomas Guthrie. 'English Canadian Literature.' *Canada and Its Provinces: A History of the Canadian People and Their Institutions.* Ed. Adam Shortt and Arthur G. Doughty, 14, sec. 2. 493–589. Toronto: Glasgow, Brook, and Company, 1914.

Marshall, Tom. *Harsh and Lovely Land: The Major Poets and the Making of a Canadian Tradition.* Vancouver: University of British Columbia Press, 1979.

Martin, Ernest. *L'Évangéline de Longfellow et la suite merveilleuse du poème.* Paris: Hachette, 1936.

Melançon, Joseph. 'L'histoire littéraire comme effet didactique.' *L'Histoire littéraire: Théories, méthodes practiques.* Ed. Clément Moisan, 77–90. Quebec: Les Presses de l'Université Laval, 1989.

Menéndez-Pidal, Ramon. *La Chanson de Roland et la tradition épique des Francs.* Trans. Irénée Cluzel. 2nd ed. Paris: Picard, 1960.

Merleau-Ponty, Maurice. *Phénoménologie de la perception.* Paris: Gallimard, 1945.

Mezei, Kathy. 'A Bridge of Sorts: The Translation of Quebec Literature into English.' *Yearbook of English Studies* 15 (1985): 201–26.

Milton, John. *The Poems of John Milton.* Ed. James Holly Hanford. New York: Ronald Press, 1936.

Mirsky, D.S. *A History of Russian Literature from Its Beginnings to 1900.* Ed. Francis J. Whitfield. 1949. New York: Vintage Books, 1958.

Miska, John. *Literature of Hungarian Canadians.* Toronto: Rákóczi Foundation, 1991.

Moisan, Clément. 'L'Histoire littéraire comme texte,' *Texte: Revue de critique et thérie littéraire* 12 (1992): 81–90.

– *Poésie des frontières: Étude comparée des poésies canadienne et québécoise.* Quebec: Editions Hurtubise HMH, 1979.

– *A Poetry of Frontiers: Comparative Studies in Quebec/Canadian Literature.* Trans. George Lang and Linda Weber. Victoria: Press Porcépic, 1983.

– *Qu'est-ce que l'histoire littéraire?* Littératures modernes. Paris: Presses Universitaires de Paris, 1987.

– 'L'Histoire littéraire comme discours scientifique.' *L'Histoire littéraire: Théories, méthodes practiques,* 25–34. Quebec: Les Presses de l'Université Laval, 1989.

– ed. *L'Histoire littéraire: Théories méthodes pratiques.* Quebec: Les Presses de l'Université Laval, 1989.

Monkman, Leslie. *A Native Heritage: Images of the Indian in English-Canadian Literature.* Toronto: University of Toronto Press, 1981.

Monière. Denis. *Le Développement des idéologies au Québec des origines à nos jours.* Montreal: Éditions Québec/Amérique, 1977.

Morison, Samuel Eliot. *Samuel de Champlain: Father of New France.* Boston: Little, Brown and Co., 1972.

Możejko, Edward. 'Ethnic or National (?): Polish Literature in Canada.' *Canadian Review of Comparative Literature/Revue canadienne de littérature comparée* 16.3–4 (1989): 809–25.

Mudge, Bradford K. 'The Man with Two Brains: Gothic Novels, Popular Culture, and Literary History.' *PMLA* 107 (1992): 92–104.

Nautet, Francis. *Histoire des lettres belges d'expression française.* 2 vols. Bibliothèque belge des connaissances modernes. Brussels: Rozez, 1892–3.

Nazarenko, Tatiana. 'To Pass Through on One's Wings: The Poetry of Oleh Zujewksij.' *Canadian Slavonic Papers / Revue canadiennes des slavistes* 37 (1996): 23–46.

Nemoianu, Virgil. *The Taming of Romanticism: European Literature and the Age of Biedermeyer.* Cambridge: Harvard University Press, 1984.

Nepveu, Pierre. *L'Écologie du réel: Mort et naissance de la littérature québécoise contemporaine.* Montreal: Boréal, 1988.

Neuman, Shirley. 'Life Writing.' *Literary History of Canada: Canadian Literature in English.* 2nd ed. Vol. 4. Ed. W.H. New, 333–70. Toronto: University of Toronto Press, 1990.

New, W.H. *A History of Canadian Literature.* London: Macmillan Education, 1989.

Niethammer, Lutz. *Posthistoire: Has History Come to an End?* 1989. Trans. Patrick Camiller. London: Verso, 1992.

Nietzsche, Friedrich. *Werke in drei Bänden.* Ed. Karl Schlechta. 1954. Darmstadt: Wissenschaftliche Buchgesellschaft, 1997.

Novák, Jan V., and Arne Novák. *Přehledné dějiny literatury české od nejstarších dob až do politického osvobození.* 3rd ed. Olomouci: R. Promberg, 1922.

O'Donovan, Joan E. *George Grant and the Twilight of Justice.* Toronto: University of Toronto Press, 1984.

O'Flaherty, Patrick. *The Rock Observed: Studies in the Literature of Newfoundland.* Toronto: University of Toronto Press, 1979.

O'Leary, Dostaler. *Le Roman canadien-français: Étude historique et critique.* Ottawa: Le Cercle du livre français, 1954.

– *Séparatisme: Doctrine constructive.* Montreal: Les Éditions des jeunesse patriotes, 1937.

Ovid. *Metamorphoseon: Libri XV.* Ed. B.A. van Proosdij. Leiden: Brill, 1959.

Owram, Doug. *Promise of Eden: The Canadian Expansionist Movement and the Idea of the West 1856–1900.* Toronto: University of Toronto Press, 1980.

The Oxford Companion to Canadian Literature. Ed. Eugene Benson and William Toye. 2nd ed. Toronto: Oxford University Press, 1997.

The Oxford Companion to Canadian Theatre. Ed. Eugene Benson and L.W. Conolly. Toronto: Oxford University Press, 1989.

Pacey, Desmond. *Creative Writing in Canada: A Short History of English-Canadian Literature.* Toronto: Ryerson Press, 1952.

Padolsky, Enoch. 'Canadian Minority Writing and Acculturation Options.' *Canadian Review of Comparative Literature / Revue canadienne de littérature comparée* 16.3–4 (1989): 600–18.

Panofsky, Erwin. '*Et in Arcadia ego:* On the Conception of Transience in Poussin and Watteau.' *History and Philosophy: The Ernst Cassirer Festschrift.* Ed. Raymond Klibansky and H.J. Paton, 223–54. Oxford: Oxford University Press, 1936.

Paré, François. *Les Littératures de l'exiguité.* Hearst, ON: Le Nordir, 1994.

Patterson, Lee. 'Literary History.' *Critical Terms for Literary Study.* Ed. Frank Lentricchia and Thomas McLaughlin, 250–62. Chicago: University of Chicago Press, 1990.

Perkins, David. *Is Literary History Possible?* Baltimore: The Johns Hopkins University Press, 1992.

Petrone, Penny. *Native Literature in Canada: From the Oral Tradition to the Present.* Toronto: Oxford University Press, 1990.

Pierce, Lorne. *An Outline of Canadian Literature (French and English).* Montreal: Louis Carrier and Co., 1927.

Pivato, Joseph. *Echo: Essays on Other Literatures.* Montreal: Guernica, 1994.

Puech, Henri-Charles. 'Gnosis and Time.' 1951. *Man and Time.* Papers from the Eranos Yearbooks. Bollingen Series 30.3. Trans. Ralph Mannheim, 38–84. Princeton, NJ: Princeton University Press, 1957.

Pugliese, Joseph. 'Literary Histories and the Ontologies of Nation.' *Canadian Review of Comparative Literature / Revue canadienne de littérature comparée* 22.3–4 (1995): 467–86.

Purdy, Anthony. *A Certain Difficulty of Being: Essays on the Quebec Novel.* Montreal: McGill-Queen's University Press, 1990.

Quinn, Herbert. *The Union Nationale: Quebec Nationalism from Duplessis to Lévesque.* 2nd ed. Toronto: University of Toronto Press, 1979.

Rashley, R.E. *Poetry in Canada: The First Three Steps.* Toronto: Ryerson Press, 1958.

Reading, Bill. *The University in Ruins.* Cambridge: Harvard University Press, 1996.

Renan, Ernest. 'Qu'est-ce qu'une nation?' 1882. *Œuvres complètes.* Ed. Henriette Psichari, 1: 887–907. Paris: Calmann-Lévy, 1947.

Report of the Royal Commission on Bilingualism and Biculturalism. Books 1–4. Ottawa: Queen's Printer, 1967–70.

Rhodenizer, V.B. *A Handbook of Canadian Literature.* Ottawa: Graphic Publishers, 1930.

Ricoeur, Paul. *Hermeneutiques and the Human Sciences.* Ed. and Trans. John B. Thompson. Cambridge: Cambridge University Press, and Paris: Éditions de la Maison des Sciences de l'Homme, 1981.

Ricou, Laurence. *Vertical Man / Horizontal World: Man and Landscape in Canadian Prairie Fiction.* Vancouver: University of British Columbia Press, 1973.

Rioux, Marcel. 'Borduas, Our Eternal Contemporary.' *artscanada: The presence of Paul-Émile Borduas* 224/5 (1978–9): 29–30.

Robert, Lucie. 'Institution, forme institutionel et droit.' *L'Institution littéraire.* Ed. Maurice Lemire, 17–26. Quebec: CRELIQ and L'Institut québécois de recherche sur la culture, 1986.

– *Le Manuel d'histoire de la littérature canadienne de Mgr. Camille Roy.* Quebec: L'Institut québécois de recherche sur la culture, 1982.

Robidoux, Réjean, and André Renaud. *Le Roman canadien-français au vingtième siècle.* Ottawa: Editions de l'Université d'Ottawa, 1966.

Roey-Roux, Françoise van. *La Littérature intime du Québec.* Trois-Rivières: Boréal Express, 1983.

Rosa, Alberto Asor, ed. *Letteratura italiana.* 11 vols. Turin: Giulio Einaudi, 1982–.

Rossel, Virgile. *Histoire de la littérature française hors de France.* Lausanne: Payot, 1895.

Roy, Camille. *French Canadian Literature: Canada and Its Provinces: A History of the Canadian People and Their Institutions.* 12, sec. 2, 435–89. Toronto: Glasgow, Brook and Company, 1914.

– *Histoire de la littérature canadienne.* Quebec: L'Action Sociale, 1930.

– *Manuel d'histoire de la littérature canadienne-française.* Quebec: L'Action Sociale, 1920.

– *Nos Origines littéraires.* Quebec: L'Action Sociale, 1909.

Said, Edward W. *Beginnings: Intention and Method.* 1975. New York: Columbia University Press, 1985.

– *Orientalism.* New York: Random House, 1978.

Saint-Jacques, Denis. 'Nationalisation et autonomisation.' *L'Histoire littéraire: Théories, méthodes practiques.* Ed. Clement Moisan, 241–48. Quebec: Les Presses de l'Université Laval, 1989.

Saul, John Ralston. *Reflections of a Siamese Twin: Canada at the End of the Twentieth Century.* Toronto: Viking, 1995.

- *The Unconscious Civilisation.* CBC Massey Lecture Series. Toronto: Anansi, 1995.
Saussure, Ferdinand de. *Cours de linguistic général.* 1915. Ed. Charles Bailly and Albert Sechehaye. Paris: Payot, 1967.
Savard, Félix-Antoine. *Menaud maître-draveur.* 1937. Bibliothèque canadienne-française. Montreal: Fides, 1978.
Schiller, Friedrich. 'Über naive und sentimentalische Dichtung.' *Sämtliche Werke.* Ed. Gerhart Fricke and Herbert G. Göpfert, 694–780. 2nd ed. Munich: Carl Hauser, 1960.
Schrimpf, Hans Joachim. *Goethes Begriff der Weltliteratur.* Stuttgart: J.B. Metzlersche Verlagsbuchhandlung, 1968.
Séguin, Maurice. *L'Idée d'indépendance au Québec: Genèse et historique.* Collection 1760. Trois Rivières: Boréal, 1968.
Sheppard, Robert. 'It's Time for an Unreality Check.' *Globe and Mail.* 31 January 1996: A13.
Smith, A.J.M., ed. *The Book of Canadian Poetry.* Chicago: University of Chicago Press, and Toronto: W.J. Gage, Ltd, 1943.
- *Modern Canadian Verse.* Toronto: Oxford University Press, 1967.
- *The Oxford Anthology of Canadian Verse.* Toronto: Oxford University Press, 1960.
- *Towards a View of Canadian Letters: Selected Critical Essays, 1928–1971.* Vancouver: University of British Colombia Press, 1973.
Smith, Goldwin. *Canada and the Canadian Question.* 1891. Toronto: University of Toronto Press, 1973.
Sœurs de Sainte-Anne. *Histoire des littératures française et canadienne.* Lachine, QC: Procure des Missions, 1954.
Stegner, Wallace. *Wolf Willow.* New York: Viking, 1955.
Stevenson, Lionel. *Appraisals of Canadian Literature.* Toronto: Macmillan, 1926.
Sutherland, Ronald. *Second Image: Comparative Studies in Québec / Canadian Literature.* Don Mills, ON: New Press, 1971.
Swales, Martin. *The German Bildungsroman from Wieland to Hesse.* Princeton, NJ: Princeton University Press, 1978.
Taine, Hippolyte. *L'Histoire de la littérature anglaise.* 5 vols. 1864. Paris: Hachette, 1916.
Taylor, M. Brook. *Promoters, Patriots, and Partisans: Historiography in Nineteenth-Century English-Canada.* Toronto: University of Toronto Press, 1989.
Thom, Martin. 'Tribes within Nations: The Ancient Germans and the History of Modern France.' *Nation and Narration.* Ed. Homi K. Bhabha, 23–43. London: Routledge, 1990.
Thomas, Brook, *The New Historicism and Other Old-Fashioned Topics.* Princeton, NJ: Princeton University Press, 1991.

Todorov, Tzvetan. *La Conquête de l'Amérique: La question de l'autre.* Paris: Seuil, 1982.

Tougas, Gérard. *Les Écrivains d'expression française et la France.* Paris: Denoël, 1973.

– *Histoire de la littérature canadienne française.* Paris: Presses Universitaires de France, 1960.

Tschofen, Monique. 'Anagrams of the Body: Hybrid Texts and the Question of Postmodernism in the Literature and Film of Canada.' PhD diss., University of Alberta, 1999.

Turnbull, Jane M. *Essential Traits of French-Canadian Poetry.* Toronto: Macmillan, 1938.

Turner, Frederick. *Beyond Geography: The Western Spirit against the Wilderness.* New York: Viking, 1980.

Tynjanov, J. 'On Literary Evolution.' *Readings in Russian Poetics: Formalist and Structuralist Poetics.* Ed. Ladislav Matejka and Krystyna Pomorska, 66–78. Cambridge: MIT Press, 1971.

Vance, Jonathan F. *Death So Noble: Memory, Meaning and the First World War.* Vancouver: UBC Press, 1997.

Viatte, Auguste. *Histoire comparée des littératures francophone.* Paris: Éditions Fernand Nathan, 1980.

– *Histoire littéraire de l'Amérique française des origines à 1950.* Quebec: Presses Universitaires Laval, and Paris: Presses Universitaires de France, 1954.

Waterston, Elizabeth. *Survey: A Short History of Canadian Literature.* Toronto: Methuen, 1973.

Watson, Sheila. *The Double Hook.* Toronto: McClelland and Stewart, 1959.

Wellek, René. *The Rise of English Literary History.* Chapel Hill: University of North Carolina Press, 1941.

White, Hayden. *Metahistory: The Historical Imagination in Nineteenth-Century Europe.* Baltimore: Johns Hopkins University Press, 1973.

Wilson, Edmund. *Axel's Castle: A Study in the Imaginative Literature of 1870–1930.* New York: Charles Scribner's Sons, 1931.

Woodcock, George. *The Meeting of Time and Space: Regionalism in Canadian Literature.* 1980 NeWest Lecture. Edmonton: NeWest Institute for Western Canadian Studies, 1981.

Zumthor, Paul. *La lettre et la voix: De la 'littérature' médiévale.* Paris: Éditions du Seuil, 1987.

Index